OLDHAM RLFC
In the 1950s
Magic or Myth?

Michael Turner

Thanks to everyone who has contributed information, anecdotes, photographs, news-clippings and other images used within this book.

ACKNOWLEDGEMENTS:

I would like to give special thanks to the following individuals who have been most helpful in the preparation of this book:

Steve Brown - Mick Harrop - Brian Walker

Tim Hughes, Dave Whitehead,
Geoff Cooke, Ian Wilson, Tom Wadsworth, Robert Gate, Alan Stacey,
Harry Edgar (Rugby League Journal), David Blackburn, John Etty,
Andy Rimmer, Joe Warham, John Warham, Alex Service , Julie Clarke,
Janice & Des McKeown, Stuart Keane, Gerard Platt, Tony Collins, Frank Jackson.

Special thanks to Karl Waddicor of Vertical Editions.

The Oldham Evening Chronicle.
The Oldham Local Studies and Archives Centre.

Cover design: Sarah Turner.

The Oldham Rugby League Heritage Trust would like to thank all of our advertisers whose continued support makes our publications possible.

3

CONTENTS:

INTRODUCTION

On December 31st 1949 Oldham made the short trip to play Belle Vue Rangers and returned having suffered a defeat by nineteen points to six. Likewise on January 2nd 1960 they again had their colours lowered with an unlikely reverse in the match at Liverpool City. Seventeen points to thirteen was the winning margin for the 'Mersey-siders'.

In between those two games was the 1950s : the period in the history of Oldham R.L.F.C. which is still the most talked about and, it would appear, the most fondly remembered. Why?

This certainly wasn't the most successful era in the club's history. The team that won successive championships in 1910 & 1911 would justifiably lay claim to that honour. Indeed, in the spell between 1905 and 1911, Oldham were the champions three times and runners-up three times, with a sprinkling of Lancashire Cup and Lancashire League successes thrown in for good measure. Then there was the team of the mid 1920s that contested four successive Challenge Cup finals, a feat that wouldn't be equalled for sixty years. Perhaps, if the move to the twin towers of Wembley had come five years earlier than the 1929 relocation to the capital, then this remarkable achievement would be more readily recognised both locally and in the annals of the history of the game. There was little for the Watersheddings' faithful to cheer in the 1930s. The club finished fourth in the 1930-31 season, going on to lose to the league leaders and eventual champions, Swinton, 16 – 3 in the play-off match at Station Road. A solitary Lancashire Cup final victory in 1933 over St Helens Recs, and a losing Challenge Cup semi-final to Widnes at the end of the same season, were the only claims to fame the Roughyeds had managed, and by the time the war-interrupted 1940s came to an end, the story was the same. Even the club's proud record against touring teams had disappeared, with the Australians being victorious in all four meetings in the 30s and 40s and the New Zealanders triumphant in the one encounter in 1947.

In spite of the accomplishments of their illustrious predecessors, it is the 1950s that are always guaranteed to arouse the fondest memories, at least amongst that diminishing number of Oldham supporters who were lucky enough to see them play. I wasn't so fortunate, having been born in December 1954; although I might have been there at Watersheddings for a few games right at the end of the decade, my memory-centres had not yet become tuned in to taking it all in! However, I do recall being taken to Frank Daley's benefit game in May 1959, and at four and a half years old, asking why was the craggy, Wigan-born stand-off was playing in the forwards? I do recall occasional mentions of the likes of Corsi, Sloman, Hilton, Rix and other luminaries from the 1920s team in the Turner household, but the names of those great champions who played in the early part of the twentieth century, Lees, Ferguson, Tyson, Wood, etc were rarely spoken.

A handbook produced by the club in 1950 seemed to hint there was a degree of optimism regarding the future as, the following passage would suggest :

"And now for the future. New players have joined us during the past two seasons whom we feel will do much to bring the club back to that high position it held during the early part of the century. Goldswain and Morgan have already received international honours and when the younger players such as Platt, Batten ,Ward, Fearnley, Leyland, Heyes and Keith are allied to the greater experience of such loyal players as Brooks, Mitchell, Ogden, Taylor and Barraclough then I think we can all look forward to the future with more optimism than in the last few years.

Not all of the above mentioned names will strike a chord with the Roughyeds' faithful but some certainly will and although it would take a few years for the prophecy to be fulfilled the seeds of the 1950s 'entertainers' were being sown!

At the beginning of the decade many clubs were still coming to terms with the deprivations that came in the aftermath of the war. Indeed, for Oldham, it was not until December, 1950 that the famous navy blue shorts, that so distinctively formed part of the Roughyeds playing colours, were able to be afforded and thus restored to the Oldham kit on a regular basis.

The game was very different then from the high intensity rugby we see today. A team in possession kept the ball until they made a handling error or kicked it away. This did lead to some very negative spectacles, when a side could literally run down the clock from well before the final whistle. However, scrums were proper contests where an experienced front-row combination, adept at raking out the ball, was an invaluable asset. There were no substitutes, so pacing the game was a skill in itself, especially for the forwards, and should one of the backs have to retire from the field, almost without exception, a forward would be withdrawn from the pack to cover for the injured man. This was a time when the vast majority of tries were scored by wings and centres, and maintaining the three-quarter line was seen as an absolute priority.

However, not all things have changed, and Rugby League then, as today, could produce totally one-sided thrashings. Equally, it could be a game of inches, where an ankle tap, a brush with the corner flag or a ricochet off the woodwork, one way or another, could decide a match or even the destination of a championship or a challenge cup.

Also then, as now, Rugby League was and remains the best spectator sport in the world, and to those of us who are enlightened it will always be... The Greatest Game!

What follows is a season-by-season, match-by-match review of the Oldham games throughout the decade. Some of the games are covered at length whereas others are summed up in no more than a few sentences. That is not to say that the effort from the players was any less in those encounters, but for various reasons some matches require more scrutiny than others.

So off we go then, back to the 1950s!

Michael Turner - July 2013.

Len McIntyre - Geoff Sims - Bryn Day - Frank Heyes - Irving Barraclough - Alan Jones - Wilson Spencer - Bob Batten - Des McKeown

Alan Jarman

Geoff Robinson

FRONT COVER

Ken Ward

Team Photo:
Back Row:
Griff Jenkins (coach), Don Vines, Derek Turner, Charlie Winslade,
Ken Jackson, Sid Little, Jack Keith, Bill Howard (president).
Middle Row:
Dick Cracknell, Alan Davies, Bernard Ganley, Dennis Ayres, John Etty.
Front Row:
Frank Daley, mascot, Frank Pitchford.

Portraits:
Top Row:
Bryn Goldswain, Frank Stirrup, Billy Mitchell, Harry Ogden, Terry O'Grady.
Bottom Row:
Arthur Tomlinson, Lawrie Platt, John Noon, Joe Warham, Alan Kellett.

Vince Nestor

Lionel Emmitt

Albert Fearnley

Herbie Goodfellow

Bob Byrne

Harold Lomas

Les Anthony

Edgar Brooks

Ian Carruthers

BACK COVER

As per border sequence.

John Watson

Jack Rogers

Bill Ratchford

Peter Goddard

Ron Rowbottom

Jim Mundy

Roland Barrow

Harold Tomlinson

Tipuna 'Smut' Smith - Geoff Kelly - Alf Murray - Jack Taylor - Bert Ambler - Joe Rea - Roger Dufty - Johnny Feather - Ike Southward

Brian Hatherall - Joe Silva - John Dean - Tommy Leyland - John Edwards

Points of note

Throughout the 1950s the scoring values were that a try was three points and a goal two points. This applied to all goals whether they were a conversion, penalty or drop goal.

No substitutes were allowed in senior matches although clubs would often jointly agree for their use in Benefit matches.

Long before the Super League trend of adopting extended club names many of the teams had nicknames some of which are used in this work.

OLDHAM - 'The Roughyeds'

Barrow - 'The Shipbuilders' or 'The Furness-men'.
Batley - 'The Gallant Youths'.
Blackpool - 'The Seasiders' or 'Borough'.
Bramley - 'The Villagers'.
Hull F.C. - 'The Airlie Birds'.
Hull K.R. - 'The Robins'.
Leeds - 'The Loiners'.
Liverpool - The 'Mersey-siders'
St. Helens - 'The Saints'.
Salford - 'The Red Devils'.
Swinton - 'The Lions'.
Warrington - 'The Wire'.
Widnes - 'The Chemics'.
York - 'The Minster-men'.

Australia - 'The Kangaroos'.
New Zealand - 'The Kiwis'.

Wigan have been known as 'The Colliers', 'The Riversiders' and 'The Cherry and Whites'.

Huddersfield - 'Fartowners' and Hunslet - 'Parksiders', had nicknames derived from their home grounds.

Other clubs would often be described by the shortened form of their official name:
Rochdale 'Hornets' - Bradford 'Northern' - Workington 'Town' - Wakefield 'Trinity' - Whitehaven 'Haven' - Featherstone 'Rovers' - Castleford 'Cas' - Liverpool 'City' or 'Stanley' - Belle Vue 'Rangers'.

In the match reports, senior games, that is those which count toward official statistics, have OLDHAM shown in capital letters. When the small case (Oldham) version is used these matches do not count toward official figures. Ironically this means that none of the Law Cup encounters against Rochdale qualify and yet these were often fiercely contested matches.

Once again I am indebted to the Oldham Evening Chronicle for their extensive archive of photographs and the skills of the photographers that caught such wonderful imagery of the Oldham team in the 1950s.
There are just a few images where a better copy could not be sourced however, I believe that this work is still enhanced by their inclusion.

OVERVIEW

As I mentioned in the introduction to all intents and purposes, I missed it!
The Oldham Rugby League team of the 1950s, most fondly remembered locally and within the greater rugby league fraternity can only reasonably be recalled if you are now well into your sixties. And yet, sometimes it is like I was there! You see I was brought up on the lore of the club and what is more never got tired of hearing the tales.

Hutton's last gasp miss at Odsal that meant the Championship came to Oldham...

Winslade throwing the ball half way across the field...

Ganley knocking the goals over from everywhere...

The cup-tie defeat at Leigh when Stirrup got hypothermia...

Tomlinson and Drake fighting all the way back to the pavilion...

Etty taking two over with him...

Little taking three over with him...

Bryn Day doing a jig as the Kiwis performed the haka...

Jack 'Rubber Legs' Keith swivelling over for a try...

Bevan coasting in from 75 yards to break Oldham hearts (again)...

Finishing work early to go to that Lancs Cup semi at Knowlsey Road in '57...

Daley's Final...

Mitchell taking the tackle while Warham scored the tries...

Davies leaving several defenders in his wake...

Stirrup bamboozling opponents and team-mates alike with his sleight of hand...

O'Grady scorching up the touchline...

Roland Barrow, did he hit the flag, or not at the Maine Road mud heap?...

The Kangaroos in 52 held to a draw by an under strength Oldham...
          in 56 demolished by a rampant Oldham...
          in 59 'mixing it' with a feast of open rugby and fighting...

Pitchford like lightening from the scrum...

Platt diving over in grand style...

Turner never a backward step...

… and there is a good place to start. The record of the club in the immediate post-war years of the late 1940s was somewhat less than impressive, and so with the new decade on the horizon the committee went on the search for some 'class' players to re-energize the playing fortunes of the team. They decided that the man to head it all off was Bryn Goldswain, whose services were secured, with a great media fanfare, from Hull Kingston Rovers in July 1949. The leadership qualities of the Welsh loose-forward were soon identified, and he was made club captain after just a few games, eventually also

taking on the coaching duties. Already on the books was a young, confident hooker from Hunslet amateur rugby, called Jack Keith. He wasn't a first team regular as the 1950s dawned, but it wouldn't take him long to become the established 'number 9' and retain the position for the next ten years. The only other personnel on the playing register who would still be there when the successes began to happen some six years later were Frank Daley and Arthur Tomlinson, although at this time they figured more regularly in the 'A' team than in the senior side. Long-established favourites Harry Ogden and Billy Mitchell were also on board, and the club was blessed with an accomplished finisher in the shape of Joe Warham, who topped the try scorers for three consecutive seasons at the start of the decade. As a crowd pleaser none did more than the flamboyant Lawrie Platt, whose dives for the try-line became legendary. Throw in the likes of Ken Ward, Tommy Leyland, Frank Heyes, Albert Fearnley and Les Anthony, and Oldham could turn out a reasonable outfit capable of giving anybody a good match - but the strength in depth wasn't yet there.

Bryn Goldswain

In January 1950 a teenage second-row forward from Maesteg in South Wales was lured north, although it would not be until October that the powerhouse that was Charlie Winslade made his senior debut. Then, on April 11th 1950, a young prop-forward, signed from the local amateur club Waterhead, made his debut at Warrington. His name was Ken Jackson, and the assemblage of the soon-to-be much-loved and renowned team had begun. A year on from the capture of Goldswain the committee pulled off arguably the finest piece of business in the history of Oldham RLFC when a young man was signed from the Dootsons amateur club in Leigh. The self-assured, seventeen year-old made an immediate impact, filling the spectators with enthusiasm and anticipation even in the pre-season trial games. Alan Davies, Oldham's 'prince of centres', had arrived. A month later a certain William Bernard Ganley joined the club, initially as an amateur before turning professional a year later after the completion of his university studies. Half-backs were deemed to be the next priority, with Frank Stirrup, like Davies and Ganley a native of Leigh, coming from Salford, and the veteran Herbert Goodfellow who was acquired from Wakefield. An undoubted talent, Goodfellow was, unfortunately for the Roughyeds, in the twilight of his career by the time he arrived at Watersheddings, but Stirrup, on the other hand, would go on to play for the club for ten years. A master tactician who could play anywhere in the back division, he was without doubt a major influence on those around him, and more than anyone the architect of the inventive playing style for which his team-mates would become so renowned. The new arrivals now provided a solid base from which to build - and it got

Frank Stirrup

better. Terry O'Grady was just sixteen when he came from the local St. Mary's club. Thrown in at the deep end against St. Helens in March 1951, the speedy winger soon showed his worth, gaining county honours against the touring New Zealanders later in the year, as did Jackson. In the forwards the fiery Bryn Day had strengthened the pack to good effect whereas the speculative signing of Ted Ward from Wigan proved to be a short sighted gamble with the player only making nine appearances.

Since the resumption of a full league championship programme after the Second World War, in time for the 1945-46 season, Oldham had been a mid-table side, but in 1951-52 they shot up to fifth place in the 31- team table, as the burgeoning talent within the side began to flourish. Not least among the

reasons for the improvement in this campaign was the fact that Bernard Ganley became the first Oldham player to achieve the total of 100 goals in a season, and although the reliable Warham still topped the try scorers with 25, O'Grady, Platt and Davies each also touched down on more than twenty occasions, proving that everything was coming together nicely and that Oldham were becoming known for playing attractive, entertaining rugby league. This was the season that the Daley / Stirrup half-back partnership was established. Between them they could tie defences in knots, with their rapport seeming at times to be verging on extra-sensory perception. It is often thought that Stirrup was the brains with Daley in the hard-man, enforcer role. Not a bit of it! Oldham's other major play-maker, Goldswain, acknowledged that it was Daley who often 'called the shots', whereas, allied to his undoubted ball-handling and game-reading skills, Stirrup was a most resolute defender invariably tackling his opponents hard and low.

Bernard Ganley

The following couple of seasons didn't quite live up to the expectations that the 1951-52 campaign hinted at, and although 8th and 12th place weren't too bad compared to what had gone before in the previous twenty years or so, it was the top four that the fans wanted. Of course, finishing at the top of the table was the aim of all clubs, but a place in the elite quartet would qualify them for the end-of-season play-off and a crack at the league championship. The reason for the play-offs was that not all clubs played each other. All the Lancashire clubs, along with the Cumberland pair of Workington and Whitehaven, played each other, and there were also four matches against Yorkshire opposition, and one club from the white rose county would be included in the Lancashire section; usually, but not exclusively, this seemed to be Halifax or Huddersfield, no doubt due to their close proximity to the county border. The rewards for such an inclusion were the potential earnings from attractive fixtures against the best of the Lancashire clubs. The recruitments continued with Walt Nicholson, Lionel Emmitt and Peter Fearis brought into the three-quarters. Full-back Bill Ratchford came from Belle Vue Rangers, half-back Johnny Feather from Leeds and in the forwards I wonder who remembers the Maori, Tipuna 'Smut' Smith and Cumbrian second-row forward, Steve Thurlow? Local lads Harold Lomas, Alf Murray, Alan Jones, Jimmy Mundy and John Watson also joined the ranks.

In February 1952, Oldham had persuaded the ex-Harlequin, Sid Little, to join the club, a master-stoke of business, as the former RAF pilot and Cumbrian county player would go on to gain international honours in Rugby League and to form a formidable partnership with Winslade for the next seven years.

Sid Little

Later that year a young, precocious scrum-half was snapped up from the Leigh St. Josephs amateur club. Frank Pitchford would make his debut on Boxing Day at Liverpool and so begin a tremendous career with the Roughyeds. Lightening quick when breaking from the scrum with the ability to deliver a pass with pin-point precision, Pitchford remains to many of those who saw him play, the best number seven ever to represent the club. In October 1953 the Huddersfield international winger, Dick Cracknell was added to the strength; a great signing for the club of a tried and tested finisher.

And still they came - Roland Barrow, Dennis Ayres, Johnny Noon, Vince Nestor. Barrow came as a centre but was selected on the wing for the 1955 Championship Final, and, but for a controversial over-rule by a touch-judge, could have been a try-scoring hero in the tight match against Warrington. Ayres came as a stand-off but would become a centre in the 1957 championship team, scoring one of the tries in the Odsal final. Noon was a no-nonsense player but with 'good hands' and a neat turn of pace, usually playing at centre but also called upon in all of the back positions, except scrum-half, proving to be equally effective wherever he played, and a good goal-kicker to boot. Likewise Nestor was a good utility back who gave the club great service for ten years. The picture was almost complete, but not quite yet.

Returning to the narrative, on August 8th 1953, Rochdale staged a tremendous late rally to win the Law Cup for the first time since 1948. The Hornets would retain the trophy by way of a draw at Watersheddings in 1954 and another success at the Athletic Ground the following season.

Dick Cracknell

Griff Jenkins

A source of pride for the Oldham supporters was the selection of local lad, Terry O'Grady, for the 1954 tour to Australia and New Zealand, but they were equally mystified by the omission of his team-mate and centre partner, Alan Davies. Nevertheless, Terry was a great success on the tour, scoring 28 tries and playing in five of the six tests.

As mentioned above, Oldham were very close in the 1954-55 season. Griff Jenkins had arrived in July as coach from Swinton, and like him or not, and plenty didn't take to the straight-talking Welshman, he had the team fit, a factor that brought about many victories late in a match, when the Roughyeds were still going strong while their opponents' energy levels were spent. The Lancashire Cup Final was reached for the first time in over 20 years, only for the team to lose to Barrow in poor conditions at Station Road, Swinton. To be fair, the 'Furness-men', under the excellent guidance of skipper Willie Horne, adapted far better to the prevailing conditions and were worthy winners for what was their first major honour. What is more, they followed it up with a triumph in the Challenge Cup final against Workington at the conclusion of the season. Injuries to Goldswain and Ganley in January denied Oldham of two of their most influential players for extended periods. However, the league leaders title looked to be in the bag as the Roughyeds concluded the season with three home matches, but, after Keighley were defeated on April 11th, Leigh came to Watersheddings and pinched a point in a drawn match five days later. Then, horror of horrors, mid-table Hull won the final league match, which enabled Warrington to take the leaders spot on points difference. The Top 4 play-off match brought Leeds to Watersheddings where, after a tight first half, the Roughyeds emerged as comfortable winners. Then there was the Championship final against Warrington at Maine Road, the home of Manchester City F.C. If the conditions were bad against Barrow then they were diabolical

John Etty

here. Two torrential downpours before the kick off left the pitch almost waterlogged and the match a mud-bath. Bath being the defining word in more ways than one, as with the teams scoring one try each, it was Warrington's Australian forward, Harry Bath who twice lifted the ball out of the Manchester mud and over the bar to win the match. As in the match against Barrow, Oldham were guilty of still trying to play their 'top-of-the-ground' open style of play far too often when a more direct and less adventurous game-plan would have served them better.

After the excitement of the '*what might have been*' season of 1954-55, the 1955-56 campaign saw Oldham slip to a disappointing ninth position in the league table. On September 3rd, Alan Davies sensationally announced his retirement from the game due to study and work commitments. However, by the end of the week, whatever reasons had caused the crisis (probably financial) had been averted, and he was back on the team-sheet for a midweek Lancashire cup tie against Leigh. Still, the form of the team was unimpressive, although the cause wasn't helped by O'Grady suffering a fractured ankle in November. However, the silver lining from this cloud emerged when John Etty, signed from Batley early in the year, was switched from centre to wing. The big Yorkshire-man was glad to be back in his favourite position and soon proved that this was where he was meant to be. Six feet tall, Etty was an awesome presence on the left wing, a dynamic finisher, a match winner!

So who was here? Ganley, Cracknell, Davies, Ayres, Etty, O'Grady, Daley, Stirrup, Pitchford, Jackson, Keith, Tomlinson, Winslade, Little, Goldswain…If more strengthening was needed, and it was, the forwards was the place where it was required and it arrived in the uncompromising shape of Derek Turner. Like Goldswain before him, he was recruited from Hull Kingston Rovers, but whereas Bryn was more of a field-marshal, Derek was an 'up and at 'em' company commander, who never knew when he was beaten. This is not to say that Goldswain couldn't put in the hard graft, or that Turner didn't have a subtle touch, but it was the added steel that the gritty Yorkshire-man brought to the team that gave Oldham that bit of extra required for landing the silverware. Don Vines also gave the Roughyeds more fire-power up front, and now the club had a winning combination so that, with Vince Nestor, John Noon, Jack Rogers and Des McKeown waiting in the wings, there was real strength in depth. Success would surely come… and it did.

Derek Turner

To start with the Law Cup was won back from Rochdale in August. On October 20th 1956 Frank Stirrup raised high the Lancashire Cup after Oldham had defeated St. Helens 10 – 3 in the final at Central Park, Wigan, so ending a 23-year gap since the last success in this, a major competition which was witnessed by just under 40,000 spectators. Wigan, Salford and Leigh had been beaten on the way to the final, all away, with the match at Wigan attracting a crowd of 28,000 plus. Two weeks after the Lancashire Cup victory, Oldham entertained the Australian touring team and despatched them 21 – 2. The Challenge Cup was a different story. After seeing off Workington Town at Derwent Park, which was probably as difficult a draw as one could have at the time, Oldham were obliged to travel again in the second round (certainly no luck with the cup draws), this time to Leigh, always a useful side but surely no match for the resurgent Roughyeds? February 23rd, 1957, to paraphrase President Roosevelt, is a date that will live in infamy amongst the Oldham supporters.

I have heard the story of this match as much as, if not more than, any other. The conditions were atrocious! It was freezing and ankle-deep in mud. Tough men like Turner and Etty pleaded with the

Frank Daley

referee Matt Coates to call the game off, but it wasn't to be. Stirrup and Pitchford both had time off the field suffering from severe cold, and the match was settled by an early penalty from Joe Hosking and a late try from Stan Owen. Credit Leigh, because the conditions were the same for them, but on any other day one would have to have fancied Oldham to progress. Indeed, six weeks later the league match at Kirkhall Lane saw Oldham victorious 40 – 13! The Lancashire League trophy was secured and this time Oldham finished as league leaders, six points clear of second -placed Hull. Once again it fell to Leeds to come to Watersheddings in the Top 4 play-off. This was a close encounter, with the result in doubt up until the closing stages, when two tries, both laid on by the irrepressible Frank Daley, saw Oldham progress to a final showdown with Hull at Odsal stadium, Bradford, on May 18th 1957. This was a match filled with passion and drama right up until the final whistle, which saw the Roughyeds scrape home by just a single point. However, a single point is enough and Oldham were the champions of the Rugby League! A splendid season by all accounts, with just the Challenge Cup slipping through the net. Every player was a hero, with each one complimenting the others.

The following 1957-58 season actually provided Oldham with a better league record. The previous campaign had the Roughyeds finish at the top of the table with 33 victories and five losses from their 38 league fixtures. This time Oldham had the same 33 wins, but one draw (against Wakefield) and four defeats left them one point better off. Bernard Ganley reached 200 goals for the season. A remarkable achievement! On March 8th 1958 Wigan finally managed to defeat the Roughyeds for the first time since November 1951. The match was the quarter-final of the Challenge Cup, when over 20,000 packed into Watersheddings to see the men from Central Park end a 14-match losing streak against the Roughyeds (0 - 8) on their way to lifting the trophy with a victory over Workington at Wembley. The Law Cup, Lancashire Cup and Lancashire League titles were retained, and the club once again finished the season at the top of the league championship table. The Lancashire Cup Final was against Wigan at Station Road, Swinton, and to the Oldham supporters will always be remembered as 'Daley's final' for the way the Oldham player dealt with the threat of Billy Boston, who had been moved to the stand-off position in the run up to the final. An awesome defensive display by Daley against his hometown club, and Boston in particular, paved the way for the victory.

However, it all went wrong in the Top 4 play off. Hull had been to Watersheddings on April 16th 1958, in the closing stages of the league season, and were hammered 43 – 9 ; yet just over a fortnight later they came to town again for the play-off match, to return triumphant 8 – 20. The match was played with a 6pm kick off so as not to clash with the televised F.A. Cup final between Bolton Wanderers and Manchester United. The usual appeal of this famous fixture was much increased due to the extraordinary interest in United in the wake of the Munich disaster, which had occurred just three months earlier. Unfortunately for the 'Reds', Bolton won 2 – 0. Likewise there was to be no fairytale for the Roughyeds, as a determined Hull outfit fully deserved their success; they went on to clinch the title with a 20 – 3 victory over Workington, with the match once again played at Odsal.

After the championship play-off defeat work soon started to erect a covered stand at the Watersheddings Street end of the ground, thus giving cover on all four sides. The work was duly finished in time for the start of the 1958-59 campaign, which was approached with an optimism born out of the success of the last two seasons and the capture of Irish Rugby Union international Sean

Quinlan. However, the Law Cup was captured by Rochdale, and before the end of September Don Vines had been transferred to Wakefield Trinity - and the break up of the team had begun. Having said that, the Lancashire Cup was won for a third consecutive season with a victory over St. Helens at Station Road, and at Christmas, Oldham were second in the league table, having won 15 of their 18 league matches so far. After that the form dipped, with the Saints exacting revenge for that Lancashire Cup defeat. They dumped Oldham out of the Challenge Cup in the first round with a single point victory at a packed Watersheddings, and then humiliated them with a 42 – 4 thrashing in the Top 4 play-off match at Knowsley Road. The Roughyeds actually beat St. Helens in the last match of the regular season (14 – 13) at Watersheddings, a result that just edged them into fourth position in the table, enough to meet the eventual champions in the play-off match. It was a strange team that took to the field that day, with Daley being brought in for only his second senior match of the season and Little playing at loose-forward. It proved to be the last match for those two players, and Cracknell also. In March, Ike Southward had been signed from Workington for a record fee of £10,650 but Turner and Etty had followed Vines to Wakefield and THE TEAM had gone. The services of Griff Jenkins were also dispensed with, and the dream was over!

As the decade drew to a close, so did Oldham's position as one of the league's revered teams. In September ten of the 12 committee men were suspended by the Rugby League authorities over alleged illegal payments to players, with scrum-half Frank Pitchford also suspended pending the repayment of a 'club loan'. In the end the Oldham officials fought their corner through the law courts, and won! All of the officials were re-instated, but relations between the club and R.L.H.Q. remained strained for some time in the aftermath of this incident, although it must be said that there was much sympathy for Oldham from other clubs, who realised that the charges levelled at the Roughyeds could indeed have been brought against most of them.

Another huge fee had brought Geoff Robinson to the club from Whitehaven, and in the first half of the season, up until the end of 1959, the performances were good enough, with only four losses and one draw out of 21 league matches while the Law Cup was recaptured from Rochdale. However, the Lancashire Cup defence failed at the first hurdle, at Whitehaven, and the touring Australians defeated the Roughyeds in a bruising encounter at Watersheddings. After Christmas it all fell apart, with another 11 league defeats before the season's end. As if it was an omen of things to come, on January 2nd 1960 Oldham went down the East Lancs Road to play lowly Liverpool City at Knotty Ash, and returned defeated. Ironically, in April, the club reached the semi-final of the Challenge Cup, something that their illustrious immediate predecessors failed to do, and many fancied their chance against Hull at Station Road, but it wasn't to be as, after a bright opening, Oldham tried to mix it with the Hull forwards when it was obvious to the spectators that a passing game would have suited them much better.

The two headlines from the Oldham Evening Chronicle that summed up the first and last matches of the 1950s.

The games were against Rochdale Hornets on January 2nd 1950 and Hull on December 28th 1959.

1950

The start of the 1949-50 season was greeted with the usual optimism but maybe this time there were genuine grounds for renewed hope due to the signing of the multi-talented Bryn Goldswain from Hull Kingston Rovers. The gifted Welsh loose forward was made club captain where his ball handling skills and thoughtful, accurate kicking game, allied to sound defensive qualities, proved to be an inspiration to his team-mates. There was no 'quick-fix' with Goldswain's arrival but the pieces of the jigsaw were beginning to assemble.

A review of the 1949-50 campaign would reveal that there was still little for the Oldham supporters to enthuse about. First round exits to Wigan in the Lancashire Cup and Bradford Northern in the Challenge Cup (although the second leg of these two game affairs was won on each occasion) did nothing to set the fans talking. However, the Law Cup had been recaptured in style with a 35 – 2 victory against Rochdale at the Athletic Grounds and the touring French combined team from the Bordeaux & Villeneuve clubs was beaten 14 - 3 on Easter Monday at a windswept Watersheddings.
A run of three consecutive away matches brought the season to an end as the campaign fizzled out with a run of five defeats. An astonishing Easter programme had seen Oldham play four matches in five days on April 7th, 8th, 10th & 11th. Three games around the holiday period was a regular occurrence but the extra 'friendly' against the French team on Easter Monday was a considerable stretch of resources. 'Hats off', to Wilson Spencer, Joe Warham, Bob Batten, Les Anthony and Albert Fearnley, who each played in all four matches.

Wilson Spencer **Joe Warham** **Bob Batten** **Les Anthony** **Albert Fearnley**

All five players played in four matches in five days during Easter 1950.

January 2nd 1950: OLDHAM 4   ROCHDALE H. 0

I. Barraclough, R. Batten, T. Williams, W. Mitchell, J. Warham, F. Heyes, G. Morgan.
L. Anthony, J. Dean, H. Tomlinson, H. Ambler, T. Leyland, A. Fearnley.
Goals: Barraclough, 2.

Attendance: 7,422   Referee: Mr. C. Appleton – Warrington.

The first match of the new decade saw Oldham without club captain Bryn Goldswain who was injured in the match at Belle Vue two days earlier. Albert Fearnley moved back to loose-forward to take his place and veteran Bert Ambler came in for his first game of the season in the second-row with Billy Mitchell taking over as skipper. The match itself was spoiled by poor weather. A. constant drizzle throughout the match limited the opportunities for open play and after a score-less first period, full-back Irving Barraclough registered the first points with a 48th minute penalty goal and added another later to clinch victory. However, the Hornets nearly stole the points in the last minute when after a mêlée under the Oldham posts, referee Appleton seemed to award a try only to reverse the decision when it emerged that the last player to rise from the mound of players with the ball was the mud-covered home prop Les Anthony.

*Albert Fearnley (13) and 'last-gasp' hero, **Les Anthony** (8) get to grips with a Rochdale player in the first match of the 1950s on a damp and muddy January day at Watersheddings.   (02.01.1950)*

January 7th 1950: OLDHAM 4   WIGAN 14

I. Barraclough, R. Batten, T. Williams, W. Mitchell, J. Warham, K. Ward, G. Morgan.
H. Ogden, J. Dean, H. Tomlinson, A. Fearnley, T. Leyland, B. Goldswain.
Goals: Barraclough, 2.

Attendance: 15,420   Referee: Mr. M. Coates – Pudsey.

A healthy crowd of over 15,000 assembled for the visit of Wigan which was all the more remarkable for on the same day at Boundary Park 31,706 gathered to witness the Latics receive a 7 – 2 hammering from Newcastle United in the F.A. Cup. Oldham had Bryn Goldswain and Harry Ogden back in the team and toiled hard against the eventual champions. Going into the last quarter they only trailed 6 - 4, again the points coming from two penalties from Barraclough, but the class of the men from Central Park told in the end, with winger Len Madden going over for a couple of tries.

January 14ᵗʰ 1950: OLDHAM 13   SWINTON 13

I. Barraclough, R. Batten, K. Ward, W. Mitchell, J. Warham, F. Heyes, G. Morgan.
H. Ogden, J. Dean, H. Tomlinson, A.Fearnley, T. Leyland, B. Goldswain.
Goals: Barraclough,2.   Tries: Warham,2. Fearnley.
Attendance: 14,700   Referee: Mr. P. Cowell - Warrington.

Barraclough opened the scoring with a penalty but against the run of play, Moran followed a kick ahead to score under the posts. 2 – 5 down at the break, Oldham looked likely to take the points after crossing for three tries, only for a late converted try by Woods that gave the 'Lions' a share of the spoils. Highlights for the home fans were the continued consistent form of winger Joe Warham, who chipped in with another two tries, and the inspirational leadership of captain, Bryn Goldswain.

Albert Fearnley is brought down by the Swinton hooker, Frank Osmond, with Harry Ogden up in support. (14.01.1950)

January 21ˢᵗ 1950: BARROW 22   OLDHAM 7

I. Barraclough, J. Warham, K. Ward, W. Mitchell, R. Batten, F. Heyes, G. Morgan.
H. Ogden, J. Dean, H. Tomlinson, A. Fearnley, T. Leyland, B. Goldswain.
Goals: Barraclough,2. Try: Warham.
Attendance: 10,263   Referee: Mr. G. Phillips – Widnes.

After three successive home games Oldham travelled up to Barrow. Only 5 -2 down at the break, they had no answer to the Willie Horne inspired home outfit in the second half. The Barrow three-quarters responded to their captain's efforts with Lewthwaite (2), Castle and Guest all crossing the whitewash. All the Roughyeds had to show was a late obstruction try awarded to Warham. Oldham had decided to switch wingers Warham and Batten from the previous games and must have deemed the exercise a success by keeping Warham on the right flank for the rest of the season.

January 28ᵗʰ should have marked the debut of the club's new signing, an 18 year old Welsh forward from Maesteg by the name of Charles Winslade. However, the match at Castleford was postponed due to frost and it would be another nine months before Charlie would start his glittering Roughyeds career.

1950

February 4th 1950: OLDHAM 5 BRADFORD N. 16
Rugby League Challenge Cup 1st Round 1st leg

I. Barraclough, J. Warham, K. Ward, W. Mitchell, R. Batten, F. Heyes, J. Silva.
H. Ogden, J. Dean, H. Ambler, A.Fearnley, T. Leyland, B. Goldswain.
Goal: Barraclough. Try: Leyland.

Attendance: 18,052   Referee: Mr. F. Cottam - Wakefield.

Oldham flattered to deceive in this cup-tie against the current holders when Ogden put Leyland over for a try after seven minutes. By half-time 'Northern' were level and by the close of the match had a nine point advantage for the second leg. However, things might have been different if Oldham had not been reduced to twelve men when Mitchell was carried off with concussion after 30 minutes. This was the last first team match for veteran forward Bert Ambler who first played for the club in 1935.

The injury to Mitchell raised once more one of the common debates in the game at the time regarding the use of substitutes. However, it would be another 14 years before the rule was introduced.

The Oldham team against Bradford Northern on February 4th 1950.

Back Row: *Johnny Dean, Ken Ward, Bert Ambler, Harry Ogden, Tommy Leyland, Albert Fearnley.*
Middle Row: *Irving Barraclough, Bob Batten, Bryn Goldswain, Billy Mitchell, Frank Heyes.*
Front Row: *Joe Silva, Joe Warham.*

OPPOSITE:
Above: *Frank Heyes picks up a loose ball watched by **Albert Fearnley** and **Emlyn Walters**.*

Below: *Bradford Northern's **Ken Traill** prepares to kick in front of the packed Watersheddings terraces. (04.02.1950)*

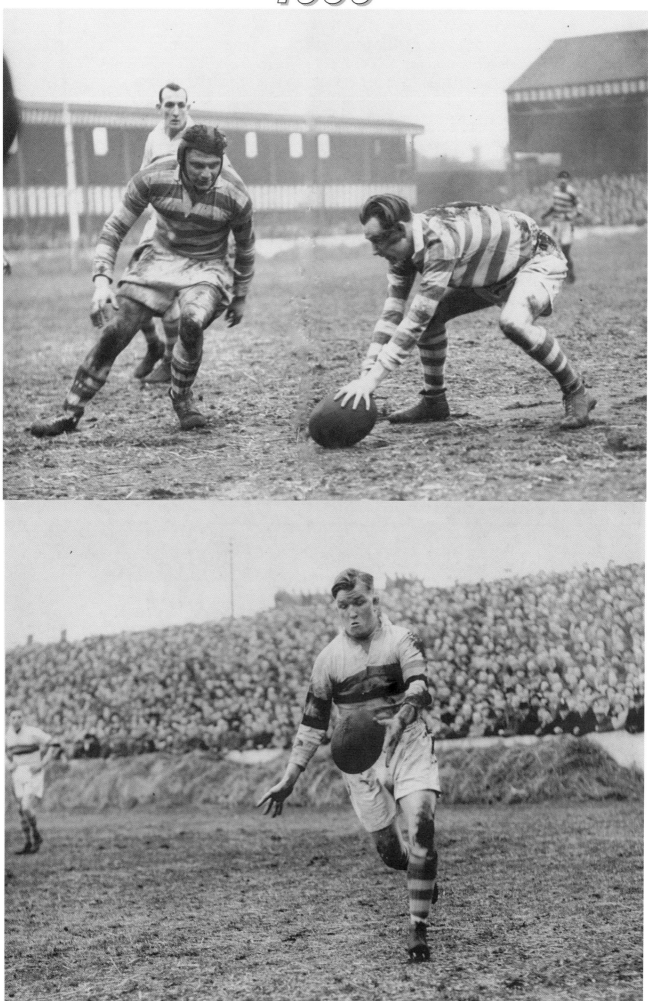

February 11th 1950: BRADFORD N. 6   OLDHAM 8
Rugby League Challenge Cup 1st Round 2nd leg
I Barraclough, J Warham, K Ward, W Mitchell, R Batten, F Heyes, J Silva.
H Ogden, J Dean, L Anthony, J Sugden, T Leyland, B Goldswain.
Goal: Barraclough. Tries: Mitchell,2.

Attendance 13,321   Referee: Mr. C. Appleton - Warrington.

A good repost from Oldham to the previous week's disappointment, which was capped by a glorious try just before half time when Ken Ward intercepted near his own line and released Heyes on a dazzling run which was finished off by Mitchell to give Oldham a 3 – 2 lead at the interval. Indeed when Mitchell went over again two minutes into the second period the home fans were worried. However, two penalty goals from Ernest Ward steadied the ship but couldn't deny the Roughyeds a deserved victory.

Charlie Winslade made his rugby league debut in the 'A' team's 23 - 0 victory at Rochdale on this day.

February 18th 1950: OLDHAM 17   WHITEHAVEN 3
I Barraclough, J Warham, K Ward, W Mitchell, R Batten, F Heyes, J Silva.
H Ogden, J Dean, L Anthony, J Sugden, T Leyland, B Goldswain.
Goal: Goldswain. Tries: Warham,3. Ward. Batten.

Attendance: 10,232   Referee: Mr L. J. Dalby - York.

This was Whitehaven's first season in the Rugby League and thus their first ever visit to Watersheddings. The mood was set as early as the second minute when Leyland and Anthony made the opening for Batten to dive in at the corner. Hooker Johnny Dean gave the Roughyeds the monopoly of scrum possession, and Warham benefited to the tune of a 'hat-trick' of tries. Indifferent goal kicking kept the score down and who knows what the score might have been had Joe Silva not had to retire through injury after half an hour with skipper Goldswain taking over at the base of the scrum.

Joe Warham scores one of his three tries to the dismay of the Whitehaven defenders.

18.02.1950

1950

March 4ᵗʰ 1950: OLDHAM 10   BELLE VUE R. 5
I Barraclough, J Warham, K Ward, W Mitchell, R Batten, J Chalmers, G Morgan.
H Ogden, J Dean, L Anthony, A Fearnley, T Leyland, B Goldswain.
Goals: Barraclough,2. Tries: Mitchell. Fearnley.
Attendance: 9,040   Referee: Mr. F. Smith Barrow.

A dour match with one of the few highlights being a smart move by Anthony and Chalmers which put Mitchell over for a first half try. A further scrambled effort by Fearnley in the second half and two Barraclough goals were all Oldham had to offer. Fortunately all Rangers could manage was a converted late score from Elwyn Gwyther. Some consolation for Belle Vue was that Gwyther and ex-Roughyed Doug Phillips were selected for the 1950 tour earlier in the week.

Ken Ward breaks away from the Belle Vue Rangers defence with Joe Warham ready for the pass on the right wing.

The Belle Vue captain, ex-Oldham favourite, Doug Phillips, is on the far right.
(04.03.1950)

Oldham in red and white hoops. Rangers in blue and white hoops. No problem for the spectators on the day, but on the photograph… oh, for those navy blue shorts!

March 11ᵗʰ 1950: SWINTON 17   OLDHAM 5
I. Barraclough, J. Warham, K. Ward, W. Mitchell, R. Batten, F. Heyes, G. Morgan.
H. Ogden, J. Dean, H. Tomlinson, A. Fearnley, T. Leyland, B. Goldswain.
Goal: Barraclough. Try: Warham.
Attendance: 10,000   Referee: Mr. L. Thorpe - Wakefield.

Oldham took the lead when a Ward breakaway opened the defence for Warham to cross for a try. Morgan and Barraclough then exchanged penalties before Holden got over for Swinton in the 35th minute. All square at the break, the 'Lions' went in front when ex-Roughyed, Vince Kenny did well to put Coburn on a run to the posts. Despite a sterling show from Ogden and Mitchell, there was no way back for Oldham. Ward also did well but Swinton finished strongly and were worthy winners.

1950

March 18th 1950: OLDHAM 4 WIDNES 4

L. Platt, J. Warham, K. Ward, W. Mitchell, R. Batten, F. Heyes, G. Morgan.
H. Ogden, J. Keith, L. Anthony, T. Leyland, A. Fearnley, B. Goldswain.
Goals: Goldswain, 2.

Attendance: 8,793   Referee: Mr. H. Squires - Ossett.

Games against the 'Chemics' were often dull affairs in this era. Indeed in the match at Widnes earlier in the season a scoreless draw was the order of the day. This was no exception with the only trouble for the scoreboard operator coming from two penalty goals for Bryn Goldswain in the first half and likewise two for Colin Hutton after the interval. A selection experiment saw Lawrie Platt tried at full back and the reintroduction of Jack Keith at hooker.

Above: Albert Fearnley and Ken Ward (3) can only watch as one of their team-mates is bundled into touch by several Widnes defenders.
An example of the sound defensive display from both teams that ensured the match remained try-less.

Right: Joe Warham chips the ball over his opposite number in a bid to break down the tight Widnes defence.

(18.03.1950)

March 25th 1950: OLDHAM 21 CASTLEFORD 9

L. Platt, J. Warham, K. Ward, W. Mitchell, R. Batten, F. Heyes, J. Silva.
H. Ogden, J. Dean, L. Anthony, A. Fearnley, T. Leyland, B. Goldswain.
Goals: Goldswain,3. Tries: Warham,2. Heyes,2. Silva.
Attendance: 6,891   Referee: Mr. S. Adams – Hull.

A brace of tries for Heyes in the first half, the first as a result of a charged kick, and Warham in the second period, combined with a cheeky effort from Silva who reportedly leaped over the full-back, were enough to see off 'Cas' on their only visit to Watersheddings in the 1950s. A try from Staines and three Langfield goals formed Castleford's reply. The match was a replay of the game abandoned on November 19th due to fog.

April 1st 1950: OLDHAM 28 BRAMLEY 5

L. Platt, J. Warham, K. Ward, W. Mitchell, W. Spencer, J. Chalmers, J. Silva.
H. Ogden, J. Keith, L. Anthony, A. Fearnley, T. Leyland, B. Goldswain.
Goals: Ogden,4. Goldswain. Tries: Anthony,2. Ward. Mitchell. Spencer. Fearnley.
Attendance: 6,770   Referee: Mr. R. Gelder - Wakefield.

After Spencer was bundled into touch just short of the line in the first minute, this went on to be a close affair for the first twenty minutes before Oldham took control and eventually took the game away from the 'Villagers'. The first try came on the half hour when Anthony snapped up a loose ball to go under the posts, and it was followed by a fine break by Chalmers who unleashed Mitchell to go around the full-back and once again score at the posts. Rhodes got Bramley on the scoreboard with a penalty but 12 - 2 up at the break, Oldham always looked comfortable. There was a notable contribution from the props in this match with two tries for Anthony and four goals kicked by Ogden. Scrum-half Caywood got a consolation try for the visitors.

April 7th 1950: OLDHAM 5 SALFORD 8

W. Spencer, J. Warham, K.Ward, W. Mitchell, R. Batten, J. Chalmers, J. Silva.
H. Ogden, J. Keith, L. Anthony, A. Fearnley, T. Leyland, B. Goldswain.
Goal: Spencer. Try: Warham.
Attendance: 18,182   Referee: Mr. L. J. Dalby – York.

The best attendance of the season assembled at Watersheddings for this 'Good Friday' encounter. After a scoreless first quarter, two unconverted tries from Danby and Harrison gave Salford a six nil interval lead.

Oldham toiled away in the second half but the 'Red Devils' held firm even though second-row forward Brown was sent off. The only time their defence was breached came from a piece of improvisation from Warham who took a quick tap penalty to sneak by a surprised defence for Oldham's only try.

Harry Ogden copes with the attentions of the Salford prop, Eynon Hawkins, as he slips the ball to Albert Fearnley who breaks clear.

(07.04.1950)

1950

April 8th 1950: ROCHDALE H. 7   OLDHAM 13

W. Spencer, J. Warham, K. Ward, W. Mitchell, R. Batten, F. Daley, J. Silva.
H. Ogden, J. Keith, L. Anthony, J. Sugden, T. Leyland, A. Fearnley.
Goals: Spencer. Ogden.   Tries: Daley,2. Sugden.
Attendance: 5,000   Referee: Mr. G. Phillips - Widnes.

It was the Oldham forwards who laid down the foundations for this 'derby' victory over Hornets. The recalled John Sugden had a storming match crashing over for a try himself and again scattering defenders to send in Daley for one of his brace. Ex-Rochdale man Fearnley also showed up well. A penalty goal by Ogden from the half-way line was the highlight of a tight first period.

April 10th 1950: Oldham 14   Bordeaux & Villeneuve 3 (Friendly)

L. Platt, J. Warham, T. Williams, W. Mitchell, R. Batten, F. Daley, W. Spencer.
H. Ogden, J. Keith, L. Anthony, A. Fearnley, J. Sugden, B. Goldswain.
Goal: Spencer.   Tries: Daley. Keith. Williams. Spencer.
Attendance: 4,901   Referee: Mr. F. Smith – Barrow.

The match against the 'select' of Bordeaux & Villeneuve played on Easter Monday 1950 was to a great degree spoiled by the weather. It was reported that as home captain, Bryn Goldswain, made the toss before the game, hailstones were swept across the pitch by a cold driving wind. Open play was at a premium and what there was of it tended to come from Oldham in the first half when they played 'with the weather'. By the time the French had the benefit of the elements in the second half they were a spent force. All they had to show for their efforts was a try from left wing, Vigouroux. In reply Oldham had tries from Daley, Keith, Williams and Spencer who also kicked the solitary goal to give them a comfortable victory.

OLDHAM EVENING CHRONICLE, Tuesday, April 11, 1950.

WEATHER WAS SPOIL-SPORT AT WATERSHEDDINGS

Forwards shone again in win over plucky French team

FIRST WIND, THEN SLEET, AND FINALLY SNOW SPOILED THE ATTRACTIVE RUGBY GAME AT WATERSHEDDINGS YESTERDAY, AND THE TALKING POINT, WHEN THOUGHTS OF THIS MATCH ARE RECALLED IN FUTURE YEARS, WILL HOW THE WEATHER ELEMENT SPOILED OLDHAM'S GAME WITH BORDEAUX & VILLENEUVE, WRITES NORTHERN.

OLDHAM
FOOTBALL CLUB

OLDHAM
V.
BORDEAUX & VILLENEUVE
(FRENCH RUGBY LEAGUE COMBINED TEAMS)
at Watersheddings
Easter Monday, 10th April, 1950
Kick-off 2-30 p.m.

Official Programme - 2d.

Gordon Whittaker Ltd., Printers, Oldham.

Below: The teams line up for the national anthems   (10.04.1950)

April 11ᵗʰ 1950: WARRINGTON 26   OLDHAM 12
W. Spencer, J. Warham, K.Ward, L. Platt, R. Batten, F. Daley, J. Silva.
K. Jackson, J. Dean, L. Anthony, A. Fearnley, J. Sugden, B. Goldswain.
Goals: Goldswain,3. Tries: Warham,2.

Attendance: 7,491   Referee: Mr. F. Smith – Barrow.

Bad handling let Oldham down in this match although Warrington, freshly qualified for the Challenge Cup final, were the better team and led 15 - 4 at the interval. However, the biggest cheer of the day was reserved for Warrington-born Joe Warham after a magnificent 75 yard dash to score after 70 minutes, and it was repeated when he side-stepped his way over again five minutes later. Twenty one year old Ken Jackson showed up well on his senior debut at prop-forward.

April 15ᵗʰ 1950: OLDHAM 11   WORKINGTON T. 31
W. Spencer, J. Warham, K. Ward, R. Batten, T. Williams, F. Daley, J. Silva.
K. Jackson, J. Keith, L. Anthony, J. Sugden, A. Fearnley, B. Goldswain.
Goal: Ward. Tries: Williams. Fearnley. Goldswain.

Attendance: 9,535   Referee: Mr. T. Armitage – Huddersfield.

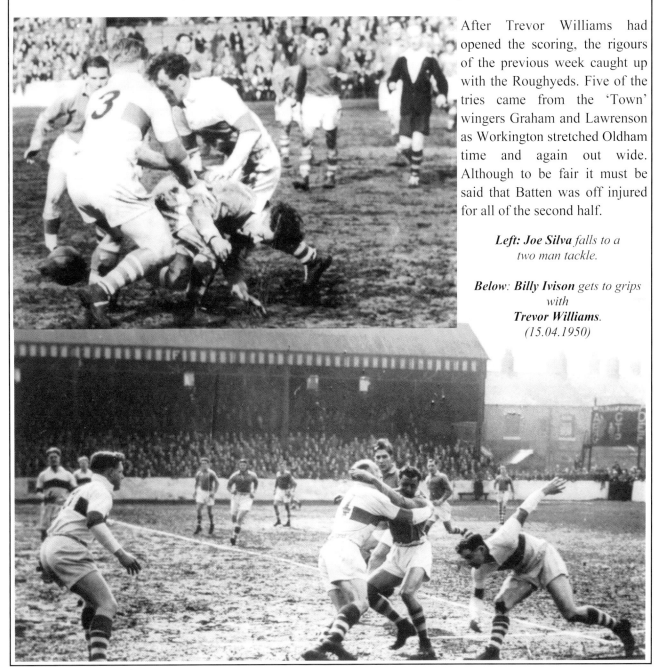

After Trevor Williams had opened the scoring, the rigours of the previous week caught up with the Roughyeds. Five of the tries came from the 'Town' wingers Graham and Lawrenson as Workington stretched Oldham time and again out wide. Although to be fair it must be said that Batten was off injured for all of the second half.

*Left: **Joe Silva** falls to a two man tackle.*

*Below: **Billy Ivison** gets to grips with **Trevor Williams**. (15.04.1950)*

1950

April 19th 1950: CASTLEFORD 7 OLDHAM 5

I. Barraclough, J. Warham, K. Ward, W. Mitchell, T. Williams, F. Daley, J. Rea.
K. Jackson, J. Keith, L. Anthony, T. Leyland, A. Fearnley, B. Goldswain.
Goal: Barraclough. Try: Warham.

Attendance: 5,000   Referee: Mr. W. E. Smith – Dewsbury.

The report in the Chronicle made much of the fact that Mr. Smith of Dewsbury, a touch judge who stood in at the last minute as referee for the scheduled official Norman Railton, did the Roughyeds no favours. Oldham brought back Joe Rea after a lengthy absence at scrum-half and maybe it was his lack of match practice that enabled Ferguson to intercept a pass from him to score the first try after six minutes. Staines added a penalty after 25 minutes and Langfield knocked over another in the first minute after the break. Tommy Leyland returned after injury and laid on the Oldham try after charging down a kick from Langfield after an hour, before putting Warham over for the score. Barraclough converted and although Oldham finished on the attack, it was to no avail as the 'Cas' defence had the resolve to see out the match.

April 22nd 1950: FEATHERSTONE R. 12 OLDHAM 3

L. Platt, J. Warham, K. Ward, W. Mitchell, R. Batten, F. Daley, J. Rea.
L. Anthony, J. Keith, E. Brooks, T. Leyland, A. Fearnley, B. Goldswain.
Try: Warham.

Attendance: 2,500   Referee: Mr. P. Cowell – Warrington.

Another fruitless visit into Yorkshire saw veteran hooker Edgar Brooks return after injury at prop-forward. Miller opened the scoring with a penalty in the 11th minute before Payne scored the only try of the first half. Ward was the pick of the Oldham players laying on the try for Warham who neatly side-stepped the full-back on his way to the line. Only trailing 7 – 3 with a few minutes to go, Leyland was pulled down just short by Blackburn before a late converted try by Gilbertson consolidated the victory for Rovers.

April 29th 1950: WHITEHAVEN 5 OLDHAM 3

I. Barraclough, J. Warham, K. Ward, W. Mitchell, W. Spencer, R. Batten, J. Rea.
J. Taylor, J. Keith, L. Anthony, T. Leyland, E. Wiggett, A. Fearnley.
Try: Batten.

Attendance: 5,000   Referee: Mr. R. Gelder – Wakefield.

Pouring rain greeted Oldham on their first trip to Whitehaven but they settled the better of the teams until Keen scored against the run of play on 14 minutes. Oldham responded with a Bob Batten try before Jack Taylor was sent off after a fracas with Dover at the end of the first half. After some indifferent kicking, home full-back McKeown settled the match with a penalty on the hour. Late on Batten and Warham both had tries disallowed. It definitely wasn't Oldham's day as Barraclough saw two goal attempts come back off the upright.

Left: Joe Rea - Scrum-half who was recalled for the last three matches of the season.

Right: Eric Wiggett - Second-row forward signed from the local Austerlands club who made his first team debut in the final match of the 1949-50 season at Whitehaven.

1950

The final league table saw Oldham in 18th position with 34 points from 15 wins, 4 draws and 17 defeats. This was however, a rise of five places from the previous season.

Most Appearances: Tommy Leyland 38 out of a possible 41.
Most tries: Joe Warham: 18.
Most goals: Irving Barraclough: 66.
Most points: Irving Barraclough: 132.

Tommy Leyland

Irving Barraclough

Joe Warham

	1949-50	Played	Won	Draw	Lost	For	Against	Points
1	Wigan	36	31	1	4	853	320	63
2	Huddersfield	36	28	1	7	694	362	57
3	Swinton	36	25	4	7	516	261	54
4	Halifax	36	25	0	11	496	251	50
5	Salford	36	24	2	10	427	306	50
6	Leigh	36	24	1	11	459	269	49
7	St. Helens	36	23	2	11	540	260	48
8	Leeds	36	24	0	12	602	365	48
9	Dewsbury	36	23	0	13	468	266	46
10	Workington T.	36	22	1	13	514	319	45
11	Warrington	36	22	0	14	579	367	44
12	Castleford	36	20	0	16	431	386	40
13	Keighley	36	20	0	16	375	390	40
14	Wakefield T.	36	19	0	17	523	447	38
15	Hunslet	36	18	1	17	405	317	37
16	Widnes	36	16	4	16	373	316	36
17	Belle Vue R.	36	16	2	18	388	393	34
18	**OLDHAM**	**36**	**15**	**4**	**17**	**395**	**411**	**34**
19	Hull	36	15	3	18	364	527	33
20	Barrow	36	14	1	21	393	464	29
21	Bradford N.	36	14	1	21	335	413	29
22	Hull K.R.	36	14	1	21	305	474	29
23	Whitehaven	36	11	4	21	262	432	26
24	Batley	36	10	0	26	346	555	20
25	Featherstone R.	36	9	2	25	300	551	20
26	Bramley	36	6	1	29	258	676	13
27	Rochdale H.	36	5	2	29	200	547	12
28	York	36	6	0	30	274	807	12
29	Liverpool S.	36	4	0	32	198	821	8

SEASON	PLAYER	APPS	TRIES	GOALS	POINTS
1949-50	T. LEYLAND	38	3		9
1949-50	R. BATTEN	37	10		30
1949-50	B. GOLDSWAIN	36	6	13	44
1949-50	K. WARD	33	8	1	26
1949-50	H. OGDEN	31	1	5	13
1949-50	W. MITCHELL	30	7		21
1949-50	I. BARRACLOUGH	29		66	132
1949-50	J. WARHAM	27	18		54
1949-50	F. HEYES	27	7		21
1949-50	A. FEARNLEY	26	5		15
1949-50	H. TOMLINSON	26	1		3
1949-50	E. BROOKS	17	1		3
1949-50	W. SPENCER	16	6	2	22
1949-50	L. ANTHONY	16	2		6
1949-50	J. KEITH	14			
1949-50	T. WILLIAMS	13	5		15
1949-50	L. PLATT	13	1		3
1949-50	J. SILVA	12	1		3
1949-50	G. GILMORE	12			
1949-50	W.G. MORGAN	12			
1949-50	J. DEAN	12			
1949-50	J. SUGDEN	11	1		3
1949-50	F. DALEY	9	3		9
1949-50	J. DONEGAN	5			
1949-50	H. GLANVILLE	4		7	14
1949-50	R. BYRNE	4			
1949-50	J. TAYLOR	4			
1949-50	J. CHALMERS	3			
1949-50	K. JACKSON	3			
1949-50	J. REA	3			
1949-50	J. TYNAN	3			
1949-50	G. WELSBY	2			
1949-50	H.D. AMBLER	2			
1949-50	E. WIGGETT	1			
1949-50	A. TOMLINSON	1			
1949-50	"WAKEFIELD" (trialist)	1			
1949-50	**TOTAL**	**533**	**86**	**94**	**446**

1950-51

There was a 'buzz' around the stands and terraces at the pre-season trial game for the 1950-51 season concerning a young centre from the Leigh area. A sprightly, dark haired, young man who oozed confidence and played with a maturity that was way beyond his seventeen years. The man in question, Alan Davies. He made his debut on the left wing against Wakefield on September 9th and right from the off he was a marked man coming in for some serious attention from the 'Trinity' defenders. Alan didn't score that day but his centre Billy Mitchell obliged with a 'hat-trick' for which I'm sure Alan would have been quick to take some credit. A new full-back, Bill Ratchford was bought from Belle Vue Rangers and another exciting young prospect was the Welsh forward Charlie Winslade from Maesteg who made his senior debut against Leigh on October 21st. Joe Warham again topped the try charts with 20 and Bryn Goldswain just nudged over the half century to finish as leading goal kicker and also made most appearances with 37, along with Ratchford.

The club reached the semi-final of the Lancashire cup losing out narrowly to Warrington in a tense cup-tie at Watersheddings. Leeds accounted for the Roughyeds in the first round of the Challenge Cup. Oldham managed to win the second leg but the Yorkshiremen had laid down a solid advantage from the first encounter. The Law Cup was retained in remarkable style with a real 'backs to the wall' victory over the Hornets which was accomplished despite having several players unable to finish the match through injury. In contrast to the previous season Oldham finished with a flourish as three straight victories elevated them to 15th position in the 29 club league which represented an improvement of three places on the 1949-50 campaign from 17 victories, 2 draws and 17 defeats.

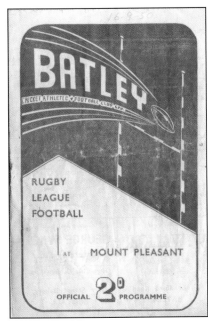  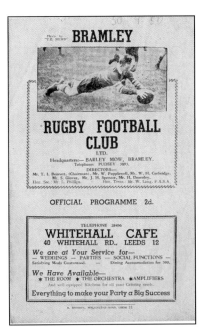

*Below: How the dramatic Law Cup victory was reported in the next home match programme and the 'hero of the hour', **Gerry Gilmore,** in what was to be his last appearance in the Oldham first team.*

WATERSHEDDINGS NEW AND VIEWS

May we compliment our team on their Annual Charity Match victory against Rochdale Hornets on Saturday last. A victory we may record equal to Rorke's Drift, a name given To a famous Test Match in Australia when England battled along with ten players against The might of Australia and won the day. This was many days ago, but the spirit still prevails in British sport, and it was a magnificent effort by our players, ten in number on the field, and of those ten, our scrum half, Gilmore, battled on with a painful thigh injury, manfully they stuck to their work, and I can assure readers that at the final whistle the victors were on the verge of exhaustion. A great victory indeed was this against odds that were overwhelming.

August 12th 1950: Oldham 10   Rochdale H. 9

Law Cup

W. Ratchford, J. Warham, K. Ward, W. Mitchell, L. Platt, F. Heyes, G. Gilmore.
L. Anthony, E. Brooks, A. Tomlinson, J. Sugden, A. Fearnley, B. Goldswain.
Goals: Ratchford. Gilmore. Tries: Mitchell. Fearnley.
Attendance: 5,359   Referee: Mr. P. Cowell – Warrington.

New signing Bill Ratchford, recruited from Belle Vue Rangers, made his debut and Gerry Gilmore was reintroduced at scrum-half for the first time since the previous December. Ken Ward paved the way for a Mitchell try which combined with a Gilmore drop goal and an opportunist try from Fearnley, after a Rochdale fumble, gave Oldham an 8 – 4 interval lead. However, Platt with a head injury and Mitchell with a broken nose failed to come out after the break so the Roughyeds were well and truly up against it! And it got worse when Sugden had to retire with a leg injury after 60 minutes and Gilmore had to soldier on with a painful thigh injury. Nevertheless the rest of the Oldham players rallied to the cause and Ratchford's second half penalty was enough to secure one of the most dramatic victories in the history of the trophy.

August 19th 1950: WHITEHAVEN 10   OLDHAM 10

W. Ratchford, J. Warham, K. Ward, W. Mitchell, R. Batten, F. Heyes, J. Rea.
L. Anthony, E. Brooks, A. Tomlinson, A. Fearnley, B. Goldswain, B. Day.
Goals: Goldswain,2. Tries: Anthony. A. Tomlinson.
Attendance: 9,547   Referee: Mr A. Hill – Dewsbury.

Signed earlier in the week from Belle Vue Rangers, Bryn Day made his Oldham debut as the Roughyeds started the new league season where they had concluded the old one and it was an unlucky day, again, for Oldham at Whitehaven! In the first half Frank Heyes had a try disallowed for a double movement and then 'Haven were awarded an obstruction try after a Ward tackle on Railton, but later a similar offence on Fearnley resulted in a penalty kick only. Despite these setbacks Tomlinson strode away to score under the posts in the first half and a late try by fellow prop Anthony who took Warham's inside pass to touch down, gave Oldham a share of the spoils.

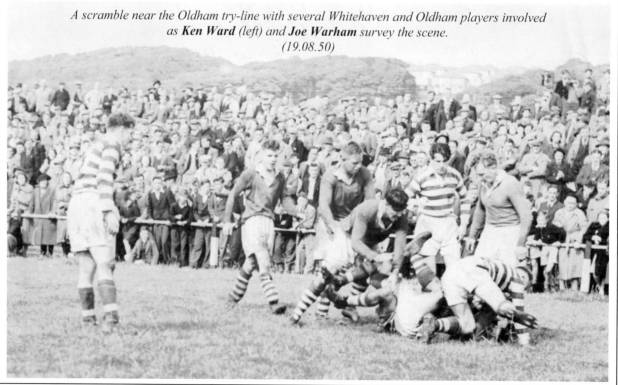

A scramble near the Oldham try-line with several Whitehaven and Oldham players involved
*as **Ken Ward** (left) and **Joe Warham** survey the scene.*
(19.08.50)

August 21st 1950: OLDHAM 7 WARRINGTON 8
W. Ratchford, J. Warham, K. Ward, W. Mitchell, R. Batten, F. Heyes, J. Silva.
L. Anthony, E. Brooks, A. Tomlinson, T. Leyland, B. Goldswain, B. Day.
Goals: Goldswain. Heyes. Try: Leyland.

Attendance: 12,327   Referee: Mr. N. T. Railton – Wigan.

By all accounts this was a splendid match with Oldham going in at the interval with a 2 – 0 advantage thanks to a Goldswain penalty goal. However, the Roughyeds were handicapped by having to play all of the second half without the injured Ward. Nevertheless, a Leyland try backed up by a Heyes drop goal looked like securing a home side victory. In the end it wasn't to be as a late drop goal from loose-forward, Palin dashed Oldham's hopes, although the drama continued to the last when Goldswain had a subsequent penalty chance to save the match but the attempt swung wide of the posts.

Harold Palin - *Match-winner for the 'Wire'.*

August 26th 1950: OLDHAM 44 YORK 2
W. Ratchford, J. Warham, R. Batten, W. Mitchell, L. Platt, F. Heyes, J. Silva.
L. Anthony, E. Brooks, A. Tomlinson, T. Leyland, B. Goldswain, B. Day.
Goals: Goldswain,7. Tries: Platt,4. Batten,2. Heyes,2. Warham. Goldswain.

Attendance: 8,373   Referee: Mr. T. Armitage – Huddersfield.

So, Oldham were three games into the season with a single point victory, a single point defeat and a draw. Something had to give and unfortunately York found themselves subject to a rich vein of Roughyeds form. The backs did the damage with nine of the ten tries. It was a particularly good day for Lawrie Platt, brought back to the side on the left wing, with four tries. Batten and Heyes also bagged a brace each with Goldswain adding a try to his seven goals, as the Oldham backs ran the 'Minster-men' ragged.

Lawrie Platt - *The local wingman was in great form against York*
with four tries and emerged as the match-winner in the next game at
Belle Vue Rangers four days later.

August 30th 1950: BELLE VUE R. 14 OLDHAM 15
W. Ratchford, J. Warham, L. Platt, W. Mitchell, W. Spencer, F. Heyes, J. Silva.
L. Anthony, E. Brooks, A. Tomlinson, T. Leyland, A. Fearnley, B. Goldswain.
Goals: Goldswain,3. Tries: Platt. Spencer. Hayes.

Attendance: 4,000 (est.)   Referee: Mr. C. Appleton – Warrington.

Another narrow squeak with Oldham prevailing again by a single point. It was the first half showing that secured the win. They led 12 – 4 at the break thanks to tries from Spencer and Heyes combined with three goals from Goldswain . However, after losing Fearnley to injury after 47 minutes possession was harder to come by and Rangers fought their way back into the match. Platt proved to be the hero again, this time forcing his way over from close range to register the decisive score.

September 2nd 1950: OLDHAM 21   ROCHDALE H. 5
Lancashire Cup 1st. Round 1st. Leg.
W. Ratchford, J. Warham, L. Platt, W. Mitchell, W. Spencer, F. Heyes, J. Silva.
L. Anthony, E. Brooks, A. Tomlinson, E. Wiggett, T. Leyland, B. Goldswain.
Goals: Goldswain,6. Tries: Platt. Heyes. A. Tomlinson.
Attendance: 10,772   Referee: Mr. T. Watkinson - Manchester.

An early try by Tomlinson set the tone for this match with the Roughyeds dominant in the first half. A further try from Platt and four Goldswain goals gave Oldham a 14 – 0 interval lead. A try from Heyes and two more goals from the inspirational Oldham skipper took the Roughyeds well clear before a late rally by Hornets gave them a little consolation before the second leg.

The Oldham team against Rochdale on September 2nd 1950.
***Back Row**: Billy Mitchell, Eric Wiggett, Arthur Tomlinson, Edgar Brooks, Tommy Leyland, Les Anthony.*
***Middle Row**: Joe Warham, Wilson Spencer, Bryn Goldswain, Lawrie Platt, Bill Ratchford,*
***Front Row**: Joe Silva, Frank Heyes.*

September 9th 1950: OLDHAM 35   WAKEFIELD T. 8
W. Ratchford, J. Warham, L. Platt, W. Mitchell, A. Davies, F. Heyes, J. Silva.
L. Anthony, E. Brooks, J. Taylor, A. Tomlinson, T. Leyland, B. Goldswain.
Goals: Goldswain,6. Mitchell. Tries: Mitchell,3. Platt,2. Warham,2.
Attendance: 11,612   Referee: Mr. L. J. Dalby – York.

A fine win for the Roughyeds and, what is more, the debut match (on the wing) for the 17½ year old, Alan Davies who reportedly came in from some rough treatment from the visitors. Goldswain was again the main danger with another fine display of ball distribution from which centres Platt and Mitchell benefited to the tune of five tries. Little went right for 'Trinity' after Duggan had given them a lead in the second minute. Mitchell supplemented his 'hat-trick' of tries with a rare drop goal.

Arthur Tomlinson on the move against Wakefield flanked by **Les Anthony, Tommy Leyland** and **Jack Taylor**.
(09.09.1950)

September 12th 1950: ROCHDALE H. 2   OLDHAM 14
Lancashire Cup 1st. Round 2nd. Leg.
W. Ratchford, J. Warham, L. Platt, W. Mitchell, A. Davies, F. Heyes, J. Silva.
L. Anthony, E. Brooks, J. Taylor, A. Tomlinson, T. Leyland, B. Goldswain.
Goal: Ratchford. Tries: Warham,2. Platt. Leyland.
Attendance: 8,000   Referee: Mr. W. Stockley - Leigh.

Hornets were 16 points adrift from the first leg and although a sixth minute penalty goal from Stockley might briefly have raised hopes, the 32nd minute dismissal of Booth, after an altercation with Tomlinson, as good as sealed their fate. Four tries to nil tells the story of Oldham's superiority with an enthusiastic display from 'young Davies' catching the eye.

September 16th 1950. BATLEY 15   OLDHAM 7
W. Ratchford, J. Warham, L. Platt, F. Daley, A. Davies, F. Heyes, J. Silva.
L. Anthony, E. Brooks, A. Tomlinson, B. Goldswain, T. Leyland, B. Day.
Goals: Goldswain,2. Try: Warham.
Attendance: 7,900   Referee: Mr. A. Cowell – Warrington.

An uninspiring match at Mount Pleasant with the home side running out worthy winners after an evenly fought first half ended level at 5 – 5 with Warham's fifth touchdown in three games the only Oldham try of the encounter. Lack of possession cost Oldham dear but it took a late try from Briggs converted by, none other than, John Etty to make the game safe for the 'Gallant Youths'. Ratchford was the pick of the Oldham players for whom Bryn Day celebrated his return from injury by being sent off late in the match!

1950-51

September 23rd 1950: OLDHAM 7 BARROW 2
W. Ratchford, J. Warham, L. Platt, W. Mitchell, R. Batten, F. Heyes, J. Silva.
J. Taylor, E. Brooks, H. Tomlinson, A. Tomlinson, B. Day, B. Goldswain.
Goals: Goldswain,2. Try: Warham.

Attendance: 10,890   Referee: Mr. S. Abram - Wigan.

Harold Tomlinson returned for his first match of the season only to leave the field injured early in the game. Lewthwaite gave Barrow the lead with a penalty but H. Tomlinson's return after a 20 minute absence rejuvenated the Roughyeds. The one real worthwhile move of the game saw all the home three-quarters combined to send in Warham for the game's only try which proved enough for the victory in another tight match.

September 25th 1950: WORKINGTON T. 8 OLDHAM 15
Lancashire Cup 2nd. Round.
I. Barraclough, R. Byrne, L. Platt, W. Mitchell, A. Davies, R. Batten, J. Tynan.
L. Anthony, E. Brooks, A. Tomlinson, T. Leyland, B. Day, B. Goldswain.
Goals: Goldswain,3. Tries: Davies,2. Leyland.

Attendance: 10,675   Referee: Mr. F. Smith – Barrow.

What was described in the press as a 'scratch' side caused a real shock with this win up in Cumberland, as the county was then known. Irving Barraclough, Bob Byrne and Jim Tynan were all making their first senior appearance of the season. Indeed it was a great night for scrum-half, Tynan who laid on all three tries, the first two for the emerging Davies in the first half and a match clincher for Leyland after the break. Two late tries for Eppie Gibson were not enough to deny Oldham a creditable cup success.

September 30th 1950: BRAMLEY 8 OLDHAM 12
W. Ratchford, J. Warham, L. Platt, W. Mitchell, R. Batten, F. Heyes, J. Tynan.
L. Anthony, J. Keith, A. Tomlinson, T. Leyland, E. Wiggett, B. Goldswain.
Goals: Ratchford,3. Tries: Platt. Tynan.

Attendance: 3,662   Referee: Mr. T. Watkinson – Manchester.

A hard fought victory was secured at the old Barley Mow ground, the highlight of which was a first half try after a bout of inter-passing between Warham and Platt. Tynan stretched the lead in the 44th minute when he kicked ahead and followed up to touch down after all the defenders over-ran the ball. A Gibson try inspired a late Bramley rally, but two Ratchford goals saw Oldham home.

October 7th 1950: OLDHAM 16 SALFORD 10
W. Ratchford, J. Warham, L. Platt, W. Mitchell, R. Batten, F. Heyes, J. Tynan.
H. Ogden, J. Keith, H. Tomlinson, T. Leyland, A. Tomlinson, B. Goldswain.
Goals: Goldswain. Ratchford.   Tries: Warham,2. Platt. Tynan.

Attendance: 12,483   Referee: Mr. N. Railton – Wigan.

Harry Ogden returned to the Roughyeds team after a spell working abroad and Frank Stirrup turned out for Salford on the left wing. Oldham scored a remarkable try after five minutes when a penalty attempt by Goldswain drifted wide and the alert Tynan raced up, took the ball 'on the full' and scored under the posts. Likewise in the second period the Roughyeds were off to a flyer! Barely a minute had elapsed before Leyland put Warham over. Salford fought back only for Ratchford to seal the victory with a late penalty goal.

Two stars of from the great side from the 1920s were present for this match in the shape of Bob Sloman, holidaying up from the West Country and former wing man Joe Corsi.

1950-51

OLDHAM v SALFORD October 7th 1950

Once again, as with the Belle Vue photograph in the previous season, with Oldham in a changed blue shirt and Salford in their traditional red, and with both teams wearing white shorts, it presents a confusing situation in these greyscale photographs.

***Left: Frank Heyes** takes on the Salford defence after a pass from **Arthur Tomlinson**.*

***Left: Harold Tomlinson** picks up a loose ball watched by namesake **Arthur** (left) and **Alan Davies**.*

***Left: Arthur Tomlinson** is tackled by **Dai Moses** and **Jim Grainger**.*

***Below Left: Frank Stirrup** playing on the Salford left wing looks to pass before going into touch.*
***Below Right: Billy Mitchell** arrives too late to stop a late Salford try from **Bryn Hartley**.*

1950-51

October 10th 1950: OLDHAM 0   WARRINGTON 5
Lancashire Cup semi-final.
W. Ratchford, J. Warham, L. Platt, W. Mitchell, A. Davies, F. Heyes, R. Batten.
H. Ogden, J. Keith, L. Anthony, T. Leyland, A. Tomlinson, B. Goldswain.
Attendance: 14,808   Referee: Mr. G. Phillips – Widnes.

The league leaders proved to be just too good for Oldham but it could have been different if penalty chances had been taken, with both Goldswain and Ratchford missing the target. Palin had given Warrington an early lead with a penalty goal before the Oldham misses. After thirty minutes the Warrington forward Jim Featherstone was dismissed after a foul on Leyland but, undeterred, the 'Wire' adapted best to the muddy conditions and increased their lead with a Brian Bevan try, who else? However, it was on defence that the great 'Bev' saved the day when he knocked down a pass from Mitchell to Davies saving a certain try.

Brian Bevan - *The scourge of Oldham, and every other team in the league, scored the only try of the match.*

October 14th 1950: KEIGHLEY 10   OLDHAM 8
W. Ratchford, J. Warham, L. Platt, W. Mitchell, R. McCormick, R. Batten, J. Silva.
H. Ogden, J. Keith, L. Anthony, T. Leyland, A. Tomlinson, B. Day.
Goal: Ratchford. Tries: Mitchell. A. Tomlinson.
Attendance: 6,000   Referee: Mr. A. Bolton – Manchester.

With Bryn Goldswain on international duty with Wales his namesake Bryn Day filled in at loose-forward and a debut was given to Roland McCormick the brother of international Stan. It was a jaded performance from Oldham no doubt due to their exertions in the cup semi-final earlier in the week. Still it was a close run thing with try scorer, Arthur Tomlinson being the pick of the pack.

On this day Bernard Ganley made his debut for the 'A' team against Pemberton Rovers.
A sign of things to come were his five goals in a 28 – 8 victory.

October 21st 1950: OLDHAM 4   LEIGH 12
W. Ratchford, J. Warham, A. Davies, W. Mitchell, L. Platt, F. Heyes, J. Silva.
H. Ogden, J. Keith, A. Tomlinson, B. Day, C. Winslade, B. Goldswain.
Goals: Goldswain,2.
Attendance: 15,538   Referee: Mr. F. Smith – Barrow.

Charlie Winslade made his first team debut in this, another inept display, from Oldham who had little to offer after an early penalty from Goldswain. Tries from Joe Egan and, former Roughyeds favourite, Norman Harris gave the visitors a comfortable interval advantage which Oldham never looked like clawing back despite Jack Keith providing a good supply of possession from the scrum.

Left: Charlie Winslade - *First team debut for Oldham.*

Right: Norman Harris*: Former Roughyeds captain who scored one of the tries for Leigh.*

October 28th 1950: WAKEFIELD T. 14   OLDHAM 10

W. Ratchford, J. Warham, L. Platt, W. Mitchell, R. Batten, F. Heyes, J. Silva.
H. Ogden, J. Keith, A. Tomlinson, T. Leyland, A. Fearnley, B. Day.
Goals: Ratchford,2. Tries: Warham. Heyes.
Attendance: 7,198   Referee: Mr. W. Stockley – Leigh.

This was a bad tempered affair and a match Oldham should have won after going in with a 10 – 0 interval lead. However, 'Trinity' started mixing it in the second-half, which the press described as a forty minute brawl! In a five minute period four players were sent off. First to go were Billy Mitchell and Herbie Goodfellow for fighting. This was Mitchell's first dismissal in a thirteen year professional career. They were followed by Booth and then the numbers were again equal when Fearnley took exception to some treatment being handed out to Silva. It was from this point on, with the Oldham scrum-half suffering from concussion, that Wakefield took command.

November 4th 1950: OLDHAM 5   BATLEY 3

W. Ratchford, J. Warham, L. Platt, A. Davies, T. Leyland, F. Heyes, J. Silva.
H. Ogden, J. Keith, H. Tomlinson, C. Winslade, B. Day, B. Goldswain.
Goal: Goldswain. Try: Keith.
Attendance: 9,213   Referee: Mr. A. S. Dobson – Pontefract.

The star players on both sides were the centre three-quarters with Platt and Davies for Oldham competing well against the more experienced Etty and Riches. Indeed it was Riches who set up the Batley score for winger Perry but not before a Goldswain penalty and a try for Keith, set up by Warham and Winslade, gave Oldham what proved to be a winning margin. The second half was scoreless with the prospect of open play being hindered by persistent rain.

Joe Warham breaks clear. Other Oldham players:
Left to Right: **Harold Tomlinson, Charlie, Winslade, Harry Ogden, Bryn Day** and **Frank Heyes.**
(04.11.1950)

November 11th 1950: ST. HELENS 7   OLDHAM 13
W. Ratchford, R. Byrne, L. Platt, A. Davies, R. Batten, F. Heyes, J. Silva.
H. Ogden, J. Keith, L. Anthony, T. Leyland, B. Day, B. Goldswain.
Goals: Goldswain,2. Tries: Davies. Batten. Keith.

Attendance: 14,000   Referee: Mr. S. Abram - Wigan.

An even contest for the first half hour started to go Oldham's way, when firstly Batten followed a kick to capitalise on some indecision in the Saints defence, and then a wonderful move involving Day, Goldswain, Heyes and Silva put Davies in the clear. Going in at the interval with a 10 – 2 lead, Keith scored another try five minutes into the second-half and, although the same player was ordered off with eleven minutes still to play, the Roughyeds had done enough to secure the victory.

November 18th 1950: OLDHAM 3   WIDNES 0
W. Ratchford, R. Byrne, L. Platt, A. Davies, J. Warham, R. Batten, J. Silva.
H. Ogden, J. Cunliffe, L. Anthony, T. Leyland, B. Day, B. Goldswain.
Try: Davies.

Attendance: 8,109   Referee: Mr. A. Bolton – Manchester.

Another stinker of a spectacle against Widnes and any late comers missed the only score of the day! Barely a minute was on the clock before Warham and Davies inter-passed for the centre to streak in at the corner. Oldham had given a debut to hooker Jim Cunliffe as Keith was suspended and it took a great cover tackle from Platt to keep out Hutton but there was little to cheer the crowd in another defence dominated encounter that the press described as "a forwards game throughout!"

*Blink and you missed it! **Alan Davies** passes out to **Joe Warham** before receiving the ball back to score the only try in the very first minute of the match .   (18.11.1950)*

November 25th 1950: SALFORD 12   OLDHAM 9
W. Ratchford, K. Ward, W. Mitchell, A. Davies, L. Platt, F. Heyes, J. Silva.
H. Ogden, E. Brooks, A. Tomlinson, T. Leyland, B. Day, B. Goldswain.
Goals: Goldswain,3.   Try: Ward.

Attendance: 7,000   Referee: Mr. J.W. Jackson – Barrow

Another close match and yet another defeat for Oldham on their travels. The experiment of playing Ken Ward on the wing didn't endear itself to either the player or the displaced Bob Batten both of whom expressed a desire to leave the club soon afterwards. Alan Davies, however, further enhanced his reputation, breaking the Salford defence to lay on the Oldham try for Ward. Furthermore, with this cloud there was a silver lining and, although the match was lost, the Oldham committee managed to come away having secured the services of Frank Stirrup. Some consolation indeed for the defeat.

December 2ⁿᵈ 1950: OLDHAM 4   KEIGHLEY 4

W. Ratchford, R. Batten, W. Mitchell, A. Davies, L. Platt, F. Heyes, J. Silva.
H. Ogden, J. Keith, A. Tomlinson, B. Day, C. Winslade, B. Goldswain.
Goals: Ratchford,2.
Attendance: 9,017   Referee: Mr. H. Harrison – Ossett.

More dour stuff in this try-less encounter. Jack Keith impressed most with a tireless display but all Oldham had to show was a Ratchford penalty in each half. The first of these was given to the dismay of the Keighley players and the amusement of the Oldham supporters, as the ball seemed to drift wide of the upright at the last second. Ratchford and Goldswain were both guilty of several penalty misses, as was Jack Mills the Keighley full-back and goal kicker.

The Oldham team against Keighley on December 2nd 1950.
Back Row: *Alan Davies, Bryn Day, Arthur Tomlinson, Harry Ogden, Jack Keith, Charlie Winslade.*
Middle Row: *Bob Batten, Billy Mitchell, Bryn Goldswain, Bill Ratchford, Lawrie Platt.*
Front Row: *Joe Silva, Frank Heyes.*

December 9ᵗʰ 1950: LIVERPOOL S. 2   OLDHAM 7

W. Ratchford, R. Byrne, W. Mitchell, A. Davies, L. Platt, F. Heyes, J. Silva.
L. Anthony, J. Keith, H. Tomlinson, B. Goldswain, A. Tomlinson, B. Day.
Goals: Goldswain,2.   Try: Heyes.
Attendance: 800   Referee: Mr. S. Abram – Wigan.

The 'Green Final' report made much of the frugal resources at Knotty Ash with the criticism balanced by an admiration for how the club managed to keep going. There was standing water on the pitch as the teams took to the field ensuring once again that open rugby would be in short supply. An early Goldswain penalty was equalised by a similar effort by Forsyth for 'Stanley'. A try from Heyes and a further goal from Goldswain gave Oldham a 7 – 2 lead at half-time and so it stayed to the end although Silva and Anthony both had second half tries disallowed.
The changing rooms were some three hundred yards from the pitch at a public baths and both teams travelled to the ground on the Oldham coach. However, they then had to wait, shivering for five minutes in the cold, until the match ball could be found..

December 25th 1950:   OLDHAM 4   SWINTON 2

W. Ratchford, R. Byrne, W. Mitchell, A. Davies, L. Platt, F. Heyes, J. Silva.
L. Anthony, J. Keith, H. Tomlinson, B. Goldswain, A. Tomlinson, B. Day.
Goals: Goldswain,2.

Attendance: 12,816   Referee: Mr. P. Cowell – Warrington.

The Roughyeds resumed after a two week break due to the snowy weather and for the first time since the war, in a regular league match,* they turned out in their traditional navy blue shorts. A Christmas present perhaps? The festive crowd saw an eighth minute penalty by Sugden give Swinton the lead. Goldswain equalised before, on 25 minutes, Keith was again sent off! Oldham therefore had the best part of an hour to cope with just twelve men. The remaining forwards stuck to the defensive task manfully with Anthony taking over at hooker, ably supported by Ratchford at full-back. On the hour mark Goldswain kicked what proved to be the winning penalty. In the match reports Davies was again singled out for special mention.
*The navy shorts were also worn in the special match against Bordeaux & Villeneuve on April 10th when the club obviously made an effort to impress their French guests.

December 26th 1950: YORK 6   OLDHAM 5

W. Ratchford, J. Warham, W. Mitchell, A. Davies, W. Spencer, F. Daley, J. Silva.
L. Anthony, J. Keith, A. Tomlinson, B. Goldswain, C. Winslade, B. Day.
Goal: Goldswain. Try: Warham.

Attendance: 6,411   Referee: Mr. J.W. Jackson – Barrow.

Another dour game reported as being 'dull and insipid'. The first half was scoreless. Warham's second half try took Oldham out to 5 – 2 but a penalty by Jenkinson reduced the deficit and then, with just five minutes remaining, Davies was penalised for obstruction and the same player kicked the winning points. This was a wake-up call for Oldham who played out the match camped on the York line but to no avail as in the last move of the game Spencer was brought down just inches short.

January 6th 1951: WARRINGTON 34   OLDHAM 2

W. Ratchford, J. Warham, W. Mitchell, A. Davies, R. Byrne, K. Ward, J. Silva.
H. Tomlinson, E. Brooks, A. Tomlinson, B. Goldswain, C. Winslade, B. Day.
Goal: Goldswain.

Attendance: 8,561   Referee: Mr. S. Abram – Wigan.

Harry Bath gave Warrington the lead with a penalty in the second minute which was equalised by Goldswain after a quarter of an hour. However, from then on it was the home side who dominated. They led 12 – 2 at half time and a late scoring burst of fifteen points in the last eight minutes emphasised their superiority. Bevan scored a 'hat-trick' which the 'Chronicle' reported was worth seeing even for the Oldham supporters.

January 20th 1951: OLDHAM 0   BELLE VUE R. 2

W. Ratchford, W. Spencer, W. Mitchell, A. Davies, L. Platt, K. Ward, F. Stirrup.
L. Anthony, E. Brooks, A. Tomlinson, C. Winslade, B. Goldswain, F. Daley.
Attendance: 8,604   Referee: Mr. N. Railton – Wigan.

Frank Stirrup made his debut and Frank Daley was tried at loose-forward in another defence dominated game. The winning score came from a Gregory penalty after twenty minutes. Stirrup started well but faded probably due to lack of match practice. Daley put Brooks through for a try in the second-half only for the referee to rule the pass forward.

January 27th 1951: WIGAN 33   OLDHAM 11
W. Ratchford, J. Warham, E. Ward, A. Davies, W. Spencer, F. Daley, F. Stirrup.
H. Ogden, E. Brooks, A. Tomlinson, C. Winslade, T. Leyland, B. Day.
Goal: Ward. Tries: Ratchford. Warham. Spencer.
Attendance: 19,000   Referee: Mr. P. Cowell – Warrington.

Earlier in the week leading up to this match Oldham had signed Ted Ward from Wigan and so it was that he made his Roughyeds debut against his former club. Oldham got off to a great start when Ratchford joined the line to score after three minutes. Wigan then took control with eighteen unanswered points but a try from Warham in the 40th minute converted by Ward gave some hope for the second half. It wasn't to be, however, and the Central Park outfit finished comfortable winners with full-back Martin Ryan chipping in with two tries.

February 2nd 1951. WORKINGTON T. 15   OLDHAM 5
W. Ratchford, W. Nicholson, L. Platt, A. Davies, J. Warham, F. Stirrup, H. Goodfellow.
H. Ogden, E. Brooks, B. Day, E. Ward, C. Winslade, F. Daley.
Goal: Ward.   Try: Warham.
Attendance: 10,241   Referee: Mr. L. Thorpe – Wakefield.

There were debuts for new signings, Walter Nicholson from Rochdale and Herbie Goodfellow from Wakefield who the 'Chronicle' described as being sturdy and tough! New signing, Ward was moved to the second row, captained the team and scored a first half penalty goal but, 7 - 2 down at the break, there was no joy again for Oldham as the slump in form continued.

February 10th 1951: LEEDS 23   ODHAM 5
Rugby League Challenge Cup 1st Round 1st Leg.
W. Ratchford, W. Nicholson, W. Mitchell, A. Davies, L. Platt, F. Stirrup, H. Goodfellow.
H. Ogden, E. Brooks, B. Day, C. Winslade, E. Ward, B. Goldswain.
Goal: Ward. Try: Davies.
Attendance: 26,000   Referee: Mr. J. Jackson – Barrow.

Goldswain and Mitchell returned to bolster the team for this Challenge Cup-tie played out at a fog shrouded Headingley. The writing was on the wall when Turnbull pounced on a wayward Oldham pass to

score after eight minutes. Ward reduced the arrears with a penalty but by half time Leeds were 18 -2 in front and the only bright note for Oldham was a Davies try in the second half which was barely visible from the press-box in the thick fog!

Bryn Goldswain brings down *Arthur Clues* in the Headingley fog. (10.02.1951)

February 17th 1951: OLDHAM 13 LEEDS 10
Rugby League Challenge Cup 1st. Round 2nd. Leg.
W. Ratchford, W. Nicholson, L. Platt, W. Mitchell, A. Davies, F. Stirrup, H. Goodfellow.
H. Ogden, J. Keith, B. Day, C. Winslade, E. Ward, B. Goldswain.
Goals: E. Ward,2. Tries: Platt. Ogden. Keith.

Attendance: 11,392   Referee: Mr. A.S. Dobson – Pontefract.

At least the losing sequence was broken in this match, although the eighteen point advantage was always going to be too much to overturn. There was some hope when first half tries from Platt and Ogden were supplemented by one from Keith after the break which stretched the lead to 13 – 5 early in the second half, but the Leeds line held firm and a further try and goal made the cup-tie safe for the 'Loiners'.

Walter Nicholson and Lawrie Platt bring down *Gordon Brown* as the Leeds full-back,
Bert Cook looks on in the Watersheddings mud.   (17.02.1951)

February 24th 1951: ROCHDALE H. 12   OLDHAM 7
W. Ratchford, W. Nicholson, L. Platt, W. Mitchell, A. Davies, F. Stirrup, H. Goodfellow.
H. Ogden, J. Keith, B. Day, C. Winslade, E. Ward, B. Goldswain.
Goals: Ward,2. Try: Platt.

Attendance: 8,680   Referee: Mr. R. Gelder – Wakefield.

Hornets included a number of Australian players for this match amongst them the Stanford brothers, Reg and Ron, who combined well to fashion the opening try for the latter in a move that originated near their own try-line. Oldham rallied to go in leading 7 – 5 at half-time but the second period belonged to Rochdale and despite a solid performance from Charlie Winslade, they held on for their first league victory against the 'old enemy' since 1935 thanks to a try from Kelly and two more goals from Lord.

March 3rd 1951: OLDHAM 16 LIVERPOOL S. 3

W. B. Ganley, W. Nicholson, K. Ward, A. Davies, W. Spencer, F. Heyes, H. Goodfellow.
H. Ogden, J. Keith, B. Day, C. Winslade, E. Ward, B. Goldswain.
Goals: Ganley, 2. Tries: Day. Davies. Spencer. Heyes.
Attendance: 7,520   Referee: Mr. F. Squires – Ossett.

Bernard Ganley made his debut in this match and was soon on target with an early penalty goal. Heitzman then gave Liverpool the lead with a touchdown on sixteen minutes. An opportunist try from Day five minutes from half-time converted by Ganley restored Oldham's advantage but all in all, bottom club, 'Stanley' gave as good as they got until they conceded three tries in the last ten minutes. Davies scored the first and laid on the next for his left-wing partner, Wilson Spencer, with another from Heyes taking the Roughyeds clear. None of these were converted which led the Chronicle to report that Ganley's kicking was not accurate!

*Head bandaged and shirt ripped, **Ken Ward** takes on **Heitzman** the Liverpool winger .*

*Alan Davies looks across to see **Wilson Spencer** touch down for Oldham's third try.*

***Bernard Ganley** breaks through the Liverpool defence on his debut match with **Wilson Spencer** in support. (03.03.1951)*

March 10th 1951: WIDNES 13   OLDHAM 8

W. B. Ganley, W. Nicholson, K. Ward, L. Platt, W. Spencer, F. Heyes, J. Tynan.
H. Ogden, J. Keith, B. Day, C. Winslade, E. Ward, B. Goldswain.
Goal: Ganley. Tries: K. Ward. Keith.

Attendance: 4,700   Referee: Mr. N. Railton – Wigan.

A Ken Ward try took Oldham in level at half time 3 – 3 in yet another tight encounter with the 'Chemics' but when his namesake Ted was sent off on the hour mark Widnes took control and held off a late Roughyeds rally to win the match.

March 17th 1951: OLDHAM 0   WORKINGTON T. 21

E. Ward, L. Platt, W. Mitchell, A. Davies, W. Spencer, F. Heyes, H. Goodfellow.
H. Ogden, J. Keith, B. Day, C. Winslade, T. Leyland, B. Goldswain.
Attendance: 8,023   Referee: Mr. T. Armitage – Huddersfield.

A try from Johnny Lawrenson was the only score in the first half. However, after the break the Cumbrians were on top form and try as they did with Heyes and Leyland particularly giving their all, the Roughyeds could make no impression on a stout Workington defence. The demolition of Oldham was a pre-cursor to an end of season surge that would see 'Town' crowned champions.

*Right: **Wilson Spencer** breaks clear.*
*Below: **Frank Heyes** gives chase to*
***Johnny Lawrenson**.*
(17.03.1951)

March 23rd 1951: SWINTON 14   OLDHAM 10

W. B. Ganley, J. Warham, L. Platt, A. Davies, W. Spencer, F. Heyes, H. Goodfellow.
H. Ogden, J. Keith, B. Day, C. Winslade, T. Leyland, B. Goldswain.
Goals: Ganley,2.   Tries: Warham,2.
Attendance: 10,000   Referee: Mr. F. Smith – Barrow.

Indiscipline again cost Oldham in this match when two tries from the recalled Warham and two Ganley goals saw Oldham 10 – 7 in front midway into the second half but the dismissal of Goldswain after sixty minutes on the intervention of the touch-judge proved the difference as Swinton finished with a flourish to take the points.

March 24th 1951: OLDHAM 11   WHITEHAVEN 2

W. B. Ganley, J. Warham, L. Platt, A. Davies, W. Spencer, F. Heyes, H. Goodfellow.
H. Ogden, J. Keith, B. Day, C. Winslade, T. Leyland, B. Goldswain.
Goal: Ganley.   Tries: Davies,2. Spencer.
Attendance: 5,922   Referee: Mr. L.J. Dalby – York.

It was back to winning ways in this match which the press described as 'drab'. The scores were level at 2 – 2 at half-time but the Roughyeds stepped up a gear in the second half with Davies going over for two tries although there was some criticism of him for trying too hard and not bringing his winger into play enough.

March 26th 1951: OLDHAM 3   ST. HELENS 0

(Abandoned at half-time - Waterlogged Pitch - see April 7th.)
W. Ratchford, J. Warham, K. Ward, A. Davies, T. O'Grady, F. Heyes, H. Goodfellow.
H. Ogden, J. Keith, A. Tomlinson, C. Winslade, T. Leyland, B. Goldswain.
Try: Warham.
Attendance: 8,375   Referee: Mr. H. Squires - Ossett

This match, played on a near waterlogged pitch, saw a debut for sixteen year old Terry O'Grady who was "buffeted into touch three times", but impressed with his enthusiasm to keep getting involved. Warham crossed in the corner for the only score before the referee abandoned the match at half–time because of the continued rain and intolerable, muddy conditions.

*Above: Taken very early in the game before the conditions became too bad, this photo shows **Harry Ogden, Jack Keith** and **Arthur Tomlinson** about to bring down a St Helens player, as **Alan Prescott** (far right) looks on.*
***Right:** It's anyone's guess who the players are as the atrocious, muddy conditions began to completely hide the players' identities.*
(26.03.19 51)

The persistent rain continued long enough after the abandoned match against St Helens that the next scheduled match at Watersheddings against Rochdale on March 31ˢᵗ was postponed due to the pitch still being waterlogged!

April 7ᵗʰ 1951: OLDHAM 17   ST. HELENS 4
W. Ratchford, J. Warham, K. Ward, A. Davies, T. O'Grady, F. Heyes, H. Goodfellow.
H. Ogden, J. Keith, B. Day, C. Winslade, T. Leyland, B. Goldswain.
Goals: Goldswain,4. Tries: Warham,2. Leyland.
Attendance: 8,093   Referee: Mr. H. Squires - Ossett.

The match against 'Saints' was replayed in much better conditions and Oldham soon took command with Leyland, who turned in a great performance, finishing off good work by Ratchford to score against his home town club. A couple of penalties by Joe Ball kept St Helens in the match but O'Grady was unlucky to be stopped inches short of the line and tries from Warham either side of the interval sealed the victory.

April 14ᵗʰ 1951: BARROW 20   OLDHAM 10
E. Ward, J. Warham, K. Ward, W. Mitchell, T. O'Grady, F. Heyes, W. Ratchford.
H. Ogden, J. Keith, A. Tomlinson, C. Winslade, T. Leyland, B. Day.
Goals: Ratchford. Leyland. Tries: Mitchell. Winslade.
Attendance: 8,481   Referee: Mr. R. Gelder - Wakefield.

Herbie Goodfellow failed to show up for this match and the reshuffle saw Ted Ward at full-back with Ratchford filling in at scrum-half. Barrow were also under strength with several of their star players missing but they led 11 – 4 at half-time after Oldham had opened the scoring with a Ratchford penalty goal. A Leyland drop-goal just before the break gave the visitors hope and despite second-half tries from Mitchell, who had taken over at scrum-half, and Winslade it wasn't to be. The main difference was the goal kicking of Jones whose seven successes from eight attempts made all the difference as the teams scored two tries each.

April 16ᵗʰ 1951. LEIGH 10   OLDHAM 5
W. Ratchford, J. Warham, K. Ward, W. Mitchell, A. Davies, F. Heyes, H. Goodfellow.
H. Ogden, J. Keith, A. Tomlinson, C. Winslade, T. Leyland, B. Day.
Goal: Ratchford. Try: Goodfellow.
Attendance: 9,000   Referee: Mr. A. Hill - Dewsbury.

No luck here for Oldham who started well and indeed dominated proceedings for the first hour. However, the Roughyeds only managed to breach the Leigh defence on one occasion with a try from Goodfellow after good approach work by Ward. Ratchford had also put over a penalty but the five point lead was scant reward for their efforts. So it was that midway through the second half Leigh began to come back into contention as Oldham began to tire. The pressure finally caught up with the visitors who succumbed to two converted tries from Allan and Baxter in the last ten minutes.

Herbie Goodfellow -
A first Roughyeds try for the ex-Wakefield favourite was not enough to win the match.

April 21ˢᵗ 1951. OLDHAM 24 BRAMLEY 11

W. Ratchford, J. Warham, K. Ward, W. Mitchell, A. Davies, F. Heyes, H. Goodfellow.
H. Ogden, J. Keith, B. Day, T. Leyland, C. Winslade, B. Goldswain.
Goals: Ratchford,2. Goldswain. Tries:Warham,2. Ogden. Mitchell. Goodfellow. Goldswain.
Attendance: 6,666　　　　　Referee: Mr. E. Hopkins - Leeds.

Oldham welcomed back Bryn Goldswain from international duty with fellow Welshman, Bryn Day reverting to the front-row. Ogden opened the scoring for the Roughyeds after fifteen minutes but Bramley were in determined mood and caught the Roughyeds by surprise when they bounced back with a Warrior try converted by Gibson. This was followed by a solid defensive effort which enabled them to hang on to their lead of 5 – 3 until the interval. Strangely the referee Mr. Hopkins called half-time after only 35 minutes. However, after some consultation with his fellow officials and some choice words from the spectators, he redressed the balance and duly played 45 minutes after the break. In the second half the Roughyeds took control aided by a monopoly of scrum possession provided by hooker, Jack Keith who

also had a fine game in the loose especially when laying on one of Warham's tries with a fine long pass. In all five tries were added after the break with play-makers, Goldswain and Goodfellow marshalling their forces well throughout the second period, their positive contribution being rewarded by the inclusion of both of them on the score-sheet.

Joe Warham reaches over in the tackle to score to the approval of Jack Keith (9) and Ken Ward.
(21.04.1951)

April 23ʳᵈ 1951. OLDHAM 16 WIGAN 2

W. Ratchford, T. O'Grady, L. Platt, W. Mitchell, A. Davies, J. Warham, H. Goodfellow.
H. Ogden, J. Keith, B. Day, T. Leyland, C. Winslade, B. Goldswain.
Goals: Ratchford,4. Day. Tries: Mitchell. Keith.
Attendance: 14,766　　　　　Referee: Mr. H. Squires - Ossett.

Wigan were slated in the press for sending an under-strength team for this match no doubt due to their upcoming Challenge Cup final and Championship play-off commitments. Nevertheless they were good

enough to go in 2 – 2 at the interval but thereafter Oldham took control. A drop goal from Day put them in front and tries from Mitchell and Keith along with two Ratchford goals saw them home comfortably.

Alan Davies is tackled by Jack Broome, watched by Harry Ogden and George Roughley with a young Brian McTigue, making his Wigan debut at centre, covering across in the background.
(23.04.1951)

April 30th 1951. OLDHAM 36 ROCHDALE H. 2

W. Ratchford, L. Platt, W. Mitchell, A. Davies, W. Spencer, J. Warham, H. Goodfellow.

H. Ogden, J. Keith, B. Day, T. Leyland, A. Tomlinson, B. Goldswain.

Goals: Ratchford,3.

Tries: Platt,3. Spencer,2. Mitchell. Keith. Leyland. Tomlinson. Goldswain.

Attendance: 7,003   Referee: Mr. P. Cowell - Warrington.

An end of season stroll for Oldham who scored ten tries but could only manage three goals. A 'hat-trick' performance from Lawrie Platt was the highlight. Fellow winger Wilson Spencer also bagged a pair with one of his tries coming from a pass from Davies who was actually over the try-line himself! However, it was in the forwards that the Roughyeds totally dominated the match with the superiority of the Oldham 'six' reflected by the fact that Keith, Leyland, Tomlinson and Goldswain all crossed the whitewash.

*John Rothwell is tackled by **Lawrie Platt** as **Bryn Goldswain** and **Harry Ogden** move up to support the wingman. (30.04.1951)*

May 8th 1951: Oldham 32 Halifax 27

W. Mitchell Benefit match.

W. Ratchford, S. McCormick*, W. Mitchell, L. Platt, T. O'Grady, J. Warham, J. Silva.

H. Ogden, J. Mundy*, A. Tomlinson, C. Winslade, T. Leyland, B. Goldswain.

* Guest Players.

Goals: Ratchford,2. Mitchell. O'Grady.

Tries: O'Grady,2. Winslade,2. Ratchford. Mitchell. Silva. Goldswain.

Attendance: 2,651

Cold and rainy conditions prevailed for this benefit game for the popular local lad, Billy Mitchell. However, the match receipts of £218. 11s 6d, would have been a welcome boost to the benefit fund. Halifax duly obliged the request to provide the opposition supplemented by Oldham players Eric Wiggett, Les Anthony and Ken Ward, himself a Halifax local. Meanwhile Stan McCormick and Jimmy Mundy guested for Oldham. A good-hearted game ensued with some unusual goal kickers being employed. Indeed when Harry Ogden lined up a conversion attempt, Joe Warham nipped in to pinch the kick. The statistics would tell us that the effort failed.

***Billy Mitchell,** Loyal servant to the Roughyeds since his senior debut in 1938.*

1950-51

	1950-51	Played	Won	Draw	Lost	For	Against	Points
1	Warrington	36	30	0	6	738	250	60
2	Wigan	36	29	1	6	774	288	59
3	Workington T.	36	27	0	9	734	328	54
4	Leigh	36	24	2	10	420	288	50
5	Leeds	36	24	0	12	678	441	48
6	St. Helens	36	22	1	13	527	359	45
7	Hunslet	36	22	1	13	526	361	45
8	Batley	36	21	1	14	391	400	43
9	Huddersfield	36	20	2	14	575	410	42
10	Wakefield T.	36	19	3	14	587	521	41
11	Halifax	36	20	0	16	523	407	40
12	Belle Vue R.	36	19	2	15	427	374	40
13	Dewsbury	36	19	2	15	440	327	40
14	Bradford N.	36	19	0	17	406	404	38
15	**OLDHAM**	**36**	**17**	**2**	**17**	**403**	**347**	**36**
16	Keighley	36	16	3	17	359	442	35
17	Swinton	36	16	1	19	395	435	33
18	Hull	36	15	2	19	351	499	32
19	Salford	36	15	1	20	380	419	31
20	Barrow	36	14	2	20	385	518	30
21	Whitehaven	36	13	3	20	257	411	29
22	Rochdale H.	36	14	1	21*	321	534	29
23	Hull K.R.	36	12	2	22	450	699	26
24	Bramley	36	11	3	22	380	530	25
25	Castleford	36	12	1	23	376	548	25
26	Featherstone R.	36	12	1	23	375	562	25
27	Widnes	36	10	1	25	265	382	21
28	York	36	8	1	27	266	706	17
29	Liverpool S.	36	2	1	33	193	712	5

Most Appearances: Bryn Goldswain and Bill Ratchford 37 out of a possible 43.
Most tries: Joe Warham 20.
Most goals: Bryn Goldswain 52.
Most points: Bryn Goldswain 113.

Bill Ratchford

Bryn Goldswain

Joe Warham

1950-51

SEASON	PLAYER	APPS	TRIES	GOALS	POINTS
1950-51	B. GOLDSWAIN	37	3	52	113
1950-51	W. RATCHFORD	37	1	21	45
1950-51	B. DAY	34	1	1	5
1950-51	L. PLATT	32	16		48
1950-51	W. MITCHELL	31	8	1	26
1950-51	A. DAVIES	31	8		24
1950-51	J. WARHAM	30	20		60
1950-51	F. HEYES	30	7	1	23
1950-51	T. LEYLAND	28	5	1	17
1950-51	A. TOMLINSON	27	4		12
1950-51	H. OGDEN	27	2		6
1950-51	J. KEITH	26	6		18
1950-51	C. WINSLADE	22	1		3
1950-51	J .SILVA	20			
1950-51	L. ANTHONY	18	1		3
1950-51	E. BROOKS	16			
1950-51	H. GOODFELLOW	14	2		6
1950-51	R. BATTEN	13	3		9
1950-51	K. WARD	12	2		6
1950-51	W. SPENCER	11	6		18
1950-51	E. WARD	9		7	14
1950-51	H. TOMLINSON	7			
1950-51	R. BYRNE	6			
1950-51	F. STIRRUP	6			
1950-51	W. NICHOLSON	6			
1950-51	F. DALEY	5			
1950-51	W.B. GANLEY	4		6	12
1950-51	J. TYNAN	4	2		6
1950-51	T. O'GRADY	4			
1950-51	A. FEARNLEY	3			
1950-51	J. TAYLOR	3			
1950-51	E. WIGGETT	2			
1950-51	J. REA	1			
1950-51	I. BARRACLOUGH	1			
1950-51	R. McCORMICK	1			
1950-51	J. CUNLIFFE	1			
1950-51	**TOTAL**	**559**	**98**	**90**	**474**

1951-52

A satisfying season in so much as there was a dramatic improvement in the league placing although the impetus could not be sustained at the same level over the following two campaigns. However, a wonderful end of season sequence of ten consecutive league victories took Oldham to fifth place in the championship table which represented their highest league placing for 21 years. The 36 league matches produced 25 victories, one draw and ten defeats, five of which came in a disastrous run between mid November and mid December when only a narrow victory over Barrow on December 1st broke the sequence.

The team was now growing ever stronger with the acquisition of Sid Little which, allied to the coming to prominence of Frank Stirrup, Alan Davies, and Charlie Winslade, put quality and balance into the side throughout the team. These were backed up by the vastly improving Frank Daley, Jack Keith, Terry O'Grady and Ken Jackson. Oldham won an exciting game against the tourists at the end of September but fell at the semi-final stage of the Lancashire Cup for the second season in a row, at home to Leigh, only frustratingly to defeat them in a league match four days later. There was a second round Challenge Cup exit to Leeds before a massive crowd at Headingley. The Law Cup was again secured against Rochdale at the Athletic Grounds.

Joe Warham ended up topping the try scorers for the third consecutive season and also appeared in most games. Indeed in this season four Oldham players - Warham, O'Grady, Platt and Davies - all scored more than 20 tries, the only time in the club's history that this has occurred. O'Grady's total of 24 from just 25 matches was particularly impressive. Throw in Bernard Ganley's achievement in hitting the magic one hundred goals total and one can clearly see that things were beginning to take shape nicely. Although in some ways this was a false dawn, for it would be a few more years before the best was seen of the team, the omens were very good indeed!

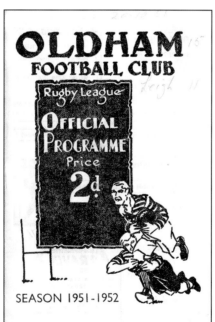

August 11ᵗʰ 1951: Rochdale H. 7 Oldham 18
Law Cup
W. Ratchford, J. Warham, A. Davies, W. Mitchell, L. Platt, K. Ward, F. Stirrup.
H. Ogden, J. Keith, B. Day, C. Winslade, T. Leyland, B. Goldswain.
Goals: Ratchford,3. Tries: Warham,2. Day. Ratchford.
Attendance: 4,434   Referee: Mr. N. Railton – Wigan.

A try by Lord after 14 minutes gave Hornets the lead but Oldham took command soon after with Warham again showing good form in scoring two tries and making the third for Ratchford who also obliged with two goals. This gave the Roughyeds a 13 – 3 advantage at the interval. Two penalties from Lord brought Rochdale back into the reckoning but the match was made safe by a last minute try from Day again converted by Ratchford. Oldham captain Bryn Goldswain duly received the trophy with the main plaudits going to Warham and Stirrup.

August 18ᵗʰ 1951: OLDHAM 11   BRADFORD N. 7
W. Ratchford, J. Warham, K. Ward, A. Davies, L. Platt, F. Stirrup. H. Goodfellow.
H. Ogden, J. Keith, B. Day, C. Winslade, A. Tomlinson, B. Goldswain.
Goal: Goldswain. Tries: Davies. Warham. Goldswain.
Attendance: 10,786   Referee: Mr. M. Coates – Pudsey.

Bradford included five New Zealanders in their starting line-up but it was Oldham who struck first after a bout of inter-passing between Platt and Davies saw the latter score the first try of the league campaign. The only further score in the first period was a Phillips penalty goal. A converted try from McLean gave 'Northern' the lead but tries from Warham and Goldswain both wide out on either wing put Oldham back in front. A late penalty goal from Goldswain concluded the scoring.

*Harry Ogden moves in on **Norman Haley** the Bradford hooker as **Bryn Day** looks on.
(18.08.1951)*

1951-52

The Oldham team that defeated Bradford Northern on August 18th 1951.
Back Row: *Alan Davies, Arthur Tomlinson, Bryn Day, Jack Keith, Harry Ogden, Charlie Winslade.*
Middle Row: *Bill Ratchford, Lawrie Platt, Bryn Goldswain, Joe Warham, Ken Ward.*
Front Row: *Herbie Goodfellow, Frank Stirrup.*

August 22nd 1951: BELLE VUE R. 7 OLDHAM 2

W. Ratchford, J. Warham, K. Ward, A. Davies, L. Platt, F. Stirrup, H. Goodfellow.
H. Ogden, J. Keith, B. Day, C. Winslade, A. Tomlinson, B. Goldswain.
Goal: Goldswain.

Attendance: 5,000   Referee: Mr. R. Gelder – Wakefield.

A dull match that produced no less than 54 scrums and although Jack Keith won that tussle by 31 to 23, it was 'Rangers' who took the points. A scoreless first half was followed by an equally hard fought second period with the only try coming after fifty minutes when former Roughyeds favourite Dai Rees carved an opening for Price to score. Gregory converted but Goldswain reduced the arrears with a penalty three minutes later. A Price drop goal was the only other score.

*Ex-Oldham scrum-half **Dai Rees (left)** who broke through the Oldham defence to lay on the decisive try for half-back partner and fellow Welshman, **Ray Price (right)** who also added a drop goal. Rare moments of skill in an otherwise uninspiring encounter.*

1951-52

August 25th 1951: KEIGHLEY 0   OLDHAM 15

W. Ratchford, J. Warham, W. Mitchell, A. Davies, L. Platt, K. Ward, F. Stirrup.
H. Ogden, J. Keith, B. Day, C. Winslade, A. Tomlinson, B. Goldswain.
Goals: Goldswain,2. Ward. Tries: Ward,2. Ogden.
Attendance: 4,000   Referee: Mr. W. Stockley – Leigh.

In contrast to the previous fixture this was a thrilling end to end affair with first Ivill for the home side and then Keith for Oldham narrowly failing to chase down kicks ahead to score. The deadlock was broken on 32 minutes when Winslade broke through for Ward to touchdown under the posts. This was followed shortly by Ogden capitalising on a 50 yard break by Platt to again score close to the posts. Goldswain converted both efforts to give Oldham a 10 – 0 margin at the break. The second half started with the Keighley forwards pounding the visitors' line. However, the Roughyeds repelled the onslaught and after Ward had dropped a goal, Stirrup put the same player through for a try after breaking clear direct from a scrum and the match was won.

August 28th 1951: OLDHAM 26   LIVERPOOL C. 0

W. Ratchford, J. Warham, W. Mitchell, A. Davies, L. Platt, K. Ward, F. Stirrup.
H. Ogden, J. Keith, B. Day, C. Winslade, T. Leyland, B. Goldswain.
Goal: Goldswain. Tries: Warham,2. Mitchell,2. Platt,2. Ratchford. Ward.
Attendance: 7,500   Referee: Mr.T. Armitage – Huddersfield.

The Oldham backs proved to be just too speedy for the 'Mersey-siders' and scored some spectacular tries as a result. The pick of these was by Ward who beat man after man on a diagonal run to the line. Another notable effort was started by Stirrup and finished by Warham after six players had handled the ball in a breathtaking movement that had the visitors chasing shadows. The rare Liverpool attacks were easily dealt with and although the forwards bossed the show, all eight of the Oldham tries were scored by the backs. The only downside was the woeful kicking which saw Ratchford and Goldswain miss nine attempts between them.

Under the watchful eye of the Law and the St John's Ambulance,
Bryn Goldswain *leads out the Roughyeds followed by* **Joe Warham** *and* **Billy Mitchell.**

September 1st 1951: ROCHDALE H. 7   OLDHAM 8
Lancashire Cup 1st Round 1st Leg.
W. Ratchford, J. Warham, W. Mitchell, A. Davies, L. Platt, K. Ward, F. Stirrup.
H. Ogden, J. Keith, B. Day, C. Winslade, T. Leyland, B. Goldswain.
Goal: Goldswain. Tries: Platt. Ward.
Attendance: 6,931   Referee: Mr. J. Jackson – Barrow.

A dour 'derby' encounter was expected and duly delivered! Lord and Goldswain exchanged penalties before Davies put Platt away to score on nineteen minutes. However, three minutes later Gibson went over to bring Hornets level. In the second half a Ward try and a Lord penalty were the only further scores to set up an intriguing second leg.

September 4th 1951: OLDHAM 21   ROCHDALE H. 5
Lancashire Cup 1st Round 2nd Leg.
W. Ratchford, J. Warham, W. Mitchell, A. Davies, T. O'Grady, F. Stirrup, H. Goodfellow.
H. Ogden, J. Keith, A. Tomlinson, C. Winslade, T. Leyland, B. Goldswain.
Goals: Ratchford,2. Goldswain. Tries: O'Grady,2. Mitchell. Davies. Winslade.
Attendance: 7,500   Referee: Mr. T. Watkinson – Manchester.

In between the two Lancashire Cup legs against Hornets Ken Ward was sold to Leeds but Oldham overcame the loss to win the tie in some style. Terry O'Grady was reintroduced to positive effect scoring two tries, the second of which was a startling interception that brought the house down. Mitchell and Davies also scored as the Roughyeds three-quarters ruled the roost.

September 8th 1951: WIGAN 41   OLDHAM 3
W. Ratchford, J. Warham, F. Daley, A. Davies, T. O'Grady, F. Stirrup, H. Goodfellow.
H. Ogden, J. Keith, A. Tomlinson, C. Winslade, J. Watson, T. Leyland.
Try: Davies.
Attendance: 18,629   Referee: Mr. M. Coates – Pudsey.

Forced to make four changes due to injuries in the previous match it was an under-strength team, including debutant John Watson, that took on the might of Wigan at Central Park. After Ken Gee had given the home side the lead with an early penalty, Oldham had a decent spell of pressure before Wigan took control. They led 23 – 0 at half time and although Davies got over for the first score of the second half, previous service was then resumed with Ernie Ashcroft scoring three tries in a one-sided match.

*A hat-trick for the Wigan left centre, **Ernie Ashcroft**.*

September 10th 1951: OLDHAM 21   WHITEHAVEN 12
W. B. Ganley, W. Ratchford, F. Daley, A. Davies, T. O'Grady, J. Warham, F. Stirrup.
H. Ogden, J. Keith, L. Anthony, C. Winslade, T. Leyland, A. Murray.
Goals: Ganley,3. Tries: O'Grady,2. Ratchford. Davies. Murray.
Attendance: 6,606   Referee: Mr. A. Howgate – Dewsbury.

Another debut this time for Alf Murray and a recall for Bernard Ganley and Les Anthony who apparently *"played with fervour, just the thing to counter the Cumbrians!"* Frank Daley drew inspiration from being made captain, turning in a solid performance, and the impressive O'Grady weighed in with two scores once more. Murray also got a try on his debut, as did Ratchford, who was selected for a rare appearance on the wing.

September 15th 1951: OLDHAM 13 ST. HELENS 7

W. B. Ganley, W. Ratchford, W. Mitchell, A. Davies, L. Platt, F. Daley, F. Stirrup.
L. Anthony, J. Keith, K. Jackson, C. Winslade, B. Day, A. Murray.
Goals: Ganley,2. Tries: Platt. Stirrup. Anthony.

Attendance: 8,721   Referee: Mr. F. Cottam – Wakefield.

Oldham's good form continued in this ill tempered game. The Roughyeds held a 10 -2 interval lead thanks to tries from Anthony and Stirrup both converted by Ganley. In the second period the match spilled over into several brawls until Mr. Cottam finally lost patience and dismissed Keith and Saints prop Bretherton. This physical challenge brought out the best in Day, Anthony and the recalled Ken Jackson with Daley also putting in a concentrated effort on defence in aid of his forwards.

Jack Keith (left) and Billy Bretherton, recipients of the early bath!

September 22nd 1951: WIDNES 9 OLDHAM 0

W. B. Ganley, J. Warham, W. Mitchell, A. Davies, L. Platt, F. Daley, F. Stirrup.
K. Jackson, L. Anthony, A. Tomlinson, B. Day, B. Goldswain, A. Murray.
Attendance: 6,000   Referee: Mr. S. Adams – Hull.

This time it was 'two off' for Oldham in another tight encounter at Naughton Park. It was 2 – 0 to Widnes at the break courtesy of a Jolley penalty goal, although the Roughyeds were unlucky when Platt was forced into touch right at the corner flag just before half-time. On 54 minutes Woodward kicked another goal for the 'Chemics' and then in the space of a few minutes just after the hour mark, first Tomlinson and then Day were ordered off! These were decisions that the press described as rash compared to the treatment

apparently doled out the week before, and also it seemed unfair that when Daley was knocked out by a 'stiff arm' the offender only received a caution, whereas his team-mates had to go. Nevertheless, Oldham stuck at it playing with a three man pack and enjoyed a good spell before a late converted try from Kemel settled the issue.

"What me sir! Never sir!"
More marching orders, this time
for likely lads, Arthur and Bryn.

September 24th 1951: OLDHAM 17 WIDNES 9
Lancashire Cup 2nd Round.

W. B. Ganley, J. Warham, W. Mitchell, L. Platt, A. Davies, F. Daley, F. Stirrup.
K. Jackson, L. Anthony, B. Day, C. Winslade, T. Leyland, B. Goldswain.
Goal: Goldswain. Tries: Platt,3. Warham. Davies.

Attendance: 6,478   Referee: Mr. J. Jackson – Barrow.

Just two days after the defeat at Widnes and Oldham had the chance to avenge the reverse in the Lancashire Cup. Things got off to a bad start as the visitors raced into a 9 – 0 lead after 17 minutes but the Roughyeds fought back to win the tie. Platt got Oldham on the score sheet before half-time and completed his 'hat-trick' in the second half. Warham and Davies also touched down with two of the tries as a direct result of astute cross-kicks by Daley.

A full account of all the Oldham matches against the touring teams can be found in the book "Kangaroos, Kiwis and Roughyeds".

September 29th 1951: OLDHAM 21 NEW ZEALAND 18

W. B. Ganley; J. Warham, W. Mitchell, A. Davies, T. O'Grady; F. Daley, F. Stirrup.
K. Jackson, L. Anthony, B. Day, C. Winslade, T. Leyland, B. Goldswain.
Goals: Ganley,3. Tries: Warham,2. Stirrup,2. O'Grady.

Attendance: 15,174   Referee: Mr. C. F. Appleton - Warrington

The Kiwis broke the deadlock after nine minutes when prop forward Johnson burst through several tackles to score under the posts. Haig added the conversion. The Roughyeds were thus stung into scoring action themselves. After being put in the clear by Davies, O'Grady rounded Berryman to score right in the corner. Ganley failed with the goal attempt. After the Kiwis were penalised it looked for all the world as if Ganley was going to go for a goal attempt but up stepped Stirrup who tapped the ball forward, inter-passed with Day and finally handed on to Warham who sidestepped through for an unconverted try. Oldham were now playing some great football with Winslade leading the way. Even when Davies had to retire injured it did not stop the Oldham momentum and after some sustained pressure it was that man Stirrup again who masterminded the Kiwis' downfall. He broke away wide from a scrum whilst half-back partner Daley came steaming up on the inside shouting for the ball. Seconds later Daley was occupying the attentions of several New Zealand defenders while his half-back partner crossed the line to score near the posts. This time Ganley was on target to give Oldham an 11 - 5 half-time lead. Within a minute of the restart the crowd were cheering again when Ganley landed a 45 yard drop goal. Next it was the now restored Davies who combined with Winslade for a fifty yard advance into Kiwi territory. This time the New Zealand defence held firm and a swift breakaway concluded with Edwards scoring at the other end. Haig missed the conversion but was on target with a penalty soon after to leave the visitors only three points in arrears. O'Grady was unlucky as he fumbled the ball when trying to re-gather his own kick ahead. However, Anthony managed to heel the resulting scrum and when the ball was moved quickly to the right Mitchell drew in the cover to send Warham over for his second try in spite of Johnson's despairing tackle. Ganley was just wide with the conversion attempt. The game was sealed when 'man of the match' Stirrup dummied his way through the defensive line then followed his kick through to score. Ganley added the

extra points. The New Zealanders, to their credit, plugged away to give the score-line some respectability and even after Richards-Jolley was carried off injured the tourists found enough reserves to go in for two late tries from McBride and Hough. Haig converted one as the Kiwis had the last word on a truly entertaining encounter.

The moment of the first Oldham try is caught here in two images taken from different angles.

*The top image shows the scramble as **Joe Warham** gets the ball down despite the tackle of **Doug Richards- Jolley** and being surrounded by a possee of Kiwi defenders and team-mates, **Charlie Winslade** on the left and **Bryn Day** who provided the final pass.*

*The lower image seems to have been taken at the same time as referee, **Charlie Appleton** points to award the score, with both of the photographers in position near the posts at the Hutchins end of the ground. (29.09.1951)*

October 6th 1951: OLDHAM 20   WARRINGTON 12

W. B. Ganley, J. Warham, W. Mitchell, L. Platt, T. O'Grady. F. Daley, F. Stirrup.
H. Ogden, L. Anthony, K. Jackson, C. Winslade, T. Leyland, B. Goldswain.
Goals: Ganley,4. Tries: Warham. Mitchell. Platt. Leyland.
Attendance: 13,197   Referee: Mr. L. J. Dalby – York.

An early Ganley penalty was answered by the Bevan boys for the 'Wire'. First Owen Bevan landed a ninth minute penalty before namesake Brian sprinted fifty yards in his own inimitable fashion to score near the posts. Owen converted to give Warrington a five point advantage. This stung Oldham into action and Mitchell and Warham combined well to send Leyland over before more pressure resulted in Mitchell going over himself to give his team a 10 – 7 lead at the break. In the second half further scores by Warham and Platt made the game safe with the Roughyeds' cause aided by the dismissal of Warrington forward Featherstone after 68 minutes. The same player was also sent off at Watersheddings last season. Notwithstanding the Oldham victory the highlight of the second half was an interception by Gerry Helme that saw the talented scrum-half race seventy yards to score.

*Future Oldham coach **Gerry Helme** scored the try of the match for Warrington.*

October 13th 1951:   LIVERPOOL C. 5   OLDHAM 25

W. B. Ganley, J. Warham, W. Mitchell, A. Davies, T. O'Grady, F. Daley, J. Silva.
H. Ogden, J. Keith, K. Jackson, C. Winslade, T. Leyland, B. Goldswain.
Goals: Ganley,5. Tries: Warham,2. Mitchell. Davies. O'Grady.
Attendance: 1,000   Referee: Mr. R. Gelder – Wakefield.

Liverpool shocked Oldham when they went into a first minute lead courtesy of a try from Australian, Ray Beythien. However, after this it was one-way traffic with the Oldham backs dominating and the three-quarter line all ending up on the score-sheet. Ogden and Keith were the pick of the forwards in a comfortable victory.

October 16th 1951: OLDHAM 10   LEIGH 14

Lancashire Cup semi-final.

W. B. Ganley, J. Warham, W. Mitchell, L. Platt, T. O'Grady, F. Daley, F. Stirrup.
H. Ogden, J. Keith, K. Jackson, C. Winslade, T. Leyland, B. Goldswain.
Goals: Ganley,2. Tries: Warham. Platt.
Attendance: 14,371   Referee: Mr. G. Phillips – Widnes.

A good, entertaining game this between two evenly matched sides. The outstanding performance on the night came from Leigh full-back Jim Ledgard who contributed four goals and a try. A Platt try and a goal from Ganley against three penalty goals from the Leigh marksman made the score 5 – 6 at half time but two tries in quick succession from Ledgard and Marston took the game away from Oldham in the second period. Warham crossed late on near the corner flag but it was to no avail as the Roughyeds fell at the semi-final stage for the second year in a row

*Leigh's international full-back **Jim Ledgard**.*
A match-winner for the visitors.

October 20th 1951: OLDHAM 15 LEIGH 11

W. B. Ganley, T. O'Grady, W. Mitchell, L. Platt, A. Davies, J. Warham, F. Stirrup.
H. Ogden, L. Anthony, K. Jackson, C. Winslade, A. Tomlinson, B. Goldswain.
Goals: Ganley,3. Tries: O'Grady. Mitchell. Davies.
Attendance: 13,822   Referee: Mr. H. Squires – Ossett.

Four days on and Leigh were back at Watersheddings, this time in a league match, and Ledgard continued where he left off with a third minute penalty. Ganley meanwhile had three failed attempts and Goldswain one before 'W.B.' opened the Roughyeds account. A try by O'Grady then nudged Oldham into a 5 – 4 interval lead. In the second half, after a further Ganley penalty goal, a converted Baxter try gave Leigh the lead. Mitchell replied for Oldham and it was 12 – 11 going into the closing minutes before a determined burst by Davies gave him the final score of the match against his home town club.

Harry Ogden breaks clear of the Leigh defence with Charlie Winslade (left) and Ken Jackson in attendance. (20.10.1951)

October 27th 1951: SALFORD 5 OLDHAM 19

W. B. Ganley, T. O'Grady, W. Mitchell, L. Platt, A. Davies, F. Daley, F. Stirrup.
H. Ogden, L. Anthony, K. Jackson, C. Winslade, A. Tomlinson, B. Goldswain.
Goals: Ganley,5. Tries: Platt. Davies. Anthony.
Attendance: 10,000   Referee: Mr. T. Armitage – Huddersfield.

The rich vein of form continued at The Willows. Davies scored on eleven minutes in the corner which Ganley converted with a great effort from the touchline. It was 10 -2 at the break and despite a determined effort from the 'Red Devils' Oldham's defence stood firm with Jackson and Daley outstanding. A late converted try from Anthony, who crashed over from close range, sealed the win.

1951-52

November 3rd 1951: OLDHAM 41   BRAMLEY 3

W. B. Ganley, T. O'Grady, L. Platt, A. Davies, J. Warham, F. Daley, F. Stirrup.
H. Ogden, L. Anthony, K. Jackson, A. Tomlinson, T. Leyland, B. Goldswain.
Goals: Ganley,7. Tries: O'Grady,3. Davies,2. Platt. Warham. Stirrup. Jackson.
Attendance: 4,882   Referee: Mr. A.S. Dobson – Pontefract.

After ten minutes Davies scored the first try of the match. However, just two minutes later, the 'Villagers' replied with an interception try from Hawkins. Shortly after this the Bramley centre Varley had to retire injured and from then on it was one-way traffic with the Oldham three-quarters making light of the rainy conditions to score seven of the nine tries. The victory took Oldham up to second place in the league table.

*Another impressive 'hat-trick' performance from young **Terry O'Grady** put the teenager in line for a Lancashire county call up against the Kiwis a few weeks later.*

November 10th 1951: WORKINGTON T. 21   OLDHAM 11

W. B. Ganley, J. Warham, W. Mitchell, L. Platt, A. Davies, F. Daley, F. Stirrup.
H. Ogden, J. Keith, K. Jackson, A. Tomlinson, T. Leyland, B. Goldswain.
Goal: Ganley. Tries: Platt,2. Warham.
Attendance: 11,300   Referee: Mr. L. Thorpe - Wakefield.

The evergreen Gus Risman gave Workington the lead with a third minute penalty before a precise kick through by Stirrup brought a try for Warham. A Lawrenson try put 'Town' back in front and the same player completed a first half 'hat-trick' with two further touchdowns in the last five minutes before the break, to put his team 11 - 8 ahead at the interval. The other Oldham points came from a Platt try and a Ganley goal. Jack Keith won the possession battle but overall the Workington forwards were on top from start to finish.

*Johnny Lawrenson -
A first half 'hat-trick' for 'Town'.*

November 17th 1951: OLDHAM 12   WIGAN 13

W. B. Ganley, J. Warham, W. Mitchell, L. Platt, A. Davies, F. Daley, F. Stirrup.
H. Ogden, J. Keith, K. Jackson, T. Leyland, L. Anthony, B. Goldswain.
Goals: Ganley,3. Tries: Warham. Mitchell.
Attendance: 16,113   Referee: Mr. R. Gelder – Wakefield.

The large crowd were entertained by the Glodwick Prize Band before the game in which a tight, though entertaining, first half finished with just a penalty goal each for Ganley and Cunliffe. Two tries from Ashcroft, the first when he intercepted a pass from Daley, and one from Hurst helped put Wigan in command and they led 13 – 4 before a converted Mitchell try gave Oldham renewed hope. Late on Stirrup conjured up a blind side move to put Warham over in the corner but Ganley's conversion attempt sailed wide and Wigan held out for the last few minutes. A great match for the spectators but little did they know that this was the last occasion the 'Colliers' would enjoy success against the Roughyeds for a long, long time!

November 24th 1951: BARROW 16   OLDHAM 9

W. B. Ganley, T. O'Grady, W. Mitchell, L. Platt, J. Warham, F. Daley, F. Stirrup.
H. Ogden, J. Keith, K. Jackson, C. Winslade, S. Thurlow, B. Goldswain.
Tries: O'Grady,2. Mitchell.

Attendance: 5,777   Referee: Mr. W. Johnson –St. Helens.

The first drama of this match occurred before the kick off when the referee, Mr. Dalby of York, failed to show up after missing his train, and so it was that the touch-judge, Mr. Johnson of St Helens, swapped his flag for the whistle. When play started the game was dominated, like so many at Craven Park, by home captain Willie Horne. He controlled the game from stand-off and his goal kicking proved the difference. Toohey and Hewson scored tries for Barrow with O'Grady and Mitchell laying on a try for each other, all before the break. However, despite Oldham scoring three tries to two with O'Grady going over again in the second half, Ganley had an off day with the boot and the points went to Barrow. New signing Steve Thurlow from Workington made his Oldham debut in the second-row.

Willie Horne - The Barrow captain and play-maker in chief.

December 1st 1951: OLDHAM 10   BARROW 7

W. B. Ganley, T. O'Grady, W. Mitchell, L. Platt, J. Warham, F. Daley, F. Stirrup.
H. Ogden, J. Keith, A. Tomlinson, C. Winslade, S. Thurlow, A. Murray.
Goals: Ganley,2. Tries: O'Grady. Platt.

Attendance: 8,967   Referee: Mr. T. Armitage – Huddersfield.

One week on and again Horne was leading the way. He opened the scoring with a forty yard penalty and after an O'Grady try had briefly given Oldham the lead, he converted a try by Castle who forced himself over near the corner flag. 7 – 3 down at the break the Roughyeds rallied well for Warham to send in Platt and this time it was Ganley who added the extra points from wide out. This gave Oldham a one point advantage. Horne failed with a drop goal attempt and a late penalty by Ganley concluded the scoring.

December 8th 1951: HALIFAX   17   OLDHAM 0

W. B. Ganley, T. O'Grady, W. Mitchell, A. Davies, W. Spencer, J. Warham, F. Stirrup.
H. Ogden, J. Keith, A. Tomlinson, C. Winslade, S. Thurlow, B. Goldswain.
Attendance: 4,000   Referee: Mr. C. Appleton – Warrington.

Ex-Oldham player Albert Fearnley turned out for Halifax and gave a sterling show against his old team-mates. Rain had fallen constantly through the day with the effect that a forty yard stretch in the middle of the pitch was almost underwater. Two tries from Daniels, one of which was converted gave the Yorkshiremen an 8 – 0 half-time advantage. The pitch deteriorated more in the second period and after three more unconverted tries took the score to 17 – 0 the referee and captains agreed to end the 'mud-bath' after 75 minutes to the relief of all present.

Albert Fearnley - In top form against his old team-mates for Halifax.

December 15ᵗʰ 1951: WHITEHAVEN 7   OLDHAM 4

W. B. Ganley, T. O'Grady, W. Mitchell, A. Davies, L. Platt, F. Daley, F. Stirrup.
H. Ogden, J. Keith, K. Jackson, C. Winslade, S. Thurlow, B. Goldswain.
Goals: Ganley,2.

Attendance: 5,000   Referee: Mr. A. Hill – Dewsbury.

Oldham started well when Ganley opened the scoring with a second minute penalty. However, this was soon equalised by McKeown. A Fearon try and a further penalty gave the Cumbrians a five point lead at the interval. It was soon evident, after the break, that this was going to be a dour forty minutes. Still, Oldham battered away at the home line in the second half only to be met by a resolute defence on every occasion. A further penalty goal was all they could manage as Whitehaven mustered all their reserves of strength to keep the Roughyeds at bay, before they made the long trip home after another fruitless visit to Cumberland.

December 22ⁿᵈ 1951: OLDHAM 27   KEIGHLEY 2

W. B. Ganley, J. Warham, A. Davies, L. Platt, T. O'Grady, F. Daley, F. Stirrup.
L. Anthony, J. Keith, K. Jackson, C. Winslade, S. Thurlow, B. Goldswain.
Goals: Ganley,3. Tries: Warham,2. Daley,2. Platt. O'Grady. Davies.
Attendance: 5,295   Referee: Mr. L.J. Dalby – York.

The Roughyeds were off to a flyer when Platt capitalised on an error to score under the posts in the first minute. Plowman slotted a penalty three minutes later but after that it was all Oldham. The backs scored all the tries with Daley being particularly impressive chipping in with a couple of touchdowns allied to his usual good defensive work

December 25ᵗʰ 1951: OLDHAM 21   SWINTON 5

W. B. Ganley, J. Warham, W. Mitchell, L. Platt, A. Davies, F. Daley, H. Goodfellow.
H. Ogden, J. Keith, L. Anthony, C. Winslade, S. Thurlow, B. Goldswain.
Goals: Ganley,3. Tries: Davies,2. Warham. Keith. Anthony.
Attendance: 8,873   Referee: Mr. A.S. Dobson - Pontefract.

A surprise recall for Goodfellow was the big news of the day as Stirrup was rested. Another fine performance from the Roughyeds with Winslade and Goldswain turning in sounds displays in the pack and Davies with two tries and Ganley the pick of the backs. The Oldham full-back stood out for his many attacking breaks coming through out of defence.

December 26ᵗʰ 1951: OLDHAM 3   WORKINGTON T. 0

W. B. Ganley, J. Warham, W. Mitchell, A. Davies, F. Stirrup, F. Daley, H. Goodfellow.
H. Ogden, L. Anthony, K. Jackson, C. Winslade, S. Thurlow, B. Goldswain.
Try: Stirrup.

Attendance: 9,068   Referee: Mr. S. Adams – Hull.

Goodfellow's solid performance had done enough the previous day to keep his place with Stirrup returning on the wing. Unlike the previous two games, this third home match in five days was a tight affair with both defences very much to the fore on a muddy pitch. The only score was a try for Stirrup on 32 minutes. The Oldham forwards worked hard to keep the Cumbrians out, none more so than Winslade and Ogden.

Frank Stirrup - *selected to play in the unusual position of left wing but still came up with the decisive score.*

December 29th 1951: BRADFORD N. 21 OLDHAM 3

W. B. Ganley, J. Warham, W. Mitchell, L. Platt, A. Davies, F. Daley, H. Goodfellow.
H. Ogden, J. Keith, L. Anthony, C. Winslade, S. Thurlow, B. Goldswain.
Try: Warham.

Attendance: 18,500   Mr. F. Smith – Barrow.

Bradford dominated the game from the start and it was very much against the run of play when Warham scooped up a loose ball to sprint home from halfway. Ganley hit the upright with the conversion attempt and that summed up Oldham's luck for the rest of the match. Two Ernest Ward penalty goals gave 'Northern' the half-time lead and they pulled away in the second period, helped in no small way by a total penalty count which read 22 – 3 in their favour!

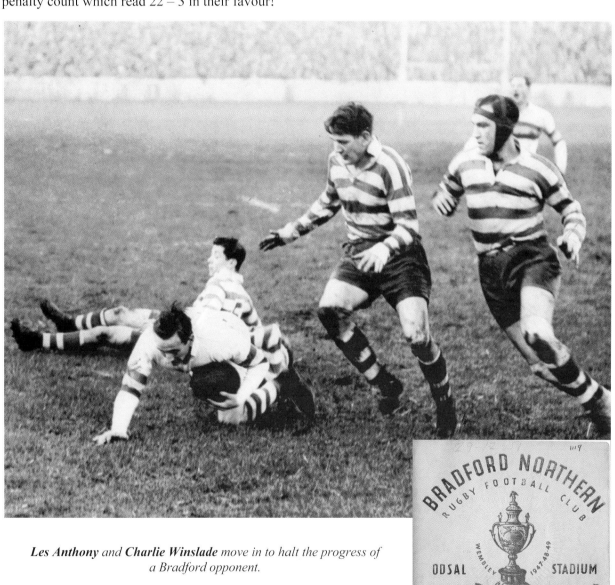

Les Anthony and *Charlie Winslade* *move in to halt the progress of a Bradford opponent.*

The match programme reflects Bradford's Challenge Cup trio of final appearances in 1947-48-49.

(2912.1951)

63

January 5th 1952: OLDHAM 24 WIDNES 7

W. B. Ganley, L. Platt, W. Mitchell, A. Davies, T. O'Grady, J. Warham, F. Stirrup.
H. Ogden, J. Keith, K. Jackson, C. Winslade, L. Anthony, B. Goldswain.
Goals: Ganley,6. Tries: O'Grady,2. Mitchell. Keith.
Attendance: 8,154   Referee: Mr. H. Squires – Ossett.

Oldham were ahead after eight minutes when Winslade kicked ahead a loose ball and the ever-alert Jack Keith was first to react to score a try. 14 -2 up at the break, the match was sealed early in the second half when Stirrup feinted to pass wide from a scrum and instead sent the ball to the wing from where Platt drew in the cover to send Mitchell over. O'Grady finished the match in style when he robbed possession from a Widnes forward and then beat a string of defenders before kicking ahead and outpacing everyone to dive on the ball for a try just before the final whistle. Ganley was in good form with six goals

Joe Warham is tackled by *Roy Hazelhurst* with *Billy Mitchell* coming up in support.
(05.01.1952)

1951-52

January 12th 1952: OLDHAM 9   SALFORD 9

W. B. Ganley, J. Warham, L. Platt, A. Davies, T. O'Grady, F. Daley, F. Stirrup.
H. Ogden, J. Keith, K. Jackson, C. Winslade, S. Thurlow, B. Goldswain.
Goals: Ganley,3. Try: Platt.

Attendance: 11,052   Referee: Mr. A. Howgate – Dewsbury.

An early long range penalty attempt by Ganley came back off the upright before Oldham took the lead on ten minutes when Stirrup and Daley combined to put Platt over. Just a minute later Hartley replied for Salford, the try being converted by Jack Davies who also put over a drop goal before Oldham responded with two penalty goals from Ganley to leave the scores level (7 - 7) at the break. Overall the Roughyeds were below par in this game and a further penalty goal each in the second half gave Salford the draw and an unexpected point. Stirrup was the pick of the Oldham players with Jack Davies having a sound game for the visitors.

February 2nd 1952: WARRINGTON 14   OLDHAM 4

W. B. Ganley, J. Warham, W. Mitchell, L. Platt, T. O'Grady, F. Stirrup, H. Goodfellow.
L. Anthony, J. Keith, K. Jackson, C. Winslade, B. Goldswain, F. Daley.
Goals: Ganley,2.

Attendance: 15,000   Referee: Mr. H. Squires – Ossett.

Tries from Lambert and Bevan offset by a Ganley penalty gave Warrington a 6 – 2 advantage in the first half. Oldham, playing into a strong wind set off well after the interval and were unlucky when O'Grady managed to get over the line only to be held up by several defenders. A further penalty goal reduced the arrears but Oldham's luck was out again when Platt had a try disallowed for a forward pass before tries from Whittaker and Helme settled the match.

February 9th 1952: HULL 8   OLDHAM 6
Rugby League Challenge Cup 1st Round 1st Leg.

W. B. Ganley, J. Warham, W. Mitchell, L. Platt, T. O'Grady, F. Daley, F. Stirrup.
H. Ogden, J. Keith, L. Anthony, C. Winslade, B. Day, B. Goldswain.
Goals: Ganley,3.

Attendance: 17,000   Referee: Mr. G. Phillips – Widnes.

The match was preceded by a minute's silence in remembrance of King George VI, who had died three days earlier on February 6th.

This was a grim cup-tie with defences dominating throughout. Ganley gave Oldham an early lead after which Mr. Phillips hammered the Roughyeds with penalties, so much so that Hart landed four first half goals to give the 'Airlie Birds' an 8 – 2 lead at the break. Ganley had a storming second half! He brought Oldham back into the match with two penalties, the first from the half-way line, and followed this up with two try-saving tackles on Burnell. A late drop goal attempt by Day was off the mark but just a two point deficit was a good return from the away leg at The Boulevard.

February 16th 1952: OLDHAM 24   HULL 0
Rugby League Challenge Cup 1st Round 2nd Leg.
W. B. Ganley, J. Warham, W. Mitchell, L. Platt, T. O'Grady, F. Daley, F. Stirrup.
H. Ogden, J. Keith, L. Anthony, C. Winslade, B. Day, B. Goldswain.
Goals: Ganley,3. Tries: Warham,2. Platt. Daley. Ogden. Winslade.
Attendance: 13,215   Referee: Mr. L. Thorpe - Wakefield.

A foggy and damp Watersheddings greeted the teams for the second leg and Oldham were soon off the mark with Platt going over. The slippery conditions were not good for open play but Oldham adapted by far the best. A Warham try concluded the first half scoring. Four further tries in the second period secured an easy victory. The best of these was a peach from Daley who out-foxed the Hull defence by way of an outrageous 'dummy'.

Jack Keith and *Joe Warham* *move in to assist their colleague who has downed one of the Hull players. (16.02.1952)*

February 23rd 1952: OLDHAM 24   HULL. K. R. 11
W. B. Ganley, J. Warham, W. Mitchell, A. Davies, T. O'Grady, F. Daley, H. Goodfellow.
H. Ogden, L. Anthony, K. Jackson, C. Winslade, S. Little, B. Day.
Goals: Ganley,3. Tries: O'Grady,3. Daley,2. Warham.
Attendance: 10,884   Referee: Mr. T. Armitage – Huddersfield.

The debut of ex-Harlequin and R.A.F. pilot, Sid Little, was the main talking point going into this match, which was Rovers' first visit to Watersheddings in the 1950s. Oldham were always comfortable in this encounter after Warham had given them an early lead. With Oldham 15 – 5 ahead at the interval, Mills gave Hull K.R. some hope with a try before O'Grady chipped in with a second half 'hat-trick'. The verdict on Little was satisfactory, with his tackling excellent.

Sid Little - *The talk of the stands and terraces on his debut against Hull Kingston Rovers.*

66

March 1st 1952: LEEDS 12   OLDHAM 9
Rugby League Challenge Cup 2nd Round.
W. B. Ganley, J. Warham, W. Mitchell, L. Platt, T. O'Grady, F. Daley, F. Stirrup.
H. Ogden, J. Keith, L. Anthony, C. Winslade, B. Day, B. Goldswain.
Goals: Ganley,3. Try: Warham.
Attendance: 34,000   Referee: Mr. F. Smith – Barrow.

A massive crowd, thought to include 10,000 Oldhamers, gathered at Headingley for this "Roses" encounter. Leeds were without skipper Arthur Clues and surprised many by preferring local teenager Jimmy Dunn at full-back. All the early pressure was with the home side and it was no surprise when Turnbull, put clear by Brown, stepped inside Ganley to score on eight minutes. It was quite against the run of play when O'Grady broke clear only to be put into touch at the corner flag. An exchange of penalty goals followed before Ryan got over in the corner in the closing seconds of the half. Dunn converted brilliantly from the touchline. The Roughyeds were charged up in the second half and a wonderful move saw them back in the match. Stirrup passed to Daley from a scrum and instead of opening out the play he passed back inside to Warham who came up at speed to score near the posts. Ganley converted and there

was another exchange of penalty goals before Oldham laid siege to the Leeds line. However, the Yorkshiremen held firm, exemplified when second-row man Scholes brought off a brilliant cover-tackle to prevent Warham from once more going under the posts. The last 25 minutes amazingly remained scoreless!

Joe Warham goes over for Oldham's only try.(01.03.1952)

Squad photo taken at training in the week leading up to the cup tie at Leeds on March 1st 1952.
Back Row: *Bernard Ganley, Les Anthony, Jack Keith, Bryn Day, Harry Ogden, Ken Jackson, Charlie Winslade.*
Middle Row: *Herbie Goodfellow, Joe Warham, Bryn Goldswain, Billy Mitchell, Terry O'Grady, Lawrie Platt.*
Front Row: *Frank Daley, Frank Stirrup, Alan Davies.*

1951-52

March 8th 1952: BRAMLEY 7   OLDHAM 12

W. B. Ganley, J. Warham, W. Mitchell, A. Davies, L. Platt, F. Daley, F. Stirrup.
H. Ogden, J. Keith, B. Day, C. Winslade, S. Little, B. Goldswain   .
Goals: Ganley,3. Tries: Mitchell. Platt.

Attendance: 2,000   Referee: Mr. W. Stockley – Leigh.

There was some complacency from the Roughyeds in this match after a ten point burst in a two minute spell midway through the first half. Stirrup and Warham combined to put Mitchell over, this being followed by the recalled Davies doing likewise for Platt. Ganley converted both to put Oldham 10 -2 ahead at the break. A Gibson try followed by Powell's second goal brought Bramley right back into it in the second half before a Ganley penalty concluded the scoring. Star man for Oldham was Sid Little, often requiring the attention of three defenders before being tackled.

March 22nd 1952: LEIGH 8   OLDHAM 11

W. B. Ganley, J. Warham, W. Mitchell, A. Davies, L. Platt, F. Daley, F. Stirrup.
H. Ogden, J. Keith, L. Anthony, B. Day, S. Little, B. Goldswain.
Goals: Ganley,4. Try: Platt.

Attendance: 14,300   Referee: Mr. H. Holland – St. Helens.

In a match that was ill-tempered from the start, Oldham scored the only try when Stirrup, Daley and Davies all handled well to put Platt over in the corner. Ganley converted magnificently from the touchline and Oldham led 9 -2 at the interval. Mossop, who was earlier cautioned after a tackle on Anthony, was dismissed on 57 minutes. Daley was having a storming game against his former club but he too was sent off along with Burke midway through the second period, in which Ledgard kicked three penalties to Ganley's one. However, the full story would reveal that the usually reliable Leigh ace kicked four out of nine attempts whereas the ever improving Ganley kicked four out of four.

The Oldham team that triumphed at Leigh on March 22nd 1952.
Back Row: *Bernard Ganley, Les Anthony, Sid Little, Jack Keith, Harry Ogden, Bryn Day, Alan Davies.*
Middle Row: *Frank Daley, Lawrie Platt, Bryn Goldswain, Joe Warham, Billy Mitchell.*
Front Row: *Frank Stirrup.*

March 29th 1952: ST. HELENS 6   OLDHAM 10

W. B. Ganley, T. O'Grady, W. Mitchell, A. Davies, L. Platt, J. Warham, F. Stirrup.
H. Ogden, J. Keith, L. Anthony, B. Day, C. Winslade, B. Goldswain.
Goals: Ganley,2. Tries: Davies. Winslade.
Attendance: 7,000   Referee: Mr. S. Adams – Hull.

Snow caused havoc with the fixtures this weekend, but Knowsley Road avoided the worst of it and Oldham continued their good form. Langfield gave Saints an early lead with a penalty goal before Winslade went over for a try, slapping aside several defenders in the process. Two further penalties gave Saints a 6 – 3 half -time lead. Ten minutes after the break Davies finished off a move that had involved six Oldham players. Ganley converted to put the Roughyeds in front. Much to the dismay of the home support, a chance to equalise late in the game was spurned by St. Helens who opted to take a 'tap' penalty rather than try a goal attempt into the strong wind. As it was Oldham quickly regained possession and within a few moments they had taken play deep into the St. Helens half, where they were awarded a penalty which Ganley slotted home for the last score of the match.

April 1st 1952: ROCHDALE H. 8   OLDHAM 22

W. B. Ganley, T. O'Grady, W. Mitchell, A. Davies, L. Platt, J. Warham, F. Stirrup.
H. Ogden, J. Keith, L. Anthony, S. Little, C. Winslade, B. Day.
Goals: Ganley,2. Tries: O'Grady,3. Davies. Platt. Little.
Attendance: 6,154   Referee: Mr. R. Gelder - Wakefield.

This was a rearranged match which was postponed for frost on January 19th. Bryn Day was made captain in Goldswain's absence and led by example with a typical no nonsense, vigorous effort. The Roughyeds were off to a great start when O'Grady scored after just four minutes. This was soon followed by Little striding over to register his first try for the club. 11 – 2 up at the interval, O'Grady gave the Hornets defence all sorts of trouble and went on to complete his 'hat-trick' in the second half as Oldham eased to a comfortable victory in spite of the fact that Ganley had an off day with the his goal kicking.

April 5th 1952: OLDHAM 17   BELLE VUE R. 3

W. B. Ganley, J. Warham, W. Mitchell, A. Davies, L. Platt, F. Daley, F. Stirrup.
H. Ogden, J. Keith, L. Anthony, A. Tomlinson, S. Little, B. Day.
Goals: Ganley,4. Tries: Mitchell. Platt. Little.
Attendance: 6,939   Referee: Mr. A. Howgate – Dewsbury.

A try from Mitchell after 14 minutes and three Ganley penalties put Oldham in control with only a Lloyd try in reply for Rangers to leave the score 9 - 3 in Oldham's favour at the interval. In the second half the Oldham forwards got on top exemplified when Little 'bulldozed' his way over the try-line scattering several defenders aside as he did so. Belle Vue's woes continued when ex-Roughyed, Doug Phillips was led off with a broken bone in his face after 65 minutes, before Platt wrapped things up with a late try. The home defence was rarely troubled after the break with Anthony and Tomlinson putting in fine defensive performances.

Doug Phillips - *The ex-Roughyed and Belle Vue Rangers captain in the wars at Watersheddings.*

April 11th 1952: SWINTON 5   OLDHAM 17

W. B. Ganley, J. Warham, W. Mitchell, A. Davies, L. Platt, F. Daley, F. Stirrup.
H. Ogden, J. Keith, B. Day, C. Winslade, S. Little, B. Goldswain   .
Goals: Ganley,4.   Tries: Warham. Platt. Daley.
Attendance: 20,000   Referee: Mr. J.P. Hebblethwaite – York.

There was a let-off for Oldham when Blan missed a first minute penalty attempt. Daley then scored to put Oldham ahead and they led 5 -2 at half time. A concerted spell of Swinton pressure on the resumption saw Burn score to level the match. The 'Lions' continued to press with Holden being held just short and Senior being denied by a forward pass ruling. Oldham rallied and sealed the victory with veteran centre Mitchell fashioning tries for first Warham and then Platt who leapt 'frog-like' over the Swinton defence to touch down. Ganley added three second half goals to stretch the margin and give the score something of an unrealistic view considering Swinton's efforts for the first hour of the game.

The Oldham team at Station Road on April 11th 1952.
Back Row: *Frank Daley, Alan Davies, Bryn Day, Sid Little, Harry Ogden, Charlie Winslade, Jack Keith, Bernard Ganley.*
Front Row: *Lawrie Platt, Billy Mitchell, Bryn Goldswain, Joe Warham, Frank Stirrup.*

April 12th 1952: OLDHAM 37   ROCHDALE H. 10

W. B. Ganley, J. Warham, W. Mitchell, A. Davies, T. O'Grady, F. Daley, F. Stirrup.
L. Anthony, J. Keith, A. Tomlinson, C. Winslade, S. Little, B. Goldswain.
Goals: Ganley,5. Tries: Davies,3. O'Grady,2. Warham. Daley. Stirrup. Keith.
Attendance: 13,570   Referee: Mr. H. Harrison – Ossett.

This was another routine win for Oldham, with five of the nine tries coming from the Davies – O'Grady left wing pairing. 13 -2 behind at the break, Hornets battled hard and Schofield did well to force his way over but it was just a temporary respite as the rampant Roughyeds, with Stirrup and Daley in top form, finished in style. Davies completed a 'hat-trick' and the ever-resourceful Keith topped an all-round fine display with a try

April 14th 1952: OLDHAM 27   HALIFAX 12

W. B. Ganley, J. Warham, W. Mitchell, A. Davies, L. Platt, F. Daley, F. Stirrup.
H. Ogden, J. Keith, L. Anthony, C. Winslade, S. Little, B. Goldswain.
Goals: Ganley,5. Stirrup. Tries: Davies,2. Warham. Platt. Anthony.
Attendance: 18,630   Referee: Mr. R. Gelder – Wakefield.

A landmark day for both Bernard Ganley and the club, as he became the first Oldham player to kick 100 goals in a season! The match itself saw Oldham's golden vein of form continue although when Lynch picked up a stray pass to score and Chalkley converted Halifax held a 5 – 3 lead following an early Davies try. Oldham then took control with Goldswain in splendid form. The big crowd were all hoping for Ganley to make the century mark and he duly obliged with a penalty eight minutes from time to rapturous applause from all around the ground. At the conclusion of the match he was carried shoulder high by his team-mates.

*A fascinating photograph of the large crowd at Watersheddings to witness the victory over Halifax and **Bernard Ganley** (inset) kick his 100th goal of the season, the first Oldham player to attain this memorable achievement. **Bryn Day** (complete with trilby) can be seen viewing from the side-lines with **Arthur Tomlinson** on his right. (14.04.1952)*

April 26th 1952: HULL K. R. 3   OLDHAM 33

W. B. Ganley, J. Warham, W. Mitchell, A. Davies, L. Platt, F. Daley, F. Stirrup.
H. Ogden, J. Keith, B. Day, C. Winslade, S. Little, B. Goldswain.
Goals: Ganley,6. Tries: Davies,2. Warham. Mitchell. Stirrup. Little. Goldswain.
Attendance: 8,000   Referee: Mr. N. Railton – Wigan.

Oldham entered this match knowing that a win would have them finish fourth, thus qualifying for the championship play-off, if Hull F.C. could win at Huddersfield on the same afternoon. There was no doubt about the first part of the equation, the Roughyeds completely dominating the match with a seven-try display of sheer quality. Davies was concussed after ten minutes but played on and indeed scored but apparently could remember little of the game afterwards. Only a try by Anderson gave Rovers any relief as Oldham finished the season with ten straight league victories.

The Oldham team had stopped for lunch at Selby en route to Craven Park and as luck would have it the Hull team were at the same place and assured them that they were going to Fartown to win!
Result: Huddersfield 45 Hull 5.

1951-52

May 6th 1952: Oldham 18 Rugby League XIII 8
J. Chalmers Benefit match.

F. Dyson,* T. O'Grady, W. Mitchell, A. Davies, T. Leyland, F. Daley, F. Stirrup.
H. Ogden, J. Keith, B. Day, C. Winslade, S. Little, B. Goldswain.
Tries: O'Grady. Mitchell. Davies. Keith. Little. Cracknell.
R. Cracknell* for Leyland at half time.* Dyson & Cracknell - Guest players.

Attendance: 5,000   Referee: Mr. T. Rees - Oldham.

An end-of-season friendly in aid of ailing Scottish half-back Jimmy Chalmers attracted a reasonable crowd to Watersheddings, despite poor weather, to watch a Rugby League XIII which featured several internationals including fellow Scotsman, Dave Valentine. Frank Dyson guested for Oldham at full-back, and was joined in the second half by Dick Cracknell who scored one of Oldham's six unconverted tries. Both of these Huddersfield stars would of course go on to become Roughyeds favourites.

Jimmy Chalmers

Most Appearances: Joe Warham 41 out of a possible 43.
Most tries: Joe Warham 25.
Most goals: Bernard Ganley 106.
Most points: Bernard Ganley 212

	1951-52	Played	Won	Draw	Lost	For	Against	Points
1	Bradford N.	36	28	1	7	758	326	57
2	Wigan	36	27	1	8	750	296	55
3	Hull	36	26	1	9	552	393	53
4	Huddersfield	36	26	0	10	785	446	52
5	**OLDHAM**	**36**	**25**	**1**	**10**	**558**	**331**	**51**
6	Warrington	36	24	1	11	622	396	49
7	Leigh	36	23	2	11	489	365	48
8	Workington T.	36	23	0	13	540	347	46
9	Hunslet	36	22	1	13	559	404	45
10	Barrow	36	21	2	13	697	345	44
11	Doncaster	36	21	1	14	422	371	45
12	Widnes	36	20	2	14	491	395	42
13	Leeds	36	19	2	15	578	514	40
14	Swinton	36	18	3	15	432	382	39
15	Salford	36	18	2	16	454	386	38
16	Wakefield T.	36	19	0	17	596	518	38
17	Batley	36	18	1	17	440	498	37
18	Dewsbury	36	18	0	18	419	439	36
19	Whitehaven	36	16	4	16	280	356	36
20	St. Helens	36	16	2	18	426	358	34
21	Halifax	36	16	2	18	474	403	34
22	Featherstone R.	36	14	2	20	431	470	30
23	Belle Vue R.	36	12	3	21	351	446	27
24	York	36	12	3	21	363	583	27
25	Hull K.R.	36	10	1	25	416	708	21
26	Rochdale H.	36	10	1	25	328	585	21
27	Bramley	36	10	1	25	300	577	21
28	Castleford	56	8	1	27	370	579	17
29	Keighley	36	8	1	27	351	617	17
30	Cardiff	36	5	0	31	342	1,024	10

1951-52

SEASON	PLAYER	APPS	TRIES	GOALS	POINTS
1951-52	J. WARHAM	41	25		75
1951-52	F. STIRRUP	40	7	1	23
1951-52	C. WINSLADE	38	3		9
1951-52	W.B. GANLEY	37		106	212
1951-52	W. MITCHELL	37	12		36
1951-52	B. GOLDSWAIN	37	2	8	22
1951-52	H. OGDEN	37	2		6
1951-52	A. DAVIES	36	22		66
1951-52	L. PLATT	35	23		69
1951-52	J. KEITH	35	3		9
1951-52	F. DALEY	33	7		21
1951-52	L. ANTHONY	26	4		12
1951-52	T. O'GRADY	25	24		72
1951-52	K. JACKSON	20	1		3
1951-52	B. DAY	20			
1951-52	A. TOMLINSON	14			
1951-52	T. LEYLAND	13	1		3
1951-52	W. RATCHFORD	9	2	2	10
1951-52	S. LITTLE	9	3		9
1951-52	H. GOODFELLOW	9			
1951-52	S. THURLOW	9			
1951-52	K. WARD	5	4	1	14
1951-52	A. MURRAY	4	1		3
1951-52	J. WATSON	1			
1951-52	J. SILVA	1			
1951-52	W. SPENCER	1			
1951-52	**TOTAL**	**572**	**146**	**118**	**674**

Joe Warham

Bernard Ganley

1952-53

After a promising start, the season somewhat fizzled out due in no small measure to an extensive injury list. The loss of influential players like Keith, Warham and especially Goldswain for lengthy periods was hard to sustain and when, on the final run-in, Ogden was also ruled out the strength in depth came up just short. In the circumstances the eighth place finish was respectable and the overall picture was encouraging. Bernard Ganley again extended the club goals and points records and Terry O'Grady topped the try scorers and registered over 20 tries for the second season running. The mercurial Frank Stirrup made the most appearances, his consistency a major factor in the club's resurgence. Alan Davies continued his progress and was becoming a real favourite with the supporters. Also in this season Alan Jones commenced his ten years service with the club.

There was a first round exit to St. Helens in the Challenge Cup over two legs and Workington accounted for the Roughyeds in the Lancashire Cup. However, the Law Cup was retained with victory over Rochdale at Watersheddings in the pre-season encounter. The eighth place in the league table was reached with 46 points coming from 22 wins, two draws and 12 defeats. The two drawn matches, against Rochdale and Whitehaven, followed on from the drawn second leg Challenge Cup tie against St. Helens in February, giving Oldham three consecutive games where the scores finished level, something which is almost unheard of in Rugby League since the very early days of the game when there tended to be much less scoring. Another drawn match was the tour game against Australia when an Oldham team, which had to replace three players at short notice because of international call-ups, put up a great display against the 1952 Kangaroos who won all but one of the matches against club sides. Only St. Helens, who went on to be champions, managed to beat the 'green-and-golds'.

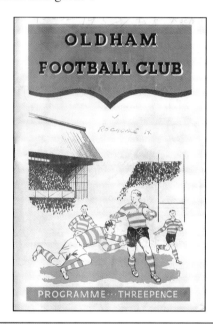

1952-53

August 16th 1952: Oldham 25 Rochdale H. 8
Law Cup

W.B. Ganley, T. O'Grady, W. Mitchell, A. Davies, L. Platt, F. Daley, F. Stirrup.
H. Ogden, J. Keith, B. Day, C. Winslade, S. Little, B. Goldswain.
Goals: Ganley,5. Tries: Stirrup,2. Winslade. Platt. O'Grady.
Attendance: 11,653   Referee: Mr. C. Appleton – Warrington.

The news going into this match was the signing of 19 year old scrum half Frank Pitchford and before the game there was a presentation by the Mayor, H.B. Whittaker, of a special plaque to Bernard Ganley for his goal kicking achievements the previous season and a Lancashire blazer to Lawrie Platt.

Ex-Roughyed, Norman Harris captained Hornets and was instrumental in laying on the first try for Stanford. Schofield converted and Rochdale were five points to the good after ten minutes. Midway through the first half Ogden scooped up a loose ball to give Winslade a walk in and later Stirrup capitalised on another Hornets fumble to put Oldham in front. Three Ganley goals left the half time score at 12 – 5. In the second half Platt scored a 'cracker' from half-way sweeping inside Cahill in the process. Rochdale scored when Ellean did well to put McGilvray over before further tries from Stirrup and O'Grady saw Oldham safely home.

Oldham v Rochdale Hornets August 16th 1952.

Back Row:
Bernard Ganley, Jack Keith, Bryn Day, Harry Ogden, Sid Little, Charlie Winslade.
Middle Row:
Terry O'Grady, Billy Mitchell, Bryn Goldswain, Alan Davies, Lawrie Platt.
Front Row:
Frank Stirrup, Frank Daley.

1952-53

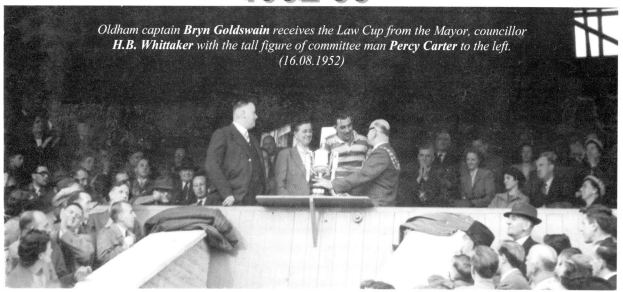

*Oldham captain **Bryn Goldswain** receives the Law Cup from the Mayor, councillor **H.B. Whittaker** with the tall figure of committee man **Percy Carter** to the left. (16.08.1952)*

August 23rd 1952: OLDHAM 32 FEATHERSTONE R. 8

W.B. Ganley, T. O'Grady, W. Mitchell, A. Davies, L. Platt, F. Daley, F. Stirrup.
H. Ogden, J. Keith, B. Day, C. Winslade, S. Little, B. Goldswain.
Goals: Ganley,7. Tries: O'Grady,3. Daley,2. Platt.
Attendance: 11,500   Referee: Mr. M. Coates – Pudsey.

Challenge Cup finalists earlier in the year, Featherstone were short of half of the team that played at Wembley and as such Oldham proved too strong from the word 'go'. Two O'Grady tries and one from Platt helped the Roughyeds to an advantage of 13 – 3 at half time. In the second period a bout of inter-passing between Mitchell and O'Grady over forty yards led to the winger's 'hat-trick' before Longley got over for his second try for Rovers. Daley was in great form and his two tries after the break were just reward for his overall performance. Ganley carried on from where he left off last season with seven goals.

***Billy Mitchell** takes on the Featherstone defence. (23.08.1952)*

August 30th 1952: OLDHAM 25   SWINTON 6
Lancashire Cup 1st Round 1st Leg.
W.B. Ganley, T. O'Grady, W. Mitchell, A. Davies, L. Platt, F. Daley, F. Stirrup.
H. Ogden, J. Keith, B. Day, A. Tomlinson, S. Little, B. Goldswain.
Goals: Ganley,5. Tries: Davies,3. O'Grady. Ogden.
Attendance: 11,500   Referee: Mr. L. Dalby – York.

Two early Ganley penalties got Oldham off to a good start prior to O'Grady increasing the lead with a try at the corner flag. Davies then sprinted sixty yards to score after Stirrup and Ganley had combined to put him clear. An Armitt penalty got the Lions on the board after the break before Davies went on to complete his 'hat-trick'. Ogden got over after a scramble near the visitors line with a couple of penalty goals from Blan the only Swinton reply. Daley was again outstanding as Oldham took a comfortable advantage into the second leg.

Harry Ogden scores as *Sid Little* and *Bryn Day* watch on.   (30.08.1952)

September 3rd 1952: SWINTON 18   OLDHAM 19
Lancashire Cup 1st Round 2nd Leg.
W.B. Ganley, J. Warham, L. Platt, A. Davies, T. O'Grady, F. Daley, F. Stirrup.
H. Ogden, J. Keith, B. Day, A. Tomlinson, S. Little, B. Goldswain.
Goals: Ganley,4. Stirrup. Tries: Warham. O'Grady. Daley.
Attendance: 6,360   Referee: Mr. R. Gelder – Wakefield.

You would think that with a nineteen point lead from the first leg there would be no problem. However, when the Roughyeds were 18 – 2 down at half time the alarm bells must have begun to ring! Three penalty goals by Blan in the first twelve minutes set the tone and when Armitt intercepted a Daley pass to score and followed it up by scooting over at the corner flag and, with both tries converted, Oldham were in trouble. The second period was totally different. A clever reverse pass from the ball-playing wizard, Stirrup had Daley going under the posts before Ganley and Davies linked up to put O'Grady through. Then it was Oldham's turn to intercept when Warham latched on to a loose pass to touch down. Ganley converted all three tries and the tie was safe. The Roughyeds weren't satisfied and when Swinton chased a failed drop goal attempt by Day over the dead ball line, Stirrup fielded the drop-out restart and fired home a drop goal from an acute angle to give Oldham victory.

September 6th 1952: OLDHAM 21   LEEDS 10

W.B. Ganley, J. Warham, W. Mitchell, A. Davies, L. Platt, F. Daley, F. Stirrup.
H. Ogden, J. Keith, L. Anthony, B. Day, S. Little, B. Goldswain.
Goals: Ganley,3. Tries: Warham,2. Mitchell. Davies. Goldswain.
Attendance: 16,700   Referee: Mr. L. J. Dalby – York.

Ogden was injured in the first minute and had to leave the field and, although he later returned, he was forced to retire again before half time. A dour first half saw Leeds take the lead with a Murphy penalty. However, Oldham had the better of the play and Davies was tackled inches short of the line. The only try of the half came when Day, who was in splendid form, broke through and from this Keith sent out a try scoring pass to Warham. The second period opened with a kicking duel between Ganley and Murphy which came to a halt with a Leeds fumble which Goldswain pounced upon to score. A try from Scholes brought Leeds back into the match but despite the sterling efforts of Clues Oldham finished stronger to take the points.

September 10th 1952: ST. HELENS 6   OLDHAM 2

W.B. Ganley, J. Warham, W. Mitchell, A. Davies, L. Platt, F. Daley, F. Stirrup.
H. Ogden, J. Keith, A. Tomlinson, S. Little, B. Day, B. Goldswain.
Goal: Ganley.
Attendance: 22,000   Referee: Mr. T. Armitage – Huddersfield.

The winning run finally came to an end at Knowsley Road in a match that despite the score-line was quite entertaining. Early on a great tackle by Warham on McCormick saved Oldham before Ganley opened the scoring with a penalty. Langfield equalised to leave the scores even at the break. The defence of both teams was magnificent and much appreciated by the massive crowd. Langfield nudged Saints ahead but Oldham's luck was out when a Ganley effort came back off the upright. A further penalty for St. Helens closed the scoring but even in defeat and try-less, Oldham earned praise from the Saints coach, the legendary Jim Sullivan, who commented after the match. *"Oldham are the best side I've seen for years"*.

*Ex-Wigan and Wales Rugby legend, and St. Helens coach in 1952, **Jim Sullivan**, lavish in his praise for Oldham after the close game at Knowsley Road.*

September 13th 1952: BARROW 13   OLDHAM 5

W.B. Ganley, J. Warham, W. Mitchell, A. Davies, L. Platt, F. Daley, F. Stirrup.
H. Ogden, J. Marre, A. Tomlinson, S. Little, B. Day, B. Goldswain.
Goal: Ganley. Try: Platt.
Attendance: 10,994   Referee: Mr. R. Gelder - Wakefield.

Oldham gave a debut to hooker John Marre, a local lad from Austerlands for the trip to Barrow. A tight first half saw Oldham in front 5 – 3 at the break courtesy of a Platt try and Ganley penalty. Oldham started well after the break but home full-back Lewthwaite was in tremendous defensive form. The Roughyeds finally ran out of steam and tries from Parker and Grundy secured victory for the 'Furness-men'. Marre obtained an equal share of the ball in the first half but the experienced McKinnell took control in the later stages of the match.

1952-53

A full account of all the Oldham matches against the touring teams can be found in the book "Kangaroos, Kiwis and Roughyeds".

September 15th 1952: OLDHAM 7 AUSTRALIA 7

W. B. Ganley; J. Warham, W. Mitchell, A. Davies, J. Watson; F. Daley, F. Stirrup;
L. Anthony, J. Keith, H. Ogden, S. Little, A. Tomlinson, A. Murray.
Goals: Ganley,2. Try: Watson.

Attendance: 19,620   Referee: Mr. F. Smith - Barrow.

Oldham were denied the services of captain, Bryn Goldswain, Bryn Day and Terry O'Grady who were selected for the England v Wales international later in the week. Les Anthony, Alf Murray and John Watson were drafted in with Frank Stirrup assuming the captaincy.

A wonderful crowd of over 19,000 turned up for the Monday evening encounter and the home crowd were soon cheering a penalty goal by Ganley. The advantage lasted only a matter of minutes before a long distance effort from Pidding brought the scores back level. Oldham soon returned to the attack and from a scrum Stirrup darted away diagonally, drawing three defenders with him before he slipped the ball out to stand-in wingman Watson who finished strongly to cross the line for a try. Ganley converted to put Oldham five points clear after nine minutes. The rest of the half was dominated by tenacious defending from both teams. Churchill looked dangerous when coming into the line, as did winger Flannery. Still the Oldham line survived to leave them with a 7 - 2 half time advantage. The visitors dominated in the early part of the second period although Pidding and Churchill were both off target with penalty attempts. Oldham responded with Little diving on a loose ball over the Australian line only to have the try disallowed. When Oldham were caught off-side Pidding was successful with a penalty attempt. The visitors were now playing with confidence and Churchill looked certain to score when he sped away up the touch line. However, when all seemed lost, Murray flung himself full length and managed to tap the full-back's ankle. More pressure from the tourists saw centre Wells cross the Oldham line only to be brought back for an obvious forward pass. After being pinned down for some time in their own quarter, Keith tried a clearing kick which was charged down by a rush of green and gold shirts. McCaffery gathered up the ball to go over for the equalising try. Luckily for Oldham the conversion from Pidding hit the post and bounced out. In the remaining minutes the ever tricky Stirrup went close for Oldham and in reply the impressive Flannery almost got over for the visitors.

*John Watson prepares to take on Kanagroos, **Ken McCaffery** and **Dennis Flannery** (3). (15.09.1952)*

1952-53

A full account of all the Oldham matches against the touring teams can be found in the book "Kangaroos, Kiwis and Roughyeds".

Above: Roughyed in trouble! **Ferris Ashton** *and* **Albert Paul** *combine to put a stop to the progress of* **Alan Davies**. *Ouch!*
Other players in the photo are **Frank Stirrup**, **Duncan Hall** *and* **Alf Murray**.　　　*(15.09.1952)*

The Oldham pack combine to bring down **Charlie Gill**.
Harry Ogden *and* **Les Anthony** *make the tackle as* **Sid Little**, **Arthur Tomlinson** *(mostly hidden) and* **Jack Keith** *move in.* **Dennis Flannery** *watches in the background.*
(15.09.1952)

September 20th 1952: OLDHAM 24   WAKEFIELD T. 7

W. Ratchford, T. O'Grady, W. Mitchell, A. Davies, L. Platt, F. Daley, F. Stirrup.
H. Ogden, J. Keith, L. Anthony, S. Little, A. Tomlinson, B. Goldswain.
Goals: Ratchford,2. Goldswain.   Tries: Platt,3. O'Grady. Daley. Stirrup.
Attendance: 12,521   Referee: Mr. A. Hill - Dewsbury.

After a run of over forty consecutive matches Bernard Ganley was absent for the visit of Wakefield to Watersheddings. Earlier in the week Oldham had signed half-back, Johnny Feather from Leeds but there was no place available in this day's match as the Daley / Stirrup combination retained their first team places. Skipper, Goldswain initially took over the goal kicking duties and opened the scoring with an early penalty. Davies then fashioned an opening for Platt to avoid the tackle of Luckman and dive over at the corner before Mortimer replied with a penalty goal for Trinity. Just before the break Daley scored after twice dummying the defence from forty yards out. A feature of the match were extended kicking duels between Ratchford and, not the full-back, but the Wakefield centre Mortimer, and when one of these broke down Stirrup, ever the opportunist nipped in to gather possession and score. Platt completed his 'hat-trick' with another try coming from O'Grady. Ratchford, who had now taken over the goal-kicking responsibilities, converted two of the tries with Burton registering the only touchdown for the visitors. This was a competent and confident display from the Roughyeds with the Stirrup, Daley, Goldswain combination in total control.

Lawrie Platt evades Wakefield full-back, *Luckman* to dive over for a spectacular try.
The first of a 'hat-trick', and typical of the flamboyant style of the Oldham winger.

(20.09.1952)

*Jack Keith is scragged by four Wakefield players as **Arthur Tomlinson, Sid Little** and **Les Anthony** look on with interest.*

(20.09.1952)

September 24th 1952: WORKINGTON T. 13   OLDHAM 10
Lancashire Cup 2nd Round.
W.B. Ganley, J. Warham, W. Mitchell, A. Davies, L. Platt, F. Daley, F. Stirrup.
H. Ogden, J. Keith, B. Day, S. Little, A. Tomlinson, B. Goldswain.
Goals: Ganley,2.   Tries: Davies. Platt.

Attendance: 8,000	Referee: Mr. R. Gelder – Wakefield.

Risman and Ganley opened the respective scoring accounts with penalty goals, after which Henderson put Town in front with a try before Platt replied for Oldham after capitalising on a kick through from Davies. A three minute spell just before the interval effectively cost the Roughyeds the match. First Ivison was allowed to skirt the touchline and score at the corner to the protests of the Oldham players who believed he took out the corner flag before touching down. Then Huddart intercepted a slack Goldswain pass to put Paskins clear. Risman converted the latter to give Workington a 13 – 5 half time lead. Try as they did after the break Oldham didn't quite manage the victory. Little was held close before Davies actually got over. Ganley converted and the Roughyeds almost snatched the match at the end when Stirrup was held up just short after a good break by Warham, but in the end it wasn't to be.

***Billy Ivison,** scorer of a controversial try for Workington.*

September 27th 1952: LEEDS 4   OLDHAM 7
W.B. Ganley, J. Warham, W. Mitchell, A. Davies, T. O'Grady, F. Daley, F. Stirrup.
H. Ogden, J. Keith, L. Anthony, B. Day, A. Tomlinson, B. Goldswain.
Goals: Ganley,2. Try: Stirrup.

Attendance: 16,000	Referee: Mr. T. Watkinson – Manchester.

By all accounts this was a dour match punctuated with rare moments of exciting play and one sublime move which produced the game's only try. It happened after seven minutes when, at a scrum in the home quarter Stirrup, Daley and Warham lined up as if to repeat the move that brought a score in the cup-tie earlier in the year. However, this time the Oldham winger was just a decoy and while he was attracting the attention of the Leeds defence, Stirrup was on his way under the posts. Two penalties, one either side of the break, were all the home side had to offer, although Turnbull was in good form but to no avail as the Roughyed's forwards repelled all comers with Ogden and Tomlinson outstanding.

October 4th 1952: WORKINGTON T. 11   OLDHAM 8

W.B. Ganley, T. O'Grady, W. Mitchell, A. Davies, L. Platt, F. Daley, F. Stirrup.
H. Ogden, J. Keith, L. Anthony, S. Little, B. Day, B. Goldswain.
Goal: Ganley. Tries: Keith. Anthony.
Attendance: 11,110   Referee: Mr. L. J. Dalby – York.

Another fruitless trip to Cumberland with Oldham rather unlucky to go down again by a narrow margin. Early in the game a Risman penalty was off target but Stirrup fumbled the kick and Dawson, following up, picked up to score. Risman converted and added a penalty goal whereas Ganley was wide with two attempts before he finally had his first success to leave the score 7 – 2 at the break. Two more Risman goals put 'Town' nine points ahead before Oldham staged a fight-back. Stirrup, eager to make up for his earlier error put in an astute kick which Keith pounced on to score. The luckless Ganley saw his effort rebound back off the upright. A late unconverted try from Anthony raised hopes but the ill fortune continued when a last gasp attack saw Huddart knock down what would have been a try scoring pass from Mitchell to O'Grady.

October 11th 1952: OLDHAM 31   WIDNES 4

W.B. Ganley, J. Warham, L. Platt, A. Davies, T. O'Grady, F. Daley, F. Stirrup.
H. Ogden, J. Keith, L. Anthony, S. Little, B. Day, B. Goldswain.
Goals: Ganley,7. Stirrup. Tries: O'Grady,3. Platt. Davies.
Attendance: 11,688   Referee: Mr. H. Squires – Ossett.

In this match Harold Tomlinson lined up with the 'Chemics' against his former club. Ganley and Sale exchanged penalty goals early on but Oldham soon took control with Stirrup, fresh from his Lancashire debut earlier in the week, once again in inspired form. Two tries from O'Grady and one from Davies saw that the Roughyeds were 17 – 4 up at half time. A super effort from Platt after the break was the highlight of the second half which also saw O'Grady complete his 'hat-trick' as Oldham eased home with plenty to spare.

October 18th 1952: WARRINGTON 0   OLDHAM 28

W.B. Ganley, L. Emmitt, W. Mitchell, A. Davies, T. O'Grady, F. Daley, F. Stirrup.
H. Ogden, J. Keith, L. Anthony, S. Little, A. Tomlinson, B. Goldswain.
Goals: Ganley,8. Tries: Emmitt. Davies. O'Grady. Tomlinson.
Attendance: 10,000 (est.)   Referee: Mr. H. Squires – Ossett.

A 'Bevan-less' Warrington had no answer to the rampant Roughyeds who gave a debut to Lionel Emmitt in for the injured Platt. Davies scored early on before Tomlinson took great delight in racing in from forty yards against his home-town club. A magnificent six goals from, the back in form, Ganley gave Oldham a lead of 18 – 0 at the interval, . The 'Wire' tightened things up in the second half but further tries from O'Grady and 'new boy', Emmitt rubber-stamped the win. Stirrup and Goldswain dictated the pace of the game and a solid defensive display from the forwards, especially props Ogden and Anthony, kept Warrington at bay.

A promising debut including a late try for
*Welshman **Lionel Emmitt**, at Wildserspool.*

1952-53

October 25th 1952: OLDHAM 27   WARRINGTON 2
W.B. Ganley, L. Emmitt, W. Mitchell, A. Davies, T. O'Grady, J. Feather, F. Stirrup.
H. Ogden, J. Keith, L. Anthony, S. Little, A. Tomlinson, A. Murray.
Goals: Ganley,6. Tries: Emmitt,2. O'Grady,2. Davies.
Attendance: 15,390   Referee: Mr. A. Howgate – Dewsbury.

Bevan was back but the outcome was the same as Warrington visited Watersheddings just a week after their defeat at Wilderspool. Johnny Feather made his debut for the injured Daley and it was his cross kick that led to the first Oldham try scored by Emmitt after a Ganley penalty had given them an early lead. A penalty from Frodsham got Warrington on the scoreboard but this was followed by a further Emmitt try. Ganley converted to put the Roughyeds 10 -2 up at half time. Five minutes into the second period Keith was sent off on the intervention of the touch judge but Oldham were undeterred and O'Grady capped a fine performance by out-sprinting wonder winger Bevan for a brace of tries.

*Lionel Emmitt narrowly avoids the touchline before passing inside to **Billy Mitchell**. (25.10.1952)*

November 1st 1952: BRAMLEY 4   OLDHAM 31
W.B. Ganley, L. Emmitt, W. Mitchell, A. Davies, T. O'Grady, F. Daley, J. Feather.
H. Ogden, L. Anthony, A. Tomlinson, C. Winslade, B. Day, B. Goldswain.
Goals: Ganley,5. Tries: O'Grady,2. Mitchell,2. Ganley. Emmitt.Goldswain.
Attendance: 4,000   Referee: Mr. G. Phillips. – Widnes.

Ganley put Oldham in front with a first minute penalty which Proctor soon equalised before putting the home side in front with another goal on sixteen minutes. Home hooker, Rippin, was monopolising possession for his team against Oldham's stand-in striker, Anthony who was in the team at hooker for the suspended Keith. However, that was it for the 'Villagers' as Oldham, in spite of consistent heavy rain, made light of the conditions to score seven unanswered tries including two from the veteran Mitchell, who defied his advancing years with a performance of real class. O'Grady also got a couple which took his total to eight in the last four matches. Ganley had an indifferent day with the conversions but was on hand for a rare touchdown after the break. This followed good work from the half-backs, Feather and the effervescent Daley who had a hand in most of Oldham's tries. On the few occasions that Bramley threatened the Oldham line. the defence held firm with Anthony making up for his lack of success in the scrums with a tireless display of tackling.

November 8th 1952: OLDHAM 9   LEIGH 2

W.B. Ganley, L. Emmitt, W. Mitchell, A. Davies, T. O'Grady, F. Daley, J. Feather.
H. Ogden, L. Anthony, A. Tomlinson, C. Winslade, B. Day, B. Goldswain.
Goals: Ganley,3. Try: Feather.

Attendance: 19,181   Referee: Mr. T. Armitage – Huddersfield.

A great crowd was in attendance for this match between two of the pace setters in the Championship. Ganley missed two early penalty chances before, once again, the two full backs engaged in a kicking duel. Feather raised Oldham hopes when he intercepted and got clear but the cheers turned to jeers when he was penalised for offside and Ledgard gave Leigh the lead. Ogden then managed to cross the line only to have the try ruled out by the referee. The score remained 2- 0 to the visitors at half time and on the resumption Ganley was off target with two more penalties and an attempted drop goal. Eventually, he succeeded after an obstruction by Clough and then gave Oldham the lead after another offence by the same player. Ledgard was unlucky when a penalty attempt came back off the upright before Feather claimed the only try of the match when he scrambled over direct from a scrum near the Leigh line. Deep into injury time Daley was sent off for a stiff arm!

A remarkable double image as **Harry Ogden** *gets over the Leigh line only for the try to be disallowed.*

Both photographs seemingly taken at exactly the same time!
(08.11.1952)

1952-53

*Arthur Tomlinson attracts the attention of Leigh defenders, **Peter Foster, Brian Chadwick** and **Rex Mossop**. The Oldham trio in the background are: **Bryn Day, Johnny Feather** and **Les Anthony**. (08.11.1952)*

November 15th 1952: WAKEFIELD T. 15   OLDHAM 4

W.B. Ganley, J. Warham, W. Mitchell, A. Davies, L. Emmitt, F. Daley, F. Stirrup.
H. Ogden, L. Anthony, A. Tomlinson, C. Winslade, S. Little, B. Goldswain.
Goals: Ganley, 2.

Attendance: 4,680   Referee: Mr. N. T. Railton – Wigan.

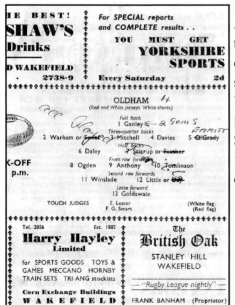

A lacklustre performance from the Roughyeds saw them concede two sloppy tries to home loose-forward Howes after handling errors which gave 'Trinity' an 8 – 2 advantage at the break. In the second period Daley was injured and went on the wing with Warham taking over at stand-off. Two penalties from Burton increased Wakefield's lead and the match was made secure when Storey won the race to touchdown after a kick ahead. As in the first half Oldham were poor when in possession and all they had to offer was a Ganley penalty goal.

*You can't please all of the people all of the time!
A copy of the match programme for the match at Wakefield with the Oldham team page adorned with the words:
" all played terrible!"*

1952-53

November 22nd 1952: OLDHAM 32 SALFORD 3

W.B. Ganley, J. Warham, W. Mitchell, A. Davies, L. Emmitt, J. Feather, F. Stirrup.
H. Ogden, L. Anthony, B. Day, C. Winslade, S. Little, B. Goldswain.
Goals: Ganley,7. Tries: Emmitt,3. Warham. Stirrup. Winslade.
Attendance: 11,755   Referee: Mr. R. Gelder – Wakefield.

Back to winning ways in convincing style, although at half time the score was just 5 – 0 thanks to a converted try scored by Stirrup. Indeed Salford could have been ahead but for some poor goal kicking attempts from Smith and Rogers. After the break Oldham found their form and swept in for a further five tries, the pick of which was a fifty yard dash by Emmitt.

*Before the match against Salford, club official **Percy Carter** presented Welsh caps to forwards **Charlie Winslade** and **Bryn Day**. (22.11.1952)*

December 6th 1952: OLDHAM 24 BELLE VUE R. 2

W.B. Ganley, J. Warham, W. Mitchell, A. Davies, L. Emmitt, J. Feather, F. Stirrup.
H. Ogden, L. Anthony, B. Day, C. Winslade, S. Little, B. Goldswain.
Goals: Ganley,6. Tries: Feather,2. Warham. Goldswain.
Attendance: 9,136   Referee: Mr. S. Adams – Hull.

The previous Saturday Oldham had travelled all the way to Whitehaven only to find the match called off for a frozen pitch and this after being reassured in the morning that the match was on!

Another comfortable win for Oldham. The highlight of the first period was a storming run by Winslade that sent Warham under the posts. Oldham had a 14 - 2 advantage at the break with Feather in splendid form. He scored a try in each half, the first after a set move from the scrum when he inter-passed with Warham and the second after an exchange with Goldswain followed by a forty yard zigzag run to the line. Ganley was back at his best with six goals.

December 20th 1952: BRADFORD N. 12 OLDHAM 9

W.B. Ganley, J. Warham, W. Mitchell, A. Davies, L. Emmitt, J. Feather, F. Stirrup.
H. Ogden, J. Keith, B. Day, C. Winslade, S. Little, B. Goldswain.
Goals: Ganley,3. Try: Davies.

Attendance: 8,500   Referee: Mr. G. Phillips. – Widnes.

Oldham stormed into the lead at Odsal with a set move from the first scrum in the second minute. In the now regular fashion, Warham came inside to receive and passed on to Mitchell and although his subsequent pass was knocked down, Davies scooped it up to score Ganley converted and then added a penalty after twelve minutes. After Phillips had missed a couple of penalty attempts, Ward took over and opened Bradford's account. Oldham led 7 – 2 at the break but ten minutes into the new half Feather was sent off on the intervention of the touch judge. Warham went to stand-off with Goldswain withdrawn from the forwards to the right wing. Howes was controversially awarded a try after diving on a loose ball with Ganley and Emmitt also in attendance. The Oldham players were convinced that one or the other of them had got there first. The winning score came after an overlap caused by the numerical advantage, due to the dismissal, led to McLean going over with five minutes to go. Ward converted well from the corner.

December 25th 1952: OLDHAM 15 SWINTON 8

W.B. Ganley, L. Platt, W. Mitchell, A. Davies, L. Emmitt, J. Warham, F. Stirrup.
H. Ogden, J. Keith, L. Anthony, C. Winslade, S. Little, B. Goldswain.
Goals: Ganley,3. Tries: Stirrup. Mitchell. Anthony.

Attendance: 15,208   Referee: Mr A. S. Dobson – Pontefract.

Three games in three days! That was the festive programme for the Roughyeds who gave Warham a run-out at stand-off half for the first time this season. An indifferent first period on a chilly Watersheddings Christmas day saw Oldham behind 8 – 5 to a determined Swinton team who scored tries through Bellard and Birkett with a goal from Blan. The Roughyeds' response was a touchdown from Stirrup combined with a Ganley goal. The second half was equally well contested but the Roughyeds edged it courtesy of the pack eventually getting the better of the 'Lions' forwards. The points were secured as Mitchell and Anthony crossed for a try each, allied to two more Ganley goals. This, combined with a solid defensive effort, which kept Swinton scoreless after the break, ensured that Oldham gave their supporters the desired Christmas cheer.

December 26th 1952: LIVERPOOL C. 2 OLDHAM 24

W. Ratchford, L. Platt, W. Mitchell, A. Davies, L. Emmitt, F. Stirrup, F. Pitchford.
L. Anthony, J. Keith, B. Day, C. Winslade, A. Tomlinson, B. Goldswain.
Goals: Ratchford,3. Tries: Platt,3. Emmitt,2. Mitchell.
Attendance: 1,000 (est)

In spite of several players being unavailable for this Boxing Day fixture, no doubt due to the festive season, a routine win was gained in appalling conditions. Half of the Knotty Ash pitch was described as being little more than a morass. Consequently the players were soon covered from head to foot in mud! Not surprisingly the damage was done on the flanks where a reasonable foothold was still possible, with the Oldham three-quarters grabbing all the tries. Notable points of the game were a 'hat-trick' for Platt and a promising debut for the young Frank Pitchford at scrum-half who defied the atrocious state of the pitch to show, even this early on his career, that he had the ability to read a game well and adapt to the prevailing conditions .

Frank Pitchford

December 27th 1952: OLDHAM 14   WIGAN 5

W.B. Ganley, L. Platt, W. Mitchell, A. Davies, L. Emmitt, J. Warham, F. Stirrup.
H. Ogden, J. Keith, L. Anthony, C. Winslade, S. Little, B. Goldswain.
Goals: Ganley,4. Tries: Platt,2.

Attendance: 18,146   Referee: Mr. A. Howgate – Dewsbury.

Although thick fog delayed Wigan's arrival and put back the kick off, the mist had lifted sufficiently for the game to commence shortly after the scheduled 2.30pm start. Stirrup was proving a thorn in Wigan's side but defences ruled in the first half with three Ganley penalties to Cunliffe's one registering a 6 – 2 half time advantage to Oldham. Two tries for Platt, both excellently laid on by the veteran, Mitchell saw Oldham take the initiative early in the second half and, though Wigan toiled away to claw the game back, a Broome try was all they had to show for their efforts.

Frank Stirrup on the move against Wigan.
(27.12.1952)

January 3rd 1952: OLDHAM 4   BARROW 7

W.B. Ganley, J. Warham, W. Mitchell, A. Davies, L. Platt, J. Feather, F. Stirrup.
H. Ogden, J. Keith, L. Anthony, C. Winslade, S. Little, B. Goldswain.
Goals: Ganley,2.

Attendance: 13,019   Referee: Mr. T. Armitage - Huddersfield.

Snow was falling as the match kicked off and two missed penalty attempts by Ganley in the first five minutes proved costly as Oldham lost their first home match in fourteen months. Once again defences were on top best demonstrated when Winslade was stopped just short of the posts after good approach work by Goldswain and Feather. Willie Horne put over a couple of penalties to give Barrow a 4 – 0 half time lead. However, in a reversal of the first period Ganley scored two penalties in the opening five minutes of the second half. A draw looked likely until, with eight minutes to go, Barrow were awarded a penalty and after initially shaping up to have a shot at goal, Horne tapped the ball forward and walked through unopposed to score. Just before the finish Warham just failed to touch down a kick through but that was it and the Barrow master, half-back had stolen the points.

January 10th 1953: WIGAN 13   OLDHAM 27

W.B. Ganley, L. Emmitt, W. Mitchell, A. Davies, L. Platt, F. Daley, F. Stirrup.
H. Ogden, J. Keith, B. Day, C. Winslade, S. Little, B. Goldswain.
Goals: Ganley,6. Tries: Day,2. Platt. Daley. Stirrup.

Attendance: 8,622   Referee: Mr. A. S. Dobson – Pontefract.

All in all this was a bizarre match. To start with, as at Watersheddings two weeks before, the ground was shrouded in fog and maybe to beat the gloom, the match started five minutes early! Gee gave Wigan an early lead with a penalty goal but Oldham were soon in front when Day secured a loose ball to go over. This was closely followed by Daley, Davies and Platt combining to put the Oldham prop in again. Ganley converted both and then added a penalty and a calmly taken drop goal to put the Roughyeds 14 – 2 up at half time. The teams commenced the second half straight away with Oldham continuing to dominate scoring three further tries, the best being another example of handling wizardry between Daley and Stirrup direct from a scrum. Wigan rallied late on to make the score respectable and the referee, for reasons unknown, played an extra ten minutes!

The view from the press-box was apparently very poor due to the fog and after the first Oldham try one of the reporters said, "I think its **Day**", *only for one of his colleagues to exclaim, "It looks like* **Night** *to me!"*

January 17th 1953: SALFORD 4 OLDHAM 8

W.B. Ganley, J. Warham, W. Mitchell, A. Davies, L. Platt, F. Daley, F. Stirrup.
H. Ogden, J. Keith, A. Tomlinson, C. Winslade, S. Little, B. Goldswain.
Goal: Ganley. Tries: Winslade. Davies.
Attendance: 11,600   Referee: Mr. M. Coates – Leeds.

This was a magnificent effort by Oldham but the victory came at a cost! After Warham had a try disallowed for a forward pass. Winslade managed to force his way over after Platt was held short. A Robson penalty reduced the arrears before disaster struck when Goldswain suffered a broken arm shortly before half time. In the second period Salford were throwing everything at a tiring Oldham but a Ganley penalty revived the team's spirits only for Ogden to suffer a dislocated and split finger. He battled on bravely for a spell before he too had to retire from the fray. In the midst of all this misfortune the Roughyeds somehow found the energy to conjure up a further try, Warham and Mitchell paving the way for Davies to accelerate away to score in the corner. Salford continued their siege on the Oldham line but a late penalty goal from Robson was all they could muster.

The Oldham team at Salford January 17th 1953.
Back Row: *Bernard Ganley, Jack Keith, Lawrie Platt, Harry Ogden, Sid Little, Arthur Tomlinson, Charlie Winslade.*
Front Row: *Alan Davies, Frank Daley, Frank Stirrup, Joe Warham, Billy Mitchell, mascot, Bryn Goldswain.*

January 24th 1953: OLDHAM 8 ROCHDALE H. 7

W.B. Ganley, J. Warham, L. Platt, A. Davies, T. O'Grady, F. Daley, F. Stirrup.
L. Anthony, J. Keith, A. Tomlinson, C. Winslade, S. Little, B. Day.
Goal: Ganley. Tries: O'Grady. Keith.
Attendance: 12,221   Referee: Mr. L. Thorpe – Wakefield.

Warham was given the captaincy in Goldswain's absence for the derby fixture with Rochdale. O'Grady put Oldham ahead on eight minutes after capitalising on a Hornets handling error. However, the visitors were in good form and when a Ganley kick was charged down Ellean won the race to ground the ball. Schofield converted and Lord added a penalty to put Rochdale 7 – 3 ahead at the interval. Once again, as at Wigan on January 10th, the teams changed right around. Warham was leading by example and it was he who began the move which saw Keith go over for a try fifteen minutes into the half. Ganley missed the conversion but slotted home a penalty soon after to give Oldham a one point advantage. And so it stayed although Lord, Schofield and Ganley all failed with penalty attempts.

1952-53

January 31st 1953: OLDHAM 4   BRAMLEY 5

W.B. Ganley, J. Warham, W. Mitchell, L. Platt, T. O'Grady, F. Daley, F. Stirrup.
K. Jackson, J. Keith, A. Tomlinson, C. Winslade, S. Little, A. Murray.
Goals: Ganley,2.

Attendance: 7,837   Referee: Mr. R. Gelder – Wakefield.

Oh dear! In the press lead up to this match there was talk of increasing the scoring average and an easy fixture before the cup-ties. However, no one told Bramley the plot and at a blustery Watersheddings one of the shock results of the season came to pass. Admittedly, Oldham suffered some ill luck when Day withdrew just before kick-off, so much so that the match had already started when replacement Murray entered the field. Then Keith was injured and had to go off after just ten minutes. Nevertheless, it was a complacent performance. A couple of long distance penalties from Ganley put Oldham ahead before a good passing move saw Harding cross for the visitors to leave them trailing by just a point at the break. Proctor missed a penalty chance to put Bramley ahead but he made amends with a terrific tackling display. One such clattered Warham into touch and left the Oldham wingman limping for the rest of the game. Warrior put over the winning penalty as Oldham toiled in vain to break down the Bramley defence.

February 7th 1953. ST. HELENS 20   OLDHAM 4

Rugby League Challenge Cup 1st Round 1st Leg.

W.B. Ganley, L. Emmitt, W. Mitchell, A. Davies, L. Platt, F. Daley, F. Stirrup.
H. Ogden, J. Mundy, A. Tomlinson, C. Winslade, S. Little, B. Day.
Goals: Ganley,2.

Attendance: 26,000   Referee: Mr. A. Hill – Dewsbury.

A greatly anticipated match that proved to be a big let-down for the Oldham faithful. Jimmy Mundy had been signed earlier in the week from Huddersfield to fill the hooking gap. The match was won by the dominance of the Saints forwards and it was two breakaways, the first from Parr and the second from Cale, that produced tries for McCormick and Greenall. Gullick also scored before half-time to leave the interval score 11 – 0. Oldham tightened things up a little after the break but a Prescott try increased the lead which, aided by three Langfield goals, gave St Helens a comfortable first leg advantage. Although Parsons was sent off, in what was a very physical encounter, two Ganley penalties was the only reply.

*Stan McCormick cuts between **Lionel Emmitt** and **Billy Mitchell**.*   *(07.02.1953)*

February 14th 1953: OLDHAM 5   ST. HELENS 5
Rugby League Challenge Cup 1st Round 2nd Leg.
W.B. Ganley, T. O'Grady, W. Mitchell, A. Davies, L. Emmitt, F. Stirrup, J. Feather.
H. Ogden, J. Mundy, A. Tomlinson, C. Winslade, S. Little, B. Day.
Goal: Ganley. Try: Feather.

Attendance: 19,780   Referee: Mr. M. Coates – Pudsey.

Two days of snow clearing enabled the match to be played and Oldham's hopes were raised when after five minutes a pass from Moses to Gullick went astray and Tomlinson gathered and forged for the line. He was stopped short but from the play the ball Feather got over. Saints replied after thirteen minutes when Honey darted away from a scrum to put Llewellyn clear. Langfield converted to more or less seal the tie. The same player then had bad luck as first a penalty came back off the upright and then a second off the crossbar. So with a 5 – 3 lead at half-time St. Helens shut up the shop effectively in the second half. Little almost broke the line but Saints held firm apart from conceding a Ganley penalty goal. There were several fiery exchanges between the forwards and after 61 minutes Day was dismissed after an altercation with Cale and it was later discovered that Tomlinson had a broken wrist.

February 21st 1953: ROCHDALE H. 7   OLDHAM 7
W.B. Ganley, W. Spencer, W. Mitchell, F. Daley, T. O'Grady, F. Stirrup, F. Pitchford.
H. Ogden, J. Mundy, L. Anthony, B. Day, S. Little, A. Murray.
Goals: Ganley,2. Try: O'Grady.

Attendance: 8,200   Referee: Mr. A. Howgate - Dewsbury.

It was an injury hit squad that took on the Hornets but Oldham were soon in front from a Ganley penalty. The improved weather conditions helped to provide for open play which was quite unexpected in this usually competitive derby game. However, despite the 'to and fro' nature of the match no tries resulted in the first half. A Lord penalty goal levelled the scores eight minutes from the break. In the opening minutes of the second half Pitchford went on the blind side at a scrum, drew in the defenders and passed to O'Grady who powered through to touch down. Rochdale bounced right back when Stanford put Oldroyd clear, he in turn chipped over Ganley and re-gathered to score. Both tries went unconverted. Ganley was unlucky after he followed an O'Grady kick through to score only to be ruled offside but he and Stanford landed penalties and the points were shared. Highlight of the match was the sparkling form of Frank Pitchford.

February 28th 1953: WHITEHAVEN 14   OLDHAM 14
W.B. Ganley, L. Emmitt, W. Mitchell, A. Davies, T. O'Grady, F. Daley, F. Stirrup.
H. Ogden, J. Mundy, L. Anthony, C. Winslade, S. Little, A. Murray.
Goals: Ganley,4. Tries: Emmitt,2.

Attendance: 7,000   Referee: Mr. L. Thorpe – Wakefield.

An entertaining match throughout. There was an early scare at both ends as, first home full-back McKeown hit the post with a penalty, closely followed by Emmitt having a try disallowed for a forward pass. McKeown was then injured and had to go on the wing, so it was Bob Nicholson who gave 'Haven' the lead with an eleventh minute penalty. Emmitt then got a legitimate try fashioned by Mitchell to put Oldham 5 – 2 up at the interval. After the break Ganley and McKeown exchanged penalty goals before a breakaway from Keen saw Nicholson score. McKeown converted but it was straight down to the other end where Stirrup put Emmitt over again. Ganley converted then added a penalty but it was no more than Whitehaven deserved when the gallant McKeown, still on the wing, touched down and converted to leave the scores equal. Incredibly, this was Oldham's third drawn match in a row!

Whitehaven hero, **John McKeown**

March 7th 1953: OLDHAM 11   BRADFORD N. 13

W.B. Ganley, L. Emmitt, W. Mitchell, A. Davies, T. O'Grady, A. Jones, F. Stirrup.
H. Ogden, J. Mundy, L. Anthony, C. Winslade, S. Little, F. Daley.
Goals: Ganley, 4.   Try: O'Grady.

Attendance: 15,644   Referee: Mr. S. Adams – Hull.

Local player, Alan Jones was given his debut and almost had a dream start after Stirrup had put Winslade through but the final pass to Jones went astray when a score looked certain. The undoubted highlight of the first half was the only try, a great effort from New Zealander, Jack McLean who eluded three Oldham defenders to score. Nevertheless three Ganley penalties left the Roughyeds 6 – 5 in front at the interval. At the start of the second half Emmitt was held just short of the line from where play switched to the other end and McLean likewise was only just denied. However, from this position Hastings got over and Phillips converted. Back came Oldham and O'Grady put in a clever kick, re-gathered and strode through to the posts. The match was settled when, five minutes from full-time, the ever dangerous McLean crossed for his second try, a score which cemented Bradford's play-off hopes and virtually ended those of Oldham.

*Left: Bradford's Kiwi winger **Jack McLean**. Scorer of two tries in an impressive display at Watersheddings.*

Right:** A first team debut for local half-back, **Alan Jones.

March 14th 1953: WIDNES 9   OLDHAM 8

W.B. Ganley, L. Emmitt, W. Mitchell, A. Davies, T. O'Grady, A. Jones, F. Stirrup.
H. Ogden, J. Mundy, L. Anthony, C. Winslade, J. Watson, F. Daley.
Goal: Ganley.   Tries: O'Grady. Stirrup.

Attendance: 3,500   Referee: Mr. F. Smith - Barrow.

The trend of close defeats continued with the visit to Naughton Park. A Simpson penalty gave Widnes the lead which was extended to seven points by half-time when Hazelhurst and ex-Roughyed, Harold Tomlinson combined to send in Todd for a converted try. A Breare penalty took the 'Chemics' further ahead before Oldham fought back with tries from O'Grady and Stirrup. Unfortunately, Ganley was only able to convert the latter to leave another frustrating narrow reverse.

*Ex-Roughyed **Harold Tomlinson** back playing with his hometown club to help set up the decisive try for Widnes.*

March 21ˢᵗ 1953: OLDHAM 19   WORKINGTON T. 9
W.B. Ganley, L. Emmitt, W. Mitchell, A. Davies, T. O'Grady, F. Daley, F. Stirrup.
H. Ogden, J. Mundy, K. Jackson, C. Winslade, J. Watson, S. Little.
Goals: Ganley,5. Tries: Emmitt. O'Grady. Little.
Attendance: 10,516   Referee: Mr. T. Armitage - Huddersfield.

After a seven match sequence without a victory since the narrow defeat of Rochdale on January 24th it was back to winning ways at last! In a try-less first half, two Ganley penalties as opposed to one from Risman gave Oldham a slight advantage. In the second half a further penalty each preceded a converted O'Grady try but 'Town' bounced right back with Gibson sprinting in from fifty yards. The Roughyeds finally took control with further tries from Emmitt and the impressive Little, who was the pick of the Oldham players ably supported by Mitchell and Stirrup.

March 28ᵗʰ 1953: FEATHERSTONE R. 7   OLDHAM 14
W.B. Ganley, T. O'Grady, W. Mitchell, J. Feather, L. Emmitt, F. Daley, F. Stirrup.
H. Ogden, J. Mundy, K. Jackson, C. Winslade, J. Watson, S. Little.
Goals: Ganley,4. Tries: O'Grady. Feather.
Attendance: 2,000   Referee: Mr. F. Smith – Barrow.

There was a fierce wind at Post Office Road which was defied by home full-back Norman Mitchell to put Rovers ahead with an eighth minute penalty. Oldham responded with a try from Feather after a side-stepping run from Stirrup. Ganley converted to leave the score 2- 5 at half-time. Three penalty goals and an O'Grady try were enough to seal victory in the second half but Rovers pressed to the end with a Derek Davies penalty and a Wildridge try adding to their total.

April 3ʳᵈ 1953: SWINTON 30   OLDHAM 12
W.B. Ganley, T. O'Grady, W. Mitchell, J. Feather, L. Emmitt, F. Daley, F. Stirrup.
H. Ogden, J. Mundy, K. Jackson, C. Winslade, J. Watson, S. Little.
Goals: Ganley,3. Tries: O'Grady. Daley.
Attendance: 14,000   Referee: Mr. R. Gelder - Wakefield.

A shoulder injury forced Ogden to retire after fourteen minutes and put him out for the rest of the season. However, Oldham managed to stay competitive in the first half with a Daley try and three Ganley goals keeping the scores level at 9 – 9 at the break. In the second period Oldham ran out of steam and the 'Lions' eased home. Two tries from Tommy Stott and six goals from the sure footed Blan being major contributing factors.

April 4ᵗʰ 1953: BELLE VUE R. 0   OLDHAM 16
W.B. Ganley, T. O'Grady, W. Mitchell, A. Davies, J. Feather, F. Daley, F. Stirrup.
K. Jackson, J. Mundy, L. Anthony, C. Winslade, A. Tomlinson, S. Little.
Goals: Ganley,2. Tries: Tomlinson,2. Mitchell. Davies.
Attendance: 4,500   Referee: Mr. S. Adams – Hull.

A comfortable win for the Roughyeds on this Easter Saturday with two tries in each half being enough to secure the points. Stirrup had a hand in the first three for Davies, Tomlinson and Mitchell, the latter of which Ganley converted from the touchline after previously being out of form. Tomlinson then wrapped up the scoring with his second try.

April 6ᵗʰ 1953: OLDHAM 15   WHITEHAVEN 3
W.B. Ganley, T. O'Grady, W. Mitchell, A. Davies, L. Emmitt, F. Daley, F. Stirrup.
K. Jackson, J. Mundy, L. Anthony, J. Watson, A. Tomlinson, S. Little.
Goals: Ganley,3. Tries: Mitchell. Emmitt. Little.
Attendance: 7,075   Referee: Mr. A. Hill – Dewsbury.

Persistent rain made for a very muddy Watersheddings and open play was consequently at a premium. Oldham were aided by a massive possession monopoly which saw Mundy heel from the first twelve scrums. Mitchell opened the scoring when he handed off Smith and then managed to keep just inside of the touchline to go over. A Ganley penalty was the only other score before the break after which Mitchell, Daley and Davies combined well to put Emmitt over. Ganley did exceptionally well in the conditions to convert from the touchline. The last try went to Little which was again made by the impressive Mitchell before Whitehaven managed a last minute consolation try from Nicholson.

April 11ᵗʰ 1953: OLDHAM 59   LIVERPOOL C. 3
W.B. Ganley, T. O'Grady, W. Mitchell, A. Davies, L. Emmitt, F. Daley, F. Stirrup.
K. Jackson, J. Mundy, L. Anthony, A. Tomlinson, J. Watson, S. Little.
Goals: Ganley,10.
Tries: Davies,2. Emmitt,2. Mundy,2. Little,2. Ganley. O'Grady. Mitchell. Daley. Watson.
Attendance: 4,919   Referee: Mr. R. Gelder - Wakefield.

Strange as it may seem, the first quarter of an hour of this match saw Liverpool in the ascendancy. They were winning the scrums and were denied a try by a forward pass ruling before Reilly missed a penalty

chance to put them ahead. Mundy then opened the scoring after good approach play from Ganley and Watson. 'City' then had the misfortune of losing Leyland and Adair to injury and Oldham capitalised immediately. They were 21 – 0 in front at the break and when Little crossed in the first minute of the second half the rout had begun. Parkes also had a spell off the field but he was reserved the biggest cheer of the day when he returned to the field and then outpaced Ganley to score after 63 minutes though the Oldham marksman had the consolation of a ten goal haul.

A study in concentration!

Bernard Ganley *kicked ten goals for the first time in the match against Liverpool City.*

April 18th 1953: OLDHAM 13   ST. HELENS 14
W.B. Ganley, J. Warham, W. Mitchell, A. Davies, L. Emmitt, F. Daley, F. Stirrup.
K. Jackson, J. Mundy, C. Winslade, A. Tomlinson, J. Watson, S. Little.
Goals: Ganley,5. Try: Mundy.
Attendance: 14,951   Referee: Mr. L. Thorpe - Wakefield.

Saints rested several first teamers ahead of their forthcoming assault on both the Challenge Cup and Championship trophies. Still, their confidence was sky high and just four minutes had passed when Langfield charged down a Ganley kick for Metcalfe to score. Langfield duly converted and later added a penalty. Ganley meanwhile kept Oldham in it with two goals and they went ahead after Stirrup went for the St. Helens line and, finding himself hemmed in, floated a pass over several defenders for Mundy to score. The try was converted to leave the Roughyeds 11 -7 in front at half time. Oldham dominated the second half in terms of possession and territory but a further Langfield goal reduced the gap and then on 68 minutes Saints found themselves with an overlap and Honey made no mistake to scoot in at the corner. Langfield goaled magnificently from the touchline. Oldham resumed their attack but a Ganley penalty seven minutes from time just wasn't enough.

*Joe Warham is just too late to touch down a kick ahead as the Saints full-back, **Glyn Moses**, closes in.*

*Oldham winger **Lionel Emmitt** is tackled by **Jimmy Honey** and **Peter Metcalfe** of St. Helens, while **Alan Davies** and **George Langfield** keep a close watch.*

(18.04.1953)

1952-53

April 22nd 1953: LEIGH 17 OLDHAM 13

W. Ratchford, J. Warham, W. Mitchell, A. Davies, T. O'Grady, F. Daley, F. Stirrup.
K. Jackson, J. Mundy, C. Winslade, A. Tomlinson, J. Watson, S. Little.
Goals: Ratchford. Mitchell. Tries: Daley. Davies. Little.

Attendance: 12,000   Referee: Mr. R. Gelder - Wakefield.

Oldham's bad luck with injuries continued right to the end of the season when the unfortunate Ratchford, playing as a stand-in for Ganley suffered a broken jaw. Chadwick opened the scoring with a try for Leigh shortly followed by Warham having a try disallowed due to a forward pass. However, Ratchford put over a penalty and a bout of Oldham pressure saw Davies score against his hometown club. Daley was, as ever, in the thick of the action on both attack and defence and increased the lead when he side-stepped through for a try. Just before the interval Wood followed up a Pawsey kick ahead to score. The incident that changed the impetus of the match happened in the 52nd minute when Pawsey barged his way over and Ratchford suffered his injury in the process. Moore converted and then Lannon scored to put Leigh further ahead. Oldham responded with a Little try and goal added by stand-in kicker, Mitchell. However, a late try from Moore sealed the win for Leigh.

Charlie Pawsey - Leigh's international forward, a powerful player who scored a try and laid on another to secure victory for Leigh.

May 16th 1953: Oldham 13 Huddersfield 20

H. Ogden Benefit match.

W.B. Ganley, J. Warham, W. Mitchell, A. Davies, T. O'Grady, F. Daley, F. Stirrup.
K. Jackson, J. Mundy, L. Anthony, A. Tomlinson, C. Winslade, S. Little.
Substitute: A. Murray.
Goals: Ganley,2. Tries: Warham,2. Davies.

Attendance: 8.000   Referee: Mr. R. Gelder - Wakefield.

Huddersfield came to Oldham as Challenge Cup holders for Harry Ogden's benefit game and a very respectable crowd of 8,000 turned up for the occasion.

The match was quite competitive compared to some of the other end of season benefit games and the Roughyeds started well with two Warham tries and a Ganley penalty giving them an 8 – 0 half time lead. However, it took two fine tackles by Mitchell on Devery and Warham on Sullivan to keep the Roughyed's line intact. After the interval Davies scored with Ganley's conversion putting Oldham thirteen points to the good. The injury hoodoo continued when Anthony broke his finger but Murray was allowed on as a replacement. Huddersfield then got to work and two tries from Sullivan, an interception from Dyson and a further score from Rylance, who converted all four tries, gave victory to the Yorkshiremen.

Harry Ogden

1952-53

Most Appearances: Frank Stirrup 40 out of a possible 42.
Most tries: Terry O'Grady 22.
Most goals: Bernard Ganley 140.
Most points: Bernard Ganley 286.

Bernard Ganley

Terry O'Grady

Frank Stirrup

	1952-53	P	W	D	L	F	A	Pts
1	St. Helens	36	32	2	2	769	273	66
2	Halifax	36	29	2	5	620	309	60
3	Bradford N.	36	28	0	8	700	32')	56
4	Huddersfield	36	27	2	7	747	366	56
5	Barrow	36	27	1	8	585	322	55
6	Leeds	36	24	0	12	690	452	48
7	Leigh	36	23	2	11	556	377	48
8	**OLDHAM**	**36**	**22**	**2**	**12**	**599**	**280**	**46**
9	Warrington	36	20	1	15	733	486	41
10	Whitehaven	36	19	3	14	465	486	41
11	Wigan	36	19	2	15	673	414	40
12	Hunslet	36	20	0	16	485	358	40
13	Salford	36	20	0	16	508	441	40
14	Swinton	36	18	0	18	441	401	36
15	Hull	36	17	2	17	461	451	36
16	Workington T.	36	16	2	18	453	460	34
17	Keighley	36	16	1	19	465	547	33
18	Wakefield T.	36	16	0	20	410	595	32
19	Dewsbury	36	15	1	20	410	440	31
20	Castleford	36	15	0	21	392	502	30
21	Batley	36	14	2	20	405	579	30
22	Rochdale H.	36	13	3	20	443	536	29
23	Widnes	36	13	2	21	336	478	28
24	Featherstone R.	36	12	1	23	415	535	25
25	York	36	10	0	26	370	496	20
26	Doncaster	36	10	0	26	377	665	20
27	Belle Vue R.	36	10	0	26	301	705	20
28	Hull K.R.	36	9	1	26	337	646	19
29	Bramley	36	6	0	30	293	898	12
30	Liverpool C.	36	4	0	32	225	837	8

1952-53

SEASON	PLAYER	APPS	TRIES	GOALS	POINTS
1952-53	F. STIRRUP	40	6	2	22
1952-53	W.B. GANLEY	39	2	140	286
1952-53	W. MITCHELL	39	8	1	26
1952-53	A. DAVIES	38	14		42
1952-53	S. LITTLE	37	5		15
1952-53	H. OGDEN	34	1		3
1952-53	F. DALEY	33	8		24
1952-53	T. O'GRADY	25	22		66
1952-53	A. TOMLINSON	25	3		9
1952-53	C. WINSLADE	25	2		6
1952-53	L. ANTHONY	25	2		6
1952-53	B. GOLDSWAIN	24	3	1	11
1952-53	L. EMMITT	23	15		45
1952-53	J. KEITH	22	2		6
1952-53	B. DAY	21	2		6
1952-53	J. WARHAM	20	5		15
1952-53	L. PLATT	19	13		39
1952-53	J. MUNDY	14	3		9
1952-53	J. FEATHER	11	5		15
1952-53	J. WATSON	9	2		6
1952-53	K. JACKSON	9			
1952-53	A. MURRAY	5			
1952-53	W. RATCHFORD	3		6	12
1952-53	A. JONES	2			
1952-53	F. PITCHFORD	2			
1952-53	J. MARRE	1			
1952-53	W. SPENCER	1			
1952-53	**TOTAL**	**546**	**123**	**150**	**669**

1953-54

Another indifferent season saw Oldham slip four places down the league table from the previous campaign after they finished in twelfth place with 38 points from 17 wins, 4 draws and 15 defeats. Right from the outset things didn't go well when Rochdale won the Law Cup for the first time since 1948 with an astonishing late rally which saw the Hornets score four tries in the last ten minutes of the match. Warrington accounted for the Roughyeds in the second round of both the Lancashire Cup at Wilderspool and the Challenge Cup at Watersheddings. Both were very close encounters with just a single point separating the sides in the Lancashire Cup match and three points in the Challenge Cup tie, with that winning margin courtesy of a 70-yard Brian Bevan interception try.

Bernard Ganley once again topped the century of goals total and Terry O'Grady led the try scorers with 27, his third consecutive season with over 20 tries. The Oldham-born winger so impressed the Rugby League authorities that he was selected for the 1954 tour to Australia and New Zealand to the delight of the Oldham supporters, who were equally mystified at the omission of centre Alan Davies. Johnny Feather had a solid season after joining the club from Leeds the previous year and there was much enthusiasm amongst the supporters with regard to the emerging talent of young Frank Pitchford. Another astute signing was that of Dick Cracknell from Huddersfield, a proven wingman who had already gained international honours.

Three great servants of the club, Lawrie Platt, Tommy Leyland and Joe Warham, played their last matches for Oldham with Warham going on to take over as manager at Rochdale.

August. 8ᵗʰ· 1953. Rochdale H. 31   Oldham 19
Law Cup
W. B. Ganley, T. O'Grady, W. Mitchell, A. Davies, J. Warham, A. Jones, F. Stirrup.
H. Ogden, J. Mundy, A. Tomlinson, S. Little, H. Lomas, B. Goldswain.
Goals: Ganley,5. Tries: O'Grady,2. Warham.
Attendance: 8,413   Referee: Mr. G. Phillips – Widnes.

The news prior to the game was the signing of Peter Fearis, a rugby union centre who had played for Bath, Dorset & Wiltshire County and the RAF. Also recruited was Harold Lomas, from the local club, Lowermoor, who went straight into the Law cup team when Charlie Winslade had to withdraw.

This was a match with a staggering turn around in fortunes. At first it was all Oldham with only a full length diving tackle from McNally denying Warham in the early stages. After a Ganley penalty put the Roughyeds in front after five minutes, ex-Roughyed Norman Harris did well to put McNally over for a converted Hornets try. O'Grady replied for Oldham following up a Mitchell kick ahead. Warham also got over before the break, by which time Oldham were 12 – 7 in front, and when Mitchell and O'Grady repeated the dose from the first half early in the second period the trophy seemed bound for Watersheddings once again. However, six more Rochdale tries, four of which came without reply in the last ten minutes, secured Hornets the cup. Undoubted man-of-the-match was home loose forward Bernard McNally who turned in a strong performance in defence and scored two tries.

August 15ᵗʰ 1953: OLDHAM 18   WIGAN 7
W. B. Ganley, T. O'Grady, W. Mitchell, A. Davies, J. Warham, A. Jones, F. Stirrup.
H. Ogden, J. Mundy, K. Jackson, S. Little, A. Tomlinson, B. Goldswain.
Goals: Ganley,5. Stirrup. Tries: Jones. Davies.
Attendance: 16,254   Referee: Mr. R. Gelder – Wakefield.

A penalty by Ganley from just inside the Wigan half opened the scoring, closely followed by Stirrup and Mitchell providing an opening for Jones to touch down for a converted try. Wigan veteran captain, Ken Gee, was held just short of the line but soon afterwards he paved the way for Ashcroft to score. Again the try was converted. A Stirrup drop goal and a further penalty saw Oldham 11 – 5 ahead at the break.

Midway through the second half an accurate, short kick by Warham enabled Davies to take it on the full and sprint to the posts. This more or less sealed the game as the visitors toiled to make much of an impression on the home defence.

Frank Stirrup looks to give Terry O'Grady a reverse pass with Billy Mitchell in support.

(15.08.1953)

1953-54

August 22nd 1953: HUDDERSFIELD 27   OLDHAM 20

W. B. Ganley, T. O'Grady, W. Mitchell, A. Davies, J. Warham, F. Daley, F. Stirrup.
H. Ogden, J. Mundy, K. Jackson, S. Little, A. Tomlinson, B. Goldswain.
Goals: Ganley,4. Tries: Warham. Davies. Stirrup. Jackson.
Attendance: 17,362   Mr. C. Appleton – Warrington.

Like the Law Cup game this was another occasion when Oldham let a comfortable lead slip away in the late stages of the match. Kicking off at 7pm, unusual for a Saturday fixture, all seemed well at first as Jackson ploughed over direct from acting half-back, then Davies cut inside to leave several defenders in his wake on his way to the posts. Later he put in a cross kick that Warham pounced on to score. This all added up to see Oldham 15 – 4 ahead at the interval and when the in-form Davies put Stirrup in under the posts just after the break, victory looked assured. The last quarter was a different story with Warham and Tomlinson both now 'passengers' due to injuries. The 'Fartowners' applied the pressure and the Roughyeds broke! Henderson twice, Pepperell, Cooper and Devery all crossed the Oldham line with the latter also finishing the match with five goals.

Ex- New Zealand 'All Black', **Peter Henderson**
scored two late tries for Huddersfield.

August 26th 1953: BRAMLEY 16   OLDHAM 9

W. B. Ganley, T. O'Grady, W. Mitchell, A. Davies, L. Platt, F. Daley, F. Stirrup.
H. Ogden, J. Mundy, K. Jackson, S. Little, J. Watson, B. Goldswain.
Goals: Ganley,3. Try: Daley.
Attendance: 4,000   Referee: Mr. T. Watkinson – Manchester.

This was a poor performance from Oldham who came up against a spirited Bramley team perhaps buoyed up from their success at Watersheddings earlier in the year. Two early penalties from Ganley saw the Roughyeds in front but after that everything went awry for the Oldham marksman. First he, Davies and Platt all failed to cope with a loose ball, enabling Nepia to score, and in the second half he sent a wayward pass that Armitage scooped up for an easy try. In Oldham's defence it has to be said that one of Nepia's goals in the first half was thought to have gone a full two feet wide and also the 'tough as teak' Daley was found to have played on for some time with a fractured arm. The same player had capitalised on good approach play by Davies and Stirrup to score a try that sent Oldham in with a 9 – 7 lead at the break.

Playing through the pain barrier.
Frank Daley, *played on with a broken arm at Bramley.*

August 29th 1953: OLDHAM 14 LEEDS 5

F. Stirrup, T. O'Grady, W. Mitchell, A. Davies, L. Platt, J. Feather, F. Pitchford.
H. Ogden, J. Mundy, K. Jackson, C. Winslade, J. Watson, B. Goldswain.
Goal: Winslade. Tries: Platt,2. Pitchford. Davies.

Attendance: 10,932   Referee: Mr. T. Armitage – Huddersfield.

Charlie Winslade and Johnny Feather played their first games of the season and Frank Stirrup was switched to full-back when Ganley had to withdraw, but the big attraction of the day was the appearance of the 'Golden Boy', Lewis Jones, for Leeds and it was he who opened the scoring with an early penalty. This prompted Oldham into action and Stirrup beat 'man after man' before putting in a slide-rule kick for Platt to follow up and score. After half an hour Stirrup again made the initial break that led to Pitchford and Davies putting Platt over again. 6 – 2 up at the break, the Roughyeds increased their lead when Pitchford darted over straight from a scrum for Winslade to add the goal. That was to be the last action for Charlie who was sent off soon afterwards, to be followed to the dressing rooms five minutes later by Gwyther. Poole forced his way over near the posts but when Jones missed the easy conversion the Leeds resolve was broken and Oldham sealed the victory with a Davies try.

*Benjamin Lewis Jones nicknamed the 'Golden Boy' after his £6,0000 switch from Rugby Union in November 1952.
This was the first appearance of the dual code international at Watersheddings.*

September 2nd 1953: WIDNES 11 OLDHAM 9

F. Stirrup, T. O'Grady, W. Mitchell, A. Davies, L. Platt, J. Feather, F. Pitchford.
H. Ogden, J. Mundy, K. Jackson, S. Little, A. Tomlinson, B. Goldswain.
Tries: Davies,2. Platt.

Attendance: 6,000   Referee: Mr. L. Garbett – Castleford.

A match Oldham should have won but for the want of a goal kicker. Widnes led 9 – 3 at the interval courtesy of three goals from Jolley and a Wilcox try. Davies scored a try in each half and also teamed up well with Feather and Goldswain to make the other touchdown for Platt but the lack of a marksman cost Oldham dear. Four players attempted shots at goal to no avail, Little being most unlucky when he was just off target with the last kick of the match. In the last two games Oldham had now scored seven tries with only one conversion!

September 5th 1953: WHITEHAVEN 13 OLDHAM 12
Lancashire Cup 1st Round 1st Leg.

W. B. Ganley, L. Emmitt, W. Mitchell, A. Davies, F. Stirrup, J. Feather, F. Pitchford.
H. Ogden, J. Mundy, K. Jackson, S. Little, A. Tomlinson, B. Goldswain.
Goals: Ganley,3. Tries: Pitchford. Emmitt.

Attendance: 5,900   Referee: Mr. R. Gelder – Wakefield.

An uneventful first period was brought to life on 28 minutes when Pitchford eluded Keen at the scrum and raced in at the corner. McKeown, who had a torrid time with goal attempts, succeeded at last with a penalty and just before the interval Gales went over to give 'Haven' the lead. After the break, Emmitt scored and Oldham had secured an 11- 8 advantage going into the final minutes when a loose pass from Morgan was hacked on by McKeown and with the Oldham players retreating a freak bounce took the ball straight into the hands of McAlone, who scored under the posts. McKeown converted and after the restart there was just time for Ganley to put over a last gasp penalty goal to close the gap to one point going into the second leg.

1953-54

September 7th 1953: OLDHAM 45   WHITEHAVEN 6
Lancashire Cup 1st Round 2nd Leg.
W. B. Ganley, L. Emmitt, W. Mitchell, A. Davies, T. O'Grady, J. Feather, F. Stirrup.
H. Ogden, J. Mundy, K. Jackson, S. Little, C. Winslade, B. Goldswain.
Goals: Ganley,12 Tries: Stirrup,2. Feather,2. Davies. Emmitt. Goldswain.
Attendance: 10,142   Referee: Mr. H. Squires- Ossett.

From the opening minutes, when Feather robbed Nicholson of the ball to put Goldswain over, this was going to be Oldham's day. The ever-alert Stirrup obliged with two tries as did his half-back partner, Feather, and Ganley equalled the club's 'goals in a match' record. The most unusual try came in the second half when Emmitt misjudged the flight of a drop-out from the Whitehaven posts; it subsequently hit his legs and bounced into the air, he took a step forward, caught the ball and sprinted 35 yards through a mesmerised defence to score. All Whitehaven's points came from McKeown penalty goals for scrum offences.

Terry O'Grady gets the 'treatment' from Bill McAlone and ex-Roughyed, Walter Nicholson as Harry Ogden and Jim Mundy move up for the play the ball.

(07.09.1953)

September 12th 1953: LEIGH 9   OLDHAM 17
W. B. Ganley, L. Emmitt, W. Mitchell, A. Davies, T. O'Grady, J. Feather, F. Stirrup.
H. Ogden, J. Mundy, L. Anthony, C. Winslade, S. Little, B. Goldswain.
Goals: Ganley,4. Tries: O'Grady. Davies. Emmitt.
Attendance: 12,000   Referee: Mr. H. Squires – Ossett.

Leigh were in the ascendancy early on and the Oldham line had a charmed life as both Kindon and Moore mishandled with the line at their mercy. The Roughyeds recovered and scored the only try of the first half when Davies scooped up a loose ball and passed to Mitchell who put O'Grady over. Ganley converted to put his side 7 – 4 up at the break. Leigh responded and Kindon atoned for his earlier error by chipping over Ganley and winning the race to touch down. Ledgard's conversion put Leigh ahead. A fine passing move paved the way for Emmitt to restore Oldham's lead before Leigh had another spell of pressure which was met with stout defence. The match was settled when Feather kicked through, for Emmitt, who also put his boot to the ball before Davies gathered to score. Ganley converted and Oldham were home and dry although misfortune hit Harry Ogden who chipped a bone in his ankle two minutes from time.

1953-54

September 19th 1953: OLDHAM 28   LIVERPOOL C. 2

W. B. Ganley, L. Emmitt, W. Mitchell, P Fearis, T. O'Grady, J. Feather, F. Pitchford.
K. Jackson, J. Keith, L. Anthony, C. Winslade, S. Little, B. Goldswain.

Goals: Ganley,5. Tries: O'Grady,2. Keith. Little. Fearis. Ganley.
Attendance: 8,106   Referee: Mr. S. Abram – Wigan.

Ex-Rugby Union centre Peter Fearis made his debut in this match and Jack Keith played for the first time since being injured against Bramley in January. Fearis was soon pleasing the fans with a 40 yard dash but it wasn't until the 14th minute that Feather unlocked the Liverpool defence and found Ganley in support; he went over for the try and then added the conversion. Little added another try before the break, by which time Oldham were 12 – 0 ahead. O'Grady got a couple in the second half but the biggest cheer was reserved for Fearis when he completed a 50 yard arcing run to score. Later he broke through again and kicked ahead and although Goldswain over-ran the ball, Keith who was following up had the simple task of touching down.

Sid Little scores Oldham's second try despite the attention of two Liverpool City defenders, to the approval of *Charlie Winslade.*

NB, the old Hutchins stand had been demolished ready for reconstruction in time for the following season.

(19.09.1953)

September 24th 1953: WARRINGTON 12   OLDHAM 11
Lancashire Cup 2nd Round.

W. B. Ganley, T. O'Grady, W. Mitchell, A. Davies, L. Emmitt, J. Feather, F. Stirrup.
L. Anthony, J. Mundy, K. Jackson, A. Tomlinson, C. Winslade, B. Goldswain.
Goals: Ganley,4. Try: Mitchell.

Attendance: 15,524   Referee: Mr. M. Coates – Pudsey.

A terrific cup-tie that saw Oldham 11 – 7 ahead at the break, aided by a two to one scrum advantage supplied by hooker Mundy. The first try went to the 'Wire' when Albert Naughton capitalised on a fumble by Feather near the Oldham line. The reply came with some style when Goldswain, Winslade, Feather and Stirrup all linked up to send in Mitchell. The decisive moment came after 48 minutes and it was Warrington's turn to show their handling skills, which culminated in Challinor scoring in the corner. The conversion by Bath was a splendid effort that went in off the upright. On the other hand the luckless Ganley saw two of his efforts hit the woodwork and bounce out!

September 26th 1953: LEEDS 27   OLDHAM 10

W. Ratchford, L. Emmitt, W. Mitchell, A. Davies, L. Platt, J. Feather, F. Stirrup.
L. Anthony, J. Mundy, K. Jackson, A. Tomlinson, S. Little, B. Goldswain.
Goals: Ratchford,2. Tries: Stirrup. Feather.

Attendance: 20,000   Referee: Mr. N. T. Railton – Wigan.

The Roughyeds were definitely second best in this match and the score does little justice to the Leeds dominance. An early penalty from Ratchford put Oldham in front and it wasn't until the 20th minute that Leeds went ahead when Clues put McLennan over. 12 - 2 up at the interval the home team went from strength to strength with Turnbull scoring the pick of their tries after a 50 yard dash. Late opportunist tries from Feather and Stirrup gave the score a sort of respectability that Oldham hardly deserved.

The Oldham team at Headingley on September 26th 1953.
Back Row: L. Anthony, F. Stirrup, A. Davies, A. Tomlinson, W. Mitchell, L. Emmitt, K. Jackson, J. Feather, S. Little.
Front Row: J. Mundy, B. Goldswain, W. Ratchford, L. Platt.

October 3rd 1953: OLDHAM 33 WIDNES 2

W. B. Ganley, L. Emmitt, P Fearis, A. Davies, L. Platt, J. Feather, F. Stirrup.
K. Jackson, J. Mundy, A. Tomlinson, C. Winslade, S. Little, B. Goldswain.
Goals: Ganley,5. Stirrup. Tries: Stirrup,2. Jackson,2. Goldswain. Little. Platt.
Attendance: 10,341   Referee: Mr. M. Coates – Pudsey.

Oldham responded to their critics with an emphatic victory over Widnes. A Stirrup drop goal after five minutes set them on their way and when a few minutes later Little forced his way over after Emmitt had been grounded just short the trend for the match was set. The lead was 15 – 0 at half time and the second period continued in the same vein with the highlight being a brace of tries from prop-forward Ken Jackson and a solid defensive display that put a stranglehold on the infrequent attacks of the 'Chemics'.

October 10th 1953: OLDHAM 11 DEWSBURY 2

W. B. Ganley, R. Cracknell, P Fearis, W. Mitchell, L. Platt, J. Feather, F. Stirrup.
K. Jackson, J. Keith, A. Tomlinson, S. Little, J. Watson, B. Goldswain.
Goal: Ganley. Tries: Platt,2. Fearis.
Attendance: 13,530   Referee: Mr. S. Adams. – Hull.

In the days leading up to this match, after several attempts, Dick Cracknell was signed from Huddersfield amid much fanfare and anticipation, his inclusion in the starting line up no doubt swelling the attendance. The new addition was soon in the action taking an inside pass from Tomlinson, but it was the rest of the three-quarter line that fashioned the first try when Fearis and Mitchell contrived to put Platt over for the only score of the half at a blustery Watersheddings. Dewsbury had given as good as they had got in the first period and it took a good tackle by Watson to deny Metcalfe. For Oldham Goldswain got over only for the try to be ruled out for a previous knock-on. Feather put Platt over again after the break before Thompson reduced the arrears with a penalty for the visitors. The final points came when Cracknell and several defenders over-ran a Feather kick through, leaving Fearis with the simple task of touching down for a try which Ganley converted.

October 17th 1953: SALFORD 11 OLDHAM 11

W. B. Ganley, R. Cracknell, A. Davies, P Fearis, L. Platt, J. Feather, F. Stirrup.
K. Jackson, J. Mundy, L. Anthony, S. Little, A. Tomlinson, B. Goldswain.
Goals: Ganley,4. Try: Fearis.
Attendance: 11,000   Referee: Mr. L. Thorpe – Wakefield.

Salford attacked early on and Keaveney was tackled close to the line in the opening minutes. Jack Davies opened the scoring with a penalty for Salford shortly before his namesake Alan saved the day for Oldham  with a great tackle on Moses. A Jack Davies drop goal increased the lead, and then Oldham hit back when Anthony got Alan Davies away to the try-line only to be buried by several defenders preventing him from grounding the ball. A Ganley penalty reduced the arrears to 4 – 2 at half time. Jack Davies added a penalty after the break and a 50 yard burst by Finan culminated with Baines scoring a try, which was converted by Rogers. Two Ganley penalties gave the Roughyeds hope going into the closing minutes but it looked as though they had missed their chance when Little was bundled into touch. However, possession was gained from the scrum and Fearis managed to scramble over in Finan's tackle. Ganley added the goal and the points were shared.

*Ex-Rugby Union man **Peter Fearis** scored the*
late try that gained a draw for Oldham.

October 24th 1953: OLDHAM 20 ROCHDALE H. 6

W. B. Ganley, R. Cracknell, W. Mitchell, A. Davies, L. Platt, J. Feather, F. Stirrup.
L. Anthony, J. Keith, K. Jackson, S. Little, A. Tomlinson, B. Goldswain.
Goals: Ganley,4. Tries: Little,2. Davies. Stirrup.
Attendance: 15,418   Referee: Mr. A. Howgate – Dewsbury.

Hornets got off to a flyer when McNally put Jones away up the wing in the third minute and he in turn put Cahill on a run to the posts. Jones then blotted his copybook by missing the conversion from straight in front. Ten minutes later Oldham were level when Davies scorched through to score and they went in front soon after when Stirrup 'bobbed and weaved' his way over direct from a scrum. The Oldham play-maker then put a deft pass out for Little to score, and by half time the lead was 13 – 3. On the resumption, as in the first half, Rochdale scored first, Jones re-gathering his own kick to sprint to the posts, but once again the conversion was missed! This time McNally was the culprit to the dismay of the Hornets players and supporters alike. Little later scored his second try as Oldham eased home. One interesting statistic was a 39 to 7 scrum advantage provided by Jack Keith, making it a debut to forget for Hornet's hooker Jack Sivill.

The Oldham team against Rochdale Hornets on October 24th 1953.

Back Row:
J. Keith,
S. Little,
A. Tomlinson,
K. Jackson,
L. Anthony,
W. B. Ganley.
Middle Row:
W. Mitchell,
A. Davies,
B. Goldswain,
L. Platt,
R. Cracknell.
Front Row:
F. Stirrup,
Mascot,
J. Feather.

October 31st 1953: DEWSBURY 6 OLDHAM 6

W. Ratchford, R. Cracknell, W. Mitchell, A. Davies, T. O'Grady, J. Feather, F. Stirrup.
L. Anthony, J. Keith, K. Jackson, S. Little, C. Winslade, B. Goldswain.
Tries: O'Grady. Mitchell.
Attendance: 4,000   Referee: Mr. J. Jackson – Barrow.

Just three weeks after the match at Oldham, the return at Crown Flatt was another tight encounter. After a quarter of an hour a fine move involving Feather, Stirrup and Davies was completed by Mitchell, who scored taking two defenders with him in the process. Two penalties to Thompson put Dewsbury ahead at the break and the second half was totally defence-dominated apart from one moment of inspiration from Cracknell, who intercepted a Dewsbury pass and raced clear before handing on to Winslade. He passed to Little who in turn gave O'Grady a run in at the corner. Like all his other goal attempts Ratchford, in for the injured Ganley, missed the conversion and Feather later missed a penalty, but late in the match Thompson found the target to earn his side a deserved draw.

November 7ᵗʰ 1953: OLDHAM 3   ST. HELENS 5

F. Stirrup, T. O'Grady, W. Mitchell, A. Davies, P Fearis, J. Feather, F. Pitchford.
L. Anthony, J. Keith, K. Jackson, S. Little, C. Winslade, B. Goldswain.
Try: O'Grady.

Attendance: 6,626   Referee: Mr. T. Armitage – Huddersfield.

Driving rain at Watersheddings made for slippery conditions which subsequently limited the prospects of open play. So it was that the first half remained scoreless. Fearis was off target with a long range penalty attempt and the same player was unlucky when he just put a foot in touch after rounding Gullick on the outside. The conditions played their part in the St. Helens try when, after Parsons kicked forward, the ball was hacked on by Llewellyn and slithered out of the reach of both Stirrup and Fearis for Parsons to follow up to score. Oldham were fortunate to draw level when O'Grady was awarded an obstruction try after being 'taken out' by Moses and although a penalty award was appropriate, it didn't seem likely that the Oldham winger would have scored. Fearis missed the conversion but Ball made no mistake with a penalty and Saints hung on for victory.

November 14ᵗʰ 1953: WHITEHAVEN 7   OLDHAM 0

J. Feather, R. Cracknell, W. Mitchell, A. Davies, T. O'Grady, F. Daley, F. Stirrup.
L. Anthony, J. Mundy, A. Tomlinson, C. Winslade, S. Little, B. Goldswain.
Attendance: 4,500   Referee: Mr. S. Adams – Hull.

Feather was tried at full-back in Ganley's extended absence and gave a good account of himself. A fifth minute penalty from McKeown was the only score in the first half although Davies missed a chance to put Cracknell over with a muffed pass. At the other end O'Grady saved the day for Oldham when he beat Harrison to secure the ball over the Roughyed's try-line. After the break Feather did well to put Nicholson into touch at the corner flag but a further penalty midway through the half and a Harrison try ten minutes from time, when he easily got past the injured Cracknell, were enough to ensure that Oldham still had to wait for their first victory at the Recreation Ground.

November 21ˢᵗ 1953: OLDHAM 35   BRAMLEY 13

J. Feather, H. Lomas, R. Barrow, A. Davies,   T. O'Grady, F. Daley, F. Stirrup.
K. Jackson, J. Keith, A. Tomlinson, T. Leyland, B. Goldswain, S. Little.
Goals: Goldswain,4. Tries: Lomas,3. Barrow,2. O'Grady,2. Leyland. Davies.
Attendance: 7,445   Referee: Mr. A. Hill – Dewsbury.

The match was delayed five minutes due to the late arrival of the Bramley team. Once underway it was a most impressive debut for local, ex-rugby union player Roland Barrow who played centre to stand in wing man, Harold Lomas, and what an impression they made. Lomas scored a 'hat-trick' and Barrow finished off a great performance with two late tries, the first coming after a 60 yard break. As early as the third

minute Daley and Barrow had put Lomas in for his first. The recalled Tommy Leyland, playing his first match in two years, also got on the score-sheet. To be fair Bramley were hampered by losing Millington to injury for all of the second half, but chipped in with three tries by Riley, Nepia and Warrior. The first was well- worked by the powerful Maori prop-forward, Tipuna 'Smut' Smith.

*A 'hat-trick' for stand-in winger **Harold Lomas**.*

November 28th 1953: BELLE VUE R. 17   OLDHAM 14
W. B. Ganley, R. Cracknell, R. Barrow, A. Davies, T. O'Grady, J. Feather, F. Pitchford.
H. Ogden, J. Keith, K. Jackson, C. Winslade, B. Goldswain, S. Little.
Goals: Ganley,4. Tries: O'Grady. Cracknell.
Attendance: 5,000   Referee: Mr. F. Smith. – Barrow.

An unexpected reverse for the Roughyeds to lowly Belle Vue Rangers seemed unlikely when O'Grady stormed over after a sweeping passing movement involving several players. However, soon afterwards, Rangers returned the compliment for winger Day to score an equally impressive try following good work form the Belle Vue back division. Tierney and Ganley had converted the tries to leave the scores level at the break. Winslade had gone off injured after 22 minutes and failed to resume after the interval, and Rangers made the extra man count with Morgan and Day scoring further tries, both converted by the sure-footed Tierney. A silver lining for Oldham was the first try for Cracknell who finished off a move started by Feather and carried on by Barrow.

December 5th 1953: OLDHAM 8   BARROW 24
W. B. Ganley, T. O'Grady, R. Barrow, A. Davies, L. Emmitt, D Ayres, F. Pitchford.
H. Ogden, J. Keith, T. Smith, A. Tomlinson, J. Watson, S. Little.
Goals: Ganley,4.
Attendance: 9,776   Referee: Mr. G. Phillips – Widnes.

The experiments continued with two more debuts in this match, local lad 18-year-old Dennis Ayres, who had a baptism of fire against international Willie Horne, and new signing Maori prop-forward Tipuna 'Smut' Smith, who had impressed at Watersheddings for Bramley two weeks earlier. However, there would be no fairy-tale ending, even though both players showed up well in the first half, which saw Oldham go in 6 – 4 in front thanks to three Ganley penalties. Two quick tries after the break from Goodwin and Wilson seemed to sap the confidence of the home side, and although Ganley added another penalty, Barrow took control from that point to win comfortably.

Tipuna Arnold 'Smut' Smith, signed from Bramley after a good display against the Roughyeds on November 21st.

December 12th 1953: ST. HELENS 21   OLDHAM 9
W. B. Ganley, R. Cracknell, W. Mitchell, A. Davies, L. Emmitt, D Ayres, F. Pitchford.
H. Ogden, J. Mundy, T. Smith, C. Winslade, S. Little, B. Goldswain.
Goals: Ganley,3. Try: Pitchford.
Attendance: 15,000   Referee: Mr. W. Stockley – Swinton.

Despite the score-line this was an improved performance from Oldham, but they met current champions St. Helens on top of their form. From the outset Saints laid siege to the Roughyeds line. The pressure eventually bore fruit when McCormick got over and when, soon afterwards, Prescott avoided Smith to barge over from close in and then Greenall scored after inter-passing with Llewellyn, the Oldham supporters feared the worst. Ganley put over a penalty and then Davies had a try disallowed for incorrect grounding just before the interval, which saw Saints 11 – 2 ahead. After the break the home side dominated once more and two further tries made the game safe, but Oldham had the consolation of a well-worked try from Pitchford after Goldswain had made the opening.

December 19th 1953: OLDHAM 10   WORKINGTON T. 22
W. B. Ganley, R. Cracknell, W. Mitchell, A. Davies, L. Emmitt, J. Feather, F. Pitchford.
H. Ogden, J. Mundy, T. Smith, C. Winslade, S. Little, B. Goldswain.
Goals: Ganley,2. Tries: Davies. Cracknell.

Attendance: 8,524   Referee: Mr. L. Thorpe – Wakefield.

Oldham actually were the better team for the first quarter and it took some good defence from 'Town', with Ivison prominent, to keep them out. However, after Thompson fashioned an opening for Southward to scorch in from 40 yards, there only ever looked like being one winner. Emmitt did well to come inside from a scrum and make an opening for Davies to score, but further tries from Bailey and Thomas put Workington 13 – 5 ahead at half time. After the break they continued to impress and ran out comfortable winners although there was some consolation when Mitchell laid on a first home try for Dick Cracknell.

*Bailey, the Workington left wing scores one of his two tries despite the tackle of **Bernard Ganley** and **John Feather**.*
(19.12.1953)

December 25th 1953: OLDHAM 23   SWINTON 0
W. B. Ganley, T. O'Grady, W. Mitchell, A. Davies, L. Emmitt, J. Feather, F. Pitchford.
H. Ogden, J. Keith, A. Tomlinson, S. Little, C. Winslade, B. Goldswain.
Goals: Ganley,4. Tries: O'Grady,2. Emmitt,2. Ganley.

Attendance: 10,931   Referee: Mr.. S. Abram – Wigan.

The annual festive fixture at Watersheddings brought the gift of an overdue victory and an emphatic one at that! One has to feel some sympathy for the 'Lions' who had to play all of the second half without Lawrenson, who had to retire with concussion. Up to then only one try had been scored, a fine passing movement putting Emmitt over. After the break the extra man advantage was exploited well, Oldham making the overlap count with three more tries to the wingers and one for Ganley coming into the line.

December 26th 1953: WORKINGTON T. 3 OLDHAM 0

W. B. Ganley, T. O'Grady, W. Mitchell, A. Davies, L. Emmitt, J. Feather, F. Pitchford.
H. Ogden, J. Keith, K. Jackson, A. Tomlinson, C. Winslade, B. Goldswain.

Attendance: 8,500 (est.)   Referee: Mr. F. Smith – Barrow.

A deluged pitch with almost as much water visible as grass did nothing to promote open play. This was reflected in a scoreless first half and there was little improvement in the second period. The only score came on 68 minutes when Gibson got the touchdown after a scramble following a kick ahead by Archer. Davies did well to stop Southward in full flight and likewise Ivison and Risman combined to push Emmitt into the corner flag in a try-saving manoeuvre. Oldham were unlucky to have tries disallowed, by Mitchell and Winslade, either side of the interval, and there was no joy for the goal kickers, either ; Ganley missed two attempts and Risman six!

Exactly two years previously, Oldham beat Workington at Watersheddings by the same score.

January 2nd 1954: HULL 23 OLDHAM 3

J. Feather, T. O'Grady, W. Mitchell, A. Davies, L. Emmitt, D Ayres, F. Pitchford.
H. Ogden, J. Keith, K. Jackson, A. Tomlinson, C. Winslade, B. Goldswain.
Try: Emmitt.

Attendance: 9,550   Referee: Mr. S. Abram – Wigan.

The Roughyeds caught Hull in top form on this day, and as early as the sixth minute, when winger Bowman rounded Keith for the first try, the pattern of the game was set. The 'Airlie Birds' had a great day with ball in hand and two further first half touchdowns to the other wingman Watts, combined with two Hutton goals, meant that Oldham were 13 – 0 down at the interval. In the second half the speedy service to the flanks continued, with Bowman adding another try and Watts passing back inside to Whiteley for another. The only highlight for the visitors was a spectacular try scored by Emmitt after a storming 50 yard break by Winslade, carried on by Pitchford

January 9th 1954: OLDHAM 2 SALFORD 2

W. B. Ganley, R. Cracknell, W. Mitchell, A. Davies, T. O'Grady, F. Daley, F. Pitchford.
T. Smith, J. Keith, L. Anthony, C. Winslade, A. Tomlinson, B. Goldswain.
Goal: Ganley.

Attendance: 7,902   Referee: Mr. W. Rigby – Leigh.

A dour match, as the score suggests, only made possible by a surprising thaw that turned what was a frozen pitch into a bog. The first half was a forward slog with attacking plays few and far between. Moses was held just short for Salford as was Cracknell for Oldham. In the second half O'Grady suffered from being served with some wayward passes when in promising positions. At the other end Cracknell did well to keep out Hartley. Ganley opened the scoring with a penalty to be followed five minutes later by a similar score from Jack Davies which crept over after bouncing on the cross-bar. However, the same player was off target with two subsequent attempts which would have won the game. Cracknell and Smith showed up best for Oldham and Roughley had an impressive debut for Salford.

This proved to be the last first team outing for the popular Welshman,
Les Anthony. *A Rugby Union international for Wales in 1948, he signed for Oldham later that year and played a total of 113 senior matches.*

January 16th 1954: OLDHAM 15   HUDDERSFIELD 4

W. B. Ganley, R. Cracknell, R. Barrow, A. Davies, T. O'Grady, F. Daley, J. Feather.
H. Ogden, J. Keith, T. Smith,   C. Winslade, A. Tomlinson, B. Goldswain.
Goals: Ganley,3. Tries: O'Grady. Davies. Cracknell.
Attendance: 12,671   Referee: Mr. A. Howgate – Dewsbury.

In contrast to the previous week this was an open match, albeit fiercely competitive. Devery had two early penalty misses and then, after 15 minutes, Cracknell showed great skill, with little room to manoeuvre, in beating a couple of defenders to score against his former club. O'Grady then had a 40 yard dash brought to an end by his opposite number Henderson, with a fine tackle. Ganley and Devery exchanged penalties to leave the Roughyeds 5 – 2 in front at the interval. Another penalty each continued the scoring until Oldham moved further ahead on the hour mark, when Ganley joined the line and passed to O'Grady who this time

sped clear of two defenders and bumped off full-back Hunter to score. Finally, when Huddersfield lost the ball, Davies was on it in a flash to go over for a converted try. Late on tempers became heated and Bawden and Winslade were cautioned before five minutes from time Ramsden was ordered off.

Dick Cracknell scores against his former club despite the attentions of *Jim Bowden.*   *(16.01.1954)*

January 23rd 1954: LIVERPOOL C. 10   OLDHAM 25

W. B. Ganley, R. Cracknell, R. Barrow, A. Davies, T. O'Grady, F. Daley, J. Feather.
H. Ogden, J. Keith, T. Smith, C. Winslade, A. Tomlinson, B. Goldswain.
Goals: Ganley,5. Tries: O'Grady,3. Davies. Barrow.
Attendance: 1,500   Referee: Mr. W. Stockley – Leigh.

Liverpool played well in the opening quarter and were every bit as dangerous as the visitors, but eventually a 50 yard break by Feather and some snappy inter-passing between Davies and O'Grady gave the opening try to the Oldham centre. O'Grady then swept in for two long range efforts himself before a Parkes try, goaled by Wood, left Oldham 15 – 5 in front at the break. O'Grady completed his hat-trick on 48 minutes and Barrow scored after an astute cross kick from Feather direct from a scrum. Wood kicked a penalty although he was off target with many other chances. Nevertheless, Liverpool battled away and Teggin went over for a last minute consolation try.

February 6th 1954: LIVERPOOL C. 5   OLDHAM 15
Rugby League Challenge Cup 1st Round 1st Leg.

W. B. Ganley, R. Cracknell, R. Barrow, A. Davies, T. O'Grady, F. Daley, J. Feather.
H. Ogden, J. Keith, T. Smith, C. Winslade, A. Tomlinson, B. Goldswain.
Goals: Ganley,3. Tries: Winslade. Goldswain. Cracknell.
Attendance: 1,000 (est.)   Referee: Mr. T. Armitage – Huddersfield.

The Oldham officials were none too happy for the game to be played, but played it was, under a covering of two inches of snow. Oldham went on the attack from the outset and after Ganley had failed with a drop-goal attempt, Cracknell went close before he was crunched into the snow by several 'City' defenders. However, a quick play the ball to Feather enabled him to put Goldswain over. Winslade then scored, shrugging off two would-be tacklers. Ganley converted and added a penalty to put the Roughyeds 10 – 0 up at the break. Liverpool started the second half well and soon scored when Wood kicked ahead a loose ball, which he followed up to touch down and also add the conversion. The home side then had ten minutes of pressure which was broken when Goldswain broke away and passed on to Barrow who, in turn, gave Cracknell a run to the posts. Ganley converted to restore the ten point advantage.

February 13th 1954: OLDHAM 18 LIVERPOOL C. 11
Rugby League Challenge Cup 1st Round 2nd Leg.
W. B. Ganley, R. Cracknell, R. Barrow, A. Davies, T. O'Grady, F. Daley, J. Feather.
H. Ogden, J. Keith, T. Smith, J. Watson, A. Tomlinson, B. Goldswain.
Goals: Ganley,3. Tries: O'Grady,2. Davies. Ganley.
Attendance: 7,492   Referee: Mr. S. Adams – Hull.

The ten point margin from the first leg was always going to be enough, and when Davies cut through from half way to put the supporting Ganley under the posts after seven minutes, the tie was as good as won. Liverpool gave it their best shot and were rewarded with a try by Adair, after Oldham lost possession near their own line, and four goals from Wood. O'Grady got a try either side of half time before Davies concluded the try scoring.

*Dick Cracknell evades **Welsby** and prepares to hand off **Collier** in the second leg of the cup tie against Liverpool. (13.02.1954)*

February 20th 1954: WARRINGTON 14 OLDHAM 2
W. B. Ganley, R. Cracknell, R. Barrow, A. Davies, T. O'Grady, J. Feather, F. Stirrup.
H. Ogden, J. Keith, T. Smith, C. Winslade, A. Tomlinson, B. Goldswain.
Goal: Ganley.
Attendance: 17,271   Referee: Mr. N. T. Railton – Wigan.

An interesting match in so much that Oldham had been drawn against Warrington in the second round of the Challenge Cup in two weeks time. The match was closer than the score suggests and Warrington were somewhat fortunate on two occasions. The first was when a kick through by McCormick after 16 minutes took an awkward bounce away from the Oldham players but right into the hands of Harry Bath, who promptly scored a try. 7 - 2 down at half time, Oldham came out with vim and vigour in the second period. Perhaps too much, as Winslade and Tomlinson were cautioned and Bath had added two penalty goals! Then Oldham's luck was out again when Stirrup kicked ahead for Goldswain to scoop up the ball and score, only to find the referee had awarded a penalty for an obstruction on Stirrup. Late in the game Helme made the match safe when he dodged over direct from a scrum.

February 27th 1954: OLDHAM 20   LEIGH 7

W. B. Ganley, R. Cracknell, R. Barrow, A. Davies, T. O'Grady, J. Feather, F. Stirrup.
T. Smith, J. Keith, A. Tomlinson, C. Winslade, S. Little, T. Leyland.
Goals: Ganley,4. Tries: O'Grady,3. Barrow.

Attendance: 9,089   Referee: Mr. G. Phillips – Widnes.

Leigh had the best of it early on before Ganley put Oldham ahead with a penalty. Ledgard then equalised after 12 minutes. Stirrup broke away from a scrum and sent a wide pass which O'Grady did well to take and score near the corner flag. Just minutes later the same combination with the help of Feather saw the Oldham winger in again. This time Ganley converted the score. The visitors hit back with a try from Kitchen following good approach play from Pawsey, McGurrin and Lowe. O'Grady was in top form and when he was hauled down just short of the line some good handling saw the ball go right across to the other wing where Cracknell passed back inside to give Barrow a run to the posts. 15 – 7 up at half time, Oldham added just one more converted try after the interval, Ganley and Davies making the ground for O'Grady to complete his 'hat-trick'.

Two post-scripts to this game were, firstly, the presence of Hector Rawson, one of the managers for the forthcoming tour to Australia, who was no doubt impressed by Terry O'Grady's excellent display.

Secondly, this proved to be the last first team outing for Tommy Leyland, a whole-hearted and dependable player, for whom the Oldham Chronicle reported for this match: "Leyland has the uncanny knack of plunging into the senior side to emerge with a credit account."

Tommy played 111 senior matches for Oldham in which he scored 15 tries and kicked two goals.

Tommy Leyland

March 6th 1954: OLDHAM 4   WARRINGTON 7
Rugby League Challenge Cup 2nd Round.

W. B. Ganley, R. Cracknell, R. Barrow, A. Davies, T. O'Grady, J. Feather, F. Stirrup.
H. Ogden, J. Keith, A. Tomlinson, C. Winslade, S. Little, B. Goldswain.
Goals: Ganley,2.

Attendance: 20,750   Referee: Mr. H. Squires – Ossett.

A big crowd gathered with all the accompanying anticipation of a fiercely fought cup-tie, and so it proved to be. In the opening minutes a Barrow breakaway led to Tomlinson being tackled ten yards short of the posts. Next there was a scare when Bevan latched on to a loose ball only to be bundled into touch by a posse of Oldham defenders. After five minutes Bath put the 'Wire' in front with a penalty, but Ganley replied with two in quick succession to give Oldham the lead after 12 minutes. The atmosphere was tense with no further scores before the break although Davies and Bevan always looked dangerous for their respective teams. Oldham started well in the second half and plugged away at the Warrington line until a slow lobbed pass from Barrow was seized by Bevan and away he went. Making light of the muddy conditions, he easily side-stepped Ganley and finished his 70 yard run scoring under the posts. Bath converted, and although there was still nearly half an hour to go, the deflated Roughyeds could make no impression on the stout Warrington defence. In general play O'Grady and Davies did a good job defending against the Warrington flyer, but one moment of magic from the 'Wizard of Aus' was enough to clinch the match and pave the way for an eventual Challenge Cup final victory in the famous replay at Odsal stadium against Halifax.

1953-54

Not this time! **Brian Bevan** *is bundled into touch by* **Terry O'Grady** *with* **Ted White** *and* **Sid Little** *in attendance.*
(06.03.1954)

March 13th 1954: BARROW 12   OLDHAM 6

W. B. Ganley, R. Cracknell, R. Barrow, A. Davies, T. O'Grady, J. Feather, F. Stirrup.
H. Ogden, J. Keith, A. Tomlinson, C. Winslade, S. Little, B. Goldswain.
Tries: O'Grady. Cracknell.

Attendance: 11,000   Referee: Mr. G. Phillips – Widnes.

A close match which had been designated as the benefit game for long serving winger Jim Lewthwaite. Barrow gradually got on top, culminating with a Horne penalty giving them the lead after 30 minutes, a score that remained unchanged at half time. The home team started strongly in the second period and after Healey and Lewthwaite were tackled just short, Grundy barged over for the opening try, converted by Horne. Two minutes later Grundy was in again after Goodwin had shaken off several defenders. Oldham got back in the game when a freak bounce took the ball away from Toohey right into the arms of O'Grady, who promptly touched down. Stirrup then fashioned a try for Cracknell and later only a forward pass decision denied Davies a further try, before a late penalty goal from Hebblethwaite settled Barrow's nerves.

An image from a different age!
Harry Ogden *and* **Bryn Goldswain** *carry out a half-time blanket collection around Craven Park for the Barrow winger, Jim Lewthwaite in his benefit year, while* **Jack Keith** *picks up the stray coins.*
(13.03.1954)

March 20th 1954: OLDHAM 21   HULL 9
W. B. Ganley, R. Cracknell, W. Mitchell, A. Davies, T. O'Grady, J. Feather, F. Stirrup.
T. Smith, J. Keith, A. Tomlinson, C. Winslade, S. Little, B. Goldswain.
Goals: Ganley,6. Tries: Cracknell,2. Mitchell.
Attendance: 9,072   Referee: Mr. A. Howgate – Dewsbury.

A fine match, played at a cracking pace. Ganley put Oldham in front with a second minute penalty, which was soon equalised by Hutton. After eight minutes a sweeping move involving Stirrup, Feather and Mitchell culminated with Cracknell side-stepping two defenders on his way to the posts. Mitchell then put Cracknell over again, and the combination almost scored a third before Hull came back into the game when a break by Jim Drake led to a converted try by Riches after half an hour. Hull then had a good spell of pressure and the match was finely poised at 12 – 9 at the interval. Three Ganley penalties eased Oldham further ahead, and when Mitchell scooped up a loose pass to coast in from 30 yards, the game was safe.

April 3rd 1954: Leigh 18   Oldham 13
Exhibition MatchPlayed at Blackpool.
W. B. Ganley, L. Platt, W. Mitchell, J. Noon, T. O'Grady, J. Feather, F. Stirrup.
H. Ogden, J. Mundy, T. Smith, C. Winslade, S. Little, B. Goldswain.
Goals: Ganley,5. Try: Mitchell.
Attendance: 2,500   Referee: Mr. K.W. Bland – Poulton.

This match was played as an exhibition in Blackpool just as the 'Seasiders' were admitted to the league for the following season. Ganley opened the scoring, on the narrow ground, with a penalty for Oldham, but then Leigh took command, with McFarlane laying on a try for Pawsey soon followed by another touchdown for Lowe. Peter Davies converted both the tries but failed when namesake Malcolm scored just before half time. Oldham rallied in the second half, Stirrup and Feather conjuring a clear run for Mitchell to score. This combined with four Ganley goals put the Roughyeds level. A late converted try by Owen after more good work from McFarlane gave Leigh the victory, but things might have been different if Platt had not had to retire with a dislocated shoulder after 60 minutes. This was to be the last first team match for this popular local player.

April 8th 1954: OLDHAM 7   WARRINGTON 7
W. B. Ganley, R. Cracknell, W. Mitchell, R. Barrow, T. O'Grady, J. Feather, F. Pitchford.
T. Smith, J. Keith, K. Jackson, C. Winslade, A. Tomlinson, B. Goldswain.
Goals: Ganley,2. Try: O'Grady.
Attendance: 7,257   Referee: Mr. A. Howgate – Dewsbury.

This matched paled in comparison to the tension in the cup tie between the two sides a month earlier, but was a close affair nevertheless. The deadlock was broken on 15 minutes when Helme broke from a scrum and passed out to Naughton, who ran strongly and managed a try-scoring pass to Price in the tackle. Bath missed the conversion but later added a penalty. Feather jinked through and lobbed out a high pass which was flicked on by Barrow for O'Grady who crashed over in a two man tackle. Like Bath previously, Ganley failed to add the extra points, but he was on target with two penalties. Bath also added another to leave the score 7 – 7 at half time. There was no further score in the second period but there was a moment of controversy when O'Grady kicked ahead and went up with Helme to catch the ball over the line. The Oldham winger got there first and tipped the ball but managed to re-gather before it hit the ground and touch down; the referee, however, ruled a knock-on and the score was ruled out. Both Ganley and Bath failed with late penalty attempts.

April 10th 1954: WIGAN 2 OLDHAM 7

W. B. Ganley, R. Cracknell, W. Mitchell, A. Davies, T. O'Grady, J. Feather, F. Stirrup.
T. Smith, J. Keith, K. Jackson, A. Tomlinson, S. Little, B. Goldswain.
Goals: Ganley,2. Try: O'Grady.

Attendance: 17,982   Referee: Mr. R. Gelder – Wakefield.

This was a rough-house of a match that saw just a penalty goal each to Ganley and Gee in the first half. Wigan started strongly after the break with McTigue looking impressive. However, the spoils went to the Roughyeds after one of the few good moves of the match saw several players handle the ball before Davies burst clear, draw Cunliffe in to tackle, and then pass to O'Grady, who duly went over for a converted try. Tempers were frayed and numerous players on both sides were cautioned as Oldham held out for victory.

April 12th 1954: OLDHAM 46 WHITEHAVEN 6

W. B. Ganley, R. Cracknell, W. Mitchell, A. Davies, T. O'Grady, J. Feather, F. Pitchford.
T. Smith, J. Keith, K. Jackson, A. Tomlinson, C. Winslade, B. Goldswain.
Goals: Ganley,8. Tries: Cracknell,3. O'Grady,2. Davies,2. Pitchford. Feather. Keith.

Attendance: 5,000   Referee: Mr. H. Squires- Ossett.

A match dominated by the emerging talent of Frank Pitchford, which saw Oldham take command after a quarter of an hour at which time they trailed by four points to two. In the next seven minutes Oldham scored three tries, the first two by Cracknell both fashioned by Pitchford after breaks direct from the scrum. Leading 20 – 4 at the interval, the Roughyeds didn't let up as Cracknell completed his 'hat-trick'. Davies looked sharp and took his tries well. Keith also had an impressive match in which he dominated the scrum possession and capped an enthusiastic display by following a Winslade break to score the final try.

*The two tries against Whitehaven for **Terry O'Grady** came midway through a six consecutive match scoring sequence that was reflective of his great form which earned him a call up for the 1954 tour to Australia and New Zealand.*

April 16th 1954: SWINTON 2 OLDHAM 15

W. B. Ganley, R. Cracknell, W. Mitchell, A. Davies, T. O'Grady, J. Feather, F. Pitchford.
T. Smith, J. Keith, K. Jackson, A. Tomlinson, S. Little, B. Goldswain.
Goals: Ganley,3. Tries: Cracknell. O'Grady. Feather.

Attendance: 12,000   Referee: Mr. V. Vacher - Lyon, France.

The French referee was apparently very lenient at the scrum in this game, which saw the scores level 2 – 2 at the interval. Three tries in a thirteen-minute spell then gave Oldham victory. The first came after a sweeping move from wing to wing, culminating in Cracknell going over after 50 minutes. Three minutes later Little laid on a converted try for O'Grady. Any hopes of a Swinton comeback were dashed when after an hour Lawrenson, the home full-back, had to retire with a dislocated shoulder. Shortly afterwards Goldswain passed to Feather who allegedly beat a 'regiment' of defenders to score. Ganley converted to complete the scoring.

April 17th 1954: OLDHAM 20 BELLE VUE R. 15

W. B. Ganley, H. Lomas, W. Mitchell, A. Davies, T. O'Grady, F. Stirrup, F. Pitchford.
T. Smith, J. Keith, K. Jackson, C. Winslade, A. Tomlinson, B. Goldswain.
Goals: Ganley,4. Tries: O'Grady. Davies. Pitchford. Jackson.
Attendance: 9,390   Referee: Mr. S. Abram – Wigan.

An early Ganley penalty put Oldham ahead, and then after 12 minutes Stirrup and Davies created an opening for O'Grady to score a converted try. Then after Winslade put Pitchford through for another converted score midway through the half all seemed set for a comfortable win. However, after Gallagher broke the Oldham defence, he found former Roughyed Trevor Williams in support and the Welshman raced home from thirty yards. Gregory converted and Rangers were back in the match. Davies scored just before half-time after good work from Pitchford to give Oldham a 15 – 5 interval lead but Belle Vue refused to capitulate and converted tries from Clancy and Jones brought them level. It took a mighty effort from Jackson to force his way over, despite appearing to be held by several defenders, to ease the nerves before a late Ganley penalty settled the match.

Alan Davies holds off the challenge of Belle Vue full-back *Arthur Gregory* to score just before half time
with *Terry O'Grady* in support.   (17.04.1954)

April 19ᵗʰ 1954: ROCHDALE H. 10   OLDHAM 7

W. B. Ganley, R. Cracknell, W. Mitchell, A. Davies, T. O'Grady, J. Feather, F. Pitchford.
T. Smith, J. Keith, K. Jackson, S. Little, A. Tomlinson, B. Goldswain.
Goals: Ganley,2. Try: O'Grady.

Attendance: 15,215   Referee: Mr. J. Jackson – Barrow.

This was the last match of the season with the early finish in place to accommodate the departure of the touring team to Australia. A robust derby game in which 'blood flowed', but also good rugby was in evidence. Twice in the first half Pitchford cut through the Hornets defence only to fall to last-ditch tackles. Home full-back Ted Cahill was in splendid defensive form and it was he who followed a Chisnall break to score the only try of the first half. He also converted it, and then added a penalty. Two Ganley goals either side of half-time kept the scores close but when Bradley pounced on a handling error by the Oldham full-back to pick up and score, it proved to be the decisive moment of the match. O'Grady got a late consolation for the Roughyeds but the man of the match was undoubtedly his fellow tourist Cahill.

*Left: **Bryn Goldswain** puts paid to a Rochdale attack.*
***Right: Terry O'Grady** evades **Walter Jones** to go over for the last try of the season. (19.04.1954)*

May 15ᵗʰ 1954: Halifax 33   Oldham 32
A. Daniels Benefit Match.

W. B. Ganley, R. Cracknell, P Fearis, A. Davies, R. Barrow, J. Feather, F. Stirrup.
T. Smith, J. Keith, K. Jackson, A. Tomlinson, S. Little, B. Goldswain.
W. Mitchell, F. Pitchford and A. Murray also played for Oldham.
Goals: Ganley,2. Fearis. Pitchford. Tries: Goldswain,2. Fearis,2. Barrow,2. Cracknell. Murray.
Attendance: 6,000   Referee: Mr. F. Seed – Halifax.

This benefit game for Halifax's Welsh winger Arthur Daniels was played very much in an end-of-season light-hearted fashion, which the healthy crowd of 6,000 took in excellent spirit. The free flowing passing and rapid scoring made for an entertaining spectacle with the best cheers reserved for the two tries scored by Daniels himself.

Substitutes were allowed and so Mitchell, Pitchford and Murray also played some part in the match.

Arthur Daniels
Halifax, Wales and Great Britain.

1953-54

Most Appearances: Bryn Goldswain 40 out of a possible 42.
Most tries: Terry O'Grady 27.
Most goals: Bernard Ganley 120.
Most points: Bernard Ganley 249.

Bryn Goldswain

Terry O'Grady

Bernard Ganley

	1953-54	Played	Won	Draw	Lost	For	Against	Points
1	Halifax	36	30	2	4	538	219	62
2	Warrington	36	30	1	5	663	311	61
3	St. Helens	36	28	2	6	672	297	58
4	Workington T.	36	29	0	7	604	333	58
5	Hull	36	25	0	11	685	349	50
6	Huddersfidd	36	24	0	12	689	417	48
7	Wigan	36	23	1	12	688	392	47
8	Barrow	36	23	0	13	574	377	46
9	Bradford N.	36	22	0	14	628	414	44
10	Leeds	36	22	0	14	766	517	44
11	Wakefield T.	36	19	1	16	671	508	39
12	**OLDHAM**	**36**	**17**	**4**	**15**	**504**	**366**	**38**
13	Leigh	36	19	0	17	547	459	38
14	Featherstonc R.	36	18	2	16	478	431	38
15	Hunslet	36	19	0	17	455	451	38
16	Widnes	36	16	3	17	420	431	35
17	York	36	17	0	19	412	401	34
18	Keighley	36	15	3	18	473	533	33
19	Rochdale H.	36	14	3	19	404	457	31
20	Dewsbury	36	14	3	19	432	508	31
21	Whitehaven	36	14	1	21	362	544	29
22	Salford	36	13	2	21	370	438	28
23	Swinton	36	13	1	22	341	513	27
24	Batley	36	13	1	22	367	658	27
25	Bramley	36	11	3	22	437	746	25
26	Castleford	36	11	1	24	437	728	23
27	Belle Vue R.	36	7	2	27	307	714	16
28	Doncaster	36	5	2	29	340	840	12
29	Hull K.R.	36	5	2	29	298	737	12
30	Liverpool C.	36	4	0	32	304	777	8

1953-54

SEASON	PLAYER	APPS	TRIES	GOALS	POINTS
1953-54	B. GOLDSWAIN	40	3	4	17
1953-54	A. DAVIES	39	16		48
1953-54	J. FEATHER	35	5		15
1953-54	W.B. GANLEY	34	3	120	249
1953-54	T. O'GRADY	34	27		81
1953-54	A. TOMLINSON	32			
1953-54	S. LITTLE	29	4		12
1953-54	W. MITCHELL	29	3		9
1953-54	J. KEITH	27	2		6
1953-54	C. WINSLADE	27	1	1	5
1953-54	K. JACKSON	26	4		12
1953-54	F. STIRRUP	25	7	2	25
1953-54	R. CRACKNELL	23	11		33
1953-54	H. OGDEN	22			
1953-54	F. PITCHFORD	18	5		15
1953-54	T. SMITH	17			
1953-54	J. MUNDY	15			
1953-54	L. EMMITT	13	6		18
1953-54	R. BARROW	12	4		12
1953-54	L. ANTHONY	10			
1953-54	F. DALEY	9	1		3
1953-54	L. PLATT	8	6		18
1953-54	P. FEARIS	5	3		9
1953-54	J. WATSON	5			
1953-54	D. AYRES	3			
1953-54	H. LOMAS	2	3		9
1953-54	W. RATCHFORD	2		2	4
1953-54	J. WARHAM	2	1		3
1953-54	T. LEYLAND	2	1		3
1953-54	A. JONES	1	1		3
1953-54	**TOTAL**	**546**	**117**	**129**	**609**

1953-54

1954-55

Definitely a season of 'might have beens' as Oldham saw the Lancashire Cup, Lancashire League, Championship League Leaders position and Championship Final all denied them at the final hurdle.

The injury to Ganley at the turn of the year deprived the club of its prime marksman and there is little doubt that with his goal-kicking expertise some of those reverses might have gone Oldham's way. Maybe an omen of what was to come came in the Law Cup contest when Hornets managed to retain the trophy by earning a draw with the last kick of the match!

Nevertheless, the signs were encouraging. Griff Jenkins was appointed coach and the team had a growing reputation for playing attractive, open rugby that was acknowledged by followers of the game both at Watersheddings and throughout the league. The emergence of Frank Pitchford as a real talent was a boost for the Oldham spectators. Who knows, had the pitch at either Maine Road in the Championship Final or Station Road in the Lancashire Cup Final resembled a rugby, rather than a 'paddy', field, Oldham's top-of-the-ground specialists might have triumphed. Still it was not to be and, in the long run, a reputation for open football is little consolation for a lack of silverware. Billy Mitchell retired after long and distinguished service for the Roughyeds and amongst those coming into the team, Alan Kellett certainly made a most promising impression towards the end of the season. Alan Davies was appointed captain and led by example by finishing top of the try scorers with 27 and Bernard Ganley still managed to top the goals and points totals in spite of only playing in half (22) of the first team games. Hooker, Jack Keith made most appearances with 43 just missing the home victory over Widnes in March.

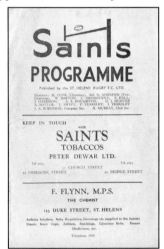

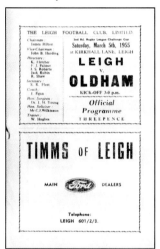

August 7th 1954: Oldham 17   Rochdale H. 17
Law Cup
W.B. Ganley, R. Cracknell, R. Barrow, A. Davies, H. Lomas, F. Daley, F. Stirrup.
T. Smith, J. Keith, A. Tomlinson, C. Winslade, J. Watson, B. Goldswain.
Goals: Ganley,4. Tries: Davies,2. Cracknell.
Attendance: 7,000   Referee: Mr. W. Stockley – Swinton.

This was the first match in charge for Griff Jenkins at Oldham and ex-Watersheddings favourite Joe Warham was now the manager at Rochdale. Two Ganley penalties in the first eight minutes opened the scoring before Hornets had a try disallowed when McArthur was adjudged to have stepped into touch. However, the same player kicked two penalties to even the scores, but another 40 yard effort from Ganley saw Oldham go in 6 – 4 in front at the break. Rochdale opened up well in the second half with McArthur sprinting 65 yards for a try he also converted. This was followed by another touchdown from Harris. Oldham responded with Smith paving the way for Cracknell to go over. Two more tries from Davies and a Ganley penalty put the Roughyeds five points clear but Hornets weren't to be denied, and with time running out Short went over near the posts, and 'man-of-the-match' McArthur levelled the scores with the last kick of the match, the draw being enough for Rochdale to retain the trophy.

Left:
*The new Oldham coach **Griff Jenkins.***

Right:
***Wallly McArthur** whose last minute goal ensured that the Law Cup stayed at the Athletic Grounds for another year.*

August 14th 1954: WAKEFIELD T. 22   OLDHAM 32
W.B. Ganley, R. Cracknell, R. Barrow, A. Davies, H. Lomas, F. Daley, F. Pitchford.
T. Smith, J. Keith, A. Tomlinson, C. Winslade, J. Watson, B. Goldswain.
Goals: Ganley,7. Tries: Davies,2. Lomas. Barrow. Pitchford. Daley.
Attendance: 4,000   Referee: Mr. S. Abram – Wigan.

A free-flowing match which swung one way then another, before the Roughyeds finally took control. Wakefield had the early pressure but the first try went to Oldham with Daley capitalising on a break by Pitchford. Holliday and Firth scored tries for 'Trinity' but a couple of solo efforts from Davies, both converted, gave the visitors a 15 – 8 lead at half time. In the second period Oldham managed to keep some distance between the scores until a late flurry of points made the game safe. Ganley converted all six Oldham tries and also landed a drop goal.

August 21st 1954: OLDHAM 16   BATLEY 3

W.B. Ganley, R. Cracknell, P. Fearis, A. Davies, H. Lomas, F. Daley, F. Pitchford.

T. Smith, J. Keith, A. Tomlinson, C. Winslade, A. Murray, B. Goldswain.

Goals: Ganley. Fearis.   Tries: Lomas,2. Davies. Fearis.

Attendance: 8,946   Referee: Mr. T. Armitage – Huddersfield.

A heavy downpour before kick-off made the overall conditions difficult. Nevertheless Oldham opened the scoring with a sweeping move from one flank to the other; it started with a break by Cracknell and finished with Lomas touching down. Cracknell also had a hand in the next two tries, for Fearis and Davies. Ganley, who was having a torrid time with the boot, converted the second to give the Roughyeds an 11 – 0 advantage at half-time. After the break there was little to shout about, although Lomas did get over for another try. Ganley finally gave up the ghost to leave Fearis to put over a penalty before MacDonald got a late consolation try for Batley.

Bryn Goldswain and *Dick Cracknell* line up a tackle on Batley's *Norman Field*.   *(21.08.1954)*

August 25th 1954: SALFORD 11   OLDHAM 2

W.B. Ganley, R. Cracknell, P. Fearis, A. Davies, H. Lomas, F. Daley, F. Stirrup.

T. Smith, J. Keith, A. Tomlinson, C. Winslade, S. Little,   B. Goldswain.

Goal: Ganley.

Attendance: 8,500   Referee: Mr. N. T. Railton – Wigan.

Salford set out to do a containing job on the Roughyeds and their plan worked a treat. The first serious threat to either try-line came on 17 minutes when Keith put Cracknell through, but the winger's kick ahead went too far and rolled away over the dead ball line. Three Jack Davies penalties to one by Ganley gave Salford a 6 – 2 lead at the interval. The 'Red Devils' skipper, Dai Moses, had marshalled his players well to nullify the attacking threat of the Roughyeds and had a hand in the only try, which came midway through the second half when he and Harrison combined to put Baines over. Salford's resolute defence allied to Oldham's frustration led to the referee giving out 14 cautions, before Davies finished the scoring with a penalty with the last kick of the match.

August 28th 1954: ST. HELENS 16   OLDHAM 23

W.B. Ganley, R. Cracknell, W. Mitchell, A. Davies, R. Barrow, F. Daley, F. Pitchford.
H. Ogden, J. Keith, A. Tomlinson, C. Winslade, S. Little, A. Murray.
Goals: Ganley,7. Tries: Cracknell,2. Pitchford.
Attendance: 17,050   Referee: Mr. C. Appleton – Warrington.

After the poor showing at Salford, Oldham made some positional changes, but the most intriguing variation was that this was the first match for which Alan Davies was appointed captain, and what a start it was in front of a good 17,000-plus crowd at Knowsley Road. Parsons was penalised at the first play-the-ball and Ganley duly obliged with the two points as he landed a great penalty goal from the touchline. Pitchford was looking lively and involved at every opportunity. A Metcalfe penalty and a try from Moses, after good play by Dickinson, put St. Helens in front, but the Oldham defence tightened up well after the try against them and Ganley was merciless in punishing Saints' indiscretions with a further three penalty goals, giving the Roughyeds an 8 – 5 advantage at the break. After 47 minutes a splendid try by Gullick after slick handling by Finnan, Moses and Carlton brought Saints back level, but this was the signal for Oldham to take control. First, Davies and Mitchell linked up well to put Cracknell over. Mitchell was injured in the build up, and had to retire briefly before returning to go on the wing with Barrow switching to centre, but Oldham

continued to press the St. Helens line and Pitchford darted over after capitalising on a handling error. Although most of the play was in the home half of the field, Saints then had a brief spell of pressure and it took a magnificent tackle from Ganley to bring down the left wing, Ratcliffe, in full flight for the try line. Davies, who was relishing the responsibility as captain, was again instrumental in sending Cracknell over under the posts for another try. Ganley converted all three of Oldham's second half tries before a couple of late touchdowns from Carlton, and a Metcalfe conversion, gave the score an air of respectability for the home team.

*Oldham's new captain, **Alan Davies** made light of the extra responsibilities to turn in a splendid display at St. Helens.*

September 4th 1954: BARROW 12   OLDHAM 17

W.B. Ganley, R. Cracknell, R. Barrow, A. Davies, J. Noon, F. Daley, F. Pitchford.
H. Ogden, J. Keith, A. Tomlinson, C. Winslade, S. Little, A. Murray.
Goals: Ganley,4. Tries: Barrow. Davies. Cracknell.
Attendance: 10,990   Referee: Mr. G. Phillips – Widnes.

Although Oldham started the match brightly it was the home side that established a commanding half-time lead with tries from Toohey and Goodwin, the latter after a wonderful flowing passing move, and three goals from Horne, that gave Barrow a 12 – 0 advantage at the interval. Oldham commenced the second half with real determination. Ganley slotted home a penalty and Noon was unlucky to just put a foot on the touch-line when going over. Still the Roughyeds were not to be denied and Roland Barrow scored near the corner flag after good approach work from Winslade. Ten minutes from time Oldham drew level when Davies brushed off Poole to go in under the posts. The match was won just before the end when Cracknell received a pass from Barrow infield and proceeded on a diagonal run which saw him score in the corner. Ganley converted all three tries, two of them from the touchline.

September 11th 1954: OLDHAM 57   Lancashire County Amateurs 17
Lancashire Cup 1st Round.
W.B. Ganley, R. Cracknell, R. Barrow, A. Davies, J. Noon, F. Daley, F. Pitchford.
H. Ogden, J. Keith, A. Tomlinson, S. Little, C. Winslade, A. Murray.
Goals: Ganley,12. Tries: Noon,4. Keith,2. Daley,2. Pitchford. Davies. Murray.
Attendance: 5,700   Referee: Mr. E. Hopkins – Leeds.

As expected this was a romp for Oldham although after two Ganley penalties the amateurs gained a shock lead when two of the Oldham representatives in the team, Hart and Maloney, combined for the latter to score, with Moores adding the conversion. Soon after this Keith opened Oldham's try account and it was a good day for Noon, who crossed four times, and for Ganley, with 12 goals. For the amateurs Maloney scored another try and all three of the local lads, Hart, Maloney and Boote, gave good accounts of themselves.

September 14th 1954: OLDHAM 28   LIVERPOOL C. 4
W.B. Ganley, R. Cracknell, R. Barrow, A. Davies, T. O'Grady, F. Daley, F. Pitchford.
H. Ogden, J. Keith, A. Tomlinson, C. Winslade, S. Little, B. Goldswain.
Goals: Ganley,5. Tries: O'Grady,2. Pitchford. Little. Cracknell. Barrow.
Attendance: 7,000 (est.)   Referee: Mr. G. Phillips – Widnes.

Another routine victory for Oldham who eased into a 10 – 4 half time lead and completed the job with a competent second half shut out of the visitors. O'Grady marked his return to action after the Lions tour with two tries and Goldswain, back in the team after a three match absence was back to form with an industrious and creative performance.

The Oldham team against Liverpool at Watersheddings on September 14th 1954.

Back Row: W.B. Ganley, K. Jackson, C. Winslade, S. Little, B. Goldswain, A. Tomlinson.
Middle Row: R. Cracknell, R. Barrow, A. Davies, T. O'Grady, J. Keith.
Front Row: F. Daley, Mascot, F. Pitchford.

September 18th 1954: BATLEY 3   OLDHAM 27
W.B. Ganley, R. Cracknell, R. Barrow, A. Davies, J. Noon, F. Daley, F. Stirrup.
H. Ogden, J. Keith, A. Tomlinson, C. Winslade, S. Little, B. Goldswain.
Goals: Ganley,6. Tries: Barrow,2. Cracknell,2. Little.
Attendance: 6,000   Referee: Mr. J. W. Jackson – Barrow.

Batley enjoyed the best of the action early on and it took a good solid tackle by Cracknell to deny Fryer, but soon afterwards they went in front when Jones capitalised on a handling error to score. Oldham responded well with Barrow going over for the first of his two tries after a fine passing move after eight minutes. By half time it was 17 – 3 to the Roughyeds and when, in the first minute of the second period, a Tomlinson kick-through led to a try for Cracknell, the points were in the bag. Stirrup put in another fine performance as did Ganley, with six successful goal attempts.

The Oldham team at Mount Pleasant, Batley on September 18th 1954.
Back Row: *J. Keith, A. Tomlinson, S. Little, B. Goldswain, J. Noon, G. Jenkins, H. Ogden, W.B. Ganley, C. Winslade.*
Front Row: *J. Heywood, F. Daley, R. Cracknell, A. Davies, F. Stirrup, R. Barrow.*

September 20th 1954: OLDHAM 20   ST. HELENS 9
Lancashire Cup 2nd Round.
W.B. Ganley, R. Cracknell, R. Barrow, A. Davies, T. O'Grady, J. Noon, F. Pitchford.
H. Ogden, J. Keith, A. Tomlinson, C. Winslade, S. Little, B. Goldswain.
Goals: Ganley,4. Tries: Cracknell,2. Pitchford. Keith.
Attendance: 16,000   Referee: Mr. R. Gelder – Wakefield.

The first half was a typical tight cup-tie. Davies broke through the Saints defence and passed to Barrow, who in turn put Cracknell clear to score. However, three penalty goals from Parsons gave the visitors a 6 – 3 lead at half-time. It wasn't until midway through the second period that Oldham gained the ascendancy, and it was an inspired spell from Pitchford that turned the tide in the Roughyeds favour. First he laid on a try for Keith, and he followed that up with a solo effort after scooping up a handling error by the visitors. Cracknell's second try sealed the tie with Goldswain again prominent as Oldham kept the Saints at bay until a last-minute consolation try from Carlton.

September 25th 1954: OLDHAM 8   WAKEFIELD T. 7
F. Stirrup, R. Cracknell, R. Barrow, A. Davies, T. O'Grady, J. Feather, F. Pitchford.
H. Ogden, J. Keith, A. Tomlinson, C. Winslade, A. Jarman, B. Goldswain.
Goal: Winslade. Tries: O'Grady. Davies.
Attendance: 10,130   Referee: Mr. E. Clay – Leeds.

There was a first team debut for local forward Alan Jarman, signed from the Higginshaw club, in this match against a determined Wakefield team who pushed Oldham all the way. In Ganley's absence Winslade opened the scoring with a penalty but that was to be the only successful kick of the game for the Roughyeds. A break by Feather made way for the opening try from O'Grady, and after 28 minutes Pitchford likewise served up another score for Davies. 'Trinity' hit back with a try by Robinson, converted by Mortimer, to leave the score 8 – 5 at half-time. The second half was a tough, uncompromising affair with defences dominant throughout, and in this respect Tomlinson was outstanding for Oldham. The only score in the second period was a further penalty from Mortimer.

September 30th 1954: WORKINGTON T. 13   OLDHAM 20
Lancashire Cup semi-final.
W.B. Ganley, R. Cracknell, R. Barrow, A. Davies, T. O'Grady, W. Mitchell, F. Pitchford.
H. Ogden, J. Keith, K. Jackson, A. Tomlinson, C. Winslade, B. Goldswain.
Goal: Ganley. Tries: Pitchford,3. Davies,2. Cracknell.
Attendance: 11,943   Referee: Mr. M. Coates – Leeds.

After a close first half, when tries from Pitchford and Cracknell against one by Faulder gave Oldham a 6 – 3 lead, a devastating spell in which the Roughyeds scored 14 unanswered points and Pitchford completed his 'hat-trick' looked to have sealed the match with ease. However, back came the Cumbrians, and going into the last ten minutes there was just four points between the teams. At this point Ogden, who had earlier retired injured, came back into the fray. This bolstered the defence and a late try from Davies saw Oldham home and into the final.

October 2nd 1954: BLACKPOOL B. 16   OLDHAM 46
W.B. Ganley, R. Cracknell, R. Barrow, A. Davies, T. O'Grady, J. Noon, F. Pitchford.
K. Jackson, J. Keith, A. Tomlinson, C. Winslade, A. Jarman, B. Goldswain.
Goals: Ganley,8. Tries: Davies,4. Jarman,2. Barrow,2. O'Grady,2.
Attendance: 7,500   Referee: Mr. W. Stockley – Swinton.

Just two days after their impressive victory at Workington, the Roughyeds made their first trip to the newly formed Blackpool club playing at St. Annes Road. A good following of Oldhamers made the trip and would have been surprised to see their favourites go 4 - 0 down to an early penalty from Peace and a drop goal by Kelly. However, the team settled down and after Pitchford had put Barrow through for the opening try, Oldham eased to a comfortable 23 – 4 half-time lead courtesy of two tries each for Davies and Jarman. A brief rally after the break saw Fisher go over for 'Borough' but soon afterwards Oldham got back into scoring mode, with Davies finishing the match with four tries.

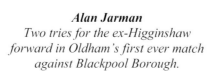

Alan Jarman
Two tries for the ex-Higginshaw
forward in Oldham's first ever match
against Blackpool Borough.

1954-55

October 9th 1954: OLDHAM 23 WORKINGTON T. 13

W.B. Ganley, R. Cracknell, R. Barrow, A. Davies, T. O'Grady, F. Daley, F. Pitchford.
K. Jackson, J. Keith, A. Tomlinson, C. Winslade, S. Little, B. Goldswain.
Goals: Ganley,4. Tries: O'Grady,3. Pitchford. Barrow.

Attendance: 14,455   Referee: Mr. A. Howgate – Dewsbury.

Barrow opened the scoring for Oldham after five minutes, and despite having an equal amount of possession and territory Workington couldn't break down the home defence. Worse was to follow for the Cumbrians as O'Grady raced over for a first half 'hat-trick' to leave the Roughyeds 16 – 2 up at the interval. Tempers were raised early in the second half, culminating in Tomlinson being sent off for retaliation just after the hour mark. Nevertheless, Oldham scored again after the dismissal through Pitchford, before late tries from Henderson, Faulder and Gibson gave the score an impression more deserving of Workington's efforts. Just before the end 'Town' winger Ivill was also ordered off.

Arthur Tomlinson battles for a loose ball as **Ken Jackson** lends his weight to the situation.   *(09.10.1954)*

October 16th 1954: ROCHDALE H. 4 OLDHAM 18

F. Stirrup, R. Cracknell, R. Barrow, A. Davies, T. O'Grady, F. Daley, F. Pitchford.
H. Ogden, J. Keith, K. Jackson, C. Winslade, S. Little, B. Goldswain.
Goals: Goldswain,3. Tries: Jackson. Davies. Barrow. Pitchford.

Attendance: 19,654   Referee: Mr. N. T. Railton – Wigan.

A marvellous attendance of just under 20,000 turned up to see if Oldham could stretch their ten-match unbeaten run, and they were rewarded with a full blooded 'derby' game which swung on a controversial try midway through the second half. Just a Goldswain penalty separated the teams at half-time, but two penalties from Les Jones then gave Hornets the lead. As the match edged into the last quarter, Cracknell made a break and, though held just short, he passed to Jackson, who lunged for the line despite the attentions of several defenders. Rochdale claimed that the ball wasn't grounded but referee Railton was right on the spot to award the score. This knocked the heart out of the 'Nets', and first Pitchford and then Barrow went in for further tries before a Davies interception wrapped up the scoring.

October 23rd 1954: BARROW 12   OLDHAM 2
Lancashire Cup Final played at Station Road, Swinton.
W.B. Ganley, R. Cracknell, R. Barrow, A. Davies, T. O'Grady, F. Daley, F. Pitchford.
H. Ogden, J. Keith, K. Jackson, C. Winslade, S. Little, B. Goldswain.
Goal: Ganley.

Attendance: 25,204   Referee: Mr. R. Gelder – Wakefield.

Oldham were their own worst enemies in this match by trying to play open, expansive rugby in spite of the terrible wet and muddy conditions. Barrow, on the other hand, adapted much better and played a tight, forward-dominated game that best suited the heavy pitch. The first score came when Ogden fumbled a pass, possession was lost, with the result that Goodwin raced over using Castle as a foil as Cracknell waited for the pass to the wingman that never came. Horne missed the conversion but was successful with a drop goal attempt soon afterwards. Then more disaster for Oldham, when a kick ahead by their opponents seemed to be well covered by Cracknell but he lost the ball in Parker's challenge, and the Barrow second-row man just had to stretch out and touch the ball, which had settled over the line, to register a try. Horne converted and the Roughyeds were well and truly up against it! Oldham came more into the match before the interval but only had a Ganley penalty goal to show for their efforts as they trailed 10 - 2 at the break. In the second half the teams pretty much cancelled each other out. Oldham were unlucky when O'Grady got clear but was recalled for a forward pass, but overall it was the 'Furness-men' who always looked the most likely to add to their total as they were invariably quickest to re-gather the often-spilled possession. As it happened there was only one further score, a late penalty goal from Horne, but the damage done in the first half was enough to give Barrow a deserved victory, and the first major honour won by the club.

The ball goes loose!

Top:
Charlie Winslade and Dick Cracknell would appear to be the favourites to gather up the ball.

Below:
This time it's Terry O'Grady, Derek Hinchley and Frank Pitchford going after the loose ball.
Wingman, Hinchley won a rare call to the first team for the inured Jim Lewthwaite.

(23.10.1954)

October 30th 1954: LIVERPOOL C. 3   OLDHAM 10

W.B. Ganley, R. Cracknell, R. Barrow, A. Davies, T. O'Grady, F. Daley, F. Pitchford.
H. Ogden, J. Keith, K. Jackson, C. Winslade, A. Tomlinson, B. Goldswain.
Goals: Ganley,2. Tries: O'Grady. Barrow.

Attendance: 1,600   Referee: Mr. G. Battersby – Barrow.

The cup final hangover didn't last long and a hard-fought victory on a near-waterlogged Knotty Ash pitch brought Oldham back to winning ways. A penalty goal from Ganley after 12 minutes put the Roughyeds in front, and the lead was extended when Barrow and Davies combined to put O'Grady over at the corner flag. Liverpool responded well, with Cox finishing off a fine passing move to score five minutes before the interval. The second half was a dour struggle, but Oldham eventually got on top, and after both Davies and O'Grady had tries disallowed, Barrow notched the clinching score after following a dribble through by Goldswain and Pitchford. A penalty from Ganley three minutes from time completed the scoring.

November 6th 1954: OLDHAM 30   B LACKPOOL B. 12

W.B. Ganley, R. Cracknell, R. Barrow, A. Davies, T. O'Grady, J. Noon, F. Stirrup.
H. Ogden, J. Keith, K. Jackson, C. Winslade, A. Tomlinson, A. Jarman.
Goals: Ganley,6. Tries: Cracknell,2. O'Grady,2. Davies. Stirrup.

Attendance: 5,304   Referee: Mr. E. P. Wilmot – Rochdale.

The first-ever visit of Blackpool to Watersheddings was marred by bad weather that kept down the crowd, which was a shame as the newly refurbished 'penny rush' stand was opened, with a pre-kick-off ceremony including the unveiling of a plaque dedicating the structure to the long time Oldham official George F. Hutchins. The visitor's full-back Peace opened the scoring with a penalty in the first minute, a lead that 'Borough' kept for a quarter of an hour until Cracknell raced over, soon to be followed by Davies, Stirrup and O'Grady. Ganley converted the first three and added a penalty, to see the Roughyeds 20 – 2 ahead at the break. Oldham eased off in the second half but Cracknell and O'Grady added further tries, the former after a thrilling 60 yard dash. Maori Kia Rika scored a couple for Blackpool but all in all it was a comfortable victory.

George F. Hutchins - Long serving Oldham club official who twice managed the Great Britain tours to Australia and New Zealand in 1928 & 1932.

November 13th 1954: WIDNES   7   OLDHAM 9

W.B. Ganley, R. Cracknell, W. Mitchell, A. Davies, R. Barrow, J. Noon   , F. Pitchford.
H. Ogden, J. Keith, K. Jackson, A. Tomlinson, C. Winslade, B. Goldswain.
Goals: Ganley,3. Try: Cracknell.

Attendance: 3,500   Referee: Mr. J. Jowett – Leeds.

Billy Mitchell came back into the Oldham team for the injured Terry O'Grady for the trip to Widnes. A dour first half saw the 'Chemics' ahead 4 – 0 at the break courtesy of two Sale penalty goals. After the interval good inter-passing between Barrow and Mitchell gave Oldham a good territorial position, from where Ganley put over a penalty goal, and after a subsequent failure he levelled the scores with his second success. Eight minutes from time Williamson got over for Widnes but a Cracknell interception try put the Roughyeds level and with time running out. Ganley converted from a difficult angle to give Oldham a hard-earned victory, which was somewhat marred by the dismissal of Tomlinson in the closing seconds after several cautions.

November 20th 1954: OLDHAM 15 WHITEHAVEN 8
W.B. Ganley, R. Cracknell, R. Barrow, W. Mitchell, T. O'Grady, J. Noon   , F. Pitchford.
H. Ogden, J. Keith, K. Jackson, C. Winslade, A. Jarman, B. Goldswain.
Goals: Ganley,3. Tries: O'Grady. Pitchford. Ogden.
Attendance: 7,713   Referee: Mr. R. Welsby – Warrington.

This was by no means the easy victory that many had imagined. It was 25 minutes before Pitchford breezed in from 40 yards after a peach of a pass from Ganley, who later added a penalty goal. However, a good break by McKeown led to a try from winger Harrison. The score remained 5 – 3 to the Roughyeds at the interval, but another McKeown break this time paved the way for Robinson to go over, and McKeown's conversion put the Cumbrians three points in front. After Barrow had a try disallowed for a forward pass, O'Grady managed a legitimate score, which Ganley converted to give Oldham the lead. Going into the closing stages there were many tense moments before a Winslade break in the last minute set up the position for Ogden to score near the posts.

November 27th 1954: WIGAN 5 OLDHAM 9
F. Stirrup, R. Cracknell, W. Mitchell, A. Davies, T. O'Grady, F. Daley, F. Pitchford.
H. Ogden, J. Keith, K. Jackson, C. Winslade, S. Little, B. Goldswain.
Goals: Goldswain,3. Try: Daley.
Attendance: 21,244   Referee: Mr. G. Phillips – Widnes.

The early exchanges were fairly even before Winslade was caught off-side and Nordgren gave Wigan the lead from the resulting penalty. Davies was constantly a threat for the Roughyeds and after Platt was penalised for obstruction Goldswain equalised for Oldham. Wigan hit back and went in front again with a controversial try. Broome put in a cross kick and although Stirrup seemed to make the ball safe, Broome

followed up and, diving on the ball, was awarded the score, to give Wigan a 5 – 2 lead at half-time. The second period saw Oldham take control and, after two more penalty goals from Goldswain put the Roughyeds in front, a try from Daley just after the hour was enough to secure the win.

Dick Cracknell is tackled by Brian Nordgren and Jack Fleming.   *(27.11.1954)*

December 11th 1954: WHITEHAVEN 2 OLDHAM 2
F. Stirrup, R. Cracknell, W. Mitchell, A. Davies, T. O'Grady, F. Daley, F. Pitchford.
H. Ogden, J. Keith, K. Jackson,   C. Winslade, S. Little, B. Goldswain.
Goal: Goldswain.
Attendance: 4,000   Referee: Mr. S. Adams – Hull.

Oldham's winning streak in league matches finally came to an end in this dour, tough encounter up at Whitehaven. A penalty goal by Goldswain after 30 minutes, closely followed by one from McKeown for the home team, were the only points scored as defences ruled supreme. Oldham had the best of it in the second half, with Pitchford and Davies each breaking through the initial defence only to be let down by a poor kick ahead. On defence Cracknell did well to stop Harrison but was then penalised for forcing him into touch. However, McKeown's effort at goal from wide out failed to hit the target. The last attacking threat saw Stirrup clear his line after McCourt tried to dribble over. That saved a point, but the Roughyeds had yet to manage that elusive victory at the Recreation Ground.

1954-55

December 18th 1954: KEIGHLEY 11 OLDHAM 15

F. Stirrup, R. Cracknell, R. Barrow, A. Davies, T. O'Grady, F. Daley, F. Pitchford.
H. Ogden, J. Keith, K. Jackson, C. Winslade, S. Little, B. Goldswain.
Goals: Goldswain,3. Tries O'Grady,2. Ogden.
Attendance: 6,000   Referee: Mr. E Clay – Leeds.

A penalty from Hollindrake opened the scoring after five minutes, but after first being denied by a forward pass ruling, O'Grady scored after a lightening break by Pitchford direct from a scrum. A further Hollindrake penalty restored Keighley's lead before, and quite against the run of play, the same player scooped up a loose pass to race 50 yards to touch down. Exhausted by his efforts, he left the conversion to Clarkson, who duly obliged to leave the half time score 9 – 3 to the West Yorkshire side. Oldham set about their comeback with a penalty by Goldswain just two minutes into the second half, and after 15 minutes he added another. It was one-way traffic by now, and the Roughyeds took the lead when Ogden barged over after good work by Daley. Goldswain added the conversion. A further try from O'Grady, once more laid on by Pitchford, put Oldham six points clear. A Clarkson penalty gave Keighley some hope, but to no avail as the Watersheddings men held on for victory.

December 25th 1954: OLDHAM 8 SWINTON 5

F. Stirrup, R. Cracknell, J. Feather, A. Davies, T. O'Grady, F. Daley, F. Pitchford.
H. Ogden, J. Keith, K. Jackson, C. Winslade, S. Little, B. Goldswain.
Goal: Feather. Tries: O'Grady. Pitchford.
Attendance: 10,452   Referee: Mr. R. Gelder – Wakefield.

The 'festive fayre' at Watersheddings saw the Roughyeds and the 'Lions' ankle deep in mud! Because of postponements, this was the first home match in a month for Oldham and the heavy conditions forced them to grind out a victory against a stubborn Swinton side who never gave up the fight. Pitchford followed up a kick through from Feather to score after 20 minutes, and the only other score in the half was a penalty from Blan, who also hit an upright with a further attempt. A penalty goal from Feather increased Oldham's lead after the break before the home backs defied the conditions to put O'Grady over in the scoreboard corner, after a sweeping move across the pitch. Back came Swinton and Blan scooped up a loose ball to go over. After this the defences ruled with Jackson and Winslade notable in their efforts for the Roughyeds.

The match against Salford on December 28th was the last for veteran centre, **Billy Mitchell** *who, ironically, spent most of the match on the wing after being injured.*

Here he looks on as **Dick Cracknell** *contests the ball with the Salford centre* **Cartwright.**

(28.12.1954)

December 28th 1954: OLDHAM 27 SALFORD 0

W.B. Ganley, R. Cracknell, W. Mitchell, A. Davies, T. O'Grady, F. Daley, F. Pitchford.
H. Ogden, J. Keith, K. Jackson, C. Winslade, A. Tomlinson, B. Goldswain.
Goals: Ganley,3. Tries Tomlinson,2. O'Grady,2. Goldswain. Winslade. Pitchford.
Attendance: 16,000   Referee: Mr. S. Abram – Wigan.

Salford had been the last team to beat Oldham in league competition back in August, but there was to be no repeat as the Roughyeds hit top form to subdue the 'Red Devils'. Straight from the kick-off, Winslade fielded the ball and set a move in motion which culminated in Goldswain going over within the first minute. Ganley converted, and it wasn't long before Winslade was on the score sheet himself after being the first to react to an Ogden kick through. Salford came back into the match, and were unlucky when Davies got away with a blatant obstruction that saved a try. With Oldham 8 – 0 up at the break, the second period was a personal triumph for Tomlinson, who scored two tries and laid on another for Pitchford. O'Grady also crossed twice as Oldham coasted home.

January 1st 1955: OLDHAM 24 BELLE VUE R. 14

W.B. Ganley, R. Cracknell, R. Barrow, A. Davies, T. O'Grady, F. Stirrup, F. Pitchford.
H. Ogden, J. Keith, K. Jackson, C. Winslade, A. Tomlinson, B. Goldswain.
Goals: Ganley,2. Goldswain. Tries: O'Grady,2. Cracknell. Goldswain. Davies. Tomlinson.
Attendance: 10,993   Referee: Mr. G. Phillips – Widnes.

This was the last time that Belle Vue would come to Watersheddings, and with the ex-Oldham pair Dai Rees and Jim Tynan at half-backs they gave a good account of themselves. The early exchanges were very even, but after 20 minutes Stirrup and Cracknell combined to put Goldswain over for the opening score, and this was soon followed by Barrow and Davies doing likewise for O'Grady. Undeterred Rangers hit back and were rewarded with a try by Day after a Stirrup kick had been charged down. None of the tries were converted, to leave Oldham 6 – 3 in front at half-time. After the break, early tries from Cracknell and O'Grady took Oldham clear, the latter, at last, being converted by Ganley, who was having an off day. Lambert got a try back for Belle Vue before Tomlinson and Davies added further tries for the Roughyeds. However, Rangers had the last say with late scores, by Lambert, again, and Brown.

Frank Pitchford
cuts through the
Belle Vue defence
with
Terry O'Grady
in support.

(01.01.1955)

January 8th 1955: LEIGH 10   OLDHAM 22

W.B. Ganley, R. Cracknell, R. Barrow, A. Davies, T. O'Grady, F. Daley, F. Pitchford.
H. Ogden, J. Keith, K. Jackson, C. Winslade, S. Little, B. Goldswain.
Goals: Ganley,2. Tries: Davies,2. Barrow,2. O'Grady. Ganley.
Attendance: 17,000   Referee: Mr. N. T. Railton – Wigan.

A tense first half saw the scores level at the interval, courtesy of an O'Grady try after five minutes, answered by a try for Moore after an awkward bounce took the ball away from the Oldham full-back. Ganley, though, kicked a penalty goal, as did Peter Davies for Leigh. Ganley's woes continued into the second period when a fumble by him led to Owen gathering the ball to score. Another Davies penalty followed but that was as good as it got for Leigh, as Oldham proceeded to take control. A break by Alan Davies laid on a try for Barrow, before he bagged two for himself. Pitchford and Daley produced a run-around move which culminated in a try for Ganley as Oldham finished in style. Keith and Pitchford were the star men.

January 15th 1955: OLDHAM 8   WARRINGTON 12

W.B. Ganley, R. Cracknell, R. Barrow, A. Davies, T. O'Grady, F. Daley, F. Pitchford.
H. Ogden, J. Keith, K. Jackson, C. Winslade, A. Tomlinson, B. Goldswain.
Goal: Ganley. Tries: O'Grady. Davies.
Attendance: 15,700   Referee: Mr. A. Howgate – Dewsbury.

Despite almost a complete cancellation of the rest of the Rugby League fixtures, a snow-covered Watersheddings was deemed playable, and so the top two teams in the championship lined up for the showdown. Hardly a minute had elapsed when the Warrington scrum-half, Helme, broke away from a scrum and veered over to the right wing where a long pass unleashed the threat that was Brian Bevan. Seconds later the ball was planted behind the Oldham line, and first blood was to the 'Wire'. The conditions didn't make for constructive rugby and it soon became obvious that points would be at a premium. As the game moved into the second quarter, Bath kicked a penalty, but the Roughyeds responded when Davies broke clear and drew in Bevan to send O'Grady in at the corner. Ganley converted magnificently from the touchline. Oldham then pressed again and Cracknell kicked ahead only for Fraser to arrive just in time to save the try. However, this was just a brief respite for Warrington as Daley smartly broke through their defences to put Davies away to score. Half-time followed with the score 8 – 5 to Oldham. After 55 minutes another Bath penalty reduced the deficit to one point, and this was soon followed by the match-clincher. Horton on the left wing broke through and, pursued by a posse of Oldham defenders, elected to kick. At first there seemed little danger, but then, like a streak of lightning from the

right wing, Bevan was there to win the race as the ball settled over the Oldham line. Bath added the conversion, and although just four points separated the teams, the Roughyeds seemed drained of their enthusiasm. As the game moved towards its conclusion, O'Grady in particular got back in the swing, but Bevan's magic had done the trick and the none-losing sequence in the league, which stretched back to August, was broken.

Brian Bevan sprints through the Watersheddings snow to score in the first minute after receiving a pass from Gerry Helme (extreme left). Terry O'Grady and Bryn Goldswain give chase, all to no avail. (15.01.1955)

January 22ⁿᵈ 1955: WORKINGTON T. 13   OLDHAM 5

F. Stirrup, J. Noon, R. Barrow, A. Davies, T. O'Grady, F. Daley, F. Pitchford.
H. Ogden, J. Keith, K. Jackson,   C. Winslade, S. Little, B. Goldswain.
Goal: Goldswain. Try: Davies.

Attendance: 8,288   Referee: Mr. J. W. Jackson – Barrow.

Cracknell and Ganley were unfit for the trip to Workington and Oldham's woes got worse when Goldswain suffered a serious injury after taking an elbow to the throat in the first half. Prior to this, Roper had intercepted a Winslade pass to put Ivill over after six minutes, but not to be outdone 'big Charlie' intercepted one himself eight minutes later and this led to a try for Davies. Goldswain converted before suffering his injury. A Paskins penalty reduced the arrears, and the same player fashioned an opening for a Southward try to leave the Cumbrians 8 – 5 in front at the interval. Playing with one man down, Oldham nevertheless tried hard to make up the deficit with Stirrup involved in much of the better moments, but a further penalty goal from Paskins and a try from Thompson were the only scores in the second half.

January 29ᵗʰ 1955: OLDHAM 11   ROCHDALE H. 9

F. Stirrup, R. Barrow, J. Etty, A. Davies, T. O'Grady, F. Daley, F. Pitchford.
H. Ogden, J. Keith, K. Jackson, C. Winslade, S. Little, J. Watson.
Goal: Pitchford. Tries: O'Grady. Keith. Stirrup.

Attendance: 14,526   Referee: Mr. C. Appleton – Warrington.

This was the debut match for John Etty, and a tough baptism it proved to be! Oldham started well, with Little carving out an opening for Davies to put O'Grady over. Winslade missed the conversion. Next it was Hornets in the ascendancy, and after a few close shaves Kelly nipped in from acting half-back. Les Jones converted to put Rochdale in front. Pitchford kicked a penalty to leave the scores level at the break. Early in the second half, Barrow and Stirrup exchanged passes before the latter crossed for a try. Winslade tried the conversion once more but again met with no success. Two further penalty goals from Jones put Hornets back in front, and things looked bleak for Oldham as Rochdale's defence, superbly marshalled by Cahill, held firm until two minutes from time, when Ogden powered to within a few yards of the Rochdale line ; a quick play-the-ball, and Keith was there to plunge over for the winning score. Again there was no goal, but the victory was secured.

*A look of despair is written on the faces of the Rochdale players as **Jack Keith** plunges over for the winning try with just two minutes left on the clock. Referee, **Charlie Appleton** has a good look before awarding the score.*
(29.01.1955)

February 5th 1955: OLDHAM 11 BARROW 5
F. Stirrup, R. Cracknell, J. Etty, A. Davies, T. O'Grady, F. Daley, F. Pitchford.
H. Ogden, J. Keith, A. Tomlinson, C. Winslade, S. Little, J. Watson.
Goal: Cracknell. Tries: Davies,2. Cracknell.
Attendance: 13,363   Referee: Mr. S. Abram – Wigan.

There was early pressure from Oldham, with Daley and Etty showing up well. Stirrup then got away and passed to Davies, who used O'Grady as a foil to ghost over for an unconverted try. Soon afterwards, Pitchford and Etty got Cracknell over, but again there was no goal to follow. A break by Grundy paved the way for Hinchley to score, and although Horne missed the conversion, he did kick a penalty soon after, to leave the score 6 – 5 at the break. The second half was a tight affair, but a touch of clever inter-passing between Davies and O'Grady led to a try by the former, and there was some relief when Cracknell managed to add the extras. That was enough for Oldham to see out the match.

The Oldham team against Barrow at Watersheddings on February 5th 1955.
Back Row: *Griff Jenkins (coach), Charlie Winslade, Arthur Tomlinson, Sid Little, John Watson, Harry Ogden, Jack Keith.*
Middle Row: *Terry O'Grady, Frank Stirrup, John Etty, Alan Davies, Dick Cracknell.*
Front Row: *Frank Daley, Frank Pitchford.*

February 12th 1955: OLDHAM 5 WIGAN 2
Rugby League Challenge Cup 1st Round.
F. Stirrup, R. Cracknell, J. Etty, A. Davies, T. O'Grady, F. Daley, F. Pitchford.

H. Ogden, J. Keith, K. Jackson, C. Winslade, S. Little, J. Watson.

Goal: Cracknell. Try: Davies.

Attendance: 22,371   Referee: Mr. R. Gelder – Wakefield.

A great sell-out, all-ticket crowd of over 22,000 saw Oldham extend their winning sequence against Wigan. This was a typical February cup-tie, with the 'fancy stuff' kept to a minimum. Oldham always looked the more likely side, and it took good defence from Bolton and Platt to keep out Cracknell and Davies, before a loose pass from Pitchford to Daley was gathered up by Davies, and, although there seemed to be little initial danger, the Oldham captain ran across the Wigan line before straightening up and diving for the line. The lead was augmented later by a 40-yard penalty goal by Cracknell, to give the Roughyeds a 5 – 0 advantage at the interval. Wigan toiled away to break the Oldham line, but to no avail. A drop goal from Platt, which scraped home off the cross-bar, was all they could muster. It did take a good tackle from Stirrup to stop McTigue in full flight, but Oldham finished the stronger, with Pitchford being brought down just short of the line near full time.

*Above: Alan Davies dives over in **Don Platt's** tackle watched by several team-mates and opponents alike on a decidedly cold-looking, Watersheddings pitch.*

*Left: **Harry Ogden** and **Jack Keith** bring down **Tommy Parr.***

(12.02.1955)

February 19th 1955: OLDHAM 9   ST. HELENS 2
F. Stirrup, R. Cracknell, J. Etty, A. Davies, T. O'Grady, F. Daley, F. Pitchford.
H. Ogden, J. Keith, K. Jackson, A. Tomlinson, S. Little, J. Watson.
Goals: Cracknell,3. Try: Cracknell.
Attendance: 14,600   Referee: Mr. M. Coates - Pudsey.

There was a covering of snow on the Watersheddings pitch as Oldham put in another good defensive display to keep their try-line intact once again. After early Oldham pressure it was St. Helens who took the lead when Ball slotted home a penalty, after Pitchford fed his own forwards at a scrum. Midway through the half Davies broke away and passed to O'Grady, who kicked ahead but was denied by a deceptive turn of pace by Prescott; he managed to reach the ball first and make it safe over the dead-ball line. Just before the interval Cracknell levelled the scores with a penalty goal. Silcock went close for Saints but, under pressure from several defenders, he lost the ball as he went to touch down. The decisive moment of the match came in the first minute of the second half, when Cracknell intercepted a pass from Parsons and sped away to the posts, before also adding the conversion. The same player concluded the scoring with another penalty four minutes from time.

Above:
An Oldham player receives some close attention from the St. Helens defence.

Left:
Alan Davies and Terry O'Grady give chase to the St. Helens winger Eric Ledger.

(19.02.1955)

142

March 5ᵗʰ 1955: LEIGH 5 OLDHAM 3
Rugby League Challenge Cup 2ⁿᵈ Round.
F. Stirrup, R. Cracknell, J. Etty, A. Davies, T. O'Grady, F. Daley, F. Pitchford.
H. Ogden, J. Keith, K. Jackson, C. Winslade, S. Little, J. Watson.
Try: O'Grady.

Attendance: 25,000 　　　　　 Referee: Mr. M. Coates – Pudsey.

Leigh sprung a surprise by naming the young 'A' teamer, Mick Martyn, in the starting line-up. The only score in the first half came just before the interval, when Malcolm Davies managed to avoid Stirrup to score wide out. Earlier, his namesake Alan had been brought back for a forward pass, after good work by Little and Daley had put him clear. A Ledgard penalty goal stretched the lead for Leigh, whose tackling was magnificent, but as the match move into the last three minutes, Oldham made one last supreme effort to rescue the tie. Pitchford went on a curving run and handed on to Davies who in turn passed to O'Grady. The winger kicked ahead and duly won the race with Ledgard to touchdown. The conversion was only about ten yards wide of the posts, but on the muddy pitch Cracknell's attempt failed, and it was another case of what might have been for the Roughyeds.

Stan Owen bumps into **Ken Jackson** as *Sid Little, Harry Ogden, Mick Martyn* and referee, **Matt Coates** watch on.
Inset: Frank Pitchford avoids the tackle of **Johnny Feather**.　　(05.03.1955)

March 12ᵗʰ 1955: BELLE VUE R. 8 OLDHAM 34
F. Stirrup, R. Cracknell, J. Etty, A. Davies, R. Barrow, A. Kellett, F. Pitchford.
H. Ogden, J. Keith, K. Jackson, C. Winslade, S. Little, B. Goldswain.
Goals: Goldswain,5. Tries: Pitchford,2. Stirrup,2. Etty. Winslade. Jackson. Goldswain.
Attendance: 4,000　　　　　 Referee: Mr. W. Rigby – Leigh.

Alan Kellett made his debut in this match, and from the first scrum he combined with Davies to set up a try for Etty. Oldham duly coasted to a 21 – 0 half-time lead. By the end of the match Oldham had scored eight tries, with Stirrup and Pitchford each grabbing a brace. Two late tries from Belle Vue winger Day were the only consolation for Rangers in this, the last-ever meeting between the clubs.

March 19th 1955: OLDHAM 36   WIDNES 2

F. Stirrup, R. Barrow, J. Etty, A. Davies, R. Cracknell, A. Kellett, F. Pitchford.
H. Ogden, R. Jennings, K. Jackson, C. Winslade, S. Little, B. Goldswain.
Goals: Goldswain,6. Tries: Cracknell,2. Jennings. Kellett. Etty. Pitchford. Davies. Jackson.
Attendance:8,972   Referee: Mr. H. Squires – Ossett.

*Before the match a minute's silence was observed in memory of the ex-Oldham half-back **John Feather**, who was tragically killed in a recent motor car accident.*

'Johnny', as he was popularly known, had last played for Oldham on Christmas Day against Swinton, and only two weeks before had been part of the Leigh side that knocked the Roughyeds out of the Challenge Cup.

In his two seasons with Oldham, John made 48 senior appearances, scoring ten tries and one goal.

The Roughyeds continued their winning ways with this comprehensive victory over Widnes. Debutant hooker Bob Jennings scored the first try after just four minutes, after Goldswain had scooped up a spilled kick by the Chemics defence. Further first half tries went to the impressive Kellett, who chased down a kick ahead by Pitchford, and Cracknell, put clear by Alan Davies. The only reply from the 'Chemics' was a penalty from Percy Davies, which left Oldham 13 – 2 up at the interval. The second half produced more of the same as the Watersheddings men, both backs and forwards, entertained the crowd with some great passing moves and eased home with a further five tries. Pitchford was in splendid form, as was Goldswain, who also slotted home six goals.

*A try-scoring debut for hooker **Bob Jennings** against Widnes.*

March 26th 1955: WARRINGTON 18   OLDHAM 4

F. Stirrup, T. O'Grady, J. Etty, A. Davies, R. Cracknell, F. Daley, F. Pitchford.
H. Ogden, J. Keith, K. Jackson, C. Winslade, S. Little, B. Goldswain.
Goals: Goldswain,2.
Attendance: 12,000   Referee: Mr. A. Hill – Dewsbury.

The score-line does little justice to a decent Oldham effort in this match. However, lessons of the past had not been learned, as Brian Bevan swooped to intercept two passes, the first from Jackson to Davies and the second from Stirrup to Cracknell, to scorch away for tries. Prior to this, Albert Naughton had opened the scoring after good work by Challinor. The Roughyeds were 4 - 10 in arrears at the break, and Bevan's second intercept took the game further away from them before the great man completed his 'hat-trick' after winning the race to collect a Naughton kick ahead. Pitchford was unlucky to have a try disallowed for incorrect grounding, and Winslade gave a good solid performance.

April 2nd 1955: OLDHAM 26   WIGAN 0
F. Stirrup, R. Cracknell, R. Barrow, A. Davies, T. O'Grady, D. Ayres, F. Pitchford.
H. Ogden, J. Keith, K. Jackson, C. Winslade, A. Tomlinson, B. Goldswain.
Goals: Goldswain,3. Stirrup. Tries Davies,2. Ayres. Keith. Cracknell. Goldswain.
Attendance: 15,127   Referee: Mr. G. Phillips – Widnes.

This match opened at a fast and furious pace, with good attacking play from both teams. Cracknell went close twice on attack and then showed good defensive qualities by being on hand to cut out a kick ahead from Bolton. The deadlock was broken after 14 minutes and it was Cracknell again who hacked ahead a loose ball and won the race to touch down. There was no conversion for this or for a try from Davies after 30 minutes, when the Oldham captain's determination saw him force his way over the line. That concluded the scoring for the first half in which Stirrup was always looking dangerous with one side-stepping run which covered over 60 yards the highlight of the first period. After the break it was one-way traffic. Oldham added four further tries, three converted by Goldswain and the last by Stirrup, as the Oldham loose -forward received attention for a cut face. Platt, the Wigan full-back, was sent off in the closing minutes.

*Above: **Alan Davies** breaks away from **Jack Broome** with **Terry O'Grady** in support.*

*Left: This time it's the Oldham left wing pair on defence combining together to bring down **Billy Boston** with **Charlie Winslade** on hand if required.*

(02.04.1955)

April 8th 1955: SWINTON 9 OLDHAM 17

F. Stirrup, R. Cracknell, R. Barrow, A. Davies, T. O'Grady, D. Ayres, F. Pitchford.
H. Ogden, J. Keith, K. Jackson,   C. Winslade, A. Tomlinson, B. Goldswain.
Goals: Goldswain,4. Tries: Cracknell. Barrow. Davies.
Attendance: 16,000   Referee: Mr. N. T. Railton – Wigan.

This match was a case of Oldham being let off the hook, as a succession of first-half missed chances for the 'Lions' kept the Roughyeds in the hunt. Cracknell scored after good work from Barrow after 25 minutes, but apart from an interception effort from Holder, Swinton had little to show for their overall dominance. As the game progressed Oldham settled down, and second half tries from Barrow and Davies gave them a victory that was not nearly as convincing as the score suggests.

Roland Barrow dives over for his try in spectacular style.   *(08.04.1955)*

April 9th 1955: HULL 11 OLDHAM 18

F. Stirrup, R. Cracknell, R. Barrow, A. Davies, T. O'Grady, F. Daley, F. Pitchford.
H. Ogden, J. Keith, K. Jackson, C. Winslade, A. Tomlinson, B. Goldswain.
Goals: Goldswain,3. Tries: Barrow,2. Jackson. Daley.
Attendance: 8,000   Referee: Mr. C. Appleton – Warrington.

A creditable win for Oldham, especially considering that they went behind to a try from Drake after just two minutes, and that Alan Davies was carried off two minutes after that! Goldswain came out of the pack to go on the right wing, with Cracknell moving to centre. Notwithstanding these set-backs, the Roughyeds set about their work, and twice the in-form Pitchford put Barrow over for tries, the first of which was converted. With the visitors 8 – 3 up at the interval, Davies returned for the second half, but was little more than a limping passenger on the wing. Oldham extended their lead when Goldswain and Barrow combined to send in Jackson near the posts, but Hull responded with a try from Watkinson, converted by Hutton. However, the joy was short-lived for the 'Airlie Birds', as Daley mesmerised the Hull defence with a side-stepping run to score a converted try, and despite a late try from Scott, Oldham had recorded a creditable victory.

John Etty releases a pass to *Dick Cracknell* as he is tackled in the match against Keighley.

(11.04.1955)

April 11th 1955: OLDHAM 23 KEIGHLEY 3

F. Stirrup, R. Cracknell, J. Etty, R. Barrow, T. O'Grady, F. Daley, F. Pitchford.
H. Ogden, J. Keith, K. Jackson, C. Winslade, A. Tomlinson, B. Goldswain.
Goals: Goldswain,4. Tries: Stirrup. O'Grady. Jackson. Barrow. Keith.
Attendance: 13,558 Referee: Mr. J. Hebblethwaite – York.

Keighley made a good fist of it in this, Oldham's third match in four days over the Easter period, and deservedly went ahead after ten minutes, when Bleasby avoided Cracknell and Stirrup to score in the corner. A few minutes later the same player looked likely to score again, but this time Stirrup got his man. Two Goldswain goals, the second a conversion of Jackson's try, put Oldham 7 – 3 up at the break, and the second half saw normal service resumed with a further four unanswered tries. Dick Cracknell was given the captaincy in the absence of Alan Davies.

April 16th 1955: OLDHAM 15 LEIGH 15

F. Stirrup, R. Cracknell, J. Etty, R. Barrow, T. O'Grady, F. Daley, F. Pitchford.
H. Ogden, J. Keith, K. Jackson, C. Winslade, A. Tomlinson, B. Goldswain,
Goals: Goldswain,3. Tries: Pitchford,2. Etty.
Attendance: 19,674 Referee: Mr. R. Gelder – Wakefield.

Oldham needed just a win from this match to be crowned champions of the Lancashire League, but as in the Challenge Cup, Leigh proved to be a thorn in the side. Two tries from Kitchen in the first quarter of an hour, one of them splendidly converted by Ledgard from the touchline, gave a clue of what was to come, although Oldham did get the score back to 7 – 8 at the break through a try from Etty, laid on by Pitchford and Goldswain, and two goals from the latter. In the second half Pitchford hit top form, and scored what the *Oldham Chronicle* called the 'try of the season' after a meandering run from his own half of the field. Not to be out-done, Leigh hit back with 15 minutes to go with a try from Davies, converted by Ledgard, but Oldham must have thought they had the title in the bag when another piece of Pitchford magic saw the scrum-half dart away to score at the Hutchins stand end, with Goldswain converting. However, a penalty given against Daley for offside gave Ledgard the chance to level the scores. His aim was true! Alas the same could not be said for Goldswain, who had an unsuccessful, long range effort in the closing minutes. For the second time in as many months, a last gasp kick was missed against Leigh.
The draw just wasn't enough and so it was Warrington who became the 1955 champions of Lancashire.

*Frank Pitchford
is congratulated
by his team-mates
after his second
try against Leigh.*

(16.04.1955)

April 18ᵗʰ 1955: OLDHAM 5   HULL 18
W.B. Ganley, R. Cracknell, J. Etty, A. Kellett, T. O'Grady, F. Daley, F. Stirrup.
H. Ogden, J. Keith, K. Jackson, S. Little, A. Tomlinson, J. Watson.
Goal: Ganley. Try: Cracknell.
Attendance: 12,500   Referee: Mr. H. Squires – Ossett.

Oldham paid the penalty for resting several players ahead of the Championship semi-final, and the situation was made worse by Kellett breaking his collar bone as early as the fifth minute. Hull were in no mood for compromise, and with the extra man for nearly all of the match they took a stranglehold on the game with some aggressive tactics. Ganley was back in the team for the first time since January after a cartilage operation, and it was he who gave Oldham the lead with a penalty, but this was soon answered by a similar effort from Watkinson. The Roughyeds re-took the lead when Daley passed out to Cracknell from a scrum, and the wingman went on an arcing run which saw him score in the left-wing corner. Watkinson then added another penalty, before Markham squeezed over for a try for Hull despite the attention of several Oldham defenders. This left the score 7 – 5 to the visitors at half-time. After the break the extra man began to tell, and Hull skipper Roy Francis scored a 'hat-trick' as the game deteriorated into a bad-tempered affair; referee Mr. Squires came in for some hefty criticism for not clamping down on the rough play early enough. Tomlinson and Jim Drake were given their marching orders in the 58ᵗʰ minute, and carried on their altercation right the way back to the pavilion. Such was the bad feeling that Francis and the other Hull players were given a police escort back to the changing rooms after the match. The defeat meant that once again Oldham were denied by Warrington, this time for the league leaders spot.

*Hull captain **Roy Francis** receives a Police escort back to the pavilion after the stormy encounter at Watersheddings.*
Francis scored a second-half 'hat-trick' as Hull triumphed 18 - 5 in this the last league match of the season.
A result that cost Oldham the league leaders title.
(18.04.1955)

April 23rd 1955: OLDHAM 25 LEEDS 6
Championship Top 4 play-off.
F. Stirrup, R. Barrow, R. Cracknell, A. Davies, T. O'Grady, F. Daley, F. Pitchford.
H. Ogden, J. Keith, K. Jackson, C. Winslade, S. Little, B. Goldswain.
Goals: Goldswain,5. Tries: Ogden. Davies. Barrow. Jackson. Cracknell.
Attendance: 17,268   Referee: Mr. R. Gelder – Wakefield.

Pitchford, Davies, Winslade and Goldswain were back for this championship semi-final as hopes were high that Oldham would contest the title decider for the first time in 33 years. On the other hand, Leeds were without two of their stars, Jeff Stevenson and Lewis Jones. The early exchanges were quite even, and it wasn't until the 26th minute that Dunn opened the scoring with a penalty goal. Goldswain equalised two minutes later, only for Dunn to once again give Leeds the lead on the half hour. This was followed by the first try, made by Davies, who burst clear and looked set to score only for Turnbull to catch and tackle the Oldham captain. Nevertheless, a quick play-the-ball to the ever-alert Goldswain paved the way for the loose-forward to give Ogden a run to the posts. Goldswain converted, but Dunn reduced the arrears with the last kick of the half, to leave the interval score 7 – 6 to the Roughyeds. The second period saw Oldham at their best. First a sweeping passing move saw Davies over. Then Cracknell, who had been switched to play right-centre, capitalised on a fumble by Scholes to kick ahead, re-gather, and lob a pass back inside to Barrow, who ran to the posts. Next, Cracknell again scooped up a Leeds handling error, but this time he went all the way himself, before Jackson went over for the final try. Goldswain added three conversions for Oldham to emerge as comfortable winners.

Alan Davies *falls to a two-man Leeds tackle with* **Harry Ogden, Terry O'Grady** *and* **Frank Pitchford** *(mostly hidden) in attendance. The return to the Oldham team of their influential captain was a great boost for the Roughyeds for this play-off match.*
(23.04.1955)

1954-55

May 14th 1955: OLDHAM 3 WARRINGTON 7
Championship Final Played at Maine Rd, Manchester City F.C.
F. Stirrup, R. Barrow, R. Cracknell, A. Davies, T. O'Grady, F. Daley, F. Pitchford.
H. Ogden, J. Keith, K. Jackson, C. Winslade, S. Little, B. Goldswain.
Try: Pitchford.

Attendance: 49,434   Referee: Mr. A. Hill - Dewsbury.

The weather was a major factor in this disappointing conclusion to the season. Heavy rain left most of the pitch a mud heap, and it was only the goal-kicking of Harry Bath that would separate the teams. However, it might all have been so different if a try by Barrow, after just five minutes, been allowed to stand. Good work by Cracknell had given his winger a run to the corner from just ten yards out. The Oldham man duly touched down, and referee Hill seemed to award the try, but as the Oldham players and supporters celebrated and the Warrington players took their place behind the posts, the touch-judge, Mr. Horsfall, raised his flag indicating that Barrow had touched the flag in Frodsham's tackle. It was a decision that was hotly disputed by the Oldham players! So it was that after 23 minutes, and quite against the run of play, Bevan got over after good approach work by Bath and Challinor. The conversion was missed, and eleven minutes later Oldham were level. First Cracknell and then Davies were both hauled into touch just short of the line, and after the scrum which followed the latter, Pitchford caught the Warrington defence by surprise to scoot over at the corner. Again there was no conversion, and half-time followed with the scores equal. There were no more tries, but Bath's two successful penalties, in the 47th and 65th minutes, were enough to win the Championship for the 'Wire'. Oldham toiled away in the mud but with Davies injured and having to play part of the match on the wing, it certainly wasn't a day when the gods or the sun shone down on the Roughyeds' cause.

Oldham in training for the 1955 Championship Final.
(Left to right)
Griff Jenkins (coach), John Etty, Terry O'Grady, Dick Cracknell, Charlie Winslade, Sid Little, Ken Jackson,
Frank Stirrup, John Watson, Alan Davies, Jack Keith, Harry Ogden, Bryn Goldswain, Frank Pitchford,
Frank Daley, Roland Barrow.

1954-55

1. The Oldham players are introduced to the **Earl of Derby**. 2. **Roland Barrow**'s controversial disallowed try. 3. **Frank Pitchford** scores for Oldham. 4. **Brian Bevan** speeds for the line with several Oldham defenders in pursuit... 5. ... the covering, **Terry O'Grady**, **Alan Davies** and **Frank Stirrup** bundled him into touch. 6. This time **Brian Bevan** scores having received the ball from **Jim Challinor**.

(14.05.1955)

1954-55

May 21st 1955: Halifax 29   Oldham 29
S. Kielty Benefit Match

F. Stirrup, R. Barrow, J. Noon, J. Etty, T. O'Grady, F. Daley, F. Pitchford.
H. Ogden, J. Keith, K. Jackson, A. Jarman, S. Little, J. Watson.
Goals: Little 4. Tries: Barrow, 2. Jarman,2. Noon. O'Grady. Little.
Attendance: 4,600   Referee: Mr. F. Seed - Halifax.

Stan Kielty - *Halifax, Yorkshire and England.*

Oldham initially named their Championship final team for this benefit match for Halifax's Stan Kielty, but there were late withdrawals, partly due to the inclusion of Winslade and Goldswain in the Welsh squad. However, it was a strong Roughyeds side that engaged in the usual end of season parade of tries that came with this type of game, in which a slightly smaller (15½oz) ball was used. Oldham led 18 – 11 at the break thanks to tries from O'Grady, Barrow, Noon and Jarman, and three goals from Sid Little! The points for Halifax came from two tries to Fearnley and one from Wilkinson, with a goal from Griffiths. After the break the scores evened up by way of further Halifax points through tries from Lynch (2), Daniels and Henderson, and goals from Kielty, Lynch and Fearnley. For Oldham, Jarman and Barrow scored tries and a late try and conversion from Little secured the draw.

	1954-55	Played	Won	Draw	Lost	For	Against	Points
1	Warrington	36	29	2	5	718	321	60
2	**OLDHAM**	**36**	**29**	**2**	**5**	**633**	**313**	**60**
3	Leeds	36	26	2	8	667	378	54
4	Halifax	36	26	1	9	579	269	53
5	Wigan	36	26	1	9	643	328	53
6	Leigh	36	25	2	9	738	399	52
7	St. Helens	36	25	1	10	631	337	51
8	Barrow	36	24	0	12	581	386	48
9	Featherstone R.	36	23	1	12	572	424	47
10	Workington T.	36	23	0	13	573	391	46
11	Huddersfield	36	22	0	14	790	483	44
12	Rochdale H.	36	20	3	13	396	346	43
13	York	36	21	0	15	439	374	42
14	Hunslet	36	20	0	16	582	477	40
15	Whitehaven	36	18	3	15	406	424	39
16	Wakefield T.	36	18	0	18	589	577	36
17	Bradford N.	36	17	2	17	476	475	36
18	Keighley	36	18	0	18	433	543	36
19	Hull	36	16	3	17	547	486	35
20	Swinton	36	16	1	19	398	451	33
21	Castleford	36	13	4	19	518	516	30
22	Widnes	36	13	0	23	325	478	26
23	Bramley	36	11	1	24	434	602	23
24	Liverpool C.	36	11	1	24	402	582	23
25	Hull K.R.	36	10	0	26	347	756	20
26	Salford	36	7	3	26	279	527	17
27	Doncaster	36	8	1	27	346	664	17
28	Batley	36	7	0	29	278	677	14
29	Blackpool B.	36	7	0	29	303	759	14
30	Belle Vue R.	36	7	0	29	248	666	14
31	Dewsbury	36	5	0	31	255	717	10

Bernard Ganley

Alan Davies

Jack Keith

Opposite*: More scenes from the 1955 Championship Final at Maine Road.*

153

1954-55

SEASON	PLAYER	APPS	TRIES	GOALS	POINTS
1954-55	J. KEITH	43	6		18
1954-55	R. CRACKNELL	42	21	5	73
1954-55	C. WINSLADE	42	2	1	8
1954-55	A. DAVIES	40	27		81
1954-55	F. PITCHFORD	40	19	1	59
1954-55	H. OGDEN	39	3		9
1954-55	B. GOLDSWAIN	34	4	47	106
1954-55	T. O'GRADY	34	24		72
1954-55	K. JACKSON	33	6		18
1954-55	R. BARROW	32	17		51
1954-55	F. DALEY	32	5		15
1954-55	F. STIRRUP	27	5	1	17
1954-55	A. TOMLINSON	27	3		9
1954-55	S. LITTLE	27	2		6
1954-55	W.B. GANLEY	22	1	84	171
1954-55	J. ETTY	11	3		9
1954-55	J. NOON	9	4		12
1954-55	W. MITCHELL	7			
1954-55	J. WATSON	7			
1954-55	A. JARMAN	4	2		6
1954-55	A. MURRAY	4	1		3
1954-55	H. LOMAS	3	3		9
1954-55	A. KELLETT	3	1		3
1954-55	T. SMITH	3			
1954-55	P. FEARIS	2	1	1	5
1954-55	D. AYRES	2	1		3
1954-55	J. FEATHER	2		1	2
1954-55	R. JENNINGS	1	1		3
1954-55	**TOTAL**	**572**	**162**	**141**	**768**

Most Appearances: Jack Keith 43 out of a possible 44.
Most tries: Alan Davies 27.
Most goals: Bernard Ganley 84 - Most points: Bernard Ganley 171.

1955-56

A disappointing season after the success of the previous year, and there can be no doubt that the lengthy injury absences for Terry O'Grady and Bernard Ganley were contributory factors to the dip in form. Much was also made of the loss of form from Frank Pitchford, who was actually dropped from the team for a spell. On the bright side the services of Derek Turner and Don Vines had been acquired and although they couldn't raise the team back into Championship contention, the team now had a real feeling of quality throughout the backs and forwards alike. Six victories in the last eight matches reinforced the view that Oldham were getting it right, as the late surge took them up to ninth place in the league table. John Etty found his try scoring touch to have the best total of 22 and Bernard Ganley still managed to top the goals and points charts. Jack Keith was Mr. Consistency at hooker and he, along with the ever-improving local lad, John Noon, made the most appearances.

August 13th 1955: Rochdale H. 23   Oldham 17

Law Cup

W.B. Ganley, R. Cracknell, R. Barrow, A. Davies, T. O'Grady, V. Nestor, F. Pitchford.
H. Ogden, J. Keith, A. Jarman, J. Watson, A. Murray, B. Goldswain.
Goals: Ganley,4. Tries: Barrow. Davies. Keith.
Attendance: 9,200   Referee: Mr. G. Phillips – Widnes.

Ganley opened the scoring with a 40 yard penalty goal, but the lead didn't last long before Les Jones made a break for Short to score. Oldham then enjoyed a good spell, with another goal from Ganley and Cracknell twice going close, before Barrow sped in from 60 yards out after a good pass from debutant, Vince Nestor. A penalty from Jones made the half time score 5 – 7 to Oldham. The second half saw the Roughyeds surge into a 17 – 10 lead before a late rally from Hornets produced three tries, with two going to second row man, Gallagher. The cup deservedly went to Rochdale, with the victory all the more creditable due to the fact that they played the last 15 minutes without their injured scrum-half, Helme.

Above:
Alan Davies tackles Alan Taylor with Terry O'Grady and Harry Ogden in the background, while Walter Jones races in to support his stand-off half (13.08.1955)

Left:
Vince Nestor played his first match for Oldham in the 1955 Law Cup match. The start of a ten year career with the Roughyeds.

1955-56

August 20th 1955: Oldham 35   Keighley 14

Friendly match arranged at short notice after Belle Vue R. resigned from the Rugby League.

F. Stirrup, R. Cracknell, R. Barrow, A. Davies, T. O'Grady, F. Daley, F. Pitchford.
H. Ogden, J. Keith, B. Goldswain, C. Winslade, S. Little, J. Rogers.
Goals: Rogers,2. Little,2.
Tries: Davies,2. Barrow. Pitchford. O'Grady. Stirrup. Cracknell. Goldswain. Rogers.
Attendance: 7,304   Referee: Mr. A. Howgate – Dewsbury.

Oldham experimented with Goldswain at prop for this swiftly-arranged friendly with Keighley, as new signing Jack Rogers came in at loose-forward. Pitchford scored early on after a break by Davies, but Keighley hit back with a try from Verrenkamp and two goals from Ward. Further tries from O'Grady and Davies put Oldham back in command and they turned around with an 11 – 9 advantage. After the break the Roughyeds found some form and added a further six tries, but unfortunately Rogers had a poor day with the boot and eventually Little took over the kicking duties.

Another debut this time for goal-kicking forward,
Jack Rogers.

August 27th 1955: BLACKPOOL B. 8   OLDHAM 18
Lancashire Cup 1st Round.

F. Stirrup, R. Cracknell, R. Barrow, A. Davies, T. O'Grady, F. Daley, F. Pitchford.
H. Ogden, J. Keith, K. Jackson, C. Winslade, S. Little, J. Rogers.
Goals: Rogers,3. Tries: Barrow. Cracknell. Pitchford. Winslade.
Attendance: 5,700   Referee: Mr. E. Clay – Leeds.

A good crowd of Oldhamers went over for a day out at the seaside to see Oldham given a good work out by a Blackpool team that featured ex-Oldham players Lionel Emmitt and Peter Fearis. Indeed, Fearis was the first to threaten a score, but he ,was soundly brought down by Stirrup. Then there was a glorious move that involved Winslade to Little to Pitchford back to Little, and finally back again to Winslade who scored, with Rogers converting. Emmitt and Ryder then combined well to lay on a try for Wright, which Bebe converted. Winslade was having a fine game and after he had made good ground, Cracknell put Barrow through for a try which left the half-time score 8 – 5 to the Roughyeds. In the second half Stirrup laid on a try for Cracknell, with Rogers adding the goal, but back came Blackpool with Emmitt scoring at the other end, and it took a late try from Pitchford, again laid on by Stirrup and converted by Rogers, to ease the nerves and see Oldham through to the next round.
Also on this day Oldham signed Derek Turner from Hull Kingston Rovers.

August 30th 1955: ROCHDALE H. 12   OLDHAM 4

W.B. Ganley, R. Cracknell, R. Barrow, J. Noon, J. Etty, F. Daley, F. Pitchford.
H. Ogden, J. Keith, K. Jackson, J. Rogers, S. Little, A. Murray.
Goals: Ganley,2.
Attendance: 15,000   Referee: Mr. A. Hill – Dewsbury.

For the second time in a month Hornets got the better of an injury-hit Oldham team, although the visitors took the lead with an early penalty goal from Ganley. Evans and Gallagher combined to put Tierney over, and this, combined with a Les Jones penalty, gave Rochdale a 5 – 2 lead at the break. In the second half Oldham had the best of it early on, but when both Pitchford and Jackson broke through the move came to nothing because of a lack of support. A Ganley penalty was cancelled out by a similar effort from Les Jones, and the match was made safe for Rochdale when Walter Jones sent an inside pass to Short, who went over for a converted try in the closing minutes.

September 3rd 1955: OLDHAM 8   HUNSLET 15

W.B. Ganley, J. Watson, J. Etty, R. Barrow, T. O'Grady, J. Noon, F. Pitchford.
H. Ogden, J. Keith, K. Jackson, S. Little, J. Rogers, D. Turner.
Goal: Ganley. Tries: Barrow. Noon.

Attendance: 12,960   Referee: Mr. R. Gelder - Wakefield.

Again Oldham were under strength, and forced to call in John Watson to play on the wing, but the talking point of the day was the much anticipated debut of Derek Turner. An early break through by Ganley broke down because of lack of support, but he did register on the scoreboard soon afterwards with a penalty goal.

Hunslet scored the first try when James shrugged off three defenders to score at the posts, and Talbot converted. The 'Parksiders' followed this up with a try by Williamson in the corner. Oldham hit back but both Pitchford and Rogers were grounded just short. The Roughyeds started the second half brightly with Noon and Pitchford fashioning a try for Barrow. However, while both Jackson and Ogden were lying injured, the Hunslet prop Hatfield forced his way over for another converted try. Oldham responded with a splendid move, where all the three-quarters handled the ball to send Noon over at the corner, but that was the last score they could muster as Hunslet held out for victory. The one pleasing aspect of the match was a good, solid performance from Turner.

The Green Final on this day led with the amazing headline "Alan Davies Retiring" but as you can see from the team for the next match the crisis was short-lived.

*The first game for **Derek Turner** in an Oldham jersey.
A dynamic loose-forward and arguably the club's
most influential player in the 1950s.*

September 7th 1955: OLDHAM 11   LEIGH 13
Lancashire Cup 2nd Round.

F. Stirrup, R. Cracknell, J. Noon, A. Davies, T. O'Grady, F. Daley, F. Pitchford.
H. Ogden, J. Keith, S. Little, C. Winslade, J. Rogers, D. Turner.
Goals: Rogers,4. Tries: O'Grady.

Attendance: 17,210   Referee: Mr. R. Gelder - Wakefield.

Ledgard opened the scoring with a penalty for Leigh in the fourth minute, and regained the lead for the visitors with a similar effort after Rogers had equalised. Oldham were playing some fine open rugby and were unlucky to have Cracknell called back when put clear by Davies, the referee ruling that a knock-on occurred in the build up. However, Oldham did take the lead just before the break, when Stirrup lobbed a high pass to O'Grady and he beat two men before passing back inside to Davies; he in turn raced clear of the rest of the Leigh defence to score at the posts. Rogers converted to give the Roughyeds a 7 – 4 interval lead. Ledgard reduced the arrears with a further penalty goal before the game-breaker, which came in the 55th minute, when Moore intercepted a pass from Turner to go over from 70 yards. Ledgard converted and he and Rogers twice exchanged penalties to leave Leigh the victors by two points.

1955-56

September 10th 1955: LEEDS 22 OLDHAM 15

F. Stirrup, R. Barrow, J. Noon, A. Davies, T. O'Grady, F. Daley, F. Pitchford.
H. Ogden, J. Keith, S. Little, J. Rogers, B. Goldswain, D. Turner.
Goals: Rogers,3. Tries: O'Grady. Ogden. Pitchford.
Attendance: 15,000   Referee: Mr. T. Watkinson – Manchester.

Oldham's woes continued with this trip to Headingley, despite having the better of the play in the early stages. Rogers gave the visitors an early lead and Little had a try disallowed when he was adjudged to have put a foot in touch before going over the line. Jones kicked a penalty before a fine Leeds move ended with McLellan putting Broughton over for Jones to convert, but thanks to two more Rogers goals, Oldham only trailed by a point at the break. A converted try by Skelton soon after the interval set the trend for the second half, however, and although Oldham scored three late tries none were converted.

Harry Ogden finds himself surrounded by a trio of Leeds players.   (10.09.1955)

September 17th 1955: OLDHAM 18 WARRINGTON 3

F. Stirrup, R. Barrow, J. Noon, A. Davies, T. O'Grady, A. Kellett, F. Pitchford.
H. Ogden, J. Keith, S. Little, J. Rogers, B. Goldswain, D. Turner.
Goals: Rogers,3. Tries: Little. Davies. Rogers. Barrow.
Attendance: 16,432   Referee: Mr. S. Abram – Wigan.

Back to winning ways at last, and against the Warrington bogey team to boot! The only try in the first half came after Turner had made a great break to find Little in support; he scampered over for the score, which Rogers converted. Oldham took full control in the second period. Tries from Davies, set up by Pitchford, and a determined effort from Rogers, who barged over from a quick play-the-ball by Keith, were answered by the almost obligatory try from Bevan before a break from Noon set up Barrow for the final score of the match.

Alan Kellett takes on Warrington prop *Dan Naughton.*
(17.09.1955)

159

1955-56

September 24th 1955: YORK 16   OLDHAM 10

W.B. Ganley, R. Cracknell, J. Noon, A. Davies, T. O'Grady, V. Nestor, F. Pitchford.
H. Ogden, J. Keith, S. Little, J. Rogers, B. Goldswain, D. Turner.
Goals: Ganley,2. Tries: O'Grady. Cracknell.
Attendance: 7,610   Referee: Mr. A. Howgate – Dewsbury.

Oldham were caught cold after six minutes when a cross-kick from Riley was snapped up by Smith; he scored and Harker converted. Just minutes later it was Riley again breaking through and putting Robinson over for a try, again converted by Harker. Ganley replied with a penalty, but then, in the 24th minute, Pitchford was sent off to the amazement of all present for what one presumes was an 'off the ball' incident. Nevertheless, after Harker had stretched York's lead with two more penalties, Oldham buckled down to their task, and after Ganley was grounded just short, quick passing enabled O'Grady to squeeze in at the corner. Then, just before the break, Nestor and Noon paved the way for Cracknell to register Oldham's second try. 14 – 10 down at the interval, Oldham suffered a further set-back midway through the second half, when Turner was dismissed on the intervention of the touch judge for speaking out of turn. However, the eleven-men Roughyeds refused to capitulate and the only further score was another Harker penalty goal, whereas Oldham were unfortunate to have a try by O'Grady disallowed for an alleged obstruction by Ganley. There was one piece of luck for the visitors, when another penalty attempt by Harker went through the posts only for the referee to disallow the goal because other York players were in front of the kicker.

The result of the sending-offs was worse than Oldham could have imagined, for not only were Turner and Pitchford suspended for four and three matches respectively, but Davies also got three matches for a remark made to the referee as the teams left the field!

Derek Turner

Frank Pitchford

Alan Davies

October 1st 1955: OLDHAM 25   FEATHERSTONE R. 6

W.B. Ganley, R. Cracknell, J. Noon, A. Davies, T. O'Grady, A. Kellett, A. Jones.
H. Ogden, J. Keith, S. Little, B. Goldswain, J. Rogers, D. Turner.
Goals: Ganley,5. Tries: Little,2. Jones. O'Grady. Keith.
Attendance: 14,752   Referee: Mr. A. Hill – Dewsbury.

After an early scare when Hulme broke through the Oldham defence, the Roughyeds soon took control of this match. Cracknell, Rogers and Davies produced a move that took play from the home line to deep into the Featherstone half, before Ganley opened the scoring with a penalty goal. And from the moment Goldswain put stand-in scrum-half Alan Jones through for a converted try, there was to be no coming back for the Yorkshire team. O'Grady got another before half-time, and a couple from Little in the second half, combined with a cracker when Keith and Cracknell inter-passed, saw Oldham home with ease. Featherstone's points came from three penalty goals from Fennell.

Terry O'Grady scores Oldham's second try against Featherstone Rovers.   (01.10.1955)

October 8th 1955: HUNSLET 11   OLDHAM 26
W.B. Ganley, R. Cracknell, J. Noon, V. Nestor, T. O'Grady, A. Kellett, F. Stirrup.
H. Ogden, J. Keith, S. Little, A. Tomlinson, J. Rogers, B. Goldswain.
Goals: Ganley,4. Tries: Nestor,3. O'Grady. Stirrup. Ogden.
Attendance: 6,300   Referee: Mr. G. Battersby – Barrow.

A re-shuffled Oldham team, as a result of the suspensions, swept aside Hunslet with the match a personal triumph for Vince Nestor, who recorded a well-taken 'hat-trick'. The first was made by Stirrup direct from a scrum, and the second came from a Little interception which was carried on by Goldswain before Nestor took the pass and, using O'Grady as a foil, veered inside to score; Ganley duly converted. Hunslet hit back with three penalty goals from Talbot, but a try for O'Grady, after Goldswain had ripped the ball from the grasp of as Hunslet player, kept Oldham in the driving seat. In truth Oldham didn't spend that much time in the Hunslet half, but they did convert their chances. On the other hand the 'Parksiders' failed to capitalise on a sterling display from loose forward Waite. 6 - 15 in arrears at the break, Hunslet started to dominate again early in the second period, but they did not have the wherewithal to turn their territorial advantage into points. At a scrum rival hookers, Smith and Keith, had their names taken amidst a slow hand-clap from the frustrated home supporters. A quarter of an hour into the second half, Kellett put Stirrup over, and this more or less sealed the match for the Roughyeds. Ogden added another try before Nestor completed his 'hat-trick'. Home stand-off half, Talbot, scored all of Hunslet's points.

October 15th 1955: OLDHAM 18   BARROW 16

W.B. Ganley, R. Cracknell, J. Noon, V. Nestor, T. O'Grady, F. Daley, F. Stirrup.
H. Ogden, J. Keith, S. Little, J. Rogers, A. Tomlinson, B. Goldswain.
Goals: Ganley,3. Tries: Ganley. Stirrup. Rogers. Cracknell.
Attendance: 13,672   Referee: Mr. S. Abram – Wigan.

A good open game which Barrow started with a 'furious attack', and it soon bore fruit, with Grundy putting Goodwin over in the corner. Horne missed the conversion and had a drop goal ruled out as the referee ruled that the ball touched an opposing player before crossing the bar. Oldham got back in the match when Nestor, O'Grady and Stirrup put together a move that ended with Ganley going over for a try that he also converted. Next it was Stirrup himself who ghosted through the Barrow defence, for another converted try.

Back came the 'Furness-men', and Jackson put Lewthwaite over, before the two of them combined to put Horne through to score. The latter score was converted, to give Barrow an 11 – 10 advantage at the break. Two minutes into the second half, Keith and Stirrup made an opening from which Rogers powered over. Once again Ganley added the extras. Castle then scored wide out. Horne couldn't convert, but he did slot over a penalty to restore a one point lead. Oldham threw everything into the closing stages and with two minutes to go, Cracknell squeezed over despite Castle's tackle for the winning score.

Dennis Goodwin - an early try for Barrow at Watersheddings.

October 22nd 1955: WARRINGTON 15   OLDHAM 13

F. Stirrup, R. Cracknell, J. Noon, A. Davies, T. O'Grady, V. Nestor, F. Pitchford.
H. Ogden, J. Keith, S. Little, J. Rogers, C. Winslade, B. Goldswain.
Goals: Rogers,5. Try: Davies.
Attendance: 17,496   Referee: Mr. T. Watkinson – Manchester.

Oldham started well in this match and two early penalties from Rogers were followed by a glorious 85 yard move which saw Davies and O'Grady inter-pass for the former to score. Rogers converted and the Roughyeds were nine points to the good. Unfortunately, a few moments later Nestor suffered a dislocated shoulder in a tackle from Bevan, and he took no further part in the match. Warrington soon began to press home their numerical advantage with Glover scoring a try converted by Bath, and then, with Cracknell lying injured, Horton put Fraser over. Bath kicked a tremendous conversion from the touch-line. In the second half Warrington resumed where they left off and after Helme was held up over the line, Horton crashed over. Two Rogers penalties brought Oldham back level, but a Bath penalty from half-way gave the home side the points.

*Maori forward, **Johnny Yates** leads the Kiwis as they perform the 'haka' at Watersheddings.*

(29.10.1955)

A full account of all the Oldham matches against the touring teams can be found in the book "Kangaroos, Kiwis and Roughyeds".

October 29th 1955: OLDHAM 13   NEW ZEALAND 15

F. Stirrup, T. O'Grady, A. Davies, F. Daley, J. Noon , A. Kellett, F. Pitchford.
H. Ogden, J. Keith, S. Little, J. Rogers, C. Winslade, B. Goldswain.
Goals: Rogers,2. Tries: O'Grady. Little. Pitchford.
Attendance: 14,422   Referee: Mr. T. Armitage – Huddersfield.

Oldham were forced to make a late change when John Etty dropped out of the side. John Noon moved over to the wing with Frank Daley coming into the team at centre. Shortly after the kick off, Atkinson intercepted a pass and raced 80 yards before being grounded just short of the line. However, just seconds later, the ball went across the field to Bakalich, who dived in at the corner for an unconverted try. The home side was unlucky when Rogers was brought back for a forward pass after racing 25 yards to touch down, and the misfortune was compounded when a short time later McKay took a pass from Sorenson to score near the posts. This time Haggie had no trouble adding the extra two points. Rogers next opened the scoring for Oldham with a penalty goal. This gave confidence to the home team, and within a matter of minutes they narrowed the lead further. Keith, who was having a storming game in the loose, completely fooled the New Zealand defence with an outrageous dummy. The Kiwi defenders managed to stop him just short, but Little was on hand to take the scoring pass and go over. Rogers missed the conversion. The next serious action saw the Kiwis break away at breath-taking pace, and this culminated in Robertson veering out to the wing before releasing a classic reverse pass to send Bakalich on a run to the posts. Haggie converted without any trouble. Just before the interval the tourists were dealt a blow when Robertson had to retire with a shoulder injury. However, a further penalty goal left them with a useful advantage. When the match resumed, the Kiwis had to adjust as Robertson was unable to continue. Nevertheless, they continued in attacking fashion. Haggie failed with a long range goal attempt before play switched to the other end and, after O'Grady narrowly failed to score, Pitchford darted through direct from a scrum without a hand being laid upon him. Rogers missed what was an easy conversion, to leave Oldham seven points in arrears. Just before full-time O'Grady squeezed in at the corner after some snappy passing, and this time Rogers made amends for his earlier effort with a glorious conversion from the touch-line. Oldham rallied for one last assault on the New Zealand line, but it wasn't to be.

Above: Frank Daley and *Jack Keith* bring down the Kiwi hooker *Trevor Kilkelly.*

Left: Vern Bakalich avoids *Terry O'Grady* to score the first try.

(29.10.1955)

1955-56

November 2nd 1955: FEATHERSTONE R. 7   OLDHAM 8
A.T.V. Cup played at Loftus Road, Queens Park Rangers F.C.
W.B. Ganley, T. O'Grady, A. Kellett, J. Noon, R. Needham, F. Daley, F. Stirrup.
K. Jackson, J. Keith, S. Little, J. Rogers, A. Tomlinson, D. Turner.
Goal: Rogers. Tries: Needham. Noon.
Attendance: 700 (est)   Referee: Mr. M. Coates - Pudsey.

This match was organised under the sponsorship of Associated Television, and the second half was screened live in the South of England. It was played at a sparsely attended Loftus Road, which wasn't surprising considering the rain-swept conditions that prevailed on the night. Oldham had all the early pressure but it was Rovers who struck first with a try by Fennell, converted by Allen. A few minutes before half-time Storey had to retire through injury, and Oldham capitalised on the extra man almost at once, with debutant Roy Needham going over for an unconverted try. Despite being down to 12 men Featherstone were playing well, and extended their lead with an Allen penalty six minutes after the break. A try from Noon narrowed the gap to one point, but with 15 minutes to go O'Grady suffered a fractured ankle injury that left him out of action for several months. Two minutes from time Rogers defied the poor conditions to land a good penalty goal from 35 yards, to give Oldham the victory.

Roy Needham

November 5th 1955: LEIGH 21   OLDHAM 30
F. Stirrup, R. Cracknell, J. Noon, A. Davies, J. Etty, F. Daley, F. Pitchford.
H. Ogden, J. Keith, S. Little, J. Rogers, B. Goldswain, D. Turner.
Goals: Goldswain,5. Rogers. Tries: Little. Turner. Noon. Cracknell. Keith. Etty.
Attendance: 11,000   Referee: Mr. G. Phillips – Widnes.

The first action of the match saw a kicking duel between Ledgard and Stirrup, and before five minutes had elapsed two penalty goals left Leigh 4 – 2 in front. Davies and Etty then combined to put Little on a 45-yard dash to the line. The try wasn't converted and the home side quickly responded when Moore broke through to put Fallon over for a converted try. Back came Oldham, and Turner and Davies managed to dribble the ball between them for a full 80 yards, culminating in a try for the Oldham loose-forward. Goldswain took over the kicking duties from Rogers and duly converted the score. However, Leigh went in front just before the break when Gullick scored after Barton was held just short. Two Ledgard penalties and a converted try from Barton seemed to have put Leigh in the clear, but in a remarkable turn-around Oldham scored 20 unanswered points to win in style. First a sweeping move from the backs paved the way for Noon to score, closely followed by a solo effort from Cracknell and a tricky Keith 'special' from close in; with all three scores converted, this put the Roughyeds on top and when Etty won the race to touch down his own kick the match was safe.

November 12th 1955: OLDHAM 22   LIVERPOOL C. 16
F. Stirrup, R. Cracknell, J. Noon, A. Davies, J. Etty, F. Daley, F. Pitchford.
K. Jackson, J. Keith, S. Little, J. Rogers, B. Goldswain, D. Turner.
Goals: Rogers,5. Tries: Cracknell. Pitchford. Davies. Little.
Attendance: 10,728   Referee: Mr. C. Appleton – Warrington.

Liverpool had the best of it early on and it was no surprise when Adair crashed over to open the scoring for 'City'. Oldham finally found their form and after Cracknell had scored, followed by a 50 yard sprint to the line from Pitchford, the match was taking the expected path, but the visitors hit back when Barton scored in the corner for Teggin to convert well from the touch-line. A converted try from Davies put Oldham 17 – 8 in front at the interval. Liverpool opened up in the second half, as they had the first, by registering the opening score when a Keith kick was charged down for Farnall to score. Teggin converted, and it was very much 'game-on'. The nerves were eased when Etty broke through to put Little over near the posts. Rogers converted, but the last say went to the 'Mersey-siders' when Turner brought down Adair, who was chasing a Hockenhull kick through, for the referee to award a penalty try.

1955-56

November 19th 1955: WIGAN 23 OLDHAM 48

F. Stirrup, R. Cracknell, J. Noon, A. Davies, J. Etty, F. Daley, F. Pitchford.
H. Ogden, J. Keith, S. Little, J. Rogers, B. Goldswain, D. Turner.
Goals:Goldswain,3. Rogers,3.
Tries: Cracknell,2. Davies,2. Daley,2. Etty. Keith. Pitchford. Noon. Rogers. Turner.
Attendance: 16,450 Referee: Mr. T. Watkinson – Pendlebury.

A great day for the Roughyeds which started as soon as the fifth minute, when a fantastic passing move involving Pitchford, Daley, Noon and Davies was finished off by Cracknell, with Rogers converting the try. Within minutes the ex-Huddersfield flyer was in again, and so the tone of the game was set. By half-time Oldham were 26 – 9 in front, with half-backs, Pitchford and particularly Daley, the main architects of Wigan's demise. Three minutes after the restart Oldham were in again, with Pitchford kidding the Wigan defence by feigning to pass one way before giving Noon a walk in. All the backs scored apart from Stirrup, and if the tries had been better complimented (only four of the twelve were converted) the already overwhelming victory would have been even more embarrassing for the hosts. The fact that Wigan also scored 23 points suggests that good defence was not the order of the day. However, for any team to score just shy of 50 points at Central Park was a truly amazing effort.

In no particular order, the ten players on the score-sheet for Oldham at Central Park
Top Row: *Frank Daley, John Etty, Frank Pitchford, Alan Davies, Jack Keith.*
Bottom Row: *Bryn Goldswain, John Noon, Dick Cracknell, Jack Rogers, Derek Turner.*

November 26th 1955: OLDHAM 24 WIDNES 5

F. Stirrup, R. Cracknell, J. Noon, A. Davies, J. Etty, F. Daley, F. Pitchford.
H. Ogden, J. Keith, S. Little, J. Rogers, B. Goldswain, D. Turner.
Goals: Rogers,2. Davies. Tries: Davies. Daley. Rogers. Pitchford. Cracknell. Etty.
Attendance: 9,469 Referee: Mr. N. T. Railton – Wigan.

Fresh from their remarkable triumph at Central Park, it was a murky day with constant drizzle that greeted Oldham back at Watersheddings. The early pressure all came from the Roughyeds but, totally against the run of play, Williamson intercepted to score a try for Widnes, converted by Sale. That spurred Oldham into renewed efforts and after Keith was unlucky to lose the ball as he went over the line, Daley split the Widnes defence to put Davies over. Rogers missed the conversion but later landed a long range penalty, to leave the scores equal at the interval. After the break the Roughyeds settled down and after Little and Turner had gone close, Keith was unlucky to be recalled for a forward pass. However, Oldham were now almost constantly on attack and the pressure finally got its reward when Pitchford put Daley over. Rogers converted, but from then on the goal-kicking was woeful, so much so that captain, Alan Davies, took one kick himself and actually scored! Alas, he too missed the next one after the final try from Etty.

December 3rd 1955: LIVERPOOL C. 16   OLDHAM 26

F. Stirrup, J. Noon, A. Kellett, A. Davies, J. Etty, F. Daley, F. Pitchford.
H. Ogden, J. Keith, S. Little, J. Rogers, B. Goldswain, D. Turner.
Goals: Rogers,4. Tries: Etty,2. Stirrup. Little. Davies. Pitchford.
Attendance: 2,500   Referee: Mr. R. Welsby – Warrington.

Oldham were soon out of the blocks at Knotty Ash when Stirrup came into the line to take Pitchford's pass to score in the opening minutes. There was no conversion and Teggin soon reduced the arrears with a penalty. The Roughyeds then took control, and after Turner gathered a loose ball near the left wing to give Etty an inside pass to touch down, they further consolidated their advantage with three more tries before the interval. All were converted by Rogers to leave them 21 – 2 ahead. However, Liverpool bounced back in the second half, and four goals from Teggin, the last a conversion of a Farnall try, gave Oldham cause for concern. It was with great relief that Davies and Etty set up Pitchford for the clinching score with ten minutes to go. 'City' did have the consolation of the last score when Grundy put Adair through in the final moments.

December 10th 1955: SALFORD 0   OLDHAM 24

F. Stirrup, R. Cracknell, J. Noon, V. Nestor, J. Etty, F. Daley, F. Pitchford.
H. Ogden, J. Keith, S. Little, J. Rogers, B. Goldswain, D. Turner.
Goals: Goldswain,4. Rogers,2. Tries: Pitchford,3. Rogers.
Attendance: 5,000   Referee: Mr. W. Rigby – Leigh.

Oldham started this match as the more lively team and continued the trend for the full 80 minutes. Turner, Cracknell, and Noon (twice) went close, but there was only one try in the first half, when Pitchford put Rogers over in a set move from a scrum close to the Salford line. This combined with three goals gave the Roughyeds a 9 – 0 advantage at the break. A second half 'hat-trick' from Pitchford, the pick of which came after a storming break away by Little, who then found his scrum-half with a deft inside pass, wrapped up the win with Goldswain and Rogers sharing the kicking duties.

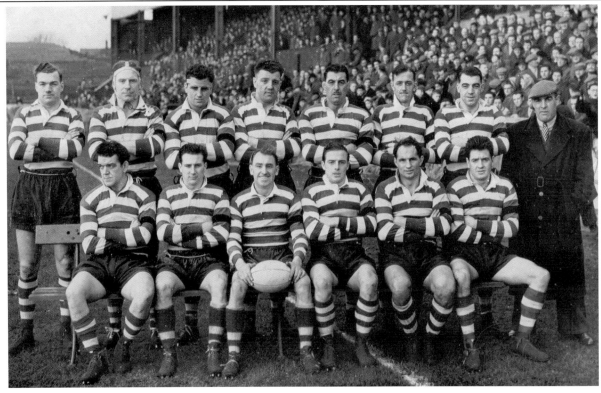

The Oldham team against Salford at Watersheddings on December 17th.
Back Row: *John Etty, Jack Rogers, Derek Turner, Harry Ogden, Bryn Goldswain, Jack Keith, Dick Cracknell, Griff Jenkins (coach).*
Front Row: *Frank Daley, Frank Pitchford, Frank Stirrup, Vince Nestor, Sid Little, John Noon. (17.12.1955)*

December 17th 1955: OLDHAM 27 SALFORD 14

F. Stirrup, R. Cracknell, J. Noon, V. Nestor, J. Etty, F. Daley, F. Pitchford.
H. Ogden, J. Keith, S. Little, J. Rogers, B. Goldswain, D. Turner.
Goals: Goldswain,3. Tries: Noon,2. Daley. Rogers. Nestor. Etty. Cracknell.
Attendance: 9,300   Referee: Mr. J. C. Clapham – Wigan.

Just a week after their triumph at the Willows Oldham entertained Salford at Watersheddings, and this time the 'Red Devils' put in an improved effort. Tries from Noon and Daley, the latter from a lovely lobbed pass from Stirrup, helped Oldham to a 10 – 5 lead at half time. However, when Cheshire crossed for his second try, Salford were right back in the match. The response from Oldham was to score a quick-fire three touchdowns that effectively sealed the contest. Rogers barged his way over from close range, and then Etty and Pitchford combined to send Nestor over, before Etty himself shook off two defenders to stroll in from ten yards out. A cause for concern was again the indifferent goal kicking, with Goldswain only managing to convert two of the seven tries and adding one penalty.

December 24th 1955: ST. HELENS 18 OLDHAM 7

F. Stirrup, R. Cracknell, J. Noon, A. Davies, J. Etty, F. Daley, F. Pitchford.
H. Ogden, J. Keith, S. Little, J. Rogers, B. Goldswain, D. Turner.
Goals: Rogers,2. Try: Davies.
Attendance: 20,000   Referee: Mr. C. Appleton – Warrington.

A tough encounter at Knowsley Road which saw Saints laying siege to the Oldham line for most of the match. From the moment that Silcock fielded a Goldswain kick to put Greenall over, the Roughyeds were up against it. Two Rogers penalties kept them in the match up to half time, when the Saints led 7 – 4, but after the interval the home side pulled away, aided by another try from McAbe and the excellent goal kicking of the teenager, Austin Rhodes. Stirrup had a great game in defence and there was a late consolation try in the corner for Davies after good work by Noon and Cracknell.

Austin Rhodes: A fine display of place kicking from the St. Helens scrum-half with six successful attempts at goal.

December 26th 1955: OLDHAM 8 SWINTON 10

F. Stirrup, R. Cracknell, J. Noon, A. Davies, J. Etty, F. Daley, F. Pitchford.
K. Jackson, J. Keith, S. Little, J. Rogers, A. Tomlinson, D. Turner.
Goal: Rogers. Tries: Etty. Cracknell.
Attendance: 12,640   Referee: Mr. H. Squires - Ossett.

No 'Boxing Day' cheer for Oldham in this fixture; they went behind to an early obstruction try awarded to Parkinson and never recovered in the heavy conditions. A further try from Hardman and two goals from Tobin were enough to secure a win for the 'Lions'. Although Oldham enjoyed the majority of possession, and created enough chances, they found it difficult to break down the stubborn Swinton defence, and when they eventually did with tries from the two wingers Etty and Cracknell, neither was converted. Indeed, goal kicking was again proving to be a major problem for Oldham with Rogers unsuccessful with a number of attempts.

1955-56

December 27th 1955: BLACKPOOL B. 9   OLDHAM 5

W.B. Ganley, R. Cracknell, J. Noon, A. Davies, J. Etty, F. Daley, F. Stirrup.
H. Ogden, J. Keith, S. Little, J. Rogers, A. Tomlinson, B. Goldswain.
Goal: Ganley. Try: Cracknell.

Attendance: 4,000 (est.)   Referee: Mr. N. T. Railton – Wigan.

This was no pleasant day-out at the seaside for the Roughyeds, as 'Borough' adapted best to the blustery and rainy conditions to shock their visitors and inflict their third consecutive defeat in what was a miserable Christmas programme. Home full-back, Stan Davies, kicked three penalties and, after a Daley fumble, Fearis kicked ahead for Peace to score a try. Oldham responded with a Cracknell try and a Ganley goal to leave the score 9 – 5 at the interval, and so it remained until the finish. The nearest either team came to adding points in the second half was when Etty just failed to avoid stepping in touch before crossing the try-line.

December 31st 1955: OLDHAM 34   WHITEHAVEN 10

F. Stirrup, R. Cracknell, J. Noon, A. Davies, J. Etty, V. Nestor, F. Pitchford.
H. Ogden, J. Keith, S. Little, J. Rogers, H. Lomas, D. Turner.
Goals: Rogers,5. Tries: Noon,2. Etty,2. Pitchford. Keith. Davies. Nestor.

Attendance: 9,787   Referee: Mr. M. Coates – Pudsey.

Back to winning ways. Whitehaven struggled to cope with the rampant Oldham back division, and the game was wrapped up by the interval, with tries from Noon, Nestor, Etty and a cracker from Pitchford seeing the Roughyeds 20 – 7 in front at the break. Whitehaven's try came just before half time when the Cumbrian forwards combined well to put Robinson over near the posts. Lowden got another for the visitors early in the second half before Oldham got on top once more. Noon and Etty were the pick of the backs and both added a further try in the second half.

January 2nd 1956: WORKINGTON T. 18   OLDHAM 4

F. Stirrup, R. Cracknell, J. Noon, A. Davies, J. Etty, V. Nestor, F. Pitchford.
H. Ogden, J. Keith, H. Lomas, J. Rogers, B. Goldswain, D. Turner.
Goals: Rogers,2.

Attendance: 9,000   Referee: Mr. R. Gelder - Wakefield.

A tough game! Moore and Rogers exchanged penalty goals early on before Southward fashioned a try for Gibson. Edgar converted to leave 'Town' 7 – 2 up at the break. Southward went on to score a couple himself in the second half, which was dominated by the aggressive Cumbrian pack of forwards. Harry Ogden was injured soon after the break and after initially trying to soldier on he left the field after 63 minutes.

This was the last ever appearance for Ogden, who had been a reliable and consistent performer in the Oldham pack since his debut in 1940. He had said two weeks previously that he intended to retire, but would stay until a replacement prop could be secured. The medical report after the match stated that both shoulders were badly injured, and he had also pulled muscles in his chest and back. A tough game!

Harry Ogden

1955-56

January 7th 1956: WHITEHAVEN 29   OLDHAM 13

F. Stirrup, R. Cracknell, J. Noon, A. Kellett, J. Etty, A. Jones, F. Pitchford.
A. Tomlinson, I Carruthers, S. Little, B. Goldswain, J. Watson, F. Daley.
Goals: Goldswain,2. Tries: Noon. Kellett. Etty.
Attendance: 4,000   Referee: Mr. E. Clay - Leeds.

More Cumbrian misery for Oldham, as an under-strength team never came to terms with the home side, and found itself 18 – 0 behind at the interval as a result of two tries for Smith and six goals from McKeown. The cause wasn't helped by the fact that Watson had to leave the fray as early as the 25th minute. Oldham did rally in the second half, with debutant hooker Ian Carruthers doing well in the battle for scrum possession, but the damage was already done.

*A promising debut for hooker, **Ian Carruthers**.*

January 21st 1956: WIDNES 11   OLDHAM 10

F. Stirrup, R. Cracknell, J. Noon, A. Davies, J. Etty, A. Kellett, F. Pitchford.
R. Rowbottom, J. Keith, K. Jackson, S. Little, J. Rogers, D. Turner.
Goals: Rogers,2. Tries: Etty,2.
Attendance: 4,900   Referee: Mr. A. Howgate – Dewsbury.

In the week leading up to this match, Ron Rowbottom had been signed, and he was included to make his debut against his former club. Rogers opened the scoring with a second minute penalty, but soon, after Myler had a try disallowed for a forward pass, Ratcliffe scored in the corner. Etty intercepted to score and regain the lead for Oldham, who were 7 – 6 up at half time. A try from Kemel, converted by Sale, was enough to secure the points for Widnes, although Rowbottom and Davies combined to put Etty in for his second try. The conversion, though, was missed, to leave the Roughyeds a point short.

January 28th 1956: OLDHAM 26   ROCHDALE H. 13

W.B. Ganley, R. Cracknell, J. Noon, A. Davies, J. Etty, F. Daley, F. Stirrup.
R. Rowbottom, J. Keith, K. Jackson, J. Rogers, D. McKeown, D. Turner.
Goals: Ganley,4. Tries: Etty,2. Noon. Cracknell. Rowbottom. Davies.
Attendance: 13,552   Referee: Mr. R. Gelder - Wakefield.

Early penalties from Ganley and Les Jones were the forerunner to Oldham taking control, with tries from Etty, Noon and Cracknell giving them a 15 – 2 lead at the break. In the opening minutes of the second period Etty's second try and one from Rowbottom finished the match as a meaningful contest, before Hornets staged a late rally. One feature of the match was a promising debut for local forward Des McKeown.

Left: The new scoreboard is used for the first time. (28.01.1956)

February 11th 1956: OLDHAM 31   DEWSBURY   2
Rugby League Challenge Cup 1st Round.
W.B. Ganley, R. Cracknell, J. Noon, A. Davies, J. Etty, F. Daley, F. Stirrup.
R. Rowbottom, J. Keith, S. Little, J. Rogers, D. McKeown, D. Turner.
Goals: Ganley,5. Tries: Stirrup,2. Etty. Noon. Davies. Cracknell. Turner.
Attendance: 10,383   Referee: Mr. E. Clay – Leeds.

Dewsbury actually took the lead with a penalty goal from Clark, but from then on it was one-way traffic. Stirrup was first to score, followed by Turner and Noon. Oldham were 15 – 2 ahead at half-time, and Cracknell soon added to the advantage when following his own kick ahead to score. Thereafter Oldham eased comfortably into the next round.

*Above: **Alan Davies** scores the final try with **John Etty** backing up.*
*Left: The ball goes loose with the Dewsbury full-back, **Dave Cox** and **John Etty** in pursuit.   (11.02.1956)*

February 18th 1956: OLDHAM 14   WIGAN 5
W.B. Ganley, R. Cracknell, J. Noon, A. Davies, J. Etty, F. Pitchford, F. Stirrup.
R. Rowbottom, J. Keith, D. Vines, S. Little, D. McKeown, D. Turner.
Goals: Ganley,4. Tries: Stirrup. Rowbottom.
Attendance: 15,137   Referee: Mr. G. Phillips. – Widnes.

After failing with a first minute penalty attempt, Ganley made amends three minutes later with a magnificent effort from all of 50 yards. Ashton soon equalised with a penalty for Wigan, and the game developed into an exciting, attacking confrontation with good play from both sides. A Cherrington break, carried on by Ashcroft, provided the space for Ashton to score in the corner, this try being sandwiched between two more Ganley penalties. Eight minutes from half-time, the ever-alert Stirrup kicked ahead when a ball went loose from a scrum, and he followed up to touch down. This left Oldham 9 – 5 in front at the break. The second half continued to be a good contest, although there was no further score until Ganley kicked his fourth goal six minutes from full time, and Oldham made the points safe when, after a Stirrup interception, some quick handling culminated in Rowbottom crossing in the corner. A good performance by Oldham, with an impressive debut by Don Vines.

*A wonderful array of talent is on view in this photograph as **Alan Davies** prepares to tackle **Billy Boston** with **Dave Bolton**, **Frank Pitchford** and **Eric Ashton** in attendance. (18.02.1956)*

February 25th 1956: FEATHERSTONE R. 14   OLDHAM 4
W.B. Ganley, T. O'Grady, J. Noon, A. Davies, J. Etty, F. Daley, J. Doughty.
R. Rowbottom, J. Keith, K. Jackson, D. McKeown, S. Little, J. Rogers.
Goals: Ganley,2.

Attendance: 5,500   Referee: Mr. C. Appleton – Warrington.

Not the ideal preparation for the cup-tie the following week, as a gritty Featherstone team made Oldham toil playing up the Post Office Road slope in the first half. Ganley gave Oldham an early lead, but a fumbled kick by O'Grady led to a try for Clamp. A good break by Doughty brought some relief, but this was followed by more Rovers pressure that brought a try for Peter Fox near the posts, converted by Fennell. When Lambert also scored in the last minute of the half, the writing was on the wall for the Roughyeds. They fared better in the second period but a Ganley penalty was all they could muster, before a try from Don Fox concluded the scoring.

March 3rd 1956: LEEDS 12   OLDHAM 7
Rugby League Challenge Cup 2nd Round.
W.B. Ganley, R. Cracknell, J. Noon, A. Davies, J. Etty, F. Daley, F. Stirrup.
R. Rowbottom, J. Keith, K. Jackson, S. Little, A. Tomlinson, D. Turner.
Goals: Ganley,2. Try: Davies.

Attendance: 33,000   Referee: Mr. T. Watkinson – Manchester.

Another cup tie at Leeds, and another massive attendance! This was a grand match, with thrilling end-to-end attacking rugby being met by resolute defence from both sides. It was a full 33 minutes before Ganley put Oldham ahead with a penalty. Dunn soon equalised, only for Ganley to re-establish the two-point lead just before half time. After the interval, a superb break from Turner paved the way for Davies to score the opening try, to put the Roughyeds further ahead. Another Dunn penalty reduced the arrears before McClellan and Stevenson forged an opening for Robinson to touch down and bring the scores level. It looked all the way like a draw, a fair result on the balance of play. However, as the match entered the final minute, a break by Poole was carried on by Scholes, and his lofted pass was taken by McClellan, who crossed for the winning score. Dunn converted and to the delight of their massed supporters Leeds were through to the next round!

March 10th 1956: OLDHAM 29   YORK 8
W.B. Ganley, T. O'Grady, A. Davies, J. Noon, J. Etty, F. Stirrup, F. Pitchford.
K. Jackson, J. Keith, D. Vines, S. Little, A. Tomlinson, D. Turner.
Goals: Ganley,7. Tries: Pitchford,2. O'Grady. Noon. Jackson.

Attendance: 10,310   Referee: Mr. G. Wilson – Dewsbury.

Oldham soon got over their cup-tie defeat, and it took just 85 seconds before Davies beat three men before putting in a kick which was gathered by Pitchford for the first try. The tricky scrum-half soon followed this

up with a second try, before he turned provider to send Noon over. 17 – 0 ahead at half time, Oldham coasted through the second half with Pitchford again being the main threat, and it was he who, early in the new half, kicked ahead for O'Grady to finish under the posts. Illingworth and Hansell later crossed for York but Oldham were never in danger.

Frank Pitchford opens the scoring in the second minute of the game with Alan Davies close by. (10.03.1956)

March 17th 1956: OLDHAM 37   BLACKPOOL B. 19

W.B. Ganley, R. Cracknell, J. Edwards, A. Davies, J. Etty, F. Stirrup, F. Pitchford.
K. Jackson, J. Keith, D. Vines, A. Tomlinson, C. Winslade, D. Turner.
Goals: Ganley,5. Tries:Etty,2. Cracknell,2. Pitchford,2. Stirrup. Keith. Turner.
Attendance: 10,016   Referee: Mr. S. Abram - Wigan.

For the second match in a row Oldham were off to a 'flyer', with Etty going over in the first minute after the opening was created by Turner and Pitchford. Despite this early setback Blackpool stuck to their task, and only trailed 13 – 7 at the interval, with ex-Roughyed Peter Fearis scoring a try with two goals from Wally McArthur. This was an incredible effort, as by half-time they were reduced to eleven men through injuries to Davies and Wood. Things were made worse after the break when Lannon also had to retire with an injured shoulder. From this point the numerical advantage began to tell, and Oldham eased to victory,

but the efforts of the beleaguered 'Seasiders' got the crowd on their side, and further tries from Bebe and Fearis were heartily cheered by the Watersheddings faithful.

Left: John Etty scores one of his two tries.

*Below Left: Despite the efforts of Blackpool second-row forward, **Charlie Armitt**, **Frank Stirrup** manages to squeeze over before hitting the corner flag.*

*Below: A debut for St. Helens born centre, **John Edwards** in the match against Blackpool (17.03.1956)*

March 24th 1956: OLDHAM 27   LEIGH 22

W.B. Ganley, R. Cracknell, J. Edwards, A. Davies, J. Etty, F. Stirrup, F. Pitchford.
K. Jackson, J. Keith, D. Vines, S. Little, C. Winslade, D. Turner.
Goals: Ganley,6. Tries: Cracknell. Pitchford. Etty. Little .Davies.
Attendance: 9,663   Referee: Mr. J. Jackson – Barrow.

Cracknell opened the scoring with a try after seven minutes, but Leigh were quick to reply, and tries from Atherton, Baxter and Kindon put them in front before Pitchford replied for Oldham just before half-time. Ganley was having the better of Ledgard in the kicking duties, so the Roughyeds enjoyed a 14 – 13 advantage at half-time. Two quick tries, by Etty and Little, gave Oldham an early boost in the second period, before a further score from Davies put them comfortably clear. Kindon got over again near the end for a Leigh consolation try.

March 30th 1956: SWINTON 7 OLDHAM 6

W.B. Ganley, R. Cracknell, J. Noon, A. Davies, J. Etty, F. Daley, F. Pitchford.
K. Jackson, J. Keith, D. Vines, S. Little, C. Winslade, D. Turner.
Tries: Noon. Etty.

Attendance: 14,500 Referee: Mr. R. Gelder - Wakefield.

The trip to Station Road produced another narrow defeat at the hands of the 'Lions' in the traditional 'Good Friday' fixture. A penalty goal by Tobin after 19 minutes was the only score in the first half. Oldham had gone close when Etty broke clear, only for Keith to put down the final pass, and it took a good tackle by Ganley to bring down Berry, who had intercepted a poor pass from Pitchford. Oldham went ahead in the second period when Davies and Ganley linked up to put Etty over, but the lead was short-lived, as soon a break from the scrum by Haynes produced an opening for Parkinson to score near the posts. Tobin duly converted. The Roughyeds went all out to retrieve the game, and quick thinking by Keith, who took a quick tap-penalty, led to a try by Noon in the corner. However, there was no conversion, and Swinton held on to their one point lead until the end of the match.

George Parkinson: scored the decisive try for Swinton. .

March 31st 1956: OLDHAM 15 LEEDS 12

W.B. Ganley, R. Cracknell, J. Edwards, A. Davies, J. Etty, D. Ayres, F. Pitchford.
K. Jackson, J. Keith, D. Vines, S. Little, C. Winslade, D. Turner.
Goals: Ganley,3. Tries: Etty. Ayres. Davies.

Attendance: 14,000 Referee: Mr. G. Scott. – Doncaster.

Four weeks on from their cup defeat, the Roughyeds were able to exact revenge on Leeds in another closely-fought encounter. Dunn opened the scoring with a penalty goal after 12 minutes, and more Leeds pressure brought a score when Stevenson skipped through the Oldham defence before sending a long pass to Scholes, who went over for an unconverted try. Oldham replied in kind when Edwards sent out a lofted pass to put Etty over. There was no conversion, but a subsequent penalty from Ganley left the scores level at the break. However, it would have been different if a successful penalty attempt by Dunn hadn't been disallowed by the referee because Tomlinson, who was steadying the ball in the windy conditions, was in front of the mark and therefore ruled to be offside. The referee recommenced the game with a scrum. Oldham started better in the second half, and after a great break up the middle by Jackson, Pitchford was on hand to give Davies a try-scoring pass. More pressure followed, and it took a good tackle from Dunn to bundle Cracknell into touch near the try-line. Leeds eventually cracked when Winslade followed his own kick and re-gathered to put Ayres over. A late try from Wilkinson, converted by Dunn, brought the visitors close but Oldham managed to keep them at bay for the last few minutes.

April 2nd 1956: BARROW 23 OLDHAM 9

W.B. Ganley, R. Cracknell, J. Noon, A. Davies, J. Etty, F. Daley, F. Pitchford.
K. Jackson, I. Carruthers, D. Vines, S. Little, D. McKeown, B. Goldswain.
Goals: Ganley,3. Try: Pitchford.

Attendance: 13,275 Referee: Mr. R. Welsby – Warrington.

After early Oldham pressure, when both Cracknell and Davies went close, it was Barrow who opened the scoring when Parker spotted a gap to race through from 15 yards. Horne converted, but two Ganley penalties brought the Roughyeds to within a point. A similar effort from Horne left the score 7 – 4 to the home side at half-time. However, the second half belonged to the 'Furness-men', with four tries, from Johnson, Castle, Rea and Harris, taking the match away from Oldham. Just before the end Pitchford swooped on a loose ball to race in from 50 yards to score a consolation try that was converted by Ganley.

April 14th 1956: OLDHAM 40 ST. HELENS 8

W.B. Ganley, J. O'Brien, J. Noon, A. Davies, J. Etty, F. Stirrup, F. Pitchford.
K. Jackson, I Carruthers, D. Vines, D. McKeown, D. Turner, F. Daley.
Goals: Ganley,8. Tries: Etty,2. Turner,2. Stirrup,2. Vines. Davies.
Attendance: 13,800   Referee: Mr. E. Clay – Leeds.

As good as this result was for the Roughyeds, it should be noted that St. Helens had played a tough Challenge Cup semi-final replay, that went into extra-time, against Barrow in mid-week. Saints had prevailed 10 – 5 after a scoreless first 80 minutes, to progress to the final against Halifax. Despite an early try from Etty, four penalties from Rhodes saw Saints in the lead, until a fine effort from Vines and Turner ended with the Welsh prop going over in the corner. The two tries, along with two Ganley penalties, saw Oldham 10 – 8 in front at the interval. After the break their cup-tie exertions began to take their toll on the visitors, and after Turner broke clear to send Stirrup under the posts after 45 minutes, there was no way back for the weary Saints. Oldham regularly kept the scoreboard ticking over. The match was a personal triumph for local second-row forward, Des McKeown, who was a constant thorn in the side of the visitors on both attack and defence.

*Left: **John Etty** touches down for one of his two tries against St. Helens.*

*Below: **Alan Prescott** and **Frank Stirrup** lead out the teams.*

(14.04.1956)

April 21st 1956: OLDHAM 32   WORKINGTON T. 8

W.B. Ganley, J. O'Brien, J. Noon, A. Davies, J. Etty, F. Stirrup, F. Pitchford.
K. Jackson, I Carruthers, D. Vines, D. Turner, D. McKeown, F. Daley.
Goals: Ganley,4. Tries: Stirrup,2. Turner,2. O'Brien,2. Davies. Noon.
Attendance: 9,800   Referee: Mr. G. Battersby – Barrow.

Oldham finished the season with a flourish, although it was Workington who were first on the attack when Archer beat three men, only to fall to a desperate ankle tap. After this Oldham settled down, and a McKeown break, carried on by Pitchford, led to a try from Davies. This was closely followed by a score from O'Brien at the corner, and when McKeown linked with Turner to put Stirrup under the posts, the game was as good as won. With the score 19 – 0 at the interval, Noon put O'Brien over again four minutes into the new half, and although the Cumbrians rallied enough for Eve and Edgar to score a try each, Oldham never looked in trouble and ran out easy winners.

*Two tries for young winger, **John O'Brien** in the final league match against Workington Town.*

April 24th 1956: Oldham 46   Rochdale H. & Guests 25
Bryn Goldswain Benefit Match.

Oldham:
E. Trumble (Roch), R. Cracknell, J. Hunter (Hud), A. Davies, T. O'Grady, F. Stirrup, F. Pitchford.
K Jackson, J. Sivill (Roch), A. Tomlinson, M. Tierney (Roch), D. Vines, D. Turner.

Rochdale & Guests:
Dyson (Hudd), Buxton, Jones, Short, Unsworth, Taylor, Banks, (Hudd).
Gill, Shaw (Wake), Jarman (Oldham), Goldswain (Oldham), Briggs (Hudd), Valentine (Hudd).
Attendance: 2,844   Referee: Mr. R.L. Thomas – Oldham.

An end-of-season romp in aid of the Bryn Goldswain benefit fund saw Oldham take on Rochdale and 'Guests'. Indeed Oldham also had four guests, three of them from Rochdale, whereas Goldswain himself and Alan Jarman lined up with the Hornets. The visitors were under the captaincy of Huddersfield's Dave Valentine. This was a light-hearted affair which contained a few positional surprises to entertain the crowd. None more so than when in the second half Vines and Tomlinson took O'Grady and Davies' slots in the three-quarters while the two international backs tried their luck in the pack! Oldham won comfortably thanks in no small measure to the seven goals and three tries scored by 'guest' Mel Tierney.

Bryn Goldswain

1955-56

Most Appearances: Jack Keith and John Noon 36 out of a possible 40.
Most tries: John Etty 22.
Most goals: Bernard Ganley 71.
Most points: Bernard Ganley 145.

| **Bernard Ganley** | **John Etty** | **Jack Keith** | **John Noon** |

	1955-56	Played	Won	Draw	Lost	For	Against	Points	%*
1	Warrington	34	27	1	6	712	349	55	80.88
2	Halifax	36	28	2	6	761	306	58	80.55
3	St. Helens	34	27	0	7	776	351	54	79.41
4	Hull	36	25	1	10	720	458	51	70.83
5	Wigan	34	22	2	10	596	402	46	67.64
6	Featherstone R.	36	23	2	11	579	464	48	66.66
7	Barrow	34	21	2	11	676	506	44	64.7
8	Bradford N.	36	22	2	12	622	455	46	63.88
9	**OLDHAM**	**34**	**20**	**0**	**14**	**658**	**455**	**40**	**58.82**
10	Swinton	34	19	2	13	441	373	40	58.82
11	Leigh	34	19	2	13	588	565	40	58.82
12	Leeds	36	21	0	15	698	564	42	58.33
13	York	36	20	0	16	503	472	40	55.55
14	Huddersfield	36	18	1	17	606	544	37	51.37
15	Workington T.	34	17	0	17	532	520	34	50
16	Keighley	36	18	0	18	495	525	36	50
17	Wakefield T.	36	17	0	19	581	539	34	47.22
18	Hunslet	36	17	0	19	511	588	34	47.22
19	Bramley	34	16	0	18	535	605	32	47.05
20	Rochdale H.	34	15	0	19	475	514	30	44.11
21	Whitehaven	34	14	1	19	482	499	29	42.64
22	Salford	34	13	1	20	391	575	27	39.7
23	Widnes	34	11	0	23	403	519	22	32.35
24	Hull K.R.	36	11	1	24	365	747	23	31.94
25	Doncaster	34	7	5	22	349	592	19	27.94
26	Blackpool B.	34	9	0	25	449	745	18	26.47
27	Castleford	36	9	0	27	452	751	18	25
28	Liverpool C.	34	8	0	26	375	685	16	23.52
29	Dewsbury	34	8	0	26	315	700	16	23.52
30	Batley	34	7	1	26	367	645	15	22.05

Due to the withdrawal of Belle Vue Rangers from the league shortly before the start of the season the championship positions were decided on a percentage basis.

1955-56

SEASON	PLAYER	APPS	TRIES	GOALS	POINTS
1955-56	J. NOON	36	14		42
1955-56	J. KEITH	36	5		15
1955-56	S. LITTLE	35	8		24
1955-56	A. DAVIES	32	16	1	50
1955-56	F. STIRRUP	32	11		33
1955-56	F. PITCHFORD	31	17		51
1955-56	R. CRACKNELL	30	16		48
1955-56	J. ROGERS	29	6	50	118
1955-56	J. ETTY	29	22		66
1955-56	D. TURNER	29	8		24
1955-56	F. DALEY	27	4		12
1955-56	H. OGDEN	22	2		6
1955-56	W.B. GANLEY	21	1	71	145
1955-56	B. GOLDSWAIN	20		17	34
1955-56	K. JACKSON	18	1		3
1955-56	T. O'GRADY	14	7		21
1955-56	D. VINES	9	1		3
1955-56	A. TOMLINSON	9			
1955-56	V. NESTOR	8	5		15
1955-56	C. WINSLADE	8	1		3
1955-56	A. KELLETT	8	1		3
1955-56	D. McKEOWN	7			
1955-56	R. ROWBOTTOM	6	2		6
1955-56	R. BARROW	5	3		9
1955-56	I. CARRUTHERS	4			
1955-56	J. EDWARDS	3			
1955-56	J. O'BRIEN	2	2		6
1955-56	A. JONES	2	1		3
1955-56	J. WATSON	2			
1955-56	H. LOMAS	2			
1955-56	NEEDHAM	1	1		3
1955-56	D. AYRES	1	1		3
1955-56	A. MURRAY	1			
1955-56	J. DOUGHTY	1			
1955-56	TOTAL	520	156	139	746

1955-56

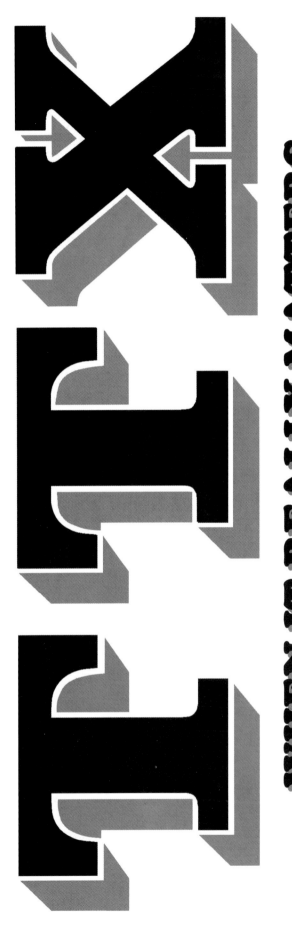

WHEN IT REALLY MATTERS

www.ttexpress.co.uk

1956-57

At last! After a 46 year wait Oldham were the champions of the Rugby League and as well as the obvious delight of the supporters at the honour in itself, it was the way in which it was achieved that made the success all the more memorable. This was a team of entertainers who played an inventive and fluent style of rugby league that endeared itself to the Roughyeds faithful and gained much respect from the other clubs' players, officials and supporters alike.

Major factors were the accuracy of the kicking of Bernard Ganley, who beat his previous record for goals in season by no less than 49 and the try scoring of John Etty whose 43 touchdowns is second only to Reg Farrar's haul of 49 in 1922. Derek Turner's dynamic leadership of the pack from loose-forward, allied to brilliant half-back play from various combinations of Daley, Stirrup and Pitchford gave a solid foundation for the rest of this superbly talented group of players to show off their undoubted skills. It is also interesting to note that no players were sent off during the entire season.

The Lancashire Cup was also won, when St. Helens were defeated in the final at Wigan, as was the Lancashire League. Add to this the fact that the Law Cup was recaptured from Rochdale and the touring Australians were well and truly trounced and you have the most successful season for the club since the halcyon days of the early 1910s. Only the Challenge Cup eluded the Roughyeds with their downfall coming in the second round, in the freezing Leigh mud, on February 23rd 1957.

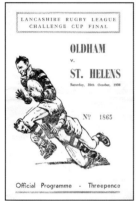  

Bernard Ganley *receives the Rugby League Championship trophy after the narrow victory over Hull at Odsal Stadium, Bradford, on May18th 1957.*

August 11th 1956: Oldham 34 Rochdale H. 5
Law Cup

W.B. Ganley, R. Cracknell, V. Nestor, A. Davies, J. Etty, F. Stirrup, F. Pitchford.
K. Jackson, J. Keith, S. Little, J. Rogers, D. Vines, D. Turner.
Goals: Ganley,5. Tries: Cracknell,3. Turner,2. Keith. Davies. Pitchford.
Attendance: 8,167   Referee: Mr. T. Watkinson – Pendlebury.

Hornets were in the driving seat early on and were unlucky when Smith was brought back for a forward pass from Tierney and then Evans had a try disallowed again when the ball was adjudged to have gone forward. Oldham finally got their act together and Cracknell was the first on the score sheet when he raced over from 45 yards. Ganley converted and from a scrum near the Rochdale line Pitchford and Nestor combined to put the Yorkshire man over again. The first half ended with an 8 – 0 advantage to Oldham and when, early in the second half, a try from Keith was followed by Cracknell completing his 'hat-trick', the Law Cup was always going to end up back in the Watersheddings trophy cupboard.

Jack 'Rubber Legs' Keith touches down for a try early in the second half.

(11.08.1956)

August 18th 1956: OLDHAM 27 BRAMLEY 11

W.B. Ganley, R. Cracknell, V. Nestor, A. Davies, J. Etty, F. Stirrup, F. Pitchford.
K. Jackson, J. Keith, C. Winslade, D. Vines, S. Little, D. Turner.
Goals: Ganley,6. Tries: Cracknell,2. Etty. Keith. Little.
Attendance: 6,611   Referee: Mr. R. Gelder. – Wakefield.

It was a rain-swept Watersheddings that hosted the first league game of the season. Nevertheless, Oldham were off to a flyer with Pitchford breaking through to put Cracknell over in the first minute for a converted try. Bramley, whose team included former Oldham forward 'Smut' Smith, hit back with a penalty from Langfield before Ganley stretched Oldham's lead with three penalty goals. Undeterred the 'Villagers' hit back with Langfield forcing his way over and then converting the try himself and when, two minutes into the second half the same player kicked another penalty goal there was just a two point difference. The Roughyeds finally got back on track with another try from Cracknell and from this point on they coped better with the atrocious conditions to secure the victory aided by an impressive performance from Pitchford.

August 20th 1956: HALIFAX 9   OLDHAM 13
F. Stirrup, R. Cracknell, V. Nestor, A. Davies, J. Etty, D. Ayres, F. Pitchford.
K. Jackson, J. Keith, D. Vines, S. Little, C. Winslade, D. Turner.
Goals: Cracknell,2. Tries: Etty,2. Davies.
Attendance: 15,706   Referee: Mr. C. Appleton – Warrington.

This was a tough, tense, nail-biting affair with the result in doubt right up to the closing seconds. After 11 minutes Pitchford picked up a fumbled pass by Leeming and put in a cross kick that Etty gathered to score. A few minutes later Cracknell added a penalty goal, which was offset by a similar effort by Schofield. Once again a Pitchford kick produced a try, this time for Davies who went over in Freeman's tackle. This put Oldham 8 – 2 up at half-time. A penalty goal for Schofield after 49 minutes reduced the arrears and shortly after this Nestor had to leave the field with a badly damaged shoulder. Halifax were now in the ascendancy and a break through by Ackerley was carried on by Turnbull who in turn transferred to Freeman who avoided Cracknell to score. Schofield converted to give the home side a one point lead. Oldham then commenced to lay siege to the Halifax line and with five minute left Jackson was hauled down just short of the line as was Vines a moment later. Nestor had returned but was little more than a passenger on the wing and unfortunately didn't have the 'legs' to finish off a superb break by Cracknell. Then, with the game moving into the final minute Turner cut clear through the Halifax defence and transferred to Davies who, with the cover closing in, passed back inside to Etty who raced in for the winning score.

August 25th 1956: ROCHDALE H. 0   OLDHAM 43
W.B. Ganley, R. Cracknell, D. Ayres, A. Davies, J. Etty, F. Stirrup, F. Pitchford.
K. Jackson, J. Keith, D. Vines, C. Winslade, S. Little, D. Turner.
Goals: Ganley,8. Tries: Ayres,3. Etty,2. Keith. Stirrup. Pitchford. Turner.
Attendance: 5,639   Referee: Mr. J. Jackson – Barrow.

Ayres was switched from stand-off in the previous match to fill in at centre for the injured Nestor. The wet conditions had transformed the Athletic Grounds into a sea of mud but this did not deter Oldham from turning on the style. However, it wasn't until the 17th minute that Ayres and Keith inter-passed for the former to register the first score. After 24 minutes Oldham exploited the extra man advantage when Unsworth was off injured for Etty to score another try and by half time the lead was stretched to 20 – 0.
To their credit Hornets started the second period well and tested the Roughyeds defence but when, in the 54th minute Turner fielded a Rochdale kick to set up another try for Ayres it was one way traffic with the experiment of switching Ayres to centre a resounding success.

August 28th 1956: OLDHAM 20   LEIGH 0
W.B. Ganley, R. Cracknell, D. Ayres, A. Davies, J. Etty, F. Stirrup, F. Pitchford.
K. Jackson, J. Keith, D. Vines, S. Little, C. Winslade, D. Turner.
Goals: Ganley,4. Tries: Etty. Ayres. Stirrup. Vines.
Attendance: 9,000   Referee: Mr. G. Philpott – Leeds.

The persistent rain of the previous weeks continued and this resulted in defences ruling the roost until the mercurial Frank Stirrup carved open the Leigh defence after 37 minutes. He headed for the touchline but as the cover came across to block off Etty on the wing, he switched direction to give Ayres a clear run to the line. Ganley converted to put the Roughyeds 5 – 0 in front at the break. After 57 minutes Etty capitalised on a dropped ball to kick ahead and dive on the ball for another converted try. After 66 minutes a Ganley penalty stretched the lead and when, straight from a scrum, Stirrup bamboozled the Leigh defence with a dummy and a side-step to score again, the game was up! Vines got over for another in the gathering gloom six minutes from time as Oldham kept a clean sheet for the second game running.

September 1ˢᵗ 1956: WIGAN 16   OLDHAM 18
Lancashire Cup 1ˢᵗ Round.
W.B. Ganley, R. Cracknell, D. Ayres, A. Davies, J. Etty, F. Stirrup, F. Pitchford.
K. Jackson, J. Keith, D. Vines, C. Winslade, S. Little, D. Turner.
Goals: Ganley,3. Tries: Etty,2. Pitchford,2.
Attendance: 28,511   Referee: Mr. G. Scott – Wakefield.

This was a great cup-tie that swung one way and then the other. Cunliffe was just wide with an ambitious penalty attempt from 55 yards in the first minute. Indeed, Wigan were having the best of it early on but that changed when Etty intercepted a pass from Broome to Boston near half way to race away for the first try

and the same player was on hand again a few minutes later to rob Broome of possession and register his second score. Cunliffe kept Wigan in the hunt with three penalty goals but a fine move started by Pitchford and carried on by Ganley and Cracknell finished with the Oldham scrum-half touching down for a converted try to leave the score 6 – 13 to the visitors at half time. The early part of the second half saw a Wigan comeback when first a speculative kick by Ashton was pounced on by Bolton for a converted try and then a break through by Parr was again finished off by the speedy Wigan stand-off. Both tries were converted by Cunliffe to put the home side ahead. Oldham were unlucky when Ayres slipped when he was clear through with the line at his mercy. Then, with four minutes to go the match winner! Pitchford broke through and put Davies on a run to the corner but with the cover closing in Davies passed back inside to his supporting scrum-half and Pitchford sped away to the posts for Ganley to convert and the cup-tie was won.

Above:
Frank Pitchford *avoids the clutches of* ***Dave Bolton*** *to score one of his two tries.*

Left:
Brian McTigue *is brought down by an Oldham player with* ***Bernard Ganley*** *and* ***Alan Davies*** *in attendance.*

(01.09.1956)

September 8th 1956: ST. HELENS 16   OLDHAM 25
W.B. Ganley, R. Cracknell, D. Ayres, A. Davies, J. Etty, F. Stirrup, F. Pitchford.
K. Jackson, J. Keith, D. Vines, S. Little, C. Winslade, D. Turner.
Goals: Ganley,5. Tries: Cracknell,2. Etty,2. Keith.
Attendance: 22,000   Referee: Mr. M. Coates – Pudsey.

The early part of the game belonged to the Saints and in spite of some firm Oldham defence, during which skipper Frank Stirrup made five tackles in succession, the home side took the lead on 13 minutes when Greenall broke through to put Carlton over. After half an hour the Roughyeds took control! First a slick bout of passing saw Etty grounded just short but 'quick hands' sent the ball right across to the other flank where Cracknell went over. Moments later another fine handling movement concluded with Ayres giving Keith the try scoring pass. Just a few seconds before the half time whistle Winslade and Davies paved the way for Etty to score again. Ganley converted the last two scores to leave Oldham 13 – 3 up at the break. Two minutes into the second half Little and Pitchford contrived to send Cracknell over at the posts and the game was as good as won. Saints did rally with tries from Carlton, Silcock and Howard but a further try from Etty in the midst of these always kept Oldham out of reach.

September 11th 1956: SALFORD 0   OLDHAM 31
Lancashire Cup 2nd Round.
W.B. Ganley, R. Cracknell, D. Ayres, A. Davies, J. Etty, F. Stirrup, F. Pitchford.
K. Jackson, J. Keith, D. Vines, S. Little, C. Winslade, D. Turner.
Goals: Ganley,8. Tries: Stirrup,2. Ayres. Ganley. Keith.
Attendance: 13,000   Referee: Mr. G. Wilson – Dewsbury.

Another impressive display as Salford were shut-out at the Willows. The first score came from a set move direct from a scrum from where Ganley came into the attacking line and provided the opening for Ayres to score and not long after the Oldham full-back touched down himself after a flowing passing movement. Salford were unlucky when Walker squeezed over only for the touch judge to rule he had put a foot in touch before grounding the ball. 22 – 0 in front at half time, Oldham continued to dominate in spite of Keith being withdrawn from the hooking position after a third caution for technical infringements. Jackson went to hooker, Little to prop with Keith going into the second row. However, the Oldham striker had the final say when he was on the end of a glorious 100 yard passing movement to score the final try and to add to Salford's woes Ganley landed two long range penalty goals.

September 15th 1956: OLDHAM 19   WAKEFIELD T. 15
W.B. Ganley, R. Cracknell, D. Ayres, A. Davies, J. Etty, F. Stirrup, F. Pitchford.
K. Jackson, J. Keith, A. Tomlinson, S. Little, C. Winslade, D. Turner.
Goals: Ganley,4. Cracknell. Tries: Etty. Keith. Little.
Attendance: 13,778   Referee: Mr. E. Clay – Leeds.

A ninth minute penalty from Ganley was answered by the same from Frank Mortimer five minute later. Bad handling was letting Oldham down but another 40 yard effort from Ganley gave Oldham the lead. They finally cracked the 'Trinity' defence when Turner broke clear, passed on to Davies who got Etty over in the corner. Ganley converted well from the touchline to leave the score 9 – 2 at the break. After the interval Winslade and Little combined to give Keith an easy touch down near the posts and it was Little himself who got over for the third Oldham try. This one was converted by Cracknell who took over the kicking duties from the injured Ganley. To their credit Wakefield did not give up and in the last ten minutes converted tries from Cooper and Froggett made for a tense finish then, when Albert Mortimer scored four minutes from time, the alarm bells began to ring! However, there was no conversion for this try and the Roughyeds managed to hang on for victory.

1956-57

September 19th 1956: LEIGH 9 OLDHAM 18
Lancashire Cup semi-final.

J. Rogers, R. Cracknell, D. Ayres, A. Davies, J. Etty, F. Stirrup, F. Pitchford.
K. Jackson, J. Keith, D. Vines, S. Little, C. Winslade, D. Turner.
Goals: Rogers,2. Cracknell. Tries: Davies,2. Stirrup. Pitchford.
Attendance: 16,000   Referee: Mr. M. Coates – Pudsey.

Oldham objected to playing this match under floodlights and so an early (5.45pm) kick-off was the order of the day. Nevertheless, a good attendance was on hand to see Oldham progress to the Lancashire Cup final. Rogers was at full-back for the injured Ganley and after Ledgard had given Leigh the lead after ten minutes with a penalty, following an altercation between Turner and Martyn, it was the emergency number one who drew the Roughyeds level with a 40 yard effort. There was then a let off for Leigh when Keith lost possession when crossing the line. Another penalty each and tries for Martyn and Davies saw the scores level at half-time. Five minutes into the second period Pitchford scooted away from a scrum before sending a reverse pass to Stirrup who scored for Cracknell to convert. Another try from Davies soon followed and the game was sewn up by a wonderful score when the ball travelled between seven pairs of hands before Pitchford touched down.

Left:
John Etty *crosses the Leigh try line only to be called back for a previous infringement.*

Below Left:
Don Vines *prepares to take a tackle from* **Mick Martyn**.

Below Right:
John Etty *attempts to stop* **Brian Fallon** *from forcing* **Alan Davies** *into touch.*

(19.09.1956)

September 22nd 1956: OLDHAM 45 BARROW 13

J. Rogers, R. Cracknell, D. Ayres, A. Davies, J. Etty, F. Stirrup, F. Pitchford.
K. Jackson, J. Keith, D. Vines, S. Little, C. Winslade, D. Turner.
Goals: Cracknell,5. Rogers. Tries: Ayres,4. Keith,2. Cracknell,2. Davies. Pitchford. Etty.
Attendance: 18,748   Referee: Mr. N. T. Railton – Wigan.

Just three days after their semi-final victory and Oldham served up something really special!
If there was a match that epitomised the open and attractive rugby league played by the Oldham team of this era then this is it! Many, many times when in the company of people recollecting the 1950s side they have mentioned this match as being the best display they have ever seen… and it took just 25 seconds for the magic to begin. Barrow kicked off, Turner fielded the ball which was transferred to Stirrup, Pitchford, Davies and Ayres in turn before the final pass saw Cracknell over the line. Then the same player scored again soon after and converted his own try. Barrow hit back with a penalty from Ball, who also converted a try from Horne to leave them just one point adrift. On 32 minutes Keith bamboozled the Barrow defence to literally walk through and score and a couple from Ayres put Oldham 21 – 7 up at the interval. And so it continued after the break with Ayres going on to score four tries in all. Harris got a couple back for the visitors but a reflection of Oldham's superiority was the fact that 11 tries were scored and only the indifferent goal-kicking of Cracknell and Rogers kept the score down to 45.

After the match the old Oldham player and secretary, Bob Wylie rated the current team as the best ever and visiting captain Willie Horne summed up the Roughyeds performance as "brilliant!"

*Three of the four tries scored by **Dennis Ayres** against Barrow.*

(22.09.1956)

September 29th 1956: LIVERPOOL C. 16   OLDHAM 8

J. Rogers, R. Cracknell, D. Ayres, A. Davies, J. Etty, F. Stirrup, A. Jones.
K. Jackson, J. Keith, D. Vines, A. Tomlinson, C. Winslade, D. Turner.
Goal: Jones. Tries: Turner. Ayres.

Attendance: 2,060   Referee: Mr. J. Manley – Warrington.

It was back to earth with a bump as Oldham suffered their first defeat of the season to lowly Liverpool and all this after the players had paid to get in! Early on Jones hit the upright with a penalty attempt but 'City' scored first when Teggin touched down. Jones pegged back two points with a penalty but this was followed by another score for the 'Merseysiders' by Walsh after a good break by Ashby. Wood converted. Oldham hit back with a try by Ayres after a good break by Turner to leave the score 8 – 5 at half time. Hockenhull opened the second half scoring after good work from his second row partner Greenhough. Wood again added the extras. There was some hope for Oldham when Turner scored with ten minutes to go but Liverpool had the last say when Curran scored after good work from 'man-of-the-match', home scrum-half, Walt Parkes.

The Oldham line up at Liverpool on September 29th 1956.

Back Row:
Don Vines,
John Etty,
Derek Turner,
Jack Rogers,
Ken Jackson,
Charlie Winslade,
Arthur Tomlinson.
Front Row:
Dennis Ayres,
Alan Jones,
Frank Stirrup,
Alan Davies,
Jack Keith,
Dick Cracknell.

October 6th 1956: WIGAN 13   OLDHAM 25

W.B. Ganley, R. Cracknell, D. Ayres, A. Davies, J. Etty, F. Stirrup, F. Pitchford.
K. Jackson, J. Keith, D. Vines, S. Little, C. Winslade, D. Turner.
Goals: Ganley,5. Tries: Cracknell,2. Ayres. Davies. Etty.

Attendance: 27,990   Referee: Mr. H. Harrison – Horbury.

It didn't take long to get over the Liverpool shock and another victory at Central Park was the perfect antidote to the debacle of the previous week. Two penalty goals from Ganley in the first ten minutes put Oldham in front but after a quarter of an hour a break by Bolton paved the way for Boston to score the opening try. Wigan were having the best of it up until the 27th minute when a loose pass from Parr was scooped up by Little who put Cracknell away for a converted try. Next Stirrup dummied his way through to provide Davies with a clear run to the line. Ganley again converted and when Turner and Davies combined to put Etty over just before the break, Oldham went in with a comfortable 5 – 17 advantage. Bolton, who had left the field injured, returned to play on the wing with Ashton moving to stand-off. Boston scored again after intercepting a Davies pass bound for Ayres but this was a temporary set-back before further tries from Ayres and Cracknell re-established Oldham's superiority. However, Boston capped a fine individual performance by completing his 'hat-trick' five minutes from time.

October 8th 1956: Leigh 26   Oldham 12

*Experimental Rules game played at Odsal. This match of two halves of 30 minutes was followed by Bradford N. v Huddersfield.

W.B. Ganley, T. O'Grady, V. Nestor, A. Davies, J. Etty, D. Ayres, J. O'Brien.

K. Jackson, J. Keith, D. Vines, C. Winslade, J. Rogers, D. Turner.

Goals: Ganley,3.   Tries: Winslade. Turner.

Attendance: 3,500 (est.)   Referee: Mr. R. Gelder – Wakefield.

A strange fixture where an experimental rule that had a player having to release the ball when tackled. The ball had then to be played by the foot, from either team, before being re-gathered. This naturally produced a lot of kicking and I'm not sure just how seriously the players took this match but the small crowd made light of the action occasionally making soccer references by shouting 'corner' etc. The experiment was deemed a failure.

October 13th 1956: OLDHAM 27   HALIFAX 6

W.B. Ganley, R. Cracknell, D. Ayres, A. Davies, J. Etty, F. Daley, F. Stirrup.

K. Jackson, J. Keith, D. Vines, S. Little, C. Winslade, D. Turner.

Goals: Ganley,9.   Tries: Little. Stirrup. Keith.

Attendance: 21,449   Referee: Mr. G. Scott – Wakefield.

An amazing match when you consider that Oldham only outscored Halifax by three tries to two but Ganley was on top form and punished any Halifax offence mercilessly with deadly accuracy. In the first half Davies gathered a stray pass to put Little over and the set move from the scrum, that brought Ganley into the attacking line, again paid dividends with Stirrup taking the final pass to score before a Henderson try got Halifax on the scoreboard. So 16 – 3 ahead at the interval, Oldham coasted through the second half no doubt with the following week's cup final in mind. An Ayres break paved the way for Keith to score under the posts while Ganley continued to rack up the penalties before Palmer got a late consolation try for the visitors.

Frank Stirrup stretches over the Halifax line to score despite the despairing tackle of a Halifax defender.

(13.10.1956)

1956-57

October 20th 1956: OLDHAM 10 ST. HELENS 3
Lancashire Cup Final at Central Park – Wigan.
W.B. Ganley, R. Cracknell, D. Ayres, A. Davies, J. Etty, F. Stirrup, F. Pitchford.
K. Jackson, J. Keith, D. Vines, S. Little, C. Winslade, D. Turner.
Goals: Ganley,2. Tries: Etty. Turner.
Attendance: 39,554   Referee: Mr. M. Coates – Pudsey.

Oldham brought back their first major honour for 23 years after this forward dominated game at Central Park. Just under 40,000 spectators bore witness to an often torrid encounter with both packs asking and receiving no quarter from the opposite 'six'. After failing with an early penalty attempt Ganley put Oldham ahead after eight minutes and the lead was stretched when Turner latched on to a poor pass from Gaskell and though held by Moses he managed to throw out a long pass to Etty who scored at the corner. The Roughyeds were well on top and playing the more attractive rugby but the St. Helens defence was up to the task and they hit back when McIntyre broke away from his own 25 yard line and passed out to Carlton. The Saints winger still had plenty to do but he avoided Cracknell and then turned inside Ganley on his way to the line. Only a desperate effort from Pitchford stopped him from going round to the posts. A good 45 yard penalty from Ganley after 30 minutes concluded the first half scoring which saw Oldham go in with a 7 – 3 lead. The second period served up more of the same with Oldham still looking the more likely to score and they were unlucky when Little was brought back for a forward pass when clear after 57 minutes. The nerves were finally eased in the final minute when Pitchford went round the blind side of the scrum and passed on to Turner who crashed over. The try wasn't converted but Oldham had done enough.

Top Left: John Etty scores the first try.
Top Right: The last minute clincher from Derek Turner.
Above: Frank Stirrup receives the cup...
Left: ... and is carried shoulder high through the Oldham fans.
(20.10.1956)

1956-57

October 27th 1956: OLDHAM 19 KEIGHLEY 5
W.B. Ganley, R. Cracknell, D. Ayres, A. Davies, T. O'Grady, F. Stirrup, F. Pitchford.
K. Jackson, I. Carruthers, D. Vines, S. Little, C. Winslade, D. Turner.
Goals: Ganley,5. Tries: Turner. Pitchford. Cracknell.
Attendance: 13,478   Referee: Mr. E. Clay - Rothwell.

Overall this was a low key performance from the Roughyeds who, although never in danger of losing the match, never really showed the flowing play that was now expected of them. They started well enough when a kick from Taylor was charged down by Davies who gathered up the ball to put Turner over for a converted try. Hollindrake pulled back a penalty for Keighley and it took a last ditch tackle from Cracknell to prevent Crewdson from scoring after a 70 yard break. A couple of penalties from Ganley and an opportunist try from Pitchford after Crewdson had lost possession pushed Oldham further ahead before a

breakaway from Brown led to a try from Lowe just before the interval which saw Oldham 14 – 5 to the good. The second half was a drab affair with a penalty from Ganley after 55 minutes and a late try from Cracknell, after Pitchford had broken straight from a scrum, the only additions to the score-line.

John Etty and Jack Keith parade the Lancashire Cup before the match against Keighley.
The two Yorkshire men were rested after the gruelling final against St. Helens the previous Saturday but took their place on the team photo below.   (27.10.1956)

Back Row: J. Etty, G. Jenkins (coach), D. Vines, I. Carruthers, K. Jackson, D. Turner, S. Little, C. Winslade, J. Keith, W Howard (pres). Middle Row: W.B. Ganley, R. Cracknell, F. Stirrup, A. Davies, T. O'Grady. Front Row: D. Ayres, mascot, F. Pitchford.

November 3rd 1956: WORKINGTON T. 7   OLDHAM 5

W.B. Ganley, R. Cracknell, J. Noon, A. Davies, J. Etty, F. Stirrup, F. Pitchford.
K. Jackson, J. Keith, D. Vines, S. Little, C. Winslade, D. Turner.
Goal: Ganley. Try: Pitchford.
Attendance: 10,012   Referee: Mr. G. Wilson – Dewsbury.

This was a tough encounter which, despite the close score, saw the Cumbrians in the ascendancy for nearly all of the game. Workington attacked right from the start and it took Oldham all their time just to get out of their own half. Stan Thompson scored the first points with a penalty after Noon was caught offside and repeated the dose when Pitchford was pulled up for 'feeding' his own forwards at the scrum. However, after half an hour the Oldham number seven made amends when he took the 'Town' defence by surprise by using Stirrup as a foil to go over straight from a scrum. Workington struck back and an Ivill cross-kick deceived Stirrup and Cracknell for Herbert to score. Only 7 – 3 at half time, Oldham were fortunate to be only four points down but in the second half it was more of the same with Workington again being the dominant force. It took a great defensive effort to keep them out but the Roughyeds were up to the task and when a loose ball was kicked ahead only the speedy Southward denied Davies from scoring a vital try. Ganley landed a penalty with seven minutes still to go, but that was the final score.

A full account of all the Oldham matches against the touring teams can be found in the book "Kangaroos, Kiwis and Roughyeds".

November 7th 1956: OLDHAM 21   AUSTRALIA 2

W.B. Ganley, T. O'Grady, D. Ayres, A. Davies, J. Etty, F. Stirrup, F. Pitchford.
K. Jackson, J. Keith, D. Vines, S. Little, C. Winslade, D. Turner.
Goals: Ganley,6. Tries: Pitchford. Etty. Turner.
Attendance: 8,956   Referee: Mr. T. Watkinson - Pendlebury.

The match opened up with the usual vigorous exchanges with the two loose-forwards Derek Turner and Kel O'Shea making the biggest impression. It was an error from Connell that produced the first score of the match. After the visitors' scrum-half had spilled the ball, O'Grady was on to it in a flash, kicking ahead and giving chase along with Turner. Clive Churchill appeared to have the situation covered but as the two Oldham men advanced, he misjudged the bounce of the ball and with all three of them scrambling on the ground up popped Pitchford to ground the ball for a try. Ganley added the goal to give Oldham a five point advantage after just six minutes. Oldham were playing well but it was Turner who was giving the Kangaroos the most trouble. Both Ganley and Churchill (twice) were off target with penalty attempts until, just after the half hour mark, the visitors were penalised at the scrum and this time Ganley was on target and then landed another to give an interval score: Oldham 9 Australia 0.

Within a minute of the restart the Australians were again pulled up for rough play and up stepped Ganley to again put the ball over the bar. There was no let-up from Oldham who took the game away from the tourists with a sparkling try two minutes later. O'Grady started the move with a cross-field run from his own quarter. Turner was on hand to take the ball and put in a precision kick ahead which Stirrup took on the first bounce to speed away towards the visitors' line. The cover managed to get to him but a slick pass just before he was grounded gave Etty a chance to beat off the last shreds of defence to run in at the corner. At least the Kangaroos were dominating the scrum possession and eventually got on the scoreboard when Oldham were caught offside and Connell put over a penalty. However, the effort was nullified almost immediately when, after another Australian indiscretion in the tackle, Ganley thumped the ball home from fully fifty yards. Thanks to their scrum monopoly, the Aussies kept battering at the Oldham line only to be met with tremendous defence from the Oldham pack. As the match drifted towards full-time the Aussies looked well and truly beaten. Only Connell, who ran himself to a standstill, Watson and the ever impressive O'Shea looked up for the task. It was fitting that the last say went to the 'man of the match'! Turner had caused the tourists much concern right from the start and after he had weaved his way through the tiring defence and kicked ahead he was tackled from behind, whereupon referee Watkinson promptly pointed for an obstruction try. Ganley converted to leave Oldham comfortable winners

Above:
Alex Watson *tries to avoid the tackle of*
John Etty

Left:
Derek Turner, Terry O'Grady *and* **Clive Churchill** *watch as the ball goes loose before Frank Pitchford (out of picture) raced up to score.*

Below:
John Etty *touches down after good play from* **Frank Stirrup** *(grounded) and* **Derek Turner** *(extreme right).*

(07.11.1956)

November 10th 1956: OLDHAM 7   WORKINGTON T. 2

W.B. Ganley, R. Cracknell, D. Ayres, A. Davies, J. Etty, F. Stirrup, F. Pitchford.

S. Little, I Carruthers, D. Vines, C. Winslade, F. Daley, D. Turner.

Goals: Ganley,2. Try: Pitchford.

Attendance: 11,520   Referee: Mr. G. Philpott – Leeds.

One week on from their defeat at Workington and just three days after that magnificent triumph over the Australian tourists, Oldham were able to exact revenge on the Cumbrians in another tough, close-fought encounter. The only try of the game went to Pitchford with stand-in, second-row man, Frank Daley putting in a marvellous defensive display and Vines also prominent. The players commented that this was their toughest match of the season so far.

November 17th 1956: KEIGHLEY 15   O LDHAM 32

W.B. Ganley, R. Cracknell, D. Ayres, V. Nestor, J. Etty, F. Stirrup, F. Pitchford.

K. Jackson, J. Keith, D. Vines, S. Little, D. Turner, F. Daley.

Goals: Ganley,7. Tries: Etty,2. Little. Pitchford. Cracknell. Daley.

Attendance: 7,587   Referee: Mr. C. Appleton – Warrington.

This was an open game from both teams from the outset and was befitting of Keighley's best attendance of the season to date. It was another competent performance from the Roughyeds. The versatile Daley, this time switched with Turner to occupy the loose-forward slot. Etty chipped in with a brace of tries and the in-form Ganley put over seven goals.

November 21st 1956: BARROW 27   OLDHAM 11

F. Stirrup, R. Cracknell, V. Nestor, J. Etty, J. O'Brien, D. Ayres, F. Pitchford.

K. Jackson, J. Keith, D. Vines, C. Winslade, A. Jarman, D. Turner.

Goal: Cracknell. Tries: O'Brien. Nestor. Etty.

Attendance: 6,650   Referee: Mr. E. Clay – Leeds.

An under strength team made the trip to Barrow for this match rearranged from the original date which had coincided with the Lancashire Cup Final. Ganley, Davies, Little and Daley were all unable to travel and although Barrow were always on top, Oldham gave it a 'good go' scoring three tries in the process though with Ganley absent only one goal was scored by Cracknell.

November 24th 1956: OLDHAM 60   BLACKPOOL B. 8

F. Stirrup, R. Cracknell, D. Ayres, A. Davies, J. Etty, A. Kellett, F. Pitchford.

K. Jackson, J. Keith, D. Vines, C. Winslade, S. Little, D. Turner.

Goals: Cracknell,9. Tries: Etty,3. Turner,3. Pitchford,2. Winslade. Kellett. Cracknell. Ayres.

Davies. Keith. Attendance: 8,971   Referee: Mr. N. Railton – Wigan.

The Roughyeds were back to winning ways with a bang in this romp against the 'Seasiders' who included three ex-Roughyeds in their line-up; Emmitt, Fearis and Mundy. Fourteen tries tells its own story with Etty passing the 'twenty for the season' mark with a 'hat-trick' of touchdowns well supported by Turner who also scored three tries. Ganley's absence did not really matter this time as Cracknell managed to hit the mark nine times.

John Etty completes his 'hat-trick' against Blackpool.
(24.11.1956)

1956-57

December 1st 1956: OLDHAM 34   YORK 12
W.B. Ganley, R. Cracknell, D. Ayres, V. Nestor, J. Etty   F. Stirrup, F. Pitchford.
K. Jackson, J. Keith, D. Vines, C. Winslade, S. Little, F. Daley.
Goals: Ganley,8. Tries: Pitchford. Etty. Daley. Stirrup. Nestor. Little.
Attendance: 8,954   Referee: Mr. A. E. Durkin – Dewsbury.

In spite of Davies and Turner being away on Test duty, Oldham once again secured a convincing victory! However, the score-line somewhat flattered the Roughyeds for York played some enterprising and entertaining rugby before the dominance of the home team came to the fore. Ganley marked his return with eight superb goals as the back division, ably marshalled by Pitchford and Stirrup, eventually proved too much for the 'Minster-men'.

December 8th 1956: OLDHAM 9   ST. HELENS 8
W.B. Ganley, R. Cracknell, D. Ayres, A. Davies, J. Etty, F. Stirrup, F. Pitchford.
K. Jackson, J. Keith, D. Vines, S. Little, C. Winslade, D. Turner.
Goals: Ganley,3. Try: Jackson.
Attendance: 16,671   Referee: Mr. J. Jackson – Barrow.

Although St. Helens scored two tries to Oldham's one, it was the Roughyeds who claimed the points thanks to three goals from Ganley. Jackson scored Oldham's try after good work by Davies and Etty and was just reward for the hard-working prop who had made a grand break just minutes earlier. Ganley converted and added two first-half penalty goals. Prescott and Finan paved the way for Steve Llewellyn to touchdown for St. Helens and a 32nd minute penalty from Rhodes left the score 9 – 5 at the break. Three minutes into the second period a loose ball was hacked on for Dickinson to follow up and score but those were the last points of the match which developed into a tense defensive struggle.

Dennis Ayres is collared by *Vince Karalius* with *Frank Carlton* on hand if required.   (08.12.1956)

193

December 15th 1956: WAKEFIELD T. 18   OLDHAM 20
W.B. Ganley, R. Cracknell, V. Nestor, D. Ayres, J. Etty, F. Stirrup, F. Pitchford.
K. Jackson, J. Keith, A. Jarman, J. Rogers, C. Winslade, F. Daley.
Goals: Ganley,4. Tries: Cracknell,3. Pitchford.
Attendance: 4,909   Referee: Mr. D. Davies – Manchester.

Oldham went into this match with Little, Turner and Davies on Test duty but opened brightly with a Ganley penalty after three minutes, closely followed by Rogers flicking out a pass to Cracknell who raced away to score from fifty yards. Ganley converted but missed a second effort a few minutes later after Cracknell again scored following good work by Winslade and Nestor. After 15 minutes home scrum-half Bullock forced his way over with the score converted by a young Neil Fox. He followed this up with a penalty before an unconverted try from Houlden left the scores level at the interval. Cracknell completed his 'hat-trick' early in the second half. There was no conversion but Ganley made amends with a fifty yard penalty soon after. 'Trinity' responded when Smith followed a kick from Holliday to score, again converted by Fox and a frantic spell of action finished with Houlden again capitalising on a cross-kick, this time from Fox, to touch down. However, the Roughyeds were not to be denied and when Cracknell was hauled down just short the ball was swiftly moved across the field and Pitchford took it at pace to score. Ganley added the extras and Oldham were home and dry.

December 22nd 1956: WARRINGTON 12   OLDHAM 2
W.B. Ganley, R. Cracknell, V. Nestor, A. Davies, J. Etty, F. Daley, F. Pitchford.
K. Jackson, J. Keith, A. Jarman, S. Little, C. Winslade, D. Turner.
Goal: Ganley.
Attendance: 8,700   Referee: Mr. A. Howgate – Dewsbury.

In a tight first half chances were few and far between, Cracknell did well to catch Gilfedder from behind after the Warrington man eluded Ganley and the same player was brought back moments later for a forward pass. Next it was Oldham's turn to be denied by the officials with Ganley having a try ruled out, again for a forward pass. However, he did register the first score with a penalty after 36 minutes. The turning point of the game came just before the break when Davies appeared to get over the line but was adjudged to have lost the ball in a crunching tackle which left him injured and unable to re-start in the second half. The 'Wire' were soon ahead after the interval when Naughton put Bevan over for Bath to convert. Still struggling with his injury, Davies came back on the field but was placed on the wing and Warrington made the game safe with a Bath penalty and conversion after Price and Bevan had combined to set up a try for Challinor.

December 29th 1956: WIDNES 7   OLDHAM 28
W.B. Ganley, R. Cracknell, V. Nestor, D. Ayres, J. Etty, F. Stirrup, F. Pitchford.
K. Jackson, J. Keith, D. Vines, C. Winslade, S. Little, D. Turner.
Goals: Ganley,5. Tries: Etty,2. Stirrup. Cracknell. Pitchford. Turner.
Attendance: 6,000   Referee: Mr. N. Railton – Wigan.

Widnes opened brightly with Dawson held just short before Oldham took the lead after Ayres was first to react to a loose ball which he gathered up to give Etty a run in at the corner. De Witt replied with a try converted by Dawson but the Roughyeds were looking the stronger team. After, first, Vines put Stirrup over closely followed by Jackson sending Pitchford through for converted tries, Oldham looked comfortable with a 13 – 5 half-time lead. Dawson kicked an early penalty but that was as good as it got for the 'Chemics' as three more tries without reply finished the match off. The pick of these was a fifty yard dash by Turner after the opening was created by Stirrup and Pitchford.

January 1st 1957: BLACKPOOL B. 7   OLDHAM 15

W.B. Ganley, R. Cracknell, J. Edwards, D. Ayres, J. Etty, F. Stirrup, F. Pitchford.

K. Jackson, J. Keith, D. Vines, S. Little, J. Rogers, D. Turner.

Goals: Ganley,3. Tries: Rogers. Ayres. Etty.

Attendance: 3,000   Referee: Mr. T. Watkinson – Manchester.

This was a rousing display from Blackpool in blustery conditions at St. Annes Road. An eighth minute try from Fearis made by Grundy was converted by Stan Davies before a Ganley penalty reduced the arrears. On 19 minutes Ayres and Etty carved open a space for Rogers to go over. Davies landed a penalty a few minutes later and Ganley did likewise before Ayres completed the first-half scoring with an unconverted try. The second half was a tight affair and a shock looked on the cards when McArthur sped away past Cracknell only to fall to a fantastic ankle-tap tackle by Stirrup which put the Blackpool flyer into touch. Six minutes from time Pitchford broke through the middle and Ayres carried on the move to give Etty the score which, added to Ganley's conversion, settled the nerves for the last few minutes.

January 5th 1957: OLDHAM 5   HUNSLET 2

W.B. Ganley, R. Cracknell, A. Davies, D. Ayres, J. Etty, F. Stirrup, F. Pitchford.

K. Jackson, J. Keith, D. Vines, S. Little, C. Winslade, D. Turner.

Goal: Ganley. Try: Etty.

Attendance: 10,360   Referee: Mr. R. Gelder – Wakefield.

"A grim battle in the mud". This was how the 'Green Final' sports paper described this match when the conditions and state of the Watersheddings pitch made for a minimum of open play. The only try came midway through the first half when Stirrup sent a cross-kick into the Hunslet 25 yard area, Etty was the first to react and on reaching the ball he hacked it on again and then won the race to touch down for Ganley to convert. The score remained 5 – 0 at half-time with the only addition being a penalty goal from Hunslet full-back Billy Langton after 58 minutes although Poole looked set to score when breaking clear only to fall to a tremendous tackle from Ganley.

January 12th 1957: OLDHAM 17   SALFORD 3

W.B. Ganley, T. O'Grady, A. Davies, D. Ayres, J. Etty, F. Stirrup, F. Pitchford.

K. Jackson, J. Keith, S. Little, C. Winslade, J. Rogers, F. Daley.

Goals: Ganley,4. Tries: O'Grady. Rogers. Jackson.

Attendance: 12,036   Referee: Mr. G. Philpott - Leeds.

Once again it was a heavy pitch that greeted the teams and it took until the 23rd minute for the first try after Ganley had opened the scoring with a 45 yard penalty goal. The try came from Rogers who latched on to a Stirrup pass to crash over. Ganley converted this and also six minutes later when O'Grady went in after

good work from Daley and Pitchford. The score remained at 12 - 0 until the interval, after which Salford enjoyed their best spell of the game in the early part of the second period and they registered a try when Moses and Keavney paved the way for Ayles to score. Oldham hit back with the impressive Rogers and Etty setting up a try for Jackson which Ganley converted to conclude the scoring.

John Etty and *Dennis Ayres,*
on the move.

January 19th 1957: WHITEHAVEN 9   OLDHAM 15

W.B. Ganley, T. O'Grady, A. Davies, D. Ayres, J. Etty, F. Daley, F. Pitchford.
K. Jackson, J. Keith, S. Little, J. Rogers, C. Winslade, D. Turner.
Goals: Ganley,3. Tries: Etty,2. Jackson.

Attendance: 5,000   Referee: Mr. A. E. Durkin – Dewsbury.

At the ninth attempt, Oldham finally gained a victory up at Whitehaven. However, it was another close affair with McKeown giving the home side the lead with a penalty after failing with two earlier attempts. Ganley equalised and although the Cumbrians had most of the play, the score remained level at the break. Oldham came out with renewed vigour in the second half and after Ganley was put into touch just short following good work from Daley and Turner, the scrum was won and Davies and Ayres combined to put Etty over in the corner. A penalty from McKeown in the 53rd minute was cancelled out by a similar effort from Ganley a minute later and the match was made safe when the mercurial Pitchford laid on tries for Jackson and Etty. Whitehaven did manage a late try from Smith but it wasn't enough and the Recreation Ground hoodoo was finally broken.

January 26th 1957: OLDHAM 18   WARRINGTON 0

W.B. Ganley, R. Cracknell, V. Nestor, D. Ayres, J. Etty, F. Stirrup, F. Pitchford.
K. Jackson, J. Keith, A. Tomlinson, J. Rogers, C. Winslade, F. Daley.
Goals: Ganley,6. Tries: Ayres. Nestor.

Attendance: 14,100   Referee: Mr. M. Coates – Pudsey.

Bevan was missing from the Warrington line-up but it is unlikely that he would have made up the difference as Oldham coasted to victory on the back of some superb kicking from Ganley. Gilfedder missed two early penalty chances to score before Ganley showed how it was done in the third minute. It took half an hour for the first try when the in-form Pitchford put Ayres clear to score. Ganley converted and had landed a further three penalties by the interval. Pitchford was mesmerising the 'Wire' defence and after nearly putting Etty over, he opened up the Warrington defence again for Nestor to go in for the clinching try converted by the irrepressible Ganley.

February 2nd 1957: SALFORD 3   OLDHAM 27

W.B. Ganley, R. Cracknell, A. Davies, D. Ayres, J. Etty, V. Nestor, F. Pitchford.
K. Jackson, J. Keith, S. Little, C. Winslade, J. Rogers, D. Turner.
Goals: Ganley,3. Tries: Nestor,2. Little. Keith. Turner. Ayres. Cracknell.

Attendance: 14,000   Referee: Mr. C. Whiteley – Ossett.

On the back of their run of success, Oldham took a huge following to the Willows and the large support were soon cheering on their favourites as the Roughyeds went on the attack from the first whistle. Winslade was in great form and after just two minutes he had paved the way for Little to score and followed it up by laying on another try for Keith with only eight minutes on the clock. Salford followed this up with a spell of attacking but the Roughyeds held firm and by half-time were 16 – 0 in front with a further two tries from Nestor. Seven minutes into the second period the home side got on the scoreboard when Keavney and Moses combined to put Garlick in for an unconverted try, but that was as good as it got for the 'Red Devils' who failed to hold the Oldham forwards which was exemplified by Turner scoring despite the attention of four defenders. None of the Roughyeds pack played better than ex-Salford player Jack Rogers.

Before the match the Oldham players sent a telegram to Terry O'Grady wishing him well in his debut match for Wigan against Whitehaven.

February 9th 1957: WORKINGTON T. 5   OLDHAM 14
Rugby League Challenge Cup 1st Round.
W.B. Ganley, R. Cracknell, A. Davies, D. Ayres, J. Etty, F. Daley, F. Pitchford.
K. Jackson, J. Keith, S. Little, J. Rogers, C. Winslade, D. Turner.
Goal: Ganley. Tries: Etty,3. Daley.

Attendance: 10,507   Referee: Mr. R. Gelder – Wakefield.

Four thousand Oldhamers made the long trip to Cumbria for this cup-tie and were rewarded with a fine performance. Workington had most of the early pressure which culminated in a failed penalty attempt by Thompson. Eventually Oldham got back into the game with Ayres and Davies both making breaks that took them deep into the Workington half and from this position Daley and Ayres paved the way for Etty to cross in the corner. After 27 minutes a fine pass from Iveson put Southward clear and the international winger made light of the heavy conditions to race away for a try converted by Thompson. Workington continued to dominate but just four minutes from the interval Etty broke clear and although held just short of the line, a quick play-the-ball saw Pitchford pass out to Daley who dummied his way over from close

range. So Oldham led 5 – 6 at the break and never looked back thanks in no small measure to Etty who was in fine form and added two more tries to clinch victory.

*Workington prop-forward, **Duggie Holland** loses possession in a double tackle by **Charlie Winslade** and **Sid Little**. **Jack Keith** scoops up the ball, with **Ken Jackson** and **Derek Turner** on hand if required.   (09.02.1957)*

February 16th 1957: OLDHAM 25   WIDNES 10
W.B. Ganley, R. Cracknell, A. Davies, D. Ayres, J. Etty, F. Daley, F. Stirrup.
A. Tomlinson, J. Keith, S. Little, C. Winslade, J. Rogers, D. Turner.
Goals: Ganley,5. Tries: Etty,2. Davies. Cracknell. Stirrup.

Attendance: 10,372   Referee: Mr. J. H. Chadwick – Batley.

This match, played with a covering of snow on the pitch, was the proverbial game of two halves with Widnes being on top for much of the first period with Dawson fashioning tries for Owen and Ratcliffe and adding a penalty goal. A Ganley penalty was the only reply as the 'Chemics' went in 8 – 2 to the good. Worse still for Oldham was the fact that Rogers was stretchered off with torn ligaments before the break,

an injury that finished his Oldham career. Whatever was said at half time did the trick and despite being a man short, early tries from Etty and Davies set the Roughyeds on their way. Widnes never got a look in and were well beaten by the time Stirrup concluded the scoring just before full-time.

*Frank Stirrup avoids the Widnes cover to score the final try.
(16.02.1957)*

February 23rd 1957: LEIGH 5   OLDHAM 0
Rugby League Challenge Cup 2nd Round.

W.B. Ganley, R. Cracknell, D. Ayres, A. Davies, J. Etty, F. Stirrup, F. Pitchford.
K. Jackson, J. Keith, S. Little, C. Winslade, D. Turner, F. Daley.
Attendance: 18,000   Referee: Mr. M. Coates – Pudsey.

According to the press in the build up to the game, Oldham would play Frank Stirrup at stand off in good conditions and Frank Daley if the going was heavy. Somewhere along the line there was a change of heart and when Oldham took the field Stirrup was leading the side from No 6 and Daley, wearing the No 13 shirt, played in the second row with Derek Turner in the No 12 shirt at loose forward? Daley being preferred to Arthur Tomlinson in the pack was a strange decision given the prevailing conditions. As the score would suggest, the match was defence dominated with Oldham's best spell coming early on when Cracknell was tackled into touch just short of the try line. Hosking gave Leigh what seemed like an insignificant lead with a fourth minute penalty. Stirrup, although already suffering from the severe cold, was in good form and created an opening for Etty who was again stopped just short. Ganley had a shot at goal from half way that fell away inches before the posts, but when a penalty much nearer the posts was awarded later, Stirrup (on coach, Jenkins instruction) elected to kick for position. There were some heated exchanges in the forwards that culminated in Turner and Martyn having their names taken after 35 minutes. The first half closed with Leigh hanging on to their two point advantage. The first action of the second half set the scene for the whole 40 minutes. Leigh kicked off and indecision within the Oldham ranks allowed home forward Stan Owen to gather the ball. With the rules of the time allowing unlimited possession, Leigh put their good fortune to maximum effect and it would be almost 20 minutes before Oldham got to grips with the ball. By this time the defensive stint had taken its toll physically and mentally, with the Oldham backs particularly, exhausted. After 60 minutes Owen, who was always in the thick of the action, had a try disallowed for a double movement. As Leigh continued their stranglehold in the Oldham half, Charlie Winslade stood out in the Oldham ranks and played with fierce determination from first to last, but overall the Leigh 'six' had the upper hand. Ten minutes from time Pitchford was carried off, suffering from the effects of the cold, but he returned a few minutes later. Then Stirrup collapsed and was taken off after being wrapped in a blanket. Just when it seemed that the one goal would be enough, Leigh put the game beyond doubt when Owen scrambled over for a try with three minutes to go. The conversion was missed but Oldham, demoralised and dejected, were out of the cup.

Stan Owen *dives through a dejected Oldham defence for the clinching score in the 77th minute.*
(23.02.1957)

March 2ⁿᵈ 1957: OLDHAM 56   LIVERPOOL C. 5

W.B. Ganley, R. Cracknell, V. Nestor, D. Ayres, J. Etty, W. Riley, F. Pitchford.
K. Jackson, J. Keith, A. Tomlinson, C. Winslade, R. Bailey, F. Daley.
Goals: Ganley,13.   Tries: Ayres,3. Cracknell,2. Etty. Winslade. Keith. Bailey. Nestor.

Attendance: 11,279   Referee: Mr. H. Harrison – Horbury.

Maybe it was just what was needed after the cup-tie defeat but the unfortunate Liverpool felt the full force of Oldham's backlash. A debut was given to second rower Reg Bailey and also to Bill Riley on trial from Batley. Ganley gave Oldham the lead with a fourth minute penalty with Riley making an inauspicious start when spilling an early pass. However, he soon made up for the error by putting Ayres clear on a 50 yard run to the line. After this the Roughyeds coasted home and hit the fifty point mark with fourteen minutes

still to play. Ayres claimed a hat-trick and Bailey scored a debut try but there would be much stiffer obstacles ahead as all the energies were now focused on the chase for the championship title.

Another good day for
***W.B.** !*

March 9ᵗʰ 1957: YORK 28   OLDHAM 4

W.B. Ganley, R. Cracknell, A. Davies, D. Ayres, J. Etty, V. Nestor, F. Pitchford.
K. Jackson, J. Keith, S. Little, C. Winslade, R. Bailey, D. Turner.
Goals: Ganley,2.

Attendance: 6,057   Referee: Mr. G. Battersby – Barrow.

There are no other words for it other than Oldham were outplayed by an enthusiastic York outfit who took the game to the Roughyeds right from the first whistle. Indeed, in the early exchanges Webster was unlucky to have a try disallowed for a forward pass but it was a brief respite as soon Robinson was putting Gordon Smith over for Dickinson to convert. A few minutes later and the same player was over again for another converted try. Oldham finally gained some time in the York half and Ganley opened the account with a penalty. Keith then has a try disallowed for a forward pass before Ganley landed his second goal after 18 minutes. Eight minutes later Webster won the race to a kick ahead from Brian Smith to give the 'Minster-men' a 13 -4 advantage at the interval. In the first minute of the second half Pitchford put Ayres clear but Etty over-ran the centre and the chance was lost and from there York took full command. Ganley had to retire with a facial injury with a quarter of an hour still to go but by that time the match was gone. The final try came from home second-row man, Hansell who ran 80 yards after latching on to a wayward pass from Turner.

March 16th 1957: OLDHAM 28   WHITEHAVEN 5

W.B. Ganley, R. Cracknell, V. Nestor, A. Davies, J. Etty, W. Riley, F. Pitchford.
K. Jackson, J. Keith, A. Tomlinson, C. Winslade, S. Little, D. Turner.
Goals: Ganley,5. Tries: Turner,3. Cracknell,2. Winslade.

Attendance: 8,000   Referee: Mr. A. Howgate – Dewsbury.

It was an under-strength Whitehaven, who had obviously rested players in view of their forthcoming Challenge Cup semi-final against Leeds, that nevertheless put in a sterling first-half performance at Watersheddings. Although Oldham had the better of the first period, they only led 4 – 2 thanks to two Ganley penalties after McKeown had given the Cumbrians an early lead. After the break Oldham set to their task in style with the forwards bossing the show. Winslade crashed over early in the second half and Turner chipped in with two in two minutes to complete his 'hat-trick', ten minutes from time in spite of the attentions of several Whitehaven defenders.

March 23rd 1957: BRAMLEY 6   OLDHAM 31

W.B. Ganley, R. Cracknell, V. Nestor, D. Ayres, J. Etty, F. Daley, F. Stirrup,.
K. Jackson, J. Keith, A. Tomlinson, C. Winslade, S. Little, D. Turner.
Goals: Ganley,5. Tries: Ayres,2. Turner. Keith. Nestor. Etty. Winslade.

Attendance: 7,000   Referee: Mr. R. Welsby – Warrington.

Another indifferent first half showing saw Bramley 4 – 3 up at the break thanks to two penalties from Wilson set against another crash-over try from Turner, although in another incident Ayres was unlucky to lose the ball in the act of scoring. Once again it was the forwards who rose to the occasion after the break. Ganley put Oldham in front with an early penalty then Turner carved out an opening for Winslade to score, followed by Jackson doing likewise for Keith to finish the move. From this point there was no stopping the Oldham momentum.

Alan Davies avoids Norman Cherrington for the match clinching try.   *(30.03.1957)*

March 30th 1957: OLDHAM 14   WIGAN 6

W.B. Ganley, R. Cracknell, V. Nestor, D. Ayres, A. Davies, F. Daley, F. Pitchford.
K. Jackson, J. Keith, D. Vines, S. Little, C. Winslade, D. Turner.
Goals: Ganley,4. Tries: Davies. Ayres.

Attendance: 19,676   Referee: Mr. A. E. Durkin – Dewsbury.

A crowd of just under 20,000 gathered at Watersheddings for the visit of Wigan and they were rewarded with a good contest in which Don Vines returned after being out for three months. Davies was played on the wing to watch Boston and although the idea proved ultimately successful the irrepressible, 'Billy' did go over for one try. Ganley opened the scoring with a 40 yard penalty goal and there was a let off for Oldham when Boston just failed to intercept a pass from Nestor to Ayres. Ganley stretched the lead with another goal before Wigan hit back midway through the half when McGurrin and Ashton spilt the defence to give Boston a walk in at the corner. Daley was instrumental in the laying on the first Oldham try when he shook off several defenders before releasing a pass to Pitchford who sent Ayres on a clear run to the line. Ganley converted well from a difficult angle. Just before half-time Ashton put in a neat chip kick but Cracknell was alert to the danger and just beat former team-mate, Terry O'Grady to the kick to make the ball safe. With defences dominant, the 9 – 3 score-line remained until the 70th minute when Daley again made the initial break for Ayres to send Davies in at the corner. Ganley sent over a great conversion from the touchline and although O'Grady scored a late try for the visitors, Oldham had done enough to win.

Above: Derek Turner puts in a kick watched by his team-mates as the Wigan defence closes in.

Right: Terry O'Grady goes over for a late try watched by the Oldham front row of Jack Keith, Ken Jackson and Don Vines.

(30.03.1957)

April 6th 1957: LEIGH 13   OLDHAM 40

W.B. Ganley, R. Cracknell, A. Davies, D. Ayres, J. Etty, F. Daley, F. Pitchford.
K. Jackson, J. Keith, D. Vines, S. Little, C. Winslade, D. Turner.
Goals: Ganley,8. Tries: Davies,3. Vines. Jackson. Turner. Little. Cracknell.
Attendance: 9,000   Referee: Mr. N. Railton – Wigan.

If only the mild conditions that prevailed for this match had been in evidence six weeks earlier... but never mind and back to the game in hand. It did appear that Oldham were motivated to put the result of February 23rd firmly behind them. A lovely break and then reverse pass from Pitchford to Davies led to the first try. Hosking replied with a penalty and after Jackson had stretched the Oldham lead, Atherton got one back for Leigh. However, further tries from Vines and Davies before the break gave the Roughyeds an 18 – 5 advantage at the interval. Four minutes into the new half Kindon reduced the arrears with a try but Oldham were not to be denied and Davies completed his 'hat-trick' as Leigh tired, no doubt deflated after the recent Challenge Cup semi-final replay loss to Barrow.

April 15th 1957: OLDHAM 38   SWINTON 13

W.B. Ganley, R. Cracknell, A. Davies, D. Ayres, J. Etty, F. Daley, F. Pitchford.
K. Jackson, J. Keith, D. Vines, S. Little, C. Winslade, D. Turner.
Goals: Ganley,7. Tries: Pitchford,3. Ayres,2. Davies,2. Etty.
Attendance: 11,800   Referee: Mr. M. Coates – Pudsey.

This match, postponed, from Christmas Day, was played on a Monday evening with Oldham knowing that two victories against the 'Lions', on this day and Good Friday later in the week, would give them the Lancashire league title. The first score came when Parkinson, the Swinton stand-off went for an interception and failed. This left space for Daley to put Pitchford on a clear run to the line. After 17 minutes the lead was increased when a peach of a pass from Winslade put Davies over. Ganley converted but Swinton hit back with Parkinson atoning for his earlier error by racing over from 60 yards for Tobin to convert. Back came the Roughyeds with Davies breaking away with Cracknell in support and just when it seemed the defence would take the Oldham winger Pitchford popped up on the inside to take a try scoring pass. Critchley got a try back for the visitors but when Daley and Davies combined to put Ayres over the game was as good as won by the interval. Ten minutes into the second half Pitchford completed his 'hat-trick' to make victory certain and so it was on to Station Road.

April 19th 1957: SWINTON 11   OLDHAM 34

W.B. Ganley, R. Cracknell, A. Davies, D. Ayres, J. Etty, F. Daley, F. Pitchford.
K. Jackson, J. Keith, D. Vines, S. Little, C. Winslade, D. Turner.
Goals: Ganley,8. Tries: Etty,2. Ayres. Ganley. Keith. Cracknell.
Attendance: 12,000   Referee: Mr. G. Scott – Dewsbury.

The Roughyeds carried on where they had left off at Watersheddings on Monday evening and in the third minute Daley, who was in a rich vein of form, was stopped just short on the right. However, a swift passing move over to the other flank culminated with Pitchford giving Ayres the scoring pass. After nine minutes Keith put Etty over. This time Ganley converted but Swinton hit back with two Tobin penalty goals. Just on half time Keith put Etty over again with Ganley on the mark with the extras. Four minutes into the new half Tobin put over another penalty closely followed by Smethurst paving the way for Berry to touch down and the 'Lions' were right back in the game. However, Oldham were not to be denied. The pick of the remaining scores was when Keith fooled all the Swinton defence to ghost over from acting half-back. The final try came from Ganley, who was up in support after Ayres and Etty had broken through and, as ever, he made a significant contribution with eight goals.

April 20th 1957: HUNSLET 12   OLDHAM 21

W.B. Ganley, R. Cracknell, J. Edwards, A. Davies, J. Etty, V. Nestor, F. Stirrup.
K. Jackson, J. Keith, A. Jarman, S. Little, C. Winslade, D. Turner.
Goals: Ganley,3. Tries: Jackson. Nestor. Etty. Turner. Little.
Attendance: 11,000   Referee: Mr. C. Appleton – Warrington.

Oldham made four changes for the second match of the Easter programme but the juggernaut was now in unstoppable, full throttle. Hunslet started well and it took a desperate lunge from Stirrup to stop Snowden from touching down a kick through in the early minutes. Talbot then put the 'Parksiders' ahead with a penalty but Oldham soon went ahead when Davies intercepted a pass from Clues to Jackson going over between the posts from where Ganley converted easily. Back came the Yorkshiremen with Snowden and Burnell capitalising on a handling error for the former to score. Talbot added the goal. Winslade and Stirrup linked up to put Nestor away and he finished well beating two defenders on the way to the line. Oldham were then on top for the rest of the half and were unlucky to have two tries disallowed. After the break they continued to dominate and after 51 minutes Stirrup and Davies got Etty over, soon followed by Turner romping in from 50 yards. Little scored the last try ten minutes later and that was it apart from a late, converted, consolation try from Stockdill.

April 22nd 1957: OLDHAM 26   ROCHDALE H. 12

W.B. Ganley, V. Nestor, A. Davies, D. Ayres, J. Etty, F. Daley, F. Pitchford.
K. Jackson, J. Keith, D. Vines, S. Little, C. Winslade, D. Turner.
Goals: Ganley,4. Tries: Etty,2. Nestor. Davies. Ayres. Pitchford.
Attendance: 15,915   Referee: Mr. E. Clay – Leeds.

Before the match the Lancashire League trophy was presented to club captain Frank Stirrup but Hornets definitely appeared to be out to spoil the party and ripped into Oldham from the start. Their pressure was rewarded after six minutes when Tierney broke through the home defence to put the supporting Fishwick in for a try, converted by Les Jones. The Roughyeds got back into the game thanks largely to the kicking skills of Turner who, first, put in a deft chip for Ayres to race through and gather the ball and give Etty the touch down. Then, a similar effort was pounced upon by Nestor for another try. In the last minute of the half Keith and Little worked an opening for Davies who tore away on a cross-field, 65 yard run to score. This broke the Rochdale spirit and by the hour mark three further tries had sealed the victory. Nine minutes from time the Hornets prop-forward, Dooney scored a consolation try converted by Jones.

Left: Frank Pitchford releases the ball to Vince Nestor when collared by a Hornets defender.
Below: John Etty sends a Rochdale player 'head over heels', as he touches down.

(22.04.1957)

May 4ᵗʰ 1957: OLDHAM 22   LEEDS 12
Championship Top 4 play-off.

W.B. Ganley, R. Cracknell, A. Davies, D. Ayres, J. Etty, F. Daley, F. Pitchford.
K. Jackson, J. Keith, D. Vines, S. Little, C. Winslade, D. Turner.
Goals: Ganley,5. Tries: Davies,2. Ayres. Cracknell.

Attendance: 20,000   Referee: Mr. R. Gelder – Wakefield.

Oldham were at full strength for this play-off decider with Frank Daley now established as the preferred stand-off to the exclusion of his good friend and club captain Frank Stirrup. It was a good start for Oldham with Ganley putting them ahead in the opening minutes with a penalty. Leeds had the chance to equalise two minutes later but Lewis Jones was off target. A kicking duel between the two full-backs then followed with the goal kicking fortunes soon reversed when Ganley failed an attempt only to see Jones successful with his next effort. Leeds then took the lead with a glorious movement from near their own line. Street shook off the initial cover to put Quinn away. At half way he kicked ahead and as the ball veered away from Cracknell, Stevenson was on it in a flash to gather and touch down. Jones converted to put the visitors five points ahead. Both the kickers were again off target with penalty attempts before Oldham had two tries disallowed! First Jackson's effort was ruled out for a forward pass and then Cracknell was adjudged to have hit the corner flag before touching down. As time ticked away Oldham did manage a legitimate score just seconds before the interval. A passing move right across the field ended with Cracknell racing clear; as he approached Jones he kicked ahead and although the Leeds man bundled him into touch, quick as a flash, he was back on his feet to re-gather and sprint away to the posts. Ganley converted and the scores were level. It was a determined Roughyeds that took the field for the second period and as early as the first minute Vines was stopped just inches from the line. Nevertheless, Leeds were putting in a tremendous defensive effort and Oldham had to wait until the 55ᵗʰ minute for a Ganley penalty to put them ahead. All seemed well when Davies touched down between the posts eight minutes later for Ganley to convert but back came the 'Loiners' and, with eight minutes left, Brown got clear only to fall to a last ditch tackle from Pitchford. As he fell the ball shot out behind him to the waiting McLellan who scooped it up to score. Jones added the goal and there were just two points in it. It was left to Daley to steady the ship. The no-nonsense Wiganer broke clear passed on to Davies who put Ayres over and Ganley's conversion settled the nerves. Then, just before full-time, Daley was through again this time he calmly drew the attention of Jones before releasing Davies on a clear run to the line. Oldham were in the Championship Final!

*Left: **Dick Cracknell** sprints away from **Lewis Jones** on his way to the first Oldham try.*
*Right: **Ken Jackson** dives over with **Sid Little** in support while, in the background, **Frank Pitchford** appeals in vain to the referee who disallowed the try for a forward pass.*
Opposite: Ticket stub and the centre page of the match programme.
(04.05.1957)

1956-57

The team have their photograph taken before the Top 4 play-off match against Leeds on May 4th 1957.
Extreme Left: Griff Jenkins. (coach) - Extreme Right: Bill Howard, (president).
Back Row: Don Vines, Derek Turner, Charlie Winslade, Ken Jackson, Sid Little, Jack Keith.
Middle Row: Dick Cracknell, Alan Davies, Bernard Ganley, Dennis Ayres, John Etty.
Front Row: Frank Daley, mascot, Frank Pitchford.

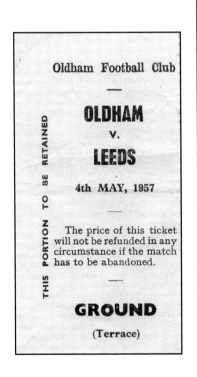

Oldham Football Club

OLDHAM
v.
LEEDS

4th MAY, 1957

The price of this ticket will not be refunded in any circumstance if the match has to be abandoned.

GROUND
(Terrace)

THIS PORTION TO BE RETAINED

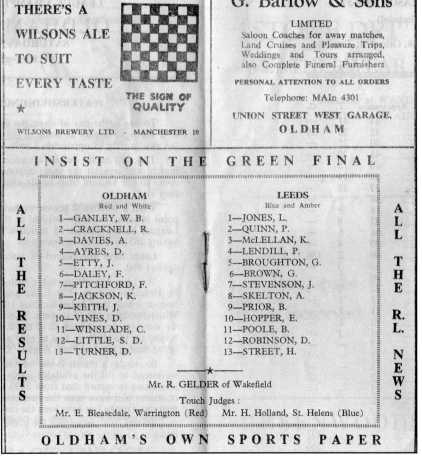

INSIST ON THE GREEN FINAL

OLDHAM	LEEDS
Red and White	Blue and Amber
1—GANLEY, W. B.	1—JONES, L.
2—CRACKNELL, R.	2—QUINN, P.
3—DAVIES, A.	3—McLELLAN, K.
4—AYRES, D.	4—LENDILL, P.
5—ETTY, J.	5—BROUGHTON, G.
6—DALEY, F.	6—BROWN, G.
7—PITCHFORD, F.	7—STEVENSON, J.
8—JACKSON, K.	8—SKELTON, A.
9—KEITH, J.	9—PRIOR, B.
10—VINES, D.	10—HOPPER, E.
11—WINSLADE, C.	11—POOLE, B.
12—LITTLE, S. D.	12—ROBINSON, D.
13—TURNER, D.	13—STREET, H.

ALL THE RESULTS

ALL THE R.L. NEWS

Mr. R. GELDER of Wakefield

Touch Judges :
Mr. E. Bleasedale, Warrington (Red)   Mr. H. Holland, St. Helens (Blue)

OLDHAM'S OWN SPORTS PAPER

May 18th 1957: OLDHAM 15 HULL 14
Championship Final at Odsal Stadium, Bradford.
W.B. Ganley, R. Cracknell, A. Davies, D. Ayres, J. Etty, F. Daley, F. Pitchford.
K. Jackson, J. Keith, D. Vines, S. Little, C. Winslade, D. Turner.
Goals:Ganley,3. Tries: Etty,2. Ayres.
Attendance: 62,217   Referee: Mr. M. Coates – Pudsey.

Eager to erase the memories of the 1955 Championship Final defeat by Warrington and the debacle at Leigh in the Challenge Cup earlier in the year, Oldham started the match as firm favourites and, unlike the two encounters mentioned above, this time the game would be played on something that looked more like a rugby pitch than a 'paddy' field. Any thoughts the Oldham supporters might have had about seeing their team enjoy a runaway victory were soon subdued. It was obvious that Hull were 'up' for the match and a Colin Hutton penalty gave them an early lead. The Roughyeds were definitely up against determined opponents whose cause was helped, in no small way, by a massive possession advantage obtained by Hull hooker Tommy Harris. The Roughyeds gradually came more into the game and after 24 minutes a defence-splitting break by Winslade paved the way for Pitchford to send out a long pass to Etty on the Oldham left wing where he evaded a last gasp tackle by Harris as he headed for the corner. However, just short of the line Etty swung round and took the ball a further 15 or so, yards closer to the posts. This was a fateful decision that made the conversion so much easier. Ganley duly obliged and Oldham held a 5 -2 lead.
Five minutes later Hutton landed another goal after Oldham were penalised for being off-side at a scrum. Next, there was some good fortune for Hull when Derek Turner was adjudged to be held up over the line after a great run by Dick Cracknell. Far from the anticipated feast of open play, the first half was a dour affair and just as the first period entered into injury time Hutton gave Hull the lead with a drop goal. Five minutes into the new half Hull increased their lead when international loose forward Johnny Whiteley put centre Carl Turner in the clear and, although Ayres got to him, his momentum was enough to score under the posts. Hutton goaled and Oldham were now 11 - 5 in arrears, with the game seemingly slipping away. Oldham reduced the deficit when the Hull forward Cyril Sykes was penalised for not playing the ball. After the decision was given it became apparent that the player was in fact injured. Nevertheless, the referee stuck to his initial ruling and Ganley kicked the goal from near half way. This lifted the Oldham team and soon after they were right back in the match after a break by Vines got Davies away. Just as the Hull cover closed in up popped fellow centre Ayres to take the pass and score near the posts. Ganley converted to give his team a single point advantage. The Oldham forwards were now well on top. Little was running strongly and from one such powerful surge he broke through and put Pitchford into the clear, only for the scrum-half to be recalled for a forward pass. However, it was a quick piece of thinking by the little number seven that increased the Oldham lead. Hull winger Cowan dropped the ball and 'Pitchy' was on it in an instant and straight away passed out to Etty who drew a defender and passed back to his supporting scrum-half who then repeated the manoeuvre for Etty to beat the cover to score in the corner. The conversion was missed but Oldham were now 4 points to the good with only 7 minutes remaining. For Pitchford it was hero turning to villain, as another attempted long pass went astray and Cowan made amends by snapping up the ball and crossing for the try. All Ganley could do was to stop him from going round to the posts. Even so the conversion was not too difficult and well within Hutton's capabilities. The crowd was hushed as the kick was taken, but it was the Oldham supporters who were left cheering as the ball sailed wide. The drama was still not over! In the very last seconds Hull made a last desperate bid to snatch the game out of the fire; Scott kicked the ball which nestled behind the Oldham try line with Etty and Dannatt in pursuit. They ran so close that their arms actually touched, but 'Big John' had enough left to win the race and make the ball dead. Thereafter the final whistle blew and Oldham were Champions for the first time since 1911.

John Etty breaks clear then avoids *Tommy Harris* to cross the line for the opening try.

(18.05.1957)

1956-57

Top Left: *Waiting for the kick off;* **Ken Jackson, Frank Pitchford, Frank Daley** *and* **John Etty**.
Top Right: **John Etty** *and* **Ken Jackson** *watch as* **Geoff Dannatt** *passes to* **Stan Cowan**.
Middle Left: Don Vines *prepares to tackle* **Johnny Whiteley**.   *(18.05.1957)*
Middle Right: Frank Pitchford *and* **Charlie Winslade** *tackle* **Geoff Dannatt**.
Below: *Two angles of* **Dennis Ayres** *going over for the second Oldham try after taking a pass from* **Alan Davies**.

1956-57

1956-57		Played	Won	Draw	Lost	For	Against	Points
1	**OLDHAM**	**38**	**33**	**0**	**5**	**893**	**365**	**66**
2	Hull	38	29	2	7	764	432	60
3	Barrow	38	29	0	9	702	481	58
4	Leeds	38	28	0	10	818	490	56
5	St. Helens	38	25	3	10	902	355	53
6	Wigan	38	26	0	12	750	417	52
7	Hunslet	38	26	0	12	688	417	52
8	Wakefield T.	38	23	1	14	747	545	47
9	Huddersfield	38	23	0	15	667	533	46
10	Warrington	38	21	1	16	571	565	43
11	York	38	21	0	17	641	538	42
12	Halifax	38	21	0	17	559	514	42
13	Salford	38	19	2	17	518	499	40
14	Workington T.	38	20	0	18	494	516	40
15	Featherstone R.	38	19	0	19	612	504	38
16	Rochdale H.	38	19	0	19	510	611	38
17	Leigh	38	18	1	19	684	608	37
18	Whitehaven	38	18	1	19	601	646	37
19	Swinton	38	18	0	20	576	594	36
20	Keighley	38	17	1	20	494	534	35
21	Bradford N.	38	17	0	21	479	672	34
22	Bramley	38	14	2	22	558	632	30
23	Widnes	38	15	0	23	439	526	30
24	Blackpool B.	38	14	0	24	470	875	28
25	Castleford	38	11	2	25	488	739	24
26	HullK.R.	38	11	2	25	395	672	24
27	Liverpool C.	38	9	1	28	356	854	19
28	Batley	38	8	0	30	399	700	16
29	Dewsbury	38	5	1	32	391	818	11
30	Doncaster	38	3	0	35	321	835	6

Lancashire League Trophy - Lancashire Cup - R.L. Championship Trophy - Law Cup

Back Row: B. Day, E. Watkins, S. Campbell, P. Carter, R.L. Thomas, E. Thomas, F. Ashworth, F. Ridgeway.
Middle Row: F.S. Holt, H. Summerscales, J. Coulthard, D. Vines, C. Winslade, J. Keith, S. Little, D. Turner, K. Jackson, A. Jarman, G. Jenkins, (coach), A. Cordwell.
Front Row: R. Cracknell, A. Davies, F. Daley, W.B. Ganley, W. Howard, F. Stirrup, F. Pitchford, D. Ayres, J. Etty.

1956-57

SEASON	PLAYER	APPS	TRIES	GOALS	POINTS
1956-57	J. ETTY	45	43		129
1956-57	J. KEITH	45	13		39
1956-57	K. JACKSON	45	5		15
1956-57	C. WINSLADE	45	4		12
1956-57	R. CRACKNELL	43	24	19	110
1956-57	D. AYRES	42	27		81
1956-57	F. PITCHFORD	42	19		57
1956-57	D. TURNER	42	16		48
1956-57	S. LITTLE	42	8		24
1956-57	W.B. GANLEY	41	2	189	384
1956-57	A. DAVIES	38	16		48
1956-57	F. STIRRUP	33	9		27
1956-57	D. VINES	32	2		6
1956-57	F. DALEY	21	3		9
1956-57	V. NESTOR	17	9		27
1956-57	J. ROGERS	11	2	3	12
1956-57	A. TOMLINSON	7			
1956-57	T. O'GRADY	4	1		3
1956-57	A. JARMAN	4			
1956-57	R. BAILEY	2	1		3
1956-57	I. CARRUTHERS	2			
1956-57	J. EDWARDS	2			
1956-57	W. RILEY	2			
1956-57	J. O'BRIEN	1	1		3
1956-57	A. KELLETT	1	1		3
1956-57	A. JONES	1		1	2
1956-57	J. NOON	1			
1956-57	**TOTAL**	**611**	**206**	**212**	**1042**

Most Appearances: John Etty, Jack Keith, Ken Jackson, Charlie Winslade 45 out of a possible 47.

Most tries: John Etty 43.

Most goals: Bernard Ganley 189 - Most points: Bernard Ganley 384.

John Etty   **Bernard Ganley**   **Jack Keith**   **Ken Jackson**   **Charlie Winslade**

1956-57

Club Captain

O D S A L   H E R O E S

210

1957-58

After the heights of 1956-57, the following campaign produced a bitterly disappointing end to what in fact had been a very good season. The Lancashire Cup and Lancashire League trophy had both been retained, as was the Law Cup in the pre-season friendly against Rochdale. Wigan finally broke their losing sequence to the Roughyeds with victory in the Challenge Cup quarter final at Watersheddings.

In the league table Oldham were top of the pile again with only four defeats and a draw compared with five defeats in the previous season. However, a totally unexpected play-off reverse against Hull took all the gloss off what had gone before with the Roughyeds' faithful fully expecting their favourites to be crowned champions once more. Bernard Ganley reached the magic 200 figure for his season goal tally and Dick Cracknell led the try scorers with 27, although no fewer than eight got into double figures including forwards, Jack Keith, Derek Turner and Sid Little. John Etty bagged 16 and was the leading appearance maker with 44 out of a possible 46.

The Oldham team before the top 4 play-off match against Hull on May 3rd 1958.

Back Row: W. Howard (pres), S. Little, R. Dufty, D. Turner, C. Winslade, K Jackson, G. Jenkins (coach).
Middle Row: A. Davies, R. Cracknell, W.B. Ganley, J. Etty, D. Ayres, J. Keith.
Front Row: F. Pitchford, A Kellett.

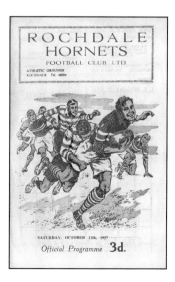

August 10th 1957: Rochdale H. 5   Oldham 31
Law Cup
W.B. Ganley, R. Cracknell, V. Nestor, D. Ayres, J. Etty, R. Moat, F. Pitchford.
K. Jackson, J. Keith, D. Vines, S. Little, R. Dufty, D. Turner.
Goals: Ganley,5. Tries: Nestor,2. Turner. Etty. Moat. Jackson. Little.
Attendance: 7,556   Referee: Mr. C. Appleton – Warrington.

Two new signings, Roger Dufty and Rowley Moat, were included in the team, but Alan Davies was out injured after suffering a severe leg strain playing for Great Britain in the World Cup in Australia; the injury would keep him side-lined for a further nine games. The inexperienced Dufty was caught off-side in the first minute and Les Jones put Hornets in front, the resulting penalty going in off the upright. Ganley equalised some ten minutes later but then, against the run of play, Rochdale re-took the lead when indecision from Pitchford and Nestor allowed Ralph to snap up a loose ball and race home from 50 yards. Oldham continued to apply pressure, however, and Pitchford, Etty and Ayres combined to put Nestor over in the corner. Then, with half an hour gone, a great break by Keith was carried on by Turner, who galloped 50 yards to the posts; Ganley converted. Hornets finished the half strongly and were unlucky when Chisnall fumbled the ball with the line at his mercy, after a clever kick ahead by Fishwick. The second half brought no better fortune for the home side when Ralph similarly spilled the ball after a good break by Trumble. Thereafter Oldham took control, running in five more tries, with the pick coming on the hour mark when Moat finished off a terrific run by Cracknell under the Hornets posts.

*Roger Dufty (left) and **Rowley Moat.**
Both played their debut match for Oldham in the
1957 Law Cup triumph.*

August 17th 1957: OLDHAM 21   HALIFAX 11
W.B. Ganley, R. Cracknell, V. Nestor, D. Ayres, J. Etty, R. Moat, F. Pitchford.
K. Jackson, J. Keith, D. Vines, S. Little, R. Dufty, D. Turner.
Goals: Ganley,6. Tries: Turner,2. Etty.
Attendance: 14,600   Referee: Mr. E. Clay – Rothwell.

Halifax got off to a good start with two penalty goals from Owen. At the other end Ganley was unlucky to see his attempt come back off the upright. However, there was better fortune for the Oldham full-back soon afterwards, when he brought off a try-saving tackle to put Freeman into touch near the line. Little made the initial break that led to the first try. After cutting through the initial cover he handed on to Turner, who chipped the ball over Owen and calmly re-gathered. The conversion was missed but Ganley made amends with two penalty goals before Owen slotted home his third goal in the last minute of the half, to leave the Roughyeds 7 – 6 in front at the break. A Ganley penalty opened the scoring in the second period, and this was followed by Pitchford and Jackson combining to send Etty over. Moments later Turner was in again for his second try and with Ganley converting both scores, the game was now safe. Halifax did stage a late rally which brought a try for Freeman, laid on by the half-back pairing of Dean and Kielty. Turner was the star of the show, ably assisted by the tireless Jackson.

August 22nd 1957: BARROW 10 OLDHAM 27

W.B. Ganley, R. Cracknell, V. Nestor, D. Ayres, J. Etty, F. Stirrup, F. Pitchford.
K. Jackson, J. Keith, D. Vines, F. Daley, R. Dufty, D. Turner.
Goals: Ganley,6. Tries: Turner,2. Ayres. Jackson. Cracknell.
Attendance: 8,000   Referee: Mr. N. Railton – Liverpool.

The Roughyeds were off to a flying start when Ayres intercepted a pass from Wilson to race 80 yards to the posts in the fifth minute. Ball replied with a penalty goal for Barrow, but Oldham were on top form, and Pitchford and Turner were soon carving an opening for Jackson to score. Three minutes later Turner crashed in at the corner, and two minutes after that Cracknell won the race to a Nestor kick, and Oldham had scored 13 points in five minutes, to lead 18 – 2 at the interval. In the second half, after a further Ganley penalty, Skeels got a couple of tries for the 'Furness-men' but the last word was with the impressive Turner, who crashed in for his second try in the final minute.

August 24th 1957: WAKEFIELD T. 12 OLDHAM 12

W.B. Ganley, R. Cracknell, V. Nestor, J. Noon, J. Etty, F. Stirrup, F. Pitchford.
K. Jackson, J. Keith, D. Vines, S. Little, A. Jarman, D. Turner.
Goals: Ganley,3. Tries: Noon. Etty.
Attendance: 11,650   Referee: Mr. F. Smith – Barrow.

After failing with two penalty attempts in the first three minutes, Ganley opened the scoring with his third effort, but the score was equalised by Mortimer after a quarter of an hour. Sustained Oldham pressure only realised another Ganley goal, in the 31st minute, but they were rocked a minute later when Rollin worked a move from a scrum near the Oldham line to put Firth over for a converted try. Still Oldham continued the pressure, and it finally told four minutes before the break when Vines and Pitchford linked up well to put Noon in at the corner. Ganley's superb conversion from the touchline gave Oldham a 9 – 7 advantage at the break. Five minutes into the second half, a Pitchford break, carried on by Noon, finished with Etty scoring in the corner. The match developed into a forward-dominated affair, and there was some controversy about Wakefield's equalising score. There is no doubt that Holliday got over the line, but the Oldham players were adamant that he was held in the tackle and didn't ground the ball. Still, the score was awarded and Mortimer's conversion levelled the match. Ganley did have a chance to snatch victory with a penalty two minutes from full-time, but the ball sailed wide and the match remained tied.

August 26th 1957: OLDHAM 7 ST. HELENS 21

W.B. Ganley, R. Cracknell, V. Nestor, J. Noon, J. Etty, F. Daley, F. Pitchford.
R. Rowbottom, J. Keith, D. Vines, S. Little, A. Jarman, D. Turner.
Goals: Ganley,2. Try: Jarman.
Attendance: 16,900   Referee: Mr. A. Howgate – Dewsbury.

This was Oldham's third match in five days and the strain finally got to them, though the deciding factor was an injury to hooker Jack Keith after just seven minutes. This, left the Roughyeds a man down with Jarman taking his place in the middle of the front row. The first score came when Carlton outpaced Nestor in a race to get to a loose ball. Forshaw added the conversion. Ganley opened Oldham's account with a 22nd minute penalty, but two tries in the last two minutes of the half swung the match towards the Saints. First Prescott and Delves carved an opening for Karalius, and then Silcock did likewise for Carlton. Forshaw converted one of the scores to leave St. Helens 13 – 2 ahead at the interval. Four minutes into the second period, hopes were raised when Jarman emerged from a ruck of players to go over near the posts for a converted try, but seven minutes later the match went away from Oldham again when Karalius scooped up a loose ball to send Forshaw in at the corner. He converted the try himself, and the final score came when Carlton completed his 'hat-trick'. It later emerged that Vines suffered a broken nose early in the game.

August 31st 1957: OLDHAM 44   BARROW 10
Lancashire Cup 1st Round.
W.B. Ganley, R. Cracknell, V. Nestor, J. Noon, J. Etty, F. Daley, F. Pitchford.
K. Jackson, I Carruthers, A. Jarman, S. Little, C. Winslade, D. Turner.
Goals: Ganley,10. Tries: Little,3. Cracknell,2. Etty. Noon. Jarman.
Attendance: 14,772   Referee: Mr. H. Harrison – Horbury.

Both teams were hit by injuries going into this cup-tie, but Oldham made light of their troubles to run the visitors ragged after struggling for the first quarter of an hour. Future Oldham favourite Len McIntyre made his debut for Barrow and put in a lively performance in an otherwise beaten pack of forwards. A penalty each by Ganley and Ball was how it stood until the 17th minute, when a forceful break by Ganley was supported by Noon, who finished off in style by dummying his way through the Barrow defence. Three more tries followed before half-time, with the pick being a 65-yard move, started by Daley, that saw the ball pass through several pairs of hands before Little planted the ball over the line in the corner. Ganley then converted superbly from the touchline. 24 – 2 in front at the break, Oldham never looked back, with Ganley having a great day with the boot in registering ten successful kicks. Barrow hit back with a couple of tries from Wilson and the hard-working McIntyre, but the result was never in doubt, with Little completing a well-deserved 'hat-trick'.

September 2nd 1957: HUDDERSFIELD 12   OLDHAM 38
W.B. Ganley, R. Cracknell, V. Nestor, J. Noon, J. Etty, R. Moat, F. Pitchford.
K. Jackson, I Carruthers, A. Jarman, S. Little, C. Winslade, D. Turner.
Goals: Ganley,10. Tries: Nestor,2. Noon. Ganley. Pitchford. Ganley.
Attendance: 18,460   Referee: Mr. D. Davies – Manchester.

This was another vintage performance from Ganley, who banged over ten goals for the second match in a row as well as chipping in with a try! The only try in the first half went to Noon, who was on hand to finish off a move involving several of the Oldham backs. 11 -2 in front at the interval, Oldham increased the lead when a long pass from Winslade to Jackson ended with Cracknell going over after 47 minutes. Soon afterwards Nestor got over for another, before a mini-revival saw Huddersfield cross for two tries, from Valentine and Henderson, both converted by Dyson. However, Ganley dismissed any thoughts of a come-back with a towering 45 yard drop goal, before three more tries in the last ten minutes re-emphasised the Roughyeds' superiority.

September 7th 1957: HALIFAX   15   OLDHAM 19
W.B. Ganley, R. Cracknell, V. Nestor, J. Noon, J. Etty, R. Moat, F. Pitchford.
K. Jackson, J. Keith, D. Vines, S. Little, C. Winslade, D. Turner.
Goals: Ganley,5. Tries: Cracknell. Etty. Nestor.
Attendance: 16,374   Referee: Mr. T. Watkinson – Manchester.

A penalty attempt by Ganley from 50 yards in the sixth minute was unsuccessful, but a minute later he was on the mark from about half the distance. Halifax then took the lead when a good break by Traill was finished off by Dean, who struggled over despite a last-ditch tackle by Pitchford. Ganley added a further two penalties, with Owen replying with one. A bout of inter-passing between Nestor and Cracknell ended with the former touching down, and the half ended with Cracknell going over in the corner after a defence-splitting pass from Winslade. Ganley converted well from the touchline, to give Oldham a 14 -5 lead at the break. Quick thinking by Kielty brought Halifax back into the match; the home scrum-half took a quick tap-penalty to catch the Oldham defence napping, before touching down for Owen to convert. Ten minutes from full-time, Pitchford and Noon created an opening for Etty to score, and once again Ganley sent over a glorious conversion from the touchline. Freeman managed a late consolation try, converted by Owen, but it was too little, too late.

September 10th 1957: OLDHAM 18   WARRINGTON   12
Lancashire Cup 2nd Round

W.B. Ganley, R. Cracknell, V. Nestor, J. Noon, J. Etty, R. Moat, F. Pitchford.
K. Jackson, J. Keith, A. Jarman, S. Little, C. Winslade, D. Turner.
Goals: Ganley,6. Tries: Little. Pitchford.
Attendance: 15,200   Referee: Mr. E. Clay - Rothwell.

Before the match Ganley had decided to 'cry-off' with a shoulder injury, but pressure from his team-mates and coach Griff Jenkins persuaded him to change his mind, and that was fortunate for Oldham as their marksman again turned in a match-winning performance with the boot. Etty was prominent on defence early on with smother tackles on centre Horton, thus stopping the ball from reaching the ever-dangerous Bevan on the wing. A couple of Ganley penalties and a conversion to a typical crash-over try from Little, against a good solo try from Edwards supplemented by a conversion and a penalty from Gilfedder, saw Oldham 9 – 7 up at the interval. Three more penalty goals from Ganley increased the lead, and Noon was unlucky to be called back by the referee when in the clear, only for the resulting penalty to go to Oldham. In the 67th minute Pitchford intercepted a pass from O'Toole to score what proved to be the clincher, although a converted try from Naughton meant Oldham had a nervous last ten minutes.

September 14th 1957: OLDHAM 17   WARRINGTON 15

W.B. Ganley, R. Cracknell, J. Noon, D. Ayres, J. Etty, R. Moat, F. Pitchford.
K. Jackson, J. Keith, D. Vines, S. Little, C. Winslade, A. Jarman.
Goals: Ganley,4. Tries: Little. Moat. Cracknell.
Attendance: 14,000   Referee: Mr. R. Gelder – Wakefield.

Just four days after the Lancashire Cup match, Warrington were back in town to provide another severe test for the Roughyeds. Gildfedder failed with a first minute penalty attempt from 40 yards, but soon afterwards Ganley was on the mark with an effort from a similar distance. After 16 minutes a break by Arnold set up an unconverted try for Gilfedder. Oldham responded positively, and after Moat was held up just short, good work from Jarman created the opening for Little to score near the posts. Ganley converted but back bounced the 'Wire', and Major broke away from a scrum 40 yards out to score, with this time Gildfedder adding the extras. Just before the break Ganley gave Oldham a single point advantage with a penalty goal. The first score of the second-half came after a break by Pitchford put Moat clear, but this was soon followed by a Warrington reply from Naughton. Both tries were converted, and, as the score suggests, there was little to choose between the teams. The best player on view was Pitchford, and it was he who fashioned the winning try for Cracknell, with assistance from Noon. Gilfedder put over a long distance penalty, but

Oldham had enough left in the tank to keep their line intact during the last few minutes.

Sid Little goes over near the posts for the first Oldham try. (14.09.1957)

September 21st 1957: OLDHAM 23 LEIGH 5

W.B. Ganley, A. Davies, V. Nestor, D. Ayres, J. Etty, R. Moat, F. Stirrup.
K. Jackson, J. Keith, D. Vines, S. Little, A. Jarman, D. Turner.
Goals: Ganley,7. Tries: Keith,2. Moat.

Attendance: 11,520   Referee: Mr. G. Scott - Wakefield.

Alan Davies returned to the team after his lengthy injury, albeit on the wing, and was faced by his brother Gwyn at full-back for Leigh. It was almost a dream start for Oldham, only for Moat to be brought back when in the clear, but then see the penalty awarded to the Roughyeds! Still, it wasn't long before a Ganley penalty opened the scoring, and this was closely followed by Stirrup releasing Nestor on a run in which he drew the last shreds of defence before putting Keith over for a converted try. On 18 minutes Little and Moat put the hooker in again, as Oldham completely dominated the game, with Ganley again in good form with the boot. For the visitors Holden looked most dangerous, and it took a good tackle by Moat on the Leigh centre to keep the Oldham line intact. With Oldham 14 – 0 up at the break, the match was made completely safe six minutes into the second period when Ayres snapped up a loose ball to put Moat in for another converted try. A late consolation try from Bright, converted by Fallon, was all Leigh had to show for their endeavours as Ganley returned another impressive seven-goal haul.

September 28th 1957: WORKINGTON T. 13 OLDHAM 24

W.B. Ganley, R. Cracknell, A. Davies, D. Ayres, J. Etty, F. Daley, F. Pitchford.
K. Jackson, J. Keith, D. Vines, C. Winslade, S. Little, D. Turner.
Goals: Ganley,6. Tries: Davies. Ayres. Cracknell. Keith.

Attendance: 6,304   Referee: Mr. C. Appleton – Warrington.

The early exchanges were quite even, but after ten minutes a sweeping 60-yard moved culminated in Eve scoring an unconverted try. Ganley replied with a penalty, but this was soon cancelled out by Stevenson with a similar effort after 20 minutes. Workington were dictating the play at this point, and it was no surprise when Ivison and Toohey laid on another try for Archer. Again there was no goal. Oldham then got back into the match with two tries in the last few minutes of the half, from Davies and Cracknell. Ganley converted both, to leave the visitors 12 – 8 to the good at the interval, and he soon opened the scoring after the break with another penalty. Then a loose pass from Winslade was seized upon by Southward, who showed the Oldham defenders a clean pair of heels on his way to the line. Stevenson missed the conversion, but he knocked over a penalty soon afterwards to leave 'Town' just a point behind. Then, as the match moved into the last five minutes, Oldham started to throw the ball about to good effect, and after

a lengthy exchange of passes, Keith was on hand to finish off in style. Two minutes later Pitchford broke clear and passed on to Ayres, who feinted to pass to Etty but hung on himself to fool the home defence and cross the line. Ganley converted both scores to give the score a slightly unbalanced reflection of an overall tight match.

Frank Pitchford and *Jack Keith* *tackle the Workington forward* **Norman Herbert.**

(28.09.1957)

1957-58

Ken Jackson avoids the
attentions of Workington's
John O'Neill and
Ike Southward to lay on a
late try for Jack Keith.

(28.09.1957)

October 2nd 1957: ST. HELENS 9   OLDHAM 29
Lancashire Cup semi-final.
W.B. Ganley, R. Cracknell, V. Nestor, A. Davies, J. Etty, F. Daley, F. Pitchford.
K. Jackson, J. Keith, D. Vines, C. Winslade, S. Little, D. Turner.
Goals: Ganley,7. Tries: Davies,2. Nestor. Etty. Winslade.
Attendance: 20,000   Referee: Mr. R. Gelder – Wakefield.

Victory was achieved after a devastating first-half blitz from the Roughyeds, who were no doubt still smarting from the defeat at Watersheddings on August 26th. Pimblett and Ganley exchanged early penalty goals before the Oldham half-backs, Daley and Pitchford, took command to lay on three tries. First the two 'Franks' combined to put Nestor away, and followed with similar service for Davies to score twice. After 36 minutes Pitchford was again involved, with Little and Turner, to enable Winslade to force his way over, and with Ganley converting all four tries the tie was as good as won. Saints did rally with a penalty by Pimblett and a try from Silcock, but the 9 – 22 score-line at the interval was proof of Oldham's dominance of the first half. The second period turned into a scrappy affair, with the only additional try coming four minutes from time when Pitchford, again, broke away to hand on to Davies, who gave Etty the try- scoring pass. The one downside to the day was the dismissal of Davies four minutes from time. He had already been cautioned twice after altercations with Karalius and Greenall, and the referee's patience finally ran out when he went to the aid of Pitchford, who was receiving some harsh treatment from the St. Helens pack.

Sid Little brings
down a Saints player
with *Jack Keith*,
Bernard Ganley,
Tom McKinney,
Walter Delves, and
Ken Jackson in
attendance.

(02.10.1957)

217

October 12th 1957: ROCHDALE H. 21   OLDHAM 29

W.B. Ganley, R. Cracknell, V. Nestor, D. Ayres, J. Noon, F. Daley, F. Pitchford.
K. Jackson, J. Keith, D. Vines, C. Winslade, S. Little, D. Turner.
Goals: Ganley,7.   Tries: Noon,2. Turner. Nestor. Cracknell.

Attendance: 13,844   Referee: Mr. T. Watkinson – Manchester.

Oldham were off to a flyer in this derby game when Winslade snapped up a loose ball to send Turner in by the posts in the first minute. It looked like the flood-gates might open when Little then stormed through the

middle to give Noon a run to the corner, from where Ganley added his second conversion. However, Hornets hit back, and an inside pass from Taylor gave Buxton a clear run to score. Kelly converted, and soon afterwards a clever delayed pass from Hanson put Short away, and he in turn put Taylor over. Ganley replied with a penalty goal, but Rochdale took the lead when Fishwick carved out an opening for Taylor to score his second try. Kelly added the goal, to leave the score 13 – 12 at the break. A penalty each early in the second half was the forerunner to a ten point blitz that saw Oldham take command. First Little and Winslade combined to put Nestor over, and then a Daley break,

followed by some slick passing, ended with Noon scoring his second touchdown.

Still Rochdale refused to give up, and they scored further tries from Buxton and Hanson, but in between these Cracknell scored the Roughyeds fifth try to maintain a clear margin between the teams. In the end, though, it was five tries apiece, so once again it was the kicking prowess of Ganley that was the difference.

Opposite Top: The crowd waits in anticipation as **Bernard Ganley** calmly leads out the team followed by **Dick Cracknell** and **Dennis Ayres** before the start of the match at Rochdale.

Above: It's the second half and **Ganley** and **Cracknell** have a more urgent expression as Oldham resume one point in arrears.

Opposite Bottom: A remarkable photo which shows nine Oldham players.
Don Vines struggles for the ball with a Rochdale player as **Jack Keith** moves in to help.
(12.10.1957)

October 19th 1957: OLDHAM 13 WIGAN 8
Lancashire Cup Final played at Station Road, Swinton.
W.B. Ganley, R. Cracknell, V. Nestor, A. Davies, J. Etty, F. Daley, F. Pitchford.
K. Jackson, J. Keith, D. Vines, C. Winslade, S. Little, D. Turner.
Goals: Ganley,2. Tries: Ganley. Pitchford. Davies.
Attendance: 42,497　　　　　Referee: Mr. M. Coates – Pudsey.

The Lancashire Cup was retained in what would become known to Oldham supporters as 'Daley's final'. The reason for this was that the craggy Wiganer blotted out the threat of Billy Boston, who had been tried at stand-off half with some success in the run up to the final. However, on this day, whenever Billy got the ball he usually got Daley as well, with a well-timed smother tackle. For a quarter of an hour the match was a typical cup-tie, with defences dominant. Pitchford was Oldham's main threat, with Ashton showing up well for Wigan. Ironically the best attack of the early exchanges came after a break from Boston, who broke out of Pitchford's tackle. He kicked ahead but the Oldham scrum-half redeemed himself by winning the race to gather the ball. After 17 minutes the Roughyeds took the lead when Little evaded three defenders to go clear; Ganley was in support to finish off under the posts, and then add the conversion. Back came Wigan, but when attacking a loose pass from Ashcroft went to ground, to be hacked on twice by Davies only for Cunliffe to kick the ball out of play just short of the Wigan line. The second try came after a scrum on the Wigan 25 yard line. Turner picked up from the back of the pack and slipped a pass to Pitchford, who streaked away to the corner to put Oldham 8 – 0 in front at the interval. Three minutes after the break Pitchford pounced on a loose ball and carved an opening through the middle, from where Jackson was on hand to put Davies over in the corner. Now it was Wigan's turn to turn on the style, and a fine passing move stretched the Oldham defence to breaking point, from where McTigue juggled with the ball as he barged over in the corner for an unconverted try, with still half an hour to go. Oldham responded with a couple of near misses when the final pass was put down. On the hour mark Ashcroft send out a suspicious -looking forward pass to O'Grady for the ex-Oldham man to kick ahead, re-gather and score. Cunliffe added the goal, and there were just three points between the teams. From here on, however, Oldham never looked like conceding again, and a late penalty goal from Ganley concluded the scoring. It later emerged that Daley played the match with a broken finger!

Alan Davies prepares to pass to **John Etty** in front of the packed stands and terraces at Station Road.

(19.10.1957)

1957-58

Lancashire Cup Final 1957

*1. **Billy Boston** breaks away with the Oldham players in pursuit.*
*2. With **Jack Keith** in support, **Bernard Ganley** races over for the first try.*
*3. **Frank Pitchford** goes in for the second.*
4. A happy dressing room of players, staff and officials pose with the trophy.   (19.10.1957)

October 26th 1957: BLACKPOOL B. 5   OLDHAM 34

W.B. Ganley, R. Cracknell, V. Nestor, A. Davies, J. Etty, F. Stirrup, F. Pitchford.
K. Jackson, J. Keith, D. Vines, S. Little, R. Dufty, D. Turner.
Goals: Ganley,8. Tries: Davies,3. Keith,2. Turner.

Attendance: 3,500   Referee: Mr. F. Smith - Barrow.

After a spirited opening from the 'Borough', Ganley opened the scoring with a tenth-minute penalty. This was followed by the first try, which came from Davies after an initial break from Jackson. Ex-Roughyed Fearis got a try back for Blackpool, but further tries from Keith and Davies saw Oldham go in with a 19 – 3 advantage at half-time. Five minutes in to the second half Davies completed his 'hat-trick', and from there Oldham coasted home with a second try for Keith and another from Turner, with just a Fearis penalty in reply for Blackpool.

November 2nd 1957: OLDHAM 23   WAKEFIELD T. 12

F. Stirrup, R. Cracknell, V. Nestor, J. Noon, J. Etty, F. Daley, F. Pitchford.
R. Rowbottom, J. Keith, D. Vines, R. Dufty, C. Winslade, A. Jarman.
Goals: Noon,4. Tries: Cracknell,2. Keith. Daley. Nestor.

Attendance: 20,028   Referee: Mr. G. Philpott - Leeds.

This was a fine performance from Oldham, who had five players away on international duty in France. 'Trinity' received from the kick off and were met straightaway by some hard tackling as the reserves sought to make their presence felt. Nevertheless, after seven minutes, when Daley fumbled a ball after a scrum on the Oldham 25 yard line, the Wakefield scrum-half Rollin was first to react, and he kicked ahead and won the race to the ball for a try. Midway through the half, Winslade broke clear and gave the supporting Keith a walk-in to the posts. Noon converted to put Oldham ahead, but by the interval Wakefield had nudged in front from two penalties from Fox. The Roughyeds had all the early pressure after the break, and it was Winslade again who split the defence to put Daley over for a converted try. This was soon followed by a slick bout of passing that finished with Nestor adding a further touch-down. Trinity hit back when Cooper intercepted a Vines pass to score. Fox converted to leave the visitors just a point in arrears, but Oldham finished strongly with two tries from Cracknell, both converted by Noon. The second of these scores was again instigated by the impressive Winslade.

*John Noon looks for an opening after taking a
pass from Vince Nestor.
(02.11.1957)*

*Left to right: John Noon, Ron Rowbottom, Frank Daley
and Frank Stirrup.
Noon and Rowbottom were drafted in to replace their
international colleagues while Stirrup switched position
to full-back for the match against Wakefield.*

1957-58

November 9th 1957: SALFORD 5 OLDHAM 14

W.B. Ganley, R. Cracknell, V. Nestor, J. Noon, J. Etty, F. Daley, F. Pitchford.
K. Jackson, J. Keith, D. Vines, C. Winslade, S. Little, D. Turner.
Goals: Ganley,4. Tries: Keith. Noon.
Attendance: 14,500   Referee: Mr. A. Howgate – Dewsbury.

Salford opened brightly, and in the first minute McArthur broke clear and passed on to Council, but with a try looking certain, Stott fumbled the final pass. However, five minutes later, Moses put Cheshire away and this time Jones was on hand to score. Ganley replied with a penalty, and then Oldham began to take control, but some stout defending kept the Salford line intact with both Cracknell and Etty being bundled into touch just short of the try-line. Eventually, though, the pressure paid off when Keith dodged over from close range, after having had a similar effort disallowed just minutes earlier for not grounding the ball correctly. The try was converted, and the last score of the half was a 45-yard penalty from McArthur, to leave the score 5 – 7 at the break. Despite the relative lack of scoring this was a good match, and the pattern continued in the second half, with Salford giving as good as they got. The game breaker came when Noon scooped up a loose ball to touchdown for a converted try.

November 16th 1957: OLDHAM 28 LIVERPOOL C. 12

W.B. Ganley, R. Cracknell, A. Davies, J. Noon, J. Etty, A. Kellett, F. Pitchford.
K. Jackson, J. Keith, D. Vines, S. Little, C. Winslade, D. Turner.
Goals:Ganley,8. Tries: Pitchford. Noon. Cracknell. Little.
Attendance: 10,376   Referee: Mr. T. Watkinson – Manchester.

Liverpool took the lead with a first minute penalty from stand-off half, Balshaw, though this was equalised by Ganley ten minutes later. Still, the 'Mersey-siders' were making a game of it and were rewarded for their determination when, after Houghton was held just short, Balshaw got over and then converted himself. It was a stroke of good fortune that brought Oldham back into the match, when Pitchford intercepted a stray pass to scoot home from 55 yards. Cracknell and Noon added two further tries before the break, by which time the lead had stretched to 21 – 7. There was little to choose between the sides after the interval, with only a converted try to each team, scored by Little and Hunt, and another penalty goal for Ganley.

November 23rd 1957: LEIGH 14 OLDHAM 24

F. Stirrup, R. Cracknell, J. Noon, D. Ayres, J. Etty, V. Nestor, F. Pitchford.
R. Rowbottom, J. Keith, D. McKeown, C. Winslade, A. Jarman, F. Daley.
Goals:Noon,6. Tries: Pitchford,2. Nestor. Keith.
Attendance: 12,000   Referee: Mr. J. Hebblethwaite – York.

Once again the Roughyeds had five players on international duty, and a close first half ensued, although Oldham did have most of the territorial advantage. An early penalty by Noon gave the visitors the lead, and this was followed by desperate Leigh defending which saw Daley, Noon and Cracknell all felled just short of the try-line. Then, against the run of play, Foster and Tabern fashioned an opening for Robinson to score, followed by a Ledgard conversion. The response was immediate, and a length-of-the-field move concluded with Nestor scoring for Noon to convert. Back came Leigh, with Fallon reacting first, scoring after a lost ball by Winslade. Again Ledgard added the extras. However, Winslade soon atoned for his error, and it was his break that put Pitchford clear for a converted try. Just before the interval a Ledgard penalty brought the scores level at 12 – 12, and shortly into the second period he gave them the lead with another. Noon soon levelled the score, but as the match moved into the last quarter it was Oldham who secured the spoils with two more long range tries, for Keith and Pitchford. Noon converted both to see the Roughyeds comfortably home.

November 30th 1957: OLDHAM 34 SALFORD 12

W.B. Ganley, R. Cracknell, J. Noon, A. Davies, J. Etty, V. Nestor, F. Pitchford.
R. Rowbottom, J. Keith, K. Jackson, S. Little, C. Winslade, D. Turner.
Goals: Ganley,5. Tries: Cracknell,2. Etty,2. Noon. Winslade. Davies. Keith.
Attendance: 14,652   Referee: Mr. M. Coates. – Pudsey.

An early penalty each for McArthur and Ganley was followed by a great break by Cheshire, providing a try for McArthur after 15 minutes, converted by Lowdon. Notwithstanding the return of his international colleagues, it was Pitchford who caught the eye with a stunning scrum-half display. It was he who laid on converted tries for Cracknell and Noon to put Oldham 12 – 7 up at half-time. As in the first half, Salford started the second period brightly, but the Roughyeds struck first when Davies dummied his way past a

couple of defenders to lay on a try for Etty. McArthur latched on to a Hartley kick ahead to touch down and reduce the arrears, but from there on Oldham pulled away, with the pick of the tries being a length-of-the-field effort started by Noon and finished by Winslade.

Frank Pitchford passes to Derek Turner.
(30.11.1957)

December 7th 1957: HUNSLET 20   OLDHAM 22

W.B. Ganley, R. Cracknell, J. Noon, A. Davies, J. Etty, V. Nestor, F. Pitchford.
R. Rowbottom, J. Keith, K. Jackson, S. Little, C. Winslade, D. Turner.
Goals: Ganley,5. Tries: Davies. Cracknell. Winslade. Noon.
Attendance: 10,500   Referee: Mr. N. Railton – Wigan.

Hunslet started well, and after first Talbot and then Shaw were grounded just short, there was no holding John Platt as he registered the first try. It was all Hunslet in the first quarter, and after 13 minutes Hatfield broke clear to put Gabbitas over for Talbot to convert. Oldham finally got in the match when Nestor raced clear to put Davies over. Ganley converted well against a strong wind. However, Hunslet were still in the ascendancy, and after 22 minutes Talbot landed a drop goal. Just two minutes later Walker put Colin over for the third Hunslet try. The Roughyeds responded with a Ganley penalty, and then it was Nestor again who was instrumental in setting up a try for Cracknell, to leave the half-time score 13 – 12 to the Yorkshiremen. After the interval Oldham got on top, but they squandered a host of chances, the worst of which was when Davies was stripped of possession when over the Hunslet try-line. To make matters worse Winslade failed to hold a pass from Rowbottom, and Colin swooped in to take the ball and race 70 yards to touch down. Talbot converted and then added a penalty. This was the signal for Hunslet to try to close the game down, and so Oldham were given

the opportunity to lay siege to the home try-line. With ten minutes to go, they were rewarded when Winslade battered his way over near the posts. Ganley converted, and there were just three points in it. Then, in the last minute, a sweeping passing movement culminated in Noon scoring the equalising try. Ganley took the conversion and, in spite of the windy conditions, the ball sailed over the bar, to give Oldham the spoils.

Brian Gabbitas escapes the clutches of John Noon to score Hunslet's second try.
(07.12.1957)

December 14th 1957: LIVERPOOL C. 11   OLDHAM 15

W.B. Ganley, J. Noon, V. Nestor, A. Davies, J. Etty, F. Stirrup, F. Pitchford.
R. Rowbottom, J. Keith, K. Jackson, F. Daley, R. Dufty, D. Turner.
Goals:Ganley,3. Tries: Nestor,2. Davies.

Attendance: 1,100   Referee: Mr. J. Clapham – Wigan.

Liverpool put up a spirited show, but were undone in the seventh minute when Pitchford and Stirrup opened up the defence for Davies to score a converted try. Balshaw slotted home a penalty before Nestor sprinted in from 70 yards for another converted score. Back came the 'Mersey-siders', with Cartledge and Teggin laying on a try for Houghton. Balshaw converted and added a penalty, to leave the score 9 – 10 at the break. The narrow pitch was restricting Oldham's attacking flair and the second half was a tight affair in which Liverpool took the lead ten minutes from time with another Balshaw penalty goal. However, with five minutes left, the Oldham half-backs again combined, with Stirrup's lobbed pass putting the in-form Nestor away. He still had much to do, but, with a change of pace and direction, he left three defenders in his wake to score the match-winning try, which was duly converted by Ganley.

December 21st 1957: OLDHAM 28   WHITEHAVEN 12

W.B. Ganley, R. Cracknell, A. Kellett, A. Davies, J. Etty, V. Nestor, F. Pitchford.
R. Rowbottom, J. Keith, K. Jackson, S. Little, R. Dufty, D. Turner.
Goals: Ganley,8. Tries: Pitchford. Davies. Kellett. Cracknell.

Attendance: 10,000   Referee: Mr. G. Wilson – Dewsbury.

In this match Oldham were going for a 19th consecutive victory (a club record), and they duly took the lead with an early Ganley penalty. However, the Cumbrians were not going to make it easy, and after a fine move from their own quarter, Robinson took the ball close to the line and released a pass in the tackle to put Stevenson over. McKeown missed the conversion but slotted home a penalty after 13 minutes. Ganley then had two penalty failures before Whitehaven struck again after 21 minutes. The ball came quickly out of a scrum, and Banks hacked it on to follow up and touch down. McKeown added the goal. Ganley atoned for his previous misses with two penalties, to leave the half time score 6 – 10. After the break he added two more, before Davies and Etty took play deep into the Whitehaven half, from where Pitchford scored direct from a scrum; Ganley converted. It was then Pitchford, again tormenting the visitors, who sent Davies racing over from 45yards. Once again Ganley added the goal, as Oldham took control. McKeown replied with a penalty on 63 minutes, but further tries from Kellett and Cracknell sealed the famous victory.

December 25th 1957: OLDHAM 9   SWINTON 15

W.B. Ganley, R. Cracknell, A. Kellett, A. Davies, J. Etty, V. Nestor, F. Pitchford.
R. Rowbottom, J. Keith, K. Jackson, S. Little, R. Dufty, F. Daley.
Goals: Ganley,3. Try: Jackson.

Attendance: 9,500   Referee: Mr. J. Manley – Warrington.

The run of victories had to end sometime! There was to be no Christmas gift from the 'Lions', who controlled the game from the off in a match in which hardly anything went right for the Roughyeds. After seven minutes a kick-through by Gowers seemed of little danger, but when Keith tried to hack the ball out of play, his kick sliced badly right into the path of Smith, who promptly touched down. Robson added the goal. Ganley got a penalty goal after 20 minutes, but soon afterwards another Gowers kick brought the second try. This time Cracknell failed to make it safe, and Doughty was on hand to score. Soon afterwards, Norburn broke clear and, with the help of Parkinson, laid on another try for Berry. Robson added his third conversion, and Oldham were in trouble. Jackson managed to barge over, after Keith had gone close, on 34 minutes, to give some hope for the second half. However, it wasn't to be, as two Ganley penalties were the only additions to the score in the second period which, like the first, was dominated by the visitors.

December 26th 1957: HULL 12 OLDHAM 5

W.B. Ganley, R. Cracknell, V. Nestor, A. Davies, J. Etty, F. Daley, L. Laverty.
R. Rowbottom, J. Keith, K. Jackson, S. Little, H. Lomas, D. Turner.
Goal: Ganley. Try: Etty.

Attendance: 26,000   Referee: Mr. T. Watkinson – Manchester.

In the wake of the Swinton reverse, it was something of a baptism of fire for young debutant Lew Laverty at high-flying Hull, and also a rare first-team slot for another local lad, Harold Lomas; not withstanding the result, both emerged from the game with much credit. It was the Hull forwards who bossed the show, with loose forward, Johnny Whiteley, instrumental in setting up the first try for winger Harrison. Four minutes later it was the turn of the Drake brothers to add to Oldham's woes, with Jim laying the foundations for brother Bill to crash over. Ganley got two points back with a penalty after 22 minutes, but the last word of the half went to the impressive Whiteley, who dodged over himself from a scrum five yards from the Oldham line. 9 – 2 behind at the interval, the Roughyeds tightened up in the second period, but not enough to hold the Hull forwards when they created an opening for Dannett to send Watts over, despite the attentions of Etty. Still, the Oldham wingman did have the last say when Jackson sent out a high pass to Davies, who duly put Etty over for an unconverted try.

Lew Laverty

December 28th 1957: WARRINGTON 14 OLDHAM 15

W.B. Ganley, R. Cracknell, V. Nestor, J. Noon, J. Etty, F. Daley, F. Stirrup.
R. Rowbottom, J. Keith, K. Jackson, S. Little, H Lomas, D. Turner.
Ganley,6. Try: Etty.

Attendance: 16,000   Referee: Mr. A. Durkin – Dewsbury.

Early on, Oldham had a lucky escape when Herbert was adjudged to have put a foot in touch before scoring. Fraser then landed a goal, only for Ganley first to equalise, and then to send the Roughyeds in front with two successful penalties. Fraser got one back, but a scrum move from the Oldham half-backs stretched the lead after 32 minutes. Stirrup took the ball and gave a wide pass to Daley, who sent the ball back inside to Etty; he ran between his half-backs to score at the posts. A wonderful score! The Warrington right flank was looking lively, and after a kick ahead by Challinor, Stirrup did well to make the ball safe. Then Lomas did well to keep out Fraser, but Warrington were now on top, and it was no surprise when Gallagher charged over in the corner. Seven minutes after the break the Warrington were in again. This time Challinor's kick was collected by Bevan for a trademark try. Ganley put Oldham back in front with three more goals, on 56, 60 and 69 minutes, and from there the defence held firm, although it was somewhat of a surprise when Fraser kicked a goal with only two minutes left, given that shortly beforehand Warrington had opted to run the ball from a similar position.

*Sid Little tackles
Robin Thompson
as Derek Turner, Vince Nestor and
Dick Cracknell (2) move in to assist.*

(28.12.1957)

January 4th 1958: OLDHAM 17   LEEDS 10

W.B. Ganley, R. Cracknell, D. Ayres, A. Davies, J. Etty, V. Nestor, F. Pitchford.
K. Jackson, J. Keith, D. Vines, S. Little, C. Winslade, D. Turner.
Goals: Ganley,4. Tries: Nestor. Ganley. Cracknell.

Attendance: 14,094   Referee: Mr. R. Gelder - Wakefield.

The first quarter was defence-dominated and quite even until Jones got the first points with a penalty goal after 17 minutes. Just three minutes later Hemmingway scored a try after what looked like a blatant forward pass from Whitehead. This stung Oldham into action, and a break from Pitchford laid on a try for Nestor, converted by Ganley, who also kicked a penalty after 33 minutes. He then topped it all off with an opportunist try after a pass from Turner was knocked down. Ganley again converted, to leave the Roughyeds 12 – 7 to the good at the break. Oldham had the best of it after the interval, and Ganley increased the lead with a penalty in the 52nd minute. A quarter of an hour later another Pitchford break set up Cracknell to score, and Gartside replied for Leeds after good approach work from Whitehead, Simms and Ward. Both tries went unconverted.

*Above: **Alan Davies** attempts to 'sell the dummy' to Leeds winger **Gary Hemmingway**.
(04.01.1958)*

The Oldham team that defeated Leeds on January 4th 1958.
Back Row:
Don Vines, John Etty, Charlie Winslade, Derek Turner, Ken Jackson, Sid Little.
Front Row:
Vince Nestor, Dennis Ayres, Alan Davies, Bernard Ganley, Dick Cracknell, Jack Keith, Frank Pitchford.

1957-58

January 11ᵗʰ 1958: OLDHAM 24   BARROW 5

W.B. Ganley, R. Cracknell, D. Ayres, A. Davies, J. Etty, F. Daley, F. Pitchford.
R. Rowbottom, J. Keith, D. Vines, S. Little, C. Winslade, D. Turner.
Goals: Ganley,3. Tries: Davies,2. Little. Etty. Cracknell. Daley.
Attendance: 13,585   Referee: Mr. M. Coates – Pudsey.

Oldham were soon in the ascendancy in this match, with Pitchford, Turner and Davies all prominent in the opening exchanges. Barrow then replied in kind, with Grundy and Jackson causing problems for the Roughyeds. In the 13ᵗʰ minute Oldham took the lead. Little made the initial break before handing on to Ayres; he found Etty on the wing, and when he was challenged, Little was following up in support to take the winger's inside pass to score a wonderful try. Ganley converted. Oldham then moved into top gear with three more tries, two from Davies and one from Etty, before the break. Barrow did have an effort from Skeels disallowed for a forward pass, but all in all it was an excellent half for the Roughyeds, who turned around 18 – 0 in front. After the break further tries from Cracknell and Daley cemented the advantage before McIntyre scored a late consolation for the visitors, converted by Ball.

Alan Davies closes in on **Phil Jackson**.
The two internationals formed the Great Britain centre three-quarter partnership at the time.
(11.01.1958)

January 18th 1958: WIDNES 2 OLDHAM 12

W.B. Ganley, R. Cracknell, D. Ayres, A. Davies, J. Etty, F. Daley, F. Pitchford.
R. Rowbottom, J. Keith, D. Vines, S. Little, C. Winslade, D. Turner.
Goals: Ganley,3. Tries: Cracknell,2.

Attendance: 5,800   Referee: Mr. C. Appleton – Warrington.

The match started in driving rain, and after some early Widnes pressure Oldham took the lead when Cracknell intercepted a pass from Derek Smith bound for Thompson. Ganley failed with the conversion, but soon afterwards put over two penalty goals in quick succession. After more Widnes pressure and a couple of missed goal attempts, Dawson finally got Widnes off the mark with a penalty. However, just minutes later, Ganley made light of the dreadful conditions to send another goal over from fully 50 yards, leaving Oldham 9 – 2 ahead at the interval. The bad weather continued after the break, and now with the wind at their backs, Widnes employed a kicking game to keep Oldham in their own half. To some extent it worked, and there was just one addition to the score. It went to the Roughyeds, when a delightful pass from Pitchford put Cracknell clear, and the winger raced on to score in the corner. Those two were the pick of the Oldham backs and Vines put in a great display in the forwards. Apparently, at half-time coach Jenkins told Keith not to worry too much about hooking the ball, as it was easier to defend and rely on the opponents' handling errors in such atrocious conditions.

February 1st 1958: WIGAN 6 OLDHAM 9

W.B. Ganley, R. Cracknell, D. Ayres, A. Davies, J. Etty, F. Daley, F. Pitchford.
K. Jackson, J. Keith, D. Vines, C. Winslade, S. Little, D. Turner.
Goals: Ganley,3. Try: Little.

Attendance: 30,764   Referee: Mr. T. Watkinson – Manchester.

Over 30,000 assembled at Central Park for this game, and it was Wigan who were soon on the attack with their impressive three-quarter line of Boston, Ashton, Sullivan and O'Grady all featuring in the early exchanges. After four minutes Cunliffe put the home side in front with a penalty after a scrum offence, but then it was Oldham's turn to go on the offensive, and after Cracknell had taken play deep into the Wigan half, Ganley was on the mark with an equalising goal. The match was played with fierce tackling from both teams and it was Wigan who stretched their lead with two further Cunliffe penalties, to leave them 6 – 2 up at half-time. After the break Oldham got on top, and after Etty had gone close, Turner and Daley created an opening for Little to come in at speed and crash over. Ganley converted to put the Roughyeds a point in

front. From here on defences dominated, and there were many unsavoury incidents with Ganley particularly coming in for some rough treatment. Nevertheless, after a couple of misses, the Oldham full-back kicked another penalty as Oldham hung on in a tense finish.

Dave Bolton looks to avoid the Oldham left wing pair of John Etty and Alan Davies.

(01.02.1958)

February 8th 1958: OLDHAM 23 HULL K. R. 6
Rugby League Challenge Cup 1st Round.

W.B. Ganley, V. Nestor, D. Ayres, A. Davies, J. Etty, F. Daley, F. Pitchford.
K. Jackson, J. Keith, D. Vines, S. Little, C. Winslade, D. Turner.
Goals:Ganley,4. Tries: Nestor,2. Pitchford,2. Little.

Attendance: 13,017   Referee: Mr. G. Wilson – Dewsbury.

Before the match there was a minute of silence observed in memory of the victims of the Munich air disaster, which included many players and officials of the Manchester United club.

Oldham had to make a late change when Cracknell cried off, so Nestor came in on the wing. The Roughyeds were soon on top and opened the scoring after ten minutes, Turner and Ayres putting Nestor over for the opening try. Ganley, who had missed two early penalty attempts, converted the score. Mageen was showing up well for Rovers, and they were unlucky when Grice crossed the try-line only to be held up by the defence. However, when Oldham were penalised soon afterwards, Kellett slotted home a penalty off the upright to open the scoring for Hull K.R. Back came the Roughyeds with Nestor, revelling in his first-team opportunity, scoring another try after good approach work by Winslade and Ayres. There was no conversion, but Ganley did add the extras when Pitchford latched on to a flicked pass from Davies to score just before the interval. Five minutes into the second half, Turner made a break and passed on to Little, who ran the last 15 yards to score. Kellett kicked another couple of penalties for the 'Robins', but the Oldham line was rarely threatened before Pitchford scored the final try of the match.

Sid Little, Jack Keith and Ken Jackson hold up Ken Grice on the try line against Hull K.R.
(08.02.1958)

1957-58

February 15th 1958: ST. HELENS 5   OLDHAM 4

W.B. Ganley, R. Cracknell, D. Ayres, A. Davies, J. Etty, F. Daley, F. Pitchford.
K. Jackson, J. Keith, D. Vines, C. Winslade, S. Little, D. Turner.
Goals: Ganley, 2.

Attendance: 28,000   Referee: Mr. R. Gelder – Wakefield.

St. Helens kicked off in driving rain, and straight away Little broke through and gave to Turner, who kicked ahead deep into the opposing half. There then followed a sustained spell of pressure from the home side, and it took stout defence by Daley and Davies to keep Silcock out. Pitchford went close midway through the first half, but all in all St. Helens were well on top and it was against the run of play when Ganley gave Oldham the lead with a penalty after half an hour. The try which swung the match came six minutes before the break, in an incident that was sheathed in controversy. A scrum was formed near the Oldham line and when the ball came out and squirted over the try-line, Pitchford touched it down to make it 'dead'. Then Murphy followed up and dived on the ball, and to the amazement of the Oldham players, referee Gelder awarded a try, which Large duly converted. To make matters worse Daley then had a try disallowed just before the interval. The rain continued into the second half, and once again Saints had most of the play, although a kick ahead by Pitchford almost brought a score for Davies. Ganley failed with two penalty attempts before putting one over, but from there on St. Helens held out for a single point victory.

*Glyn Moses prepares to pass to **Nat Silcock** as he is tackled while **Derek Turner** looks on.*
(15.02.1958)

231

February 22nd 1958: BLACKPOOL B. 5   OLDHAM 12
Rugby League Challenge Cup 2nd Round.
W.B. Ganley, R. Cracknell, D. Ayres, A. Davies, J. Etty, F. Daley, F. Pitchford.
K. Jackson, J. Keith, D. Vines, C. Winslade, S. Little, D. Turner.
Goals: Ganley,3. Tries: Ayres. Cracknell.
Attendance: 5,000   Referee: Mr. E. Clay – Leeds.

A good contingent of Oldhamers travelled over to a wintry Blackpool for this cup-tie, with the home-side fielding several ex-Roughyeds. It was two of them, Emmitt and Fearis, who figured prominently in Blackpool's early attacks as the 'Seasiders' gave Oldham plenty to think about in the first half. After 12 minutes a break by Healey put Brennan in for the first try under the posts, from where Fearis had no trouble in adding the conversion. Soon afterwards, Brennan went close once more before the play was switched into the Blackpool half for a spell of Oldham pressure, but the 'Borough' defence held firm. Both Ganley and Fearis missed goal attempts before Ganley finally got Oldham on the board with a 40-yard effort in the last minute of the half. Snow started to fall as the teams came out for the second period, and Oldham resumed on attack, though they could not pierce the home defence until midway through the half, when Ganley slotted home another penalty. Two minutes later Ganley failed with another effort, and it was a sign of the desperation of the Oldham team that this effort was from 58 yards out! Bad handling was letting the Roughyeds down until finally, the brave Blackpool effort faltered, and with fourteen minutes to go Pitchford put Ayres over. Cracknell then added a second try in the closing minutes. Ganley added one conversion and a relieved Oldham were through.

Above: Alan Davies passes to John Etty in Lionel Emmitt's tackle as Frank Pitchford moves up in support.

Right: Ex-Roughyed, Peter Fearis falls to a tackle from Dennis Ayres in the tense cup-tie played at Blackpool's, St. Annes Road ground. (22.02.1958)

March 1st 1958: OLDHAM 21   BLACKPOOL B. 11

F. Stirrup, R. Cracknell, D. Ayres, J. Noon, J. Etty, V. Nestor, F. Pitchford.
R. Rowbottom, I Carruthers, D. Vines, C. Winslade, R. Dufty, F. Daley.
Goals: Noon,3. Tries: Cracknell,3. Nestor. Vines.
Attendance: 11,063   Referee: Mr. H. Harrison – Horbury.

Once again Blackpool put up a good show against a re-jigged Oldham line-up that brought in several reserve players, partly due to four again being in France on international duty. Four minutes into the game a 75 yard move culminated in Nestor racing in from half-way for an unconverted try. Eight minutes later a kick deep into the Oldham half was fielded by Stirrup, who set off on a 40 yard run; this then led to another try for Cracknell. However, Blackpool were not to be left behind, and after Dunn had a try disallowed for a previous knock-on by Healey, Fearis got the visitors on the scoreboard with a penalty. The play then swayed from one end of the field to the other, but the only score went to Blackpool when, after Dunn had gone close, Brennan battled his way over. The conversion attempt by Fearis came back off the post, to leave Oldham 6 – 5 in front at the interval. Early in the second half Fearis missed a penalty, before a break by Carruthers set up a try for Vines. Noon's conversion attempt split the touch-judges, but 'no goal' was the ruling. From here Oldham gradually got on top, with two more tries from Cracknell sealing the win. Noon finished with three goals, and Fearis added a further try and goal for the visitors.

The Oldham team against Blackpool Borough on March 1st 1958.

Back Row: *Vince Nestor, Frank Stirrup, Ron Rowbottom, Roger Dufty, Charlie Winslade, Frank Daley, Don Vines.*

Front Row: *Frank Pitchford, Dennis Ayres, Dick Cracknell, John Etty, John Noon, Ian Carruthers.*

March 8th 1958: OLDHAM 0 WIGAN 8
Rugby League Challenge Cup 3rd Round.
W.B. Ganley, R. Cracknell, D. Ayres, A. Davies, J. Etty, F. Daley, F. Pitchford.
K. Jackson, J. Keith, D. Vines, C. Winslade, S. Little, D. Turner.
Attendance: 23,000   Referee: Mr. M. Coates – Pudsey.

It had to happen some time and it was just Oldham's luck that it would happen in the Challenge Cup! Wigan finally ended their run of 14 consecutive defeats to the Roughyeds in this fiercely-fought quarter-final. Oldham lost the toss and kicked off into a strong wind. Keith was penalised at an early scrum, and Cunliffe took play close to the Oldham line with the resulting penalty. From the scrum, Bolton went close before McTigue barged his way over. Cunliffe converted with only two minutes on the clock. Oldham then controlled the rest of the half, but could find no way through the Wigan defence. Davies was injured and swapped places with Etty to go on the wing. Tempers were raised, with first Etty and Bolton and then

Daley and Ashton receiving cautions from the referee. A defence-dominated second half saw Davies go over to the right wing with Cracknell going to left centre. Ganley missed a long range shot at goal after 46 minutes, but Oldham rarely troubled the Wigan line. Bolton was in splendid form for the visitors and went close on a couple of occasions, before Boston ensured victory with a last minute try. This would be the last time that the thirteen players who played in the championship final at Odsal in May 1957 would form the Oldham team.

Above:
Under the watchful eye of referee **Matt Coates**, **Derek Turner** *and* **Frank Daley** *bring down* **Dave Bolton.**

Right:
The relief is there for all to see in the faces of the Wigan supporters who rushed on to the pitch at the final whistle, as the losing sequence against Oldham is finally broken with the last minute match clincher, **Billy Boston** *the centre of attention.*

(08.03.1958)

Top: *There were just two minutes on the clock when **Brian McTigue** ploughed over despite the attention of several defenders. The delight is obvious in his Wigan team-mates with equal resignation from **Frank Pitchford, Bernard Ganley, Sid Little** and **Jack Keith** as the referee awards the try.*

Middle: John Etty *tackles* **Eric Ashton.**

Bottom: Alan Davies *gets a pass away to* **John Etty** *when confronted by* **Eric Ashton** *and* **Billy Boston.** *(08.03.1958)*

1957-58

March 15th 1958: WHITEHAVEN 11   OLDHAM 13

W.B. Ganley, R. Cracknell, D. Ayres, J. Noon, J. Etty, A. Kellett, F. Pitchford.
K. Jackson, J. Keith, D. McKeown, S. Little, R. Dufty, D. Turner.
Goals: Ganley,2. Tries: Pitchford. Ayres. Little.

Attendance: 5,000   Referee: Mr. J. Chadwick – Batley.

In the opening ten minutes Bill McKeown kicked two penalties for Whitehaven to offset a try by Pitchford, who beat three defenders direct from a scrum. The player of the half was undoubtedly Alan Kellett, who caused constant trouble for the Cumbrian defence and was instrumental in putting Ayres and Little in for further tries. Ganley converted the latter, and added a penalty just before the break, to leave Oldham 13 – 4 ahead. The visitors opened the second half brightly, but Whitehaven gradually got back into the match, and two more goals from McKeown kept them in touch. Left wing King missed a chance when he spilled a pass from McMenemy with the line open, but later he made amends by getting over for McKeown to convert and so leave 'Haven' just two points in arrears. Oldham, however, managed to hang on for a victory.

March 22nd 1958: OLDHAM 27   ROCHDALE H. 0

W.B. Ganley, R. Cracknell, V. Nestor, D. Ayres, J. Etty, A. Kellett, F. Pitchford.
K. Jackson, I Carruthers, D. McKeown, C. Winslade, S. Little, D. Turner.
Goals: Ganley,6. Tries: Etty,2. Cracknell. Turner. Pitchford.

Attendance: 11,693   Referee: Mr. G. Wilson – Dewsbury.

The opening quarter was a typical tight 'derby' affair, with just a couple of Ganley penalties separating the teams, but in the 22nd minute Kellett beat two men and then lobbed a pass out to Cracknell. He in turn passed back inside to Nestor, and was then still in support to receive the ball back and race over in the corner. Ganley converted well from the touchline. Six minutes later, Kellett was again involved, with Pitchford and Ayres, in setting up another try, this time in the opposite corner, for Etty. Once again Ganley was on the mark, to leave Oldham 14 – 0 ahead at the break. As in the first half, Rochdale put up a good show for the first 20 minutes of the second, but when Turner won the race to dive on an Etty kick-ahead to score, the match was as good as won. Etty got his second try a few minutes later, after good approach work by Winslade and McKeown, and Pitchford finished the try-scoring with a fine individual effort, in which he evaded several defenders on a run to the corner.

Frank Pitchford goes over for the final try.

(22.03.1958)

236

March 25th 1958: OLDHAM 17   WIDNES 15

W.B. Ganley, R. Cracknell, J. Noon, D. Ayres, J. Etty, A. Kellett, F. Pitchford.
K. Jackson, J. Keith, D. McKeown, F. Daley, C. Winslade, D. Turner.
Goals: Ganley,4. Tries: Etty. Ayres. Ganley.

Attendance: 6,083   Referee: Mr. T. Watkinson – Manchester.

After a time pinned in their own half, a break by Jackson, carried on by Pitchford, saw Etty go over for a converted try. Dawson got Widnes on the board with a couple of penalties, before Ganley replied with one for Oldham after good breaks by Noon and Pitchford had taken play deep into the Widnes half. There then followed an inspired spell of play by Frank Myler, who first sped in from 50 yards and then, after taking a defence splitting pass from Thompson, repeated the effort from half the distance. Neither try was converted, but when a snappy bout of passing saw Ratcliffe go over for the third Widnes try, Dawson was on the mark to put the 'Chemics' eight points clear. This finally snapped Oldham into action, and it was Pitchford breaking away to the left who created space for Ayres to score, and then Kellett and Turner who combined to create a gap for Ganley to steam in under the posts. Both conversions were added and the Roughyeds managed to hang on for the last five minutes.

Dennis Ayres releases the ball in the tackle of *Harry Dawson.*   *(25.03.1958)*

April 4th 1958:   SWINTON 18   OLDHAM 28

W.B. Ganley, R. Cracknell, V. Nestor, A. Davies, J. Etty, A. Kellett, F. Pitchford.
K. Jackson, I Carruthers, R. Dufty, C. Winslade,   S. Little, D. Turner.
Goals: Ganley,8. Tries: Nestor,2. Davies. Jackson.

Attendance: 12,000   Referee: Mr. R. Gelder – Wakefield.

Open play was the order of the day in this feast of football at Station Road. It took just six minutes for Kellett and Davies to open up the Lions defence, putting Nestor over for the score. Quick as a flash the home team hit back, with Norburn going in for Swinton. Then Kellett again, this time aided by Winslade, created another opening for Nestor to get his second try. No sooner had the cheering stopped than Parkinson was scooping up a loose pass from Pitchford to keep the scoreboard ticking over, and soon it was Parkinson again, this time intercepting a Kellett pass to send Roberts on his way to the line. Into the second period and Pitchford, who did not have a happy first half, found his form to put Davies over. Back came Swinton, with Mather touching down after good work by Norburn and Blan. Oldham's response was for Turner to charge through the Swinton defence to give Jackson a clear run to the line. So there it was : four tries each! The difference… Ganley! Whereas Swinton struggled with the boot, Bernard was popping them over from everywhere ; eight goals in total, and during those successes he beat his own club record of 189, set in the previous season.

April 5th 1958: OLDHAM 19   WIGAN 7

W.B. Ganley, R. Cracknell, V. Nestor, A. Davies, J. Etty, A. Kellett, F. Pitchford.
K. Jackson, J. Keith, R. Dufty, C. Winslade, S. Little, D. Turner.
Goals: Ganley,5. Tries: Kellett,2. Pitchford.

Attendance: 15,031   Referee: Mr. T. Watkinson – Manchester.

Wigan moved Billy Boston to the right centre position, to cover for the injured Eric Ashton, where he formed a three-quarter partnership with ex-Oldham favourite Terry O'Grady. After a flurry of attacks from both sides, Oldham took the lead with a sixth-minute penalty from Ganley. Cunliffe missed a chance to equalise, but soon afterwards Bolton broke clear through some slack Oldham defence to put Sullivan over for Cunliffe to convert. Bad handling was letting both teams down but, after 30 minutes, a scrum move between Kellett and Pitchford saw the latter score. Ganley converted to give the Roughyeds a 7 – 5 advantage at the interval. There was almost a sensational start to the second half when Winslade and Keith inter-passed for over half the length of the field. It finished with Winslade touching down, only for the referee to rule the final pass forward. A penalty goal each followed, before Oldham took control in the last quarter, after O'Grady had been sent off. Once again it was the Oldham half-backs that caused the problems for the visitors. On 68 minutes Pitchford put Kellett through, but the stand-off had plenty to do, managing to beat three defenders to touch down. Just before the end the pair repeated the dose, with Ganley adding one conversion and a penalty to seal the win.

Above Left:
Sid Little breaks clear pursued by
Terry O'Grady.

Above Right:
Alan Kellett scores one of his two tries.

Left:
Billy Boston releases a pass when
challenged by *Derek Turner.*

(05.04.1958)

Above: *Dick Cracknell* races clear as **Mick Sullivan** tackles **Vince Nestor**
Below: This time **Nestor** receives from **Cracknell** as **Sullivan** again makes the tackle. *(05.04.1958)*

April 7ᵗʰ 1958: OLDHAM 27 HUDDERSFIELD 3

W.B. Ganley, R. Cracknell, D. Ayres, A. Davies, V. Nestor, A. Kellett, F. Pitchford.
K. Jackson, J. Keith, R. Dufty, C. Winslade, S. Little, D. Turner.
Goals: Ganley,3. Tries: Pitchford,2. Cracknell,2. Little,2. Nestor.
Attendance: 14,645   Referee: Mr. G. Wilson – Dewsbury.

Oldham went on the attack from the start, and were soon on the scoreboard when Pitchford was in support of a Little breakthrough to score a converted try. The second score came after 16 minutes, with Turner, Pitchford and Ayres all handling to set up a Cracknell touchdown. Huddersfield responded, and after Breen had broken clear down the right, some quick handling set up Plunkett to send Barrow over, against his former club, with a well-timed pass. However, that was it for the 'Fartowners', and after Cracknell scored his second try, Turner and Jackson both had tries disallowed for incorrect grounding. Nevertheless, the Roughyeds coasted through the rest of the match and should really have won by a bigger margin. Turner was the star of the show as he laid on second-half tries for Pitchford and Nestor.

*Left: **Derek Turner** loses the ball in a two man tackle as he attempts to touch down under the posts.*

*Below: It's **Derek Turner** again as he sprints through the Huddersfield defence with **Tommy Smales** and **Roland Barrow** in pursuit. (07.04.1958)*

Bernard Ganley sends out a pass when challenged by the Huddersfield defence.
(07.04.1958)

April 12th 1958: OLDHAM 38   HUNSLET 13

W.B. Ganley, R. Cracknell, D. Ayres, A. Davies, J. Etty, A. Kellett, F. Pitchford.
K. Jackson, J. Keith, R. Dufty, C. Winslade, S. Little, D. Turner.
Goals: Ganley,7. Tries: Davies,2. Etty,2. Ayres. Keith. Turner. Dufty.
Attendance: 13,602   Referee: Mr. H. Harrison – Horbury.

The Roughyeds had this match wrapped up by half-time, by which time they led 23 – 0. The first try came on six minutes, when Pitchford and Kellett broke quickly from a scrum 25 yards out to put Davies over. Five minutes later Ganley started a move which finished with a try for Ayres. Next there was an obstruction try awarded to Etty, who was pushed out of the way by Langton as he chased down a Davies kick. Hunslet raised their game for the second half, with stand-off Brian Gabbitas in good form, scoring one try and making others for Tate and Colin. Oldham replied with a late flurry of points, and there was prolonged applause for Bernard Ganley when he broke Jim Sullivan's record of 204 goals in a season in all matches (club and representative).

Bernard Ganley slots home the record breaking 204th goal of
the season watched by *Dennis Tate* and *Brian Gabbitas*
from under the cross-bar.
(12.04.1958)

1957-58

April 16th 1958: OLDHAM 43 HULL 9

W.B. Ganley, R. Cracknell, D. Ayres, A. Davies, J. Etty, A. Kellett, F. Pitchford.
K. Jackson, J. Keith, R. Dufty, C. Winslade, S. Little, D. Turner.
Goals: Ganley,8. Tries: Keith,2. Cracknell. Etty. Pitchford. Davies. Little. Ayres. Turner.
Attendance: 14,008   Referee: Mr. E. Clay – Rothwell.

This mid-week clash of two of the league's top four teams was looked forward to with much anticipation by the Oldham fans, and for a quarter-of-an-hour the match lived up to its star billing. After just two minutes Turner broke away and put Davies clear. The international centre veered over to the right and passed to Cracknell, who scored in the corner. Ganley converted, but Hull then enjoyed some time in the Oldham half, during which Bateson kicked two penalty goals. From then on Oldham took full control, and it was something of a procession to the Hull line with Etty, Pitchford and Davies all going over before the interval. Five more tries followed after the break, including a brace for the in-form Jack Keith, with only a 75th minute consolation try for Sykes, converted by Bateson, in reply from the 'Airlie Birds'.

*Above: **John Etty** races clear of **Frank Broadhurst** and the Hull defence...*

Left: ... and heads for the try line at the pavilion end of Watersheddings.
(16.04.1958)

April 19th 1958: LEEDS 11 OLDHAM 26

V. Nestor, R. Cracknell, D. Ayres, A. Davies, J. Etty, A. Kellett, F. Pitchford.
K. Jackson, J. Keith, R. Dufty, C. Winslade, S. Little, D. Turner.
Goals: Cracknell,4. Tries: Pitchford,2. Davies. Jackson. Nestor. Turner.
Attendance: 21,000   Referee: Mr. C. Appleton – Warrington.

Ganley was a late withdrawal from the team, so Nestor filled in at full-back. There were early handling errors from both teams but Leeds settled down first, Stevenson setting up the first try for Broughton, converted by Jones. Oldham responded almost immediately with Winslade setting up a try for Pitchford, who in turn laid on the next two tries, first for Davies and then Jackson. Cracknell, who got the kicking duties, missed the first two conversions but slotted home the third, albeit off the post. However, he did add twp penalties to leave the score 15 – 5 to Oldham at the break. In the second half the Roughyeds took up where they left off, and after Etty had a try disallowed in the first minute, Pitchford touched down for a legitimate score two minutes later. Leeds hit back with tries from Robinson and the hard-working Tomlinson, but a length-of-the-field effort by Nestor soon put paid to any hopes of a revival, before Turner concluded the scoring late on.

April 26th 1958: OLDHAM 10   WORKINGTON T. 8

W.B. Ganley, R. Cracknell, D. Ayres, A. Davies, J. Etty, A. Kellett, F. Pitchford.
K. Jackson, J. Keith, R. Dufty, C. Winslade, S. Little, D. Turner.
Goals: Ganley,2. Tries: Dufty. Jackson.

Attendance: 14,682   Referee: Mr. G. Scott – Leeds.

Oldham expected a tough test from the Cumbrians, and they got it! After some tit-for-tat attacking in the first five minutes, Kellett had an unsuccessful drop-goal attempt, but Ganley put over a penalty shortly afterwards. The ever- alert Pitchford then kicked ahead a fumble by Archer and re-gathered the ball to put Dufty over for the opening try. Ganley converted, only for the Cumbrians to repay the Roughyeds in kind when Southward swooped in when Turner failed to hold a pass, to scoop up the ball and coast home from

75 yards out. Etty had a try disallowed for a forward pass before Oldham stretched their lead after 35 minutes. Ganley broke down the right and after the ball was then switched to the left, Little was held short, but Jackson barged over on the next play to leave the score 10 – 3 at half time. The second period was a tight affair, with the only score coming from Roper, who went over direct from a scrum without a hand being laid upon him. Southward converted but that was it, as the defences cancelled each other out and, to be fair, it was Oldham who dominated most of the remaining play.

Left: Ike Southward attempts to escape the clutches of John Etty.

Below: Alan Davies and Roger Dufty bring down Cec Thompson as Charlie Winslade looks on.

(26.04.1958)

May 3rd 1958: OLDHAM 8   HULL 20
Championship Top 4 play-off.
W.B. Ganley, R. Cracknell, D. Ayres, A. Davies, J. Etty, A. Kellett, F. Pitchford.
K. Jackson, J. Keith, R. Dufty, C. Winslade, S. Little, D. Turner.
Goals: Ganley. Tries: Dufty. Ayres.

Attendance: 21,000   Referee: Mr. M. Coates - Pudsey.

It is hard to believe the events at Watersheddings this day, when only two weeks previously Hull had been trounced by more than 40 points. However, the lessons were learned, and Oldham were caught cold, with Hambling and Finn combining to put Watts over after only three minutes. Surely this was a minor setback, and so it seemed when some crisp handling between Keith, Turner, Jackson and Etty paved the way for Dufty to equalise on 14 minutes. Ten minutes later a Bateson penalty put Hull back in front, and there then followed three tries before half-time that took the game away from the Roughyeds. First Sykes broke clear up the middle to put Cooper in for a converted try. Then Watts did likewise for Drake to score, and finally, just before the break, Whiteley opened up the shell-shocked Oldham defence once more for Sykes to score. Bateson added another conversion for the last try to leave the Roughyeds a mountain to climb with the score 3 – 18 at half-time. After 56 minutes Bateson added another penalty, and midway through the half, as tempers became heated, Harris was sent off for striking Pitchford. Shortly afterwards a Kellett break led to a try by Ayres, converted by Ganley, but from that point Hull battened down the hatches and held out for an unexpected but thoroughly deserved victory.

*Above: **John Etty** breaks away from **Ivor Watts** and **Brian Cooper** with back up from **Alan Davies** and **Frank Pitchford**.*

*Left: **Frank Pitchford** makes a tackle with **Dick Cracknell** and **Roger Dufty** ready to lend a hand.*

(03.05.1958)

1957-58

Most Appearances: John Etty, 44 out of a possible 46.
Most tries: Dick Cracknell 27.
Most goals: Bernard Ganley 200 - Most points: Bernard Ganley 412.

John Etty

Bernard Ganley

Dick Cracknell

	1057-58	Played	Won	Draw	Lost	For	Against	Points
1	**OLDHAM**	**38**	**33**	**1**	**4**	**803**	**415**	**67**
2	St. Helens	38	32	0	6	842	336	64
3	Workington T.	38	28	2	8	685	356	58
4	Hull	38	27	2	9	920	431	56
5	Wigan	38	27	0	11	815	430	54
6	Halifax	38	25	2	11	819	441	52
7	Leigh	38	24	0	14	625	457	48
8	Featherstone R.	38	23	1	14	606	497	47
9	Wakefield T.	38	22	2	14	729	477	46
10	Widnes	38	23	0	15	608	453	46
11	Hunslet	38	22	1	15	611	569	45
12	York	38	19	4	15	627	489	42
13	Warrington	38	19	1	18	669	529	39
14	Leeds	38	18	1	19	657	662	37
15	Salford	38	18	1	19	471	542	37
16	Hull K.R.	38	17	2	19	477	570	36
17	Whitehaven	38	17	1	20	559	579	35
18	Huddersfield	38	17	1	20	531	675	35
19	Rochdale H.	38	17	1	20	466	642	35
20	Bradford N.	38	16	2	20	574	594	34
21	Barrow	38	16	2	20	579	688	34
22	Keighley	38	15	2	21	576	527	32
23	Bramley	38	14	2	22	477	728	30
24	Swinton	38	13	3	22	506	589	29
25	Blackpool B.	38	12	0	26	488	726	24
26	Batley	38	10	0	28	434	722	20
27	Liverpool C.	38	9	1	28	442	728	19
28	Dewsbury	38	6	4	28	375	944	16
29	Castleford	38	7	1	30	443	893	15
30	Doncaster	38	4	0	34	246	971	8

1957-58

SEASON	PLAYER	APPS	TRIES	GOALS	POINTS
1957-58	J. ETTY	44	16		48
1957-58	R. CRACKNELL	43	27	4	89
1957-58	F. PITCHFORD	43	17		51
1957-58	W.B. GANLEY	42	4	200	412
1957-58	J. KEITH	41	12		36
1957-58	D. TURNER	41	10		30
1957-58	S. LITTLE	40	13		39
1957-58	K. JACKSON	40	5		15
1957-58	C. WINSLADE	34	3		9
1957-58	V. NESTOR	31	17		51
1957-58	A. DAVIES	28	18		54
1957-58	D. AYRES	25	8		24
1957-58	D. VINES	24	1		3
1957-58	F. DALEY	23	2		6
1957-58	J. NOON	19	9	13	53
1957-58	R. DUFTY	17	3		9
1957-58	A. KELLETT	14	3		9
1957-58	R. ROWBOTTOM	13			
1957-58	A. JARMAN	9	2		6
1957-58	F. STIRRUP	9			
1957-58	R. MOAT	6	2		6
1957-58	I. CARRUTHERS	5			
1957-58	D. McKEOWN	4			
1957-58	H. LOMAS	2			
1957-58	L. LAVERTY	1			
1957-58	**TOTAL**	**598**	**172**	**217**	**950**

Some consolation for Oldham was the presentation of the Lancashire League trophy after the play-off defeat to Hull.
Bernard Ganley *received the trophy from Mr C. Horsfield the Halifax member of the Rugby League Management committee with club president Mr. W. Howard also in attendance.   (03.05.1958)*

1958-59

Although the Law Cup went to Rochdale in the pre-season friendly, the Lancashire Cup was retained for the third consecutive year in the final against St. Helens at Swinton. The Saints gained revenge by defeating Oldham in the first round of the Challenge Cup at Watersheddings and after a promising run of nine victories in the last ten league matches put the Roughyeds up to fourth position in the league table, there was a devastating end to the season as Oldham were hammered at St. Helens in the Championship play-off.

Watersheddings now had cover on all four sides after the completion of the new stand behind the goals at the pavilion end of the ground. However, by the season's end, the great side had disintegrated with Turner, Vines and Etty all gone to Wakefield, Little, Daley and Cracknell retired and the likes of Ayres and Stirrup yet to play in only a handful of games for Oldham. Bernard Ganley still managed to bang over 190 goals and was the leading appearance maker with 41 out of a possible 44 in senior matches with Alan Kellett, now firmly established in the team, just one behind with 40. Dick Cracknell once again topped the try chart with 20 touchdowns.

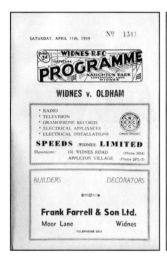   

1958-59

August 9ᵗʰ 1958: Rochdale H. 25   Oldham 10
Law Cup
W.B. Ganley, R. Cracknell, V. Nestor, D. Ayres, J. Etty, A. Kellett, A. Jones.
R. Rowbottom, J. Keith, H. Lomas, C. Winslade, S. Little, F. Daley.
Goals: Ganley,2. Tries: Jones,2.
Attendance: 6,471   Referee: Mr. K. Rathbone - St Helens.

Hornets started brightly and after a good break by Bailey was brought to a halt by an Etty smother tackle, Les Jones of Rochdale was off target with a penalty attempt following an infringement by his namesake, Oldham's Alan. Hornets took the lead in the 13ᵗʰ minute when Fishwick broke clear and was fortunate when his kick ahead took a ricochet off Ganley's back for him to pick up and score. After two missed penalty attempts by Ganley, Rochdale scored another try with Fishwick again involved making the final scoring pass to Smith. This time Les Jones added the conversion. Not to be out-done, Oldham's Alan hit back with two tries! First he was up in support of a Winslade break and then finished off a move started by Ayres and Nestor. Ganley converted both tries after which he and Bailey were lectured by the referee. Oldham's two point half-time lead was soon wiped out by a Jones penalty and Hornets took the lead when Fishwick again cut through the Oldham defence to set up a try for Chisnall. The same player was over again two minutes later when he followed up a kick ahead by Smith. Rochdale were now dominating the match completely. Etty was put clear by a long pass only to be tackled just short of the line but this was a rare excursion into Hornets territory and late on Short scored to make the match safe. Les Jones converted all the second half tries.

*Briers puts an early penalty attempt wide in
front of the new Watersheddings stand.*

(16.08.1958)

August 16th 1958: OLDHAM 21   HALIFAX 10

W.B. Ganley, R. Cracknell, J. Noon, D. Ayres, V. Nestor, A. Kellett, A. Jones.
H. Lomas, J. Keith, D. Vines, C. Winslade, D. McKeown, D. Turner.
Goals: Ganley,6. Tries: Kellett. Nestor. Cracknell.
Attendance: 12,319   Referee: Mr. A. Durkin – Dewsbury.

An early penalty miss by Briers was followed by a successful attempt by Ganley. However, Halifax were testing the Oldham line in the early stages. In the 11th minute Ganley added another penalty before Kellett received a pass from Jones direct from a scrum to scorch through for a try against his home town club. Ganley added the conversion but Briers was off target once more with a shot for Halifax. This prompted a change of kicker and Dean duly obliged with the next effort to put the visitors on the scoreboard. Oldham responded with a try from Nestor in the corner and, although the conversion failed, Ganley added another penalty to leave Oldham 14 – 2 in front at the break. In the second half Halifax initially enjoyed territorial advantage on the back of several penalties in their favour and the pressure told in the 55th minute when Dean put Burnett over for a try converted by Briers. Four minutes later Palmer scored another after a good 40 yard break down the right wing. The conversion was missed and Ganley stretched the Roughyeds lead with another penalty. The turning point in the match came when Williams looked set to score before a desperate tackle by Noon caused him to hit the corner flag as he went over the line. The nerves were finally settled by a converted late try from Cracknell.

*Right: **Bernard Ganley** tackles **Brian Sparks**.*

*Below: Action sequence - **Vince Nestor** goes for the line but is smothered by the Halifax defence just short of the posts.*
(16.08.1958)

August 19th 1958: BLACKPOOL B. 12   OLDHAM 34

W.B. Ganley, R. Cracknell, V. Nestor, D. Ayres, J. Noon, A. Kellett, F. Stirrup.
R. Rowbottom, J. Keith, D. Vines, C. Winslade, D. McKeown, D. Turner.
Goals: Ganley,8. Tries: Keith,2. McKeown. Rowbottom. Turner. Cracknell.
Attendance: 3,500   Referee: Mr. R. Welsby – Warrington.

Blackpool put in a tremendous display in the first half and took the lead after ten minutes with a Maughan penalty which was increased when prop forward Fitton lobbed a high pass to Emmitt who rounded Noon to score a converted try. Ganley kept Oldham in the hunt with three penalty goals before the Roughyeds found their form with a second half blitz from the forwards that brought three quick tries to McKeown, Keith and Rowbottom. Blackpool added a further penalty from Maughan and a second try for Emmitt but Oldham always looked comfortable for the rest of the match with Turner in exceptional form.

August 23rd 1958: WAKEFIELD T. 23   OLDHAM 7

W.B. Ganley, R. Cracknell, J. Edwards, D. Ayres, G. Sims, A. Kellett, F. Stirrup.
R. Rowbottom, J. Keith, D. Vines, C. Winslade, D. McKeown, D. Turner.
Goals: Ganley,2. Try: McKeown.

Attendance: 13,200   Referee: Mr. J. Manley – Warrington.

Oldham were second best in this match with Wakefield dominating from the early stages. After four minutes Kelly was stopped inches short after a good pass from Traill and it took a great tackle from debutant Geoff Sims to bring down Smith. Fox opened the scoring with a penalty before the Oldham line was breached after 14 minutes when a break by Poynton laid on a score for Rollin at the posts for Fox to convert. Ganley and Fox exchanged penalty goals and in the last minute of the half Houlden scored in the corner to leave 'Trinity' 12 – 2 up at the interval. In the second half Smith intercepted an Edwards pass to put Rollin over for his second try before the home scrum-half completed his 'hat-trick' beating four Oldham players in the process. The only consolation was a late try from McKeown who barged over with three defenders hanging on.

August 30th 1958: OLDHAM 49   WHITEHAVEN 5
Lancashire Cup 1st Round.

W.B. Ganley, R. Cracknell, A. Davies, D. Ayres, G. Sims, A. Kellett, F. Stirrup.
S. Little, J. Keith, D. Vines, C. Winslade, D. McKeown, D. Turner.
Goals: Ganley,8. Tries: Davies,4. Sims,2. Cracknell. Keith. Little. Ayres. Winslade.

Attendance: 12,000   Referee: Mr. G. Wilson – Dewsbury.

Alan Davies announced his return back from the summer tour to Australia and New Zealand by scoring the opening try after ten minutes, following good work from McKeown and Kellett, and went on to score another three in this one-sided affair. Cracknell, Little, Keith and another from Davies together with five goals from Ganley made it 25 – 0 at half-time. After the break the rout continued with Sims showing up well on his home debut with two tries.

The moment of an Oldham try is captured in a photograph taken from the main stand.

(30.08.1958)

250

1958-59

Alan Davies - Attack and defence!
Above: *Leaving several defenders in his wake and with* **Alan Kellett** *in support, he scores one of his four tries.*
Below: *This time preparing to bring down the Whitehaven winger* **Bill Smith.**
(30.08.1958)

1958-59

September 2nd 1958: OLDHAM 30   WORKINGTON T. 4

W.B. Ganley, G. Sims, A. Davies, J. Edwards, R. Cracknell, A. Kellett, F. Stirrup.
D. McKeown, J. Keith, D. Vines, C. Winslade, S. Little, D. Turner.
Goals: Ganley,6. Tries: Davies. Keith. Cracknell. Sims. Kellett. Winslade.
Attendance: 11,721   Referee: Mr. E. Clay – Rothwell.

Workington took an early lead with a first minute penalty from Stephenson who added another six minutes later as Oldham struggled to make an impression through a lack of possession. Ganley kicked a penalty goal after 17 minutes but it wasn't until five minutes from the interval that the first try was scored when Kellett beat four men before sending Davies in with a reverse pass. The conversion left Oldham 7 – 4 in

front at the break. The second half was a different story with the Roughyeds adding a further five tries, the pick of which were a 50 yard run by Kellett and a typical effort from Winslade where he touched down despite the attentions of several defenders.

*Left: **Derek Turner** prepares to meet the tackle of Workington's **Billy Ivison**.*

*Below: Referee, **Eric Clay** keeps an eye on the action as **Sol Roper** makes a tackle with **Des McKeown** standing by.*

(02.09.1958)

Déjà vous! (no it's not a repeat of the photo from the previous match)
Alan Davies *once again leaves the defence in tatters before heading for the posts.*
(02.09.1958)

September 6th 1958: HALIFAX 11   OLDHAM 27

W.B. Ganley, G. Sims, A. Davies, R. Cracknell, J. Etty, A. Kellett, F. Stirrup.
R. Dufty, J. Keith, D. McKeown, C. Winslade, S. Little, D. Turner.
Goals: Ganley,6. Tries: Kellett. Winslade. Davies. Little. Ganley.
Attendance: 15,301   Referee: Mr. F. Smith – Barrow.

There was a let-off for Oldham when Pearce took the ball straight from the kick off and put Williams clear only for the winger to be recalled for a forward pass. Then, likewise, in the sixth minute McKeown and Little combined to put Stirrup over, only for the referee to again rule out the score for a forward pass. After ten minutes a Ganley penalty put Oldham in front before Kellett stunned his home town club with a spectacular solo try. There was then a lengthy delay for an injury to Turner. When play resumed Marchant looked likely to score when he snapped up a loose pass from Winslade only to fall to a double tackle from Ganley and Sims. Stirrup then left the field with a head injury but Oldham went further ahead with tries from Winslade and Little and by half-time the lead was 17 – 0. Stirrup had his wound stitched and returned wearing a scrum-cap. Halifax did better in the second period with tries from Sparks, Williams and Palmer but Oldham were never in danger with Ganley capping a fine performance with the final try.

Alan Kellett *avoids two defenders to score the opening try.*
(06.09.1958)

September 13th 1958: OLDHAM 28 WAKEFIELD T. 11

W.B. Ganley, R. Cracknell, A. Davies, J. Noon, J. Etty, A. Kellett, B Hatherall.
R. Rowbottom, J. Keith, R. Dufty, C. Winslade, D. McKeown, D. Turner.
Goals: Ganley,5. Tries: Etty,2. Dufty. Noon. Cracknell .Kellett.

Attendance: 14,543   Referee: Mr. G. Wilson – Dewsbury.

Oldham gave a debut to scrum-half, Brian Hatherall and were eager to avenge the defeat at Belle Vue just three weeks previous. They were off to a good start when a lobbed pass from Kellett gave Noon the opportunity to put Etty over for a try in the corner. A Ganley penalty was followed by a try from Dufty

after some sleight-of-hand from Keith close to the 'Trinity' line. Fox got Wakefield on the board with a penalty but there was no holding the Roughyeds as Hatherall, showing up well in his first match, and Davies gave Noon the chance to power his way over for another try. A Further try from Cracknell against an interception from Rollin saw Oldham 18 – 5 to the good at half-time. The lead was increased by a Kellett special from half way and another for Etty before late scores from Holliday and Round gave the Trinity score an air of respectability.

*Left: **Alan Kellett** breaks through the 'Trinity' **defence.***

BELOW:
Left : Brian Hatherall** loses the ball when challenged by **Gerry Round.**
Right: John Noon** stumbles through the tackle of **Neil Fox.

(13.09.1958)

September 16th 1958: OLDHAM 19 WIGAN 7
Lancashire Cup 2nd Round.

W.B. Ganley, R. Cracknell, A. Davies, J. Noon, J. Etty, A. Kellett, F. Pitchford.
R. Rowbottom, J. Keith, R. Dufty, C. Winslade, S. Little, D. Turner.
Goals: Ganley,5. Tries: Davies. Keith. Pitchford.
Attendance: 20,543   Referee: Mr. R. Gelder – Wakefield.

Over 20,000 packed into Watersheddings for this Tuesday evening cup-tie and the majority were rewarded with a great defensive display from Oldham who wore down Wigan's forward dominated tactics in a tight first half to take control in the second period. A dour first 40 minutes saw Wigan with a big possession advantage met by a robust stint of tackling by the Roughyeds. Two penalties each for Ganley and Cunliffe saw the scores level at the break. However, just two minutes into the second half a scrum 30 yards from the Wigan line saw Pitchford dart away to gave Davies a clear run to the line for Ganley to convert. Next a break by Boston led to Sullivan racing clear only to be recalled for a forward pass. Ganley then failed with an attempt at a drop goal but soon after Turner slipped a delightful pass for Keith to scamper over with Ganley adding the extras. The game was up for Wigan when Collier dropped a pass which Pitchford scooped up to race away and score leaving several defenders in his wake. Late on Bolton and Evans laid on a try from the hard working Sayer but Oldham's victory was secure with the back row outstanding ably assisted by the tricky Pitchford.

Alan Davies prepares to take on *Brian McTigue* as *Jack Keith, Derek Turner* and *Bill Sayer* watch the action.
(16.09.1958)

September 20th 1958: ROCHDALE H. 13   OLDHAM 14

W.B. Ganley, R. Cracknell, A. Davies, J. Noon, G. Sims, A. Kellett, F. Pitchford.
R. Rowbottom, J. Keith, R. Dufty, C. Winslade, S. Little, D. Turner.
Goals: Noon,4. Tries: Davies. Kellett.

Attendance: 9,533   Referee: Mr. G. Battersby – Barrow.

Oldham started well and were unlucky to have a try disallowed in the second minute when the final pass of a 50 yard move from Keith to Dufty was ruled forward. Then Hornets enjoyed a good spell and soon after Short had intercepted a Kellett pass, Bailey dummied his way through the Oldham defence to score. The attacks were going from one side to another but the game erupted on 22 minutes when Ganley and Smith, the Rochdale stand-off half, were both sent off for apparently ignoring the referee's instruction to stop fighting. A minute later referee Battersby cautioned Winslade and Buxton as the match threatened to heat over. After 34 minutes Oldham had another try disallowed, this time Little being brought back for a forward pass but a minute later Davies was on hand to take a Pitchford pass and score for Noon to convert. Two minutes from the break Rochdale regained the lead when Hanson broke through strongly to put Short over for Richardson to convert leaving Hornets 8 – 5 in front at half-time. Noon brought Oldham to within a point with a penalty goal but bad handling was letting them down until Pitchford and Kellett covered 70 yards between them for the latter to score. Once again Noon added the conversion. Soon after Oldham had their third try disallowed for a forward pass with Dufty again denied by Mr. Battersby. After 73 minutes Hornets scored a great try with Short putting Buxton over for another 70 yards special, this time for Rochdale. Richardson's conversion put them one point up but three minutes later Oldham had the last say when Noon thumped over a 45 yard penalty to give victory to the Roughyeds.

September 27th 1958: OLDHAM 44   BLACKPOOL B. 3

L. Mee, R. Cracknell, A. Davies, J. Noon, G. Sims, F. Stirrup, B Hatherall.
R. Rowbottom, J. Keith, R. Dufty, S. Little, D. McKeown, D. Turner.
Goals: Noon,7. Tries: Noon,2. Cracknell,2. Sims,2. Little,2. Stirrup. Keith.

Attendance: 10,391   Referee: Mr. C. Whiteley – Warrington.

Oldham gave a debut to young Leigh born full-back, Len Mee to cover for Ganley's absence through suspension for his sending off the previous week. There was a shock for the Roughyeds when Blackpool took the lead after Dunn surprised the home defence by cutting inside to give Lannon the try scoring pass. Lowe missed the easy conversion. After 15 minutes the scores were level after Cracknell broke through and, although caught by Lowe, he managed to get the ball to Noon who touched down but could not convert his own score. However, he did add the extra points to a Stirrup try, made by Davies, to leave Oldham 8 – 3 up at the interval, although, Lowe had missed five shots at goal and Dunn one on a sad day for the 'Borough' kickers. After the break the Roughyeds settled down and began to turn on the style. Cracknell started the procession to the Blackpool line and the match was a personal triumph for Noon who finished with a twenty points haul from two tries and seven goals.

John Noon - Enjoyed a good day with a twenty point haul against Blackpool.

September 30th 1958: OLDHAM 9   WIDNES 4
Lancashire Cup semi-final
W.B. Ganley, R. Cracknell, A. Davies, J. Noon, G. Sims, A. Kellett, F. Pitchford.
R. Rowbottom, J. Keith, R. Dufty, C. Winslade, S. Little, D. Turner.
Goals: Ganley,3. Try: Pitchford.
Attendance: 13,674   Referee: Mr. M. Coates – Pudsey.

This was always likely to be a low scoring game due to the appalling weather conditions with driving rain sweeping across the Watersheddings' pitch. Oldham's answer was to employ a kicking game designed to keep Widnes in their own half and capitalise on any mistakes. At the break there were only a couple of points in it with Ganley knocking over two penalty goals to one from Dawson. The only try came after the Widnes prop forward Reg Smith put down a pass near the half way line to which the ever-alert Pitchford was first to react. He hacked the ball forward and after it had spun its way through several puddles it rested just short of the try line. However, with three defenders in pursuit, the Oldham scrum-half pulled off a

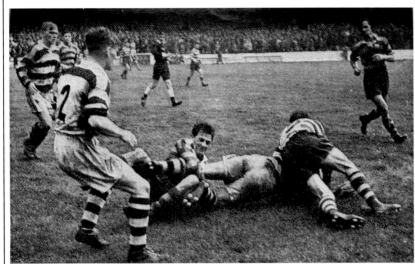

marvellous pick up in the slippery conditions to go over for a converted try. Widnes had the most of the second half possession but the Oldham defence held firm and just another penalty goal from Dawson was conceded. In fact the nearest to another try was when Cracknell kicked ahead only to be obstructed by Kinsey.

John Noon and *Geoff Sims*
bring down Reg Smith.
(30.09.1958)

October 4th 1958: WARRINGTON 13   OLDHAM 20
W.B. Ganley, R. Cracknell, A. Davies, J. Noon, J. Etty, A. Kellett, F. Pitchford.
R. Rowbottom, J. Keith, R. Dufty, C. Winslade, S. Little, D. Turner.
Goals: Ganley,4. Tries: Noon. Etty. Davies. Keith.
Attendance: 16,627   Referee: Mr. M. Coates – Pudsey.

Fraser missed an early penalty chance to put Warrington ahead and they were soon in arrears when, after eight minutes, Winslade latched on to a loose pass from Pitchford to make good ground before releasing the ball to Noon who scored in the corner. The 'Wire' hit back ten minutes later when Major paved the way for Challinor to cross near the posts for Fraser to convert. Then after half an hour, Ganley saw a penalty come back off the upright but within a couple of minutes Pitchford and Noon combined well to put Etty over and this time Ganley was on the mark with the conversion. Five minutes later Winslade was again instrumental in putting Davies over by the posts for a converted try but in the last minute of the half Bevan kept Warrington in it with a try to leave the half-time score 8 – 13 in the Roughyeds' favour. Stand-off, Jackie Edwards was in good form for Warrington for whom a Fraser penalty narrowed the deficit. A Ganley penalty stretched Oldham's lead and then came the score that settled the match. It started with a breakaway by Winslade in the Oldham half, Pitchford got with him and fed the ball on to the supporting Keith and, although he still had 45 yards to go, the Oldham hooker proved too quick for the fleet footed Warrington wingers, Bevan and O'Grady, to race away to the line. Ganley converted and despite a late try from the impressive Edwards, Oldham were always in command.

257

October 11ᵗʰ 1958: OLDHAM 22   ROCHDALE H. 18
W.B. Ganley, R. Cracknell, A. Davies, J. Noon, J. Etty, A. Kellett, F. Pitchford.
K. Jackson, J. Keith, R. Dufty, C. Winslade, D. McKeown, S. Little.
Goals: Ganley,5. Tries: Davies. Cracknell. Pitchford. Keith.
Attendance: 13,096   Referee: Mr. J. Flanagan – Keighley.

Oldham welcomed back Ken Jackson for his first match after being injured on the Australian tour. The early exchanges were quite even and after both Ganley and Jones had missed penalty attempts, it was the Oldham full back who opened the scoring in the 13ᵗʰ minute after a Rochdale obstruction. The game was scrappy with lots of whistle from the referee who hauled both hookers out for a lecture after a succession of scrum penalties. The Roughyeds finally broke the deadlock when Dufty broke away and although he was caught, from the advantage gained Kellett sent Davies racing round Cahill for the opening try. Ganley converted and just before the break sent over a magnificent 50 yard penalty goal to leave Oldham 9 – 0 in front. In the early part of the new half both teams had tries disallowed but sandwiched between these Cracknell got a legitimate score after a good break by McKeown. After 58 minutes Pitchford weaved his way over direct from a scrum for a converted try but Hornets hit back with a couple from Smith and Parr. After 75 minutes Keith scored to put Oldham 22 – 8 ahead but credit Hornets fighting spirit which brought them ten points in the last four minutes with converted tries from Fishwick and Chisnall.

*Above: **Frank Pitchford** avoids **Les Jones** to touch down.*
*Right: 'Back in Action' - **Ken Jackson** tackles **Alan Scholes**.*
*Below: **John Etty** brings down a Hornets attacker with **Des McKeown** and **John Noon** in support.*
(11.10.1958)

October 18th 1958: LIVERPOOL C. 13   OLDHAM 28

W.B. Ganley, G. Sims, A. Davies, J. Noon, J. Etty, A. Kellett, F. Stirrup.
K. Jackson, J. Keith, D. McKeown, C. Winslade, S. Little, D. Turner.
Goals: Ganley,8. Tries: Kellett,2. Sims. Stirrup.

Attendance: 2,000   Referee: Mr. T. Watkinson – Pendlebury.

After a bright start by the home team, Oldham opened the scoring with a magnificent penalty by Ganley from well inside his own half of the field and within minutes he had added a conversion after Kellett intercepted a loose pass to send Stirrup over. Liverpool were monopolising possession but only had two penalty goals from Twiss to show for it, whereas Ganley had added another three successes by the break. Three more penalty goals by Twiss brought Liverpool right back in the game before, midway through the half, Winslade and Davies carved an opening for Sims to race 70 yards for a converted try. That seemed to settle the Oldham nerves and despite of a try for Fishwick, a couple from Kellett either side of that score saw the Roughyeds comfortably home.

October 25th 1958: OLDHAM 12   ST. HELENS 2

Lancashire Cup Final played at Station Road, Swinton.

W.B. Ganley, R. Cracknell, A. Davies, J. Noon, J. Etty, A. Kellett, F. Pitchford.
R. Rowbottom, J. Keith, K. Jackson, C. Winslade, D. McKeown, D. Turner.
Goals: Ganley,2. Kellett. Tries: Kellett. Davies.

Attendance: 38,780   Referee: Mr. R. Gelder – Wakefield.

A 'hat-trick' of Lancashire Cup victories for the Roughyeds was achieved in this somewhat dour encounter with St. Helens whose cause was not helped by an injury to hooker McKinney that left him a passenger for most of the game. Injuries to Dufty and Little saw Rowbottom and McKeown drafted in to the team. The first real attacking chance went to Saints when Murphy broke from half way passed on for Howard and Large to put Carlton clear only for Cracknell to pull off a try saving tackle that sent the Saints winger into touch a yard short of the line. St. Helens continued to put pressure on the Oldham line and after Fearis had missed a 40 yard penalty in the eleventh minute, Ganley did well to bring down Howard, who had snapped up a loose pass from Winslade. The injured McKinney had handed the hooking duties over to Delves but it was still St. Helens in the ascendancy although Fearis missed another penalty chance, as did Ganley moments later. The deadlock was broken in the 27th minute when Kellett surprised the defence when he stopped in his tracks and coolly landed a drop goal. Fearis equalised with a penalty two minutes later and was unlucky a minute after that when he re-gathered his own kick ahead only to step in touch as he broke into the clear. Five minutes from the break Turner put Winslade away and the Welshman burst through towards the right wing from where Davies took his inside pass to go over at the posts. Ganley converted to leave Oldham 7 – 2 up at the interval. As in the first half it was St. Helens who were the first on the attack with Greenall putting Van Vollenhoven clear but a classic cover tackle from Kellett sent the South African flyer hurtling into touch. As the match went on Oldham looked the more likely to add to their score and, after a 59th minute penalty goal from Ganley, the match was made safe when, six minutes later, Pitchford put in a speculative grubber kick after Oldham had won a scrum and, although Fearis seemed to have it covered, Kellett was in like a flash to kick ahead once more and drop on the ball over the try-line. Try as they might the in the last quarter of an hour Saints could find no way through the Roughyeds defence.

Left: Alan Davies turns in towards the posts to score the first try.
Right: Davies again this time making a tackle on Peter Fearis.
(25.10.1958)

1958-59

Lancashire Cup Final 1958

*Above: **Alex Murphy** gets a kick away when challenged by **Derek Turner.***

Below: Two views of the celebrating Oldham players and officials.

(25.10.1958)

November 1st 1958: FEATHERSTONE R. 8   OLDHAM 30

W.B. Ganley, R. Cracknell, A. Davies, J. Noon, J. Etty, A. Kellett, F. Pitchford.
R. Rowbottom, J. Keith, K. Jackson, C. Winslade, D. McKeown, D. Turner.
Goals: Ganley,6. Tries: Davies,2. Cracknell. Pitchford. Kellett. Noon.
Attendance: 8,000   Referee: Mr. C. Appleton – Warrington.

Featherstone opened brightly with Clamp prominent on attack. Fox was off target with a penalty before Ganley slotted one over for Oldham. However, a minute later, direct from a scrum, the ball was moved to Smith who passed on to the injured Woolford on the wing who managed to avoid the cover and literally limp over for a try. Then, midway through the half, Clamp dummied his way through the initial Oldham defence and rounded Ganley for another try. This time Fox added the conversion. It was all Rovers at this point but the Roughyeds held firm. Ganley added another penalty and four minutes from the break Davies broke clear and from this position Pitchford sent a long pass for Cracknell to go over in the corner. This left Featherstone 8 – 7 in front at the interval but after the break Oldham took control immediately with Davies going clear in the first minute to draw in Cooper before giving Pitchford a walk in at the posts. Next, it was Pitchford the provider as he burst through to put Kellett over, again at the posts. Ganley was on target with both conversions and Oldham were safe. Davies chipped in with a couple of tries before Turner, who was the subject of much attention from the Rovers forwards, received his marching orders in the 72nd minute having been cautioned twice previously. Even with a man short Oldham still managed another try three minutes from full time when Noon reacted quickest to a charged kick to touch down.

November 8th 1958: OLDHAM 12   FEATHERSTONE R. 7

F. Stirrup, R. Cracknell, A. Davies, J. Noon, G. Sims, A. Kellett, F. Pitchford.
R. Rowbottom, J. Keith, K. Jackson, C. Winslade, D. McKeown, D. Turner.
Goals: Noon,3. Tries: Sims. Cracknell.
Attendance: 11,043   Referee: Mr. G. Wilson – Dewsbury.

Seven days on and it was an injury hit Featherstone who visited Watersheddings and proved to be a severe test for the Roughyeds. Once again the Yorkshiremen started the game well with Sims having to bring off two try saving tackles in the opening exchanges but after nine minutes Rovers took the lead when Greatorex scrambled over near the posts for Fox to convert. Oldham gradually got in the match and had two tries disallowed, first Sims was adjudged to have been held up over the line and then Davies was said to have grounded incorrectly. Stirrup, deputising for Ganley at full back, was having a fine game in defence and put in some pinpoint field kicks. Shortly before the interval Noon put Oldham on the scoreboard with a penalty. Featherstone were now a man short when Fox failed to come out for the second half. Noon reduced the arrears with another penalty and then converted after a Winslade break produced a try for Sims. Cooper got a penalty back for Rovers before Turner had a try disallowed on 70 minutes. However, just a minute later, Stirrup and Kellett laid on a try for Cracknell in the corner. However, there was a scare when, in the last minute, Kinsey intercepted and kicked ahead. The ball stopped on the Oldham try-line but the reliable Stirrup just got to the ball first and the match was won.

*A scramble as **Alan Davies** loses the ball near the Featherstone line. (08.11.1958)*

November 15th 1958: SALFORD 14   OLDHAM 9

W.B. Ganley, R. Cracknell, A. Davies, J. Noon, J. Etty, A. Kellett, F. Pitchford.
R. Rowbottom, J. Keith, K. Jackson, C. Winslade, R. Dufty, G. Kelly.
Goals: Ganley,3. Try: Winslade.

Attendance: 6,000   Referee: Mr. L. Wingfield – Normanton.

With Turner suspended for three matches after his sending off two weeks earlier, Oldham moved quickly to sign Geoff Kelly from Rochdale and the newcomer was soon in the action, driving into the heart of the Salford defence. However, it was against the run of play when, after 14 minutes, Winslade waded through four defenders to score at the posts for Ganley to convert. Although Oldham had a try from Noon disallowed for a forward pass, Salford were having by far the better of the play but by the break they only had a Lowdon penalty to show for their efforts. After the interval things got better immediately for the 'Red Devils' when Preece avoided Davies to score an unconverted try in the first minute. Five minutes later McGuinness scored another with Lowdon adding the extras. Bad handling let Oldham down time and again, with the effect that the only additions to the score were two penalties by Ganley. In between these Lowdon got another for Salford and concluded the scoring with a last minute drop goal.

November 22nd 1958: OLDHAM 13   LEEDS 12

W.B. Ganley, R. Cracknell, J. Noon, A. Davies, S. Quinlan, A. Kellett, F. Pitchford.
K. Jackson. J. Keith. D. McKeown. C. Winslade. S. Little. G. Kelly.
Goals: Ganley,2. Tries: Cracknell. Noon. Winslade.

Attendance: 13,417   Referee: Mr. A. Howgate – Dewsbury.

This was the debut match for the former Rugby Union international, Sean Quinlan and the Irishman received some vigorous attention when receiving an early pass from Kellett. A penalty was awarded but Ganley was wide of the mark. Lewis Jones had better luck when opening the scoring for Leeds soon after but by the 17th minute Ganley had missed another two. A sensational try from Cracknell gave Oldham the lead when the wingman broke clear of Hodgkinson and Jones and then rounded Quinn on a 60 yard run to the line. This time Ganley converted but he was again off the mark when another terrific break by Cracknell led to a try for Noon. Leeds then had some territorial advantage with hooker, Simms prominent in their attacks. Just before half-time they were rewarded when Lendill latched on to a Ward cross-kick to score. Jones converted to leave the score 13 – 7 at the break. A scrappy second period saw Oldham again missing several chances due to bad handling, although Kelly was unlucky to have a try disallowed for a double movement. Tomlinson barged his way over at the posts for Leeds with seven minutes left, but the Oldham defence held firm for a narrow victory.

Above: Geoff Kelly is brought down just short of the Leeds line.

Left: Sean Quinlan is tackled with Frank Pitchford and Ken Jackson looking on. (22.11.1958)

November 29th 1958: WIGAN 19 OLDHAM 7

W.B. Ganley, R. Cracknell, A. Davies, J. Noon, J. Etty, A. Kellett, F. Pitchford.
K. Jackson, J. Keith, R. Dufty, C. Winslade, S. Little, G. Kelly.
Goals: Ganley,2. Try: Etty.

Attendance: 24,782   Referee: Mr. J. Manley – Warrington.

Oldham started well with Winslade putting Kellett clear in the fourth minute, Pitchford was up in support to hand on to Etty who scored in the corner. Ganley converted magnificently from the touchline. Wigan hit back just three minutes later with Bolton, Thomas and Ashton laying on a chance for Boston to score wide out and as if to mirror Oldham's efforts, Cunliffe again knocked over a difficult conversion. This was a good, open match but the only other score of the half was another penalty from Cunliffe. After the interval Ganley levelled the scores in the 44th minute after which Wigan started to dominate proceedings with the veteran half-back Rees Thomas running the show. He put in a cross kick to which Sayer won the race to touch down and later slotted over a drop goal as Wigan edged clear. Oldham's fate was sealed near the end when a Cunliffe penalty hit an upright and bounced right back to Collier who duly scored. It later emerged that Jackson had soldiered on to finish the match after breaking a bone in his wrist.

December 6th 1958: OLDHAM 44 WIDNES 8

W.B. Ganley, R. Cracknell, A. Davies, D. Ayres, J. Etty, A. Kellett, F. Pitchford.
R. Rowbottom, J. Keith, S. Little, C. Winslade, G. Kelly, D. Turner.
Goals: Ganley,9. Turner. Tries: Cracknell,2. Kellett,2. Keith,2. Winslade. Ayres.

Attendance: 9,038   Referee: Mr. A. Durkin – Dewsbury.

After some early Widnes pressure this was an easy victory for the Roughyeds with two early penalties from Ganley followed by a Cracknell try laid on by Davies after 15 minutes. From there it was plain sailing with the speedy Kellett chipping in with a couple, as did hooker Keith. Myler scored a superb solo try for Widnes after 36 minutes but by half time it was 19 – 3 to Oldham and the second period continued in the same way. Winslade barged over five minutes into the new half with a humorous highlight being Turner's decision to drop a goal much to the amusement of the crowd.

Alan Davies breaks clear as *Frank Myler* moves in to tackle.   *(06.12.1958)*

December 13th 1958: WORKINGTON T. 0   OLDHAM 23
W.B. Ganley, R. Cracknell, J. Noon, D. Ayres, J. Etty, A. Davies, F. Pitchford.
S. Little, J. Keith, D. McKeown, C. Winslade, G. Kelly, D. Turner.
Goals: Ganley,4. Tries: Kelly. Ayres. Little. Noon. Pitchford.
Attendance: 6,031   Referee: Mr. A. Howgate – Dewsbury.

A strange match of two halves with Workington definitely superior in the first half, although the only score went to the Roughyeds as early as the fourth minute. After Ayres had gained good position, the Oldham forwards took over with McKeown, Winslade and Turner all involved in driving for the line before Kelly broke through to score. That was it for the first period, although Huddart and McDowell had tries disallowed and Kelly did well to nail Southward just short of the Oldham line. Bad handling let down both teams but 'Town' were unlucky to go in on the wrong side of the score-line. Two tries in the first ten minutes of the second half put Oldham in the ascendancy. First, Etty fielded a kick from Stephenson and

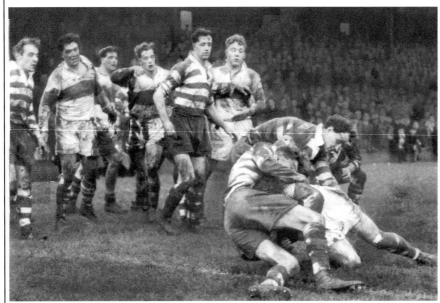

made good ground before putting Ayres in, then a superb inside pass from Davies put Little over. Further tries from Noon and Pitchford cemented the victory but in the closing stages the Roughyeds were left with only nine fit players after Turner and Pitchford had gone off injured while Cracknell and Kelly were both limping badly.

Players from both teams look on as the Oldham defence stop **McDowell** *near the try line. (13.12.1958)*

December 20th 1958: OLDHAM 21   WIGAN 18
W.B. Ganley, V. Nestor, A. Davies, D. Ayres, J. Etty, A. Kellett, F. Pitchford.
R. Rowbottom, J. Keith, S. Little, C. Winslade, G. Kelly, D. Turner.
Goals: Ganley,6. Tries: Davies,2. Kellett.
Attendance: 15,200   Referee: Mr. E. Clay – Rothwell.

This was a fine, open game with attacking play from the opening minutes when Sullivan was pulled into touch near the Oldham line. Griffiths and Ganley exchanged penalty goals before a break and kick ahead by Nestor produced a try for Davies. There was no conversion but Ganley obliged with a 23rd minute penalty. Then came a great solo effort from Boston who bumped off man after man on the way to the line.

Again there was no conversion but a penalty from Griffiths and two more tries from Sullivan put Wigan in front 13 – 7 at the interval. In the second period Kellett intercepted a Collier pass to score at the posts and then linked up with Ayres to put Davies in with Ganley converting both and then adding another penalty goal. Back came Wigan with Sullivan just denied his 'hat-trick' by some good defence which held him up just short of the try-line but from this position Evans scored with the conversion by Griffiths leaving the visitors just a point behind. Ganley was on target again in the 68th minute, his 100th goal of the season, and that was it. However, late in the match a 20 yard pass by Thomas to Sullivan looked set to level the match before the Oldham defence mustered en bloc to take the test wingman into the corner flag.

Mick Sullivan - *Two tries and an overall impressive performance for Wigan.*

December 25th 1958: OLDHAM 8   SWINTON 7
W.B. Ganley, R. Cracknell, D. Ayres, A. Davies, S. Quinlan, A. Kellett, F. Pitchford.
R. Rowbottom, G. Kelly, S. Little, C. Winslade, D. McKeown, D. Turner.
Goals: Ganley,4.

Attendance: 15,093   Referee: Mr. N. Railton – Billinge.

A hard fought victory for the 'try-less' Roughyeds, against a determined Swinton outfit. Jack Keith had cried off just before kick off with Geoff Kelly standing in as a makeshift hooker. Gowers opened the scoring with a penalty in the third minute and overall Swinton were the more lively outfit, although Oldham were unlucky when Pitchford put Cracknell over only for the winger to be recalled for a forward pass. Critchley got the only try after a good, long pass from Blan. This was converted and it was left to Ganley to keep Oldham in the hunt with three first half penalties. The one point advantage to Swinton at the break was reversed when Ganley landed his fourth goal on 50 minutes and from there defences

dominated as the Roughyeds hung on for the narrowest of victories. Haynes and Norburn were outstanding for the 'Lions' with Winslade, as usual, putting everything in for the Roughyeds' cause.

Dick Cracknell looks to release the ball to Dennis Ayres.

December 26th 1958: HUNSLET 14   OLDHAM 14
W.B. Ganley, S. Quinlan, A. Davies, D. Ayres, J. Etty, V. Nestor, F. Pitchford.
R. Rowbottom, P. Goddard, K. Lloyd, C. Winslade, S. Little, D. Turner.
Goals: Ganley,4. Tries: Pitchford. Quinlan.

Attendance: 11,000   Referee: Mr. T. Watkinson – Pendlebury.

With Keith still injured, Peter Goddard got his chance at hooker with Kevin Lloyd also making his Oldham debut in the second row. Langton opened the scoring with a penalty but this was followed by some powerful attacking play from Oldham. Winslade was having a grand game and it was a neat pass in the tackle from the Welshman that put Pitchford in for the first try, converted by Ganley. After 23 minutes it was Winslade again who paved the way for Davies to send in Quinlan for his first try for Oldham. Two more Ganley penalties against one to Langton gave the Roughyeds a 12 – 4 advantage at the break. Stockdill latched on to an handling error near the Oldham try-line to score a converted try for Hunslet but Oldham still looked comfortable. The match changed midway through the second half when Davies was sent off after an intervention by the touch-judge. This was the signal for Hunslet to hammer away at the Oldham line and two minutes into injury time Gunney broke clear and Stockdill got with him to score near the posts for Langton to slot home the equalising conversion.

1958-59

December 27th 1958: ST. HELENS 22   OLDHAM 6

W.B. Ganley, V. Nestor, A. Davies, D. Ayres, J. Etty, A. Kellett, F. Pitchford.
R. Rowbottom, P. Goddard, D. McKeown, C. Winslade, G. Kelly, D. Turner.
Goals: Ganley,3.

Attendance: 28,000   Referee: Mr. A. Durkin – Dewsbury.

Oldham won the toss and played with the wind and were soon on the attack with Kelly being held just short. From this position Saints were penalised for offside and Ganley opened the scoring. There were some fierce exchanges with the referee taking the names of Rowbottom and Vince Karalius in the first quarter. Dennis Karalius made the break that led to the first try and although Davies managed to bring him down, Murphy got over a minute later from a scrum close to the Oldham line. Rhodes converted but both he and Ganley missed subsequent penalty attempts before each registered one more to leave the half time score 7 – 4 to St. Helens. The match had ebbed and flowed between the two teams in a so far evenly matched contest. However, the send period belonged to the home team with impressive displays from Murphy and Huddart who scored a try, laid on another for Greenall and put in some great tackles. Prinsloo also crossed for Saints whereas a solitary penalty from Ganley was all Oldham had to offer as St. Helens ran out worthy winners.

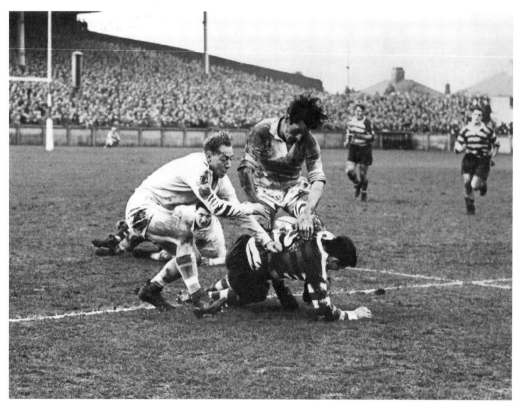

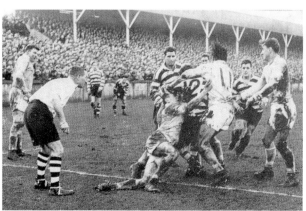

*Above: **Vince Karalius** and **Jan Prinsloo** haul down **Alan Davies**.*

*Opposite: It's **Karalius** again this time releasing a pass in the tackle*

*Left: **Geoff Kelly** is halted near the St. Helens try-line, backing up is **Derek Turner** during his last match for Oldham.*

(27.12.1958)

January 3rd 1959: OLDHAM 19 LEIGH 16
W.B. Ganley, G. Sims, A. Davies, V. Nestor, J. Etty, A. Kellett, F. Pitchford.
R. Rowbottom. J. Keith, H. Lomas, C. Winslade, S. Little, G. Kelly.
Goals: Ganley,5. Tries: Etty. Davies. Pitchford.
Attendance: 10,063   Referee: Mr. K. Rathbone - St. Helens.

A close match with had the result in doubt right up to the end. The first try came after 13 minutes when Pitchford broke from a scrum and threw a long ball out to Etty who met it on the burst and scattered several defenders on a 40 yard run to the line. Ganley converted but ten minutes later Leigh were back in the game when Dickens broke through to send Robinson crashing over for an unconverted try. Kellett made a great break of 60 yards which culminated with Kelly sending out a smart pass for Davies to score. Ganley was again on the mark with the conversion. Not to be outdone the visitors hit right back again with, this time, the powerful Owen forcing his way over for Fallon to convert and leave Oldham 10 – 8 in front at the interval. It was Owen again who paved the way for Martyn to score and give Leigh the lead. Fallon added the extras and after Ganley had scored a penalty, followed it up with a try again from a break by Owen. With ten minutes to go, a magnificent break away by Winslade was carried on by Pitchford who sailed round the full-back to score at the posts. Ganley converted and added a late penalty as Oldham scraped home.

January 31st 1959: LEEDS 18 OLDHAM 15
W.B. Ganley, R. Cracknell, V. Nestor, J. Noon, J. Etty, A. Kellett, F. Pitchford.
R. Rowbottom, J. Keith, H. Lomas, C. Winslade, S. Little, G. Kelly.
Goals: Ganley,3. Tries: Nestor. Pitchford. Etty.
Attendance: 20,000   Referee: Mr. D. Davies - Manchester.

After Kellett nearly opened the scoring when he just failed to hold on to an interception after six minutes, it was the pace of the Leeds backs that was Oldham's undoing. Midway through the half full-back, Quinn linked up with the three-quarters and passed on to Hemmingway who showed Etty a clean pair of heels on his way to the line. Ganley and Jones exchanged penalties, then two minutes before the interval, Brown broke clear and kicked ahead, Hallas hacked the ball on with Etty, Pitchford and Ganley in pursuit but once again it was the fleet-footed Hemmingway that won the race to touch down. Next Robinson scooped up a loose pass to put Garside over. Oldham replied with tries from Nestor and Pitchford before Skelton scored for Leeds on 73 minutes. However, the Roughyeds refused to capitulate and a minute later Etty was over after a great ball from Pitchford direct from a scrum but it was too little, too late.

1958-59

February 7th 1959: OLDHAM 19   WARRINGTON 8

W.B. Ganley, G. Sims, A. Kellett, J. Noon, J. Etty, F. Daley, F. Pitchford.
K. Jackson, J. Keith, H. Lomas, C. Winslade, S. Little, D. McKeown.
Goals: Ganley,5. Tries: Kellett. Noon. Sims.
Attendance: 12,000   Referee: Mr. G. Philpott – Leeds.

Frank Daley was brought back into the team exactly ten years after his debut match while Alan Kellett reluctantly moved to centre. Warrington were unlucky to lose their hooker, Harper after just four minutes but they did take the lead with a Fraser penalty. Daley was showing that he had lost none of his defensive skills whereas Kellett defied his unaccustomed position to score a glorious try when he broke through, kicked ahead and re-gathered to touch down. This was followed by a sweeping move where Pitchford, Jackson, Sims and Keith all handled before Noon finished off for Ganley to convert. The Oldham marksman then added two penalty goals to give the Roughyeds a 12 – 2 lead at half-time. There was a strange try to open the second half scoring when Pitchford put Sims clear but as three Warrington defenders looked set to crunch the Oldham winger, he somehow bounced off all of them and promptly ran in to score at the posts. After 54 minutes things got worse for the 'Wire' when O'Grady went off injured but notwithstanding this latest setback Warrington set about getting back in the match. First, Regan went through a huge gap in the Oldham defence to put Fraser over and then, after O'Grady had returned to the field, Edwards broke through and kicked ahead for Bevan to win the race to touch down. However, neither try was converted and Ganley closed the scoring with a last minute penalty.

*Left: **Eric Fraser** releases a pass as the Oldham defence closes in.*

*Below Left: **Des McKeown** is tackled in mid-field.*

*Opposite: **Bobby Greenough** and **Harry Major** tackle **John Noon** with **Sid Little, John Etty** and **Brian Bevan** close by.*

*Below : **Alan Kellett** breaks clear.*

(07.02.1959)

1958-59

The Oldham team against Warrington. *(07.02.1959)*
Back Row: *Des McKeown, Charlie Winslade, Sid Little, Harold Lomas, Ken Jackson, Jack Keith.*
Middle Row: *Geoff Sims, John Noon, Bernard Ganley, John Etty, Alan Kellett.*
Front Row: *Frank Daley, Frank Pitchford.*

1958-59

February 14th 1959: LEIGH 11   OLDHAM 7
A. Kellett, G. Sims, J. Noon, D. Ayres, J. Etty, V. Nestor, F. Pitchford.
K. Jackson, P. Goddard, S. Little, C. Winslade, R. Dufty, D. McKeown.
Goals: Noon,2. Try: Nestor.

Attendance: 10,000   Referee: Mr. C. Appleton – Warrington.

In Ganley's absence Charlie Winslade was given the captaincy and Kellett further showed his versatility by filling in at full-back. Noon opened the scoring with a magnificent penalty goal from 55 yards and added another after ten minutes with Fallon replying with a goal for Leigh between the two. The only try in a tight first half came after Little broke through to send Nestor in at the corner. Fallon put over another penalty to leave Oldham 7 – 4 up at the break and added another three minutes into the second period. Leigh were hampered when Robinson had to leave with a wound that required four stitches but they were the more lively of the two teams with Owen, Martyn and Tabern showing up well. The deciding score came after 63 minutes when Martyn crashed over although the Oldham players protested that he was 'held up' without grounding the ball. Nevertheless, the score stood to which Fallon added the conversion. The home team were off target with two late drop goal attempts but hung on for a deserved victory.

Oldham on Defence!

Left: Peter Goddard, Des McKeown and *Sid Little* *bring down Walt Tabern.*

Below: Stan Owen is *brought to a halt by Ken Jackson, Des McKeown* and *Roger Dufty.*

(14.02.1959)

February 21ˢᵗ 1959: OLDHAM 6   ST. HELENS 7
Rugby League Challenge Cup 1ˢᵗ Round.
W.B. Ganley, R. Cracknell, V. Nestor, A. Davies, J. Etty, A. Kellett, F. Pitchford.
K. Jackson, J. Keith, S. Little, C. Winslade, R. Dufty, D. McKeown.
Goals: Ganley, 3.
Attendance: 23,000   Referee: Mr. E. Clay – Leeds.

A big crowd gathered at Watersheddings for this cup tie but they, like the players, had to put up with miserable, wet conditions. The opening exchanges were even but the decisive moment of the match came on 16 minutes when the Saints prop-forward, Terry, slipped a tackle to break away. The lightening-fast Murphy got with him and veered over to the wing to put Greenall in at the corner. There was no conversion but Oldham were ruled offside at the restart and Fearis landed a penalty from half way. He got another one on 35 minutes, whereas the normally reliable Ganley missed five attempts in a first half to forget. In the second period Ganley fared much better with three successes. Davies was held just short twice after a set move from the scrum and in spite of the Oldham crowd roaring on the team after Ganley's last penalty on 72 minutes, it was St. Helens who dominated possession in the closing stages to see out the match.

A scramble in the mud near the Oldham try-line.
(21.02.1959)

February 28ᵗʰ 1959: WHITEHAVEN 14   OLDHAM 3
W.B. Ganley, R. Cracknell, A. Davies, J. Noon, J. Etty, V. Nestor, F. Pitchford.
K. Jackson, L McIntyre, R. Smith, D. McKeown, R. Dufty, G. Kelly.
Try: Nestor.
Attendance: 4,000   Referee: Mr. C. Appleton – Warrington.

Muddy conditions greeted the teams in this match when Oldham had a new-look front row with debuts for the newly signed, Len McIntyre and local lad, Dick Smith. The star of the match was home stand-off, Brian Davies who opened the scoring with a try in the eighth minute and followed it up by putting in a precise kick ahead that enabled Hughes to send in Baker for the second try. McIntyre was showing up well but Whitehaven were in total control and it was no more than they deserved when Davies took a quick tap penalty to send in Tembey for the third try which, after two previous failures, he managed to convert to give his team an 11 – 0 advantage at the break. Oldham were better after the interval but Whitehaven scored again when Gibson and Tembey put Smith over. Ironically, the Roughyeds then produced the best try of the game when Pitchford 'sold the dummy' to several defenders to break away from his own half and then send Nestor clear on a 40 yard run to the line. In keeping with the rest of the performance Ganley's conversion came back off the cross-bar.

Dick Smith (left) and Len McIntyre both made their first appearance for the Roughyeds at Whitehaven.

March 14th 1959: HULL 20 OLDHAM 8

W.B. Ganley, R. Cracknell, V. Nestor, J. Noon, G. Sims, A. Kellett, F. Pitchford.
K. Jackson, J. Keith, D. McKeown, C. Winslade, S. Little, R. Pugsley.
Goal: Ganley. Tries: Noon. Nestor.

Attendance: 10,000　　　　　　　Referee: Mr. D. Davies. – Manchester.

Another debut on this day for Welshman Bob Pugsley at loose forward. After 25 minutes two penalty goals by Keegan separated the teams but then a loose pass from Pitchford was snapped up by Boustead who put Matthews clear for a converted try. Oldham got back in the match after a thumping tackle from McKeown dislodged the ball from Sutton. Kellett was on to it in a flash to race 60 yards before sending Noon in for a try converted by Ganley. Just before the interval another Keegan penalty left the score 11 – 5 at the break. After a scoreless third quarter there was a carbon copy of the first score with Boustead again capitalising on a handling error to give Matthews his second try. The next score went to Watts who kicked ahead and re-gathered to score after indecision in the Oldham defence. Nestor gave Oldham some hope when he broke though and shaped as if to kick but held on to go in for the try. The score was unconverted and the pattern of the day continued with Boustead scoring the last try after another Oldham handling error. Sykes, who took over the kicking for the injured Keegan, had no luck with any of the second half conversions.

March 21st 1959: OLDHAM 39 BARROW 13

W.B. Ganley, I. Southward, A. Davies, V. Nestor, G. Sims, A. Kellett, F. Pitchford.
K. Jackson, J. Keith, H. Lomas, C. Winslade, S. Little, R. Pugsley.
Goals: Ganley,9. Tries: Lomas,2. Davies. Pitchford. Sims. Southward. Keith.

Attendance: 10,220　　　　　　　Referee: Mr. G. Wilson – Dewsbury.

Yet another debut, this time for the international winger Ike Southward signed from Workington for a world record fee of £10,650. Barrow took the lead in the fourth minute when Hanley and Ball combined well to put Rea over. Ball converted but then Oldham blitzed the 'Furness-men' with 20 points in 18 minutes to take control of the match. The first try went to Lomas after good work by fellow prop, Jackson. Then, Davies took a Pitchford pass at pace to cut through the Barrow defence. Next, it was Pitchford himself inter-passing with Kellett to register the third try and then Nestor put Sims clear for the fourth. Ganley converted the lot and added a couple of penalties to leave the Roughyeds 24 – 5 up at the break. Fifteen more points in the first eleven minutes of the second half reinforced Oldham's superiority. Lomas got his second try with the crowd particularly cheering a touchdown for Southward before Keith concluded the Oldham try tally. Ganley was on the mark again with all the conversions before Dawes and Delves got late consolation scores for the visitors.

*Above: Ike Southward on his debut
match against Barrow.*

Left: Alan Davies scores under the posts

(21.03.1959)

March 27th 1959: SWINTON 8   OLDHAM 19

W.B. Ganley, I. Southward, A. Davies, J. Noon, G. Sims, A. Kellett, F. Pitchford.
K. Jackson, J. Keith, H. Lomas, C. Winslade, S. Little, R. Pugsley.
Goals: Ganley,5. Tries: Southward. Davies. Keith.
Attendance: 14,000   Referee: Mr. G. Philpott – Leeds.

After a fifth minute penalty from Ganley, Swinton hit back when Cartwright charged down a kick from the Oldham full-back to score for Gowers to convert. However, the Roughyeds were the faster team in this encounter with first half tries from Southward, quickly starting to repay the huge fee invested in him, Davies and Keith. Kellett had a hand in all of the tries as the 'Lions' struggled to cope with the pace of the speedy stand-off. Ganley chipped in with five goals as Oldham went in with a 19 – 5 lead at half-time. The only points of a dull second period came in the 59th minute when McGowan snapped up a loose ball and sprinted to the try line.

March 30th 1959: OLDHAM 5   HULL 0

W.B. Ganley, I. Southward, A. Davies, J. Noon, V. Nestor, A. Kellett, F. Pitchford.
K. Jackson, J. Keith, D. McKeown, H. Lomas, S. Little, R. Pugsley.
Goal: Ganley. Try: Noon.
Attendance: 15,321   Referee: Mr. R. Gelder – Wakefield.

This was a tough, uncompromising, forward dominated encounter with the only score in the first half coming from a 15th minute Ganley penalty. Oldham were unlucky to have a try ruled out after a McKeown break was finished off by a bout of inter-passing between Southward and Davies only for the final pass to be ruled forward. The move that settled the match came with just six minutes left when McKeown again made the initial break through, then handed on to Southward who passed back inside to Pugsley who had Pitchford in support. The Oldham scrum-half then picked out Noon coming through with a forceful burst to score at the corner for the match clincher.

Bernard Ganley breaks away up the left wing with **Stan Cowan** in pursuit.   (30.03.1959)

April 4th 1959: OLDHAM 67   LIVERPOOL C. 6

W.B. Ganley, R. Cracknell, V. Nestor, J. Noon, G. Sims, A. Kellett, F. Pitchford.
K. Jackson, J. Keith, H. Lomas, D. McKeown, S. Little, R. Pugsley.
Goals: Ganley,14. Tries: Cracknell,4. Kellett,4. Jackson. Pitchford. Sims. Little. Noon.
Attendance: 9,401   Referee: Mr. T. Watkinson – Pendlebury.

A record score and a record of 'goals in a match' for Bernard Ganley! Liverpool actually took the lead with a first minute penalty from Simpson but after a lobbed pass from Keith sent Jackson in for the first try, which ironically Ganley failed to convert, it was one way traffic with the Roughyeds well in command by half-time with a 32 – 6 lead. Kellett and Cracknell both bagged four tries with Ganley's record breaking goal coming in the last minute. The pick of the tries was a 60 yard special from Kellett with Cracknell also adding two long range efforts.

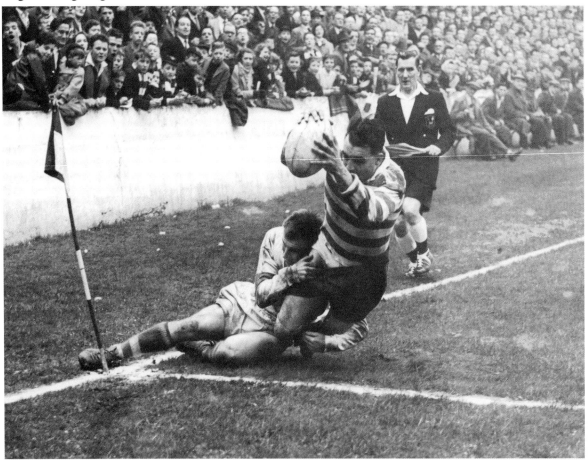

Above: Dick Cracknell scores his fourth try.

Left: Vince Nestor cuts through the Liverpool defence. (04.04.1959)

April 7th 1959: OLDHAM 25 SALFORD 10

W.B. Ganley, I. Southward, A. Davies, V. Nestor, R. Cracknell, A. Kellett, F. Pitchford.
K. Jackson, J. Keith, D. McKeown, R. Dufty, H. Lomas, R. Pugsley.
Goals: Ganley,5. Tries: Cracknell,2. Davies. Southward. Pitchford.
Attendance: 8,177 Referee: Mr. G. Wilson – Dewsbury.

Persistent rain had left the pitch in a treacherous condition but the 8,000 plus hardy souls who braved the elements were treated to some decent rugby with Pitchford the star of the show. Ganley knocked over two early penalties but Salford hit back when Banks opened up the Oldham defence to send Preece over for Lowdon to convert. The lead was restored when Davies brought off a wonderful one handed take from a Pitchford pass to score a converted try. After the break Keith created an opening for Cracknell who took three defenders over with him for a splendid try. Bettinson got one back for the 'Red Devils' but Oldham were always in control and after Southward and Cracknell added further tries, it was left to Pitchford who made light of the heavy conditions to skip through the Salford defence for the final touchdown.

Referee, **George Wilson** *points for the try after* **Alan Davies** *grounded the ball before being dragged over the dead ball line, against Salford.*

(07.04.1959)

April 11th 1959: WIDNES 28 OLDHAM 6

W.B. Ganley, I. Southward, A. Davies, J. Noon, V. Nestor, A. Kellett, F. Pitchford.
K. Jackson. J. Keith. S. Little. R. Dufty. H. Lomas. R. Pugsley.
Tries: Southward,2.
Attendance: 6,939 Referee: Mr. J. Jowett – Leeds.

A bad day at the office for Oldham who started brightly enough with Nestor being denied by a great cover tackle from Thompson and only an awkward bounce from a Southward cross-kick stopping either the supporting Keith or Noon from touching down. However, once Bate had put Myler through with a slick pass in the 27th minute there was only going to be one winner. Myler added a second try and Pimblett a third and also two goals to leave Widnes 13 – 0 up at the break. Five minutes into the second half Southward was called back for a forward pass from Kellett and although he later got two legitimate scores, Widnes remained in control with Myler completing a deserved 'hat-trick'.

1958-59

April 14th 1959: OLDHAM 32 HUNSLET 12

W.B. Ganley, I. Southward, A. Davies, J. Noon, R. Cracknell, A. Kellett, F. Pitchford.
R. Rowbottom, J. Keith, H. Lomas, C. Winslade, R. Dufty, D. McKeown.
Goals: Ganley,10. Tries: Southward,2. Kellett. Noon.
Attendance: 12,442   Referee: Mr. A. Howgate – Dewsbury.

This was likely to be a tricky match against high-flying Hunslet, with Oldham needing victory in all their remaining matches to keep their play-off hopes alive.

Langton and Ganley exchanged penalty goals before what looked like a blatant obstruction from Robbins went unpunished leaving Colin to score the first try converted by Langton. Three more Ganley goals kept the score close then right on half-time referee Howgate again upset the Oldham crowd by failing to whistle for a knock on with Colin once again touching down. Two minutes after the break the Roughyeds showed their intent with a sweeping move involving Pitchford, Kellett and Davies who handed on to Southward and though still with much to do, the Cumbrian winger left Hunslet clutching at shadows on his way to the line. From here Oldham were always in command with Ganley's 'ten from ten' goal attempts being a major factor in the victory.

*Above: Ike Southward brings down **Kevin Doyle** with **Des McKeown** and **Roger Dufty** in attendance.*

*Below: Which way will he go? **Brian Shaw** contemplates the next move for Oldham centre, **Alan Davies**. (14.04.1959)*

276

1958-59

April 18ᵗʰ 1959: OLDHAM 29   WHITEHAVEN 19

W.B. Ganley, I. Southward, A. Davies, J. Noon, R. Cracknell, A. Kellett, F. Pitchford.
K. Jackson, J. Keith, H. Lomas, C. Winslade, R. Dufty, R. Pugsley.
Goals: Ganley,7. Tries: Southward,2. Pitchford,2. Cracknell.
Attendance: 11,078   Referee: Mr. H. Harrison – Horbury.

Whitehaven had the best of the first half with Geoff Robinson, in fine form, barging through to score under the posts in the sixth minute. Davies put Southward clear and the wingman kicked ahead and won a 50 yard race to touch down as the ball nestled over the try-line. Four goals from Forster gave the Cumbrians an 11 – 7 advantage at the interval. After Robinson and Davies had put Stephenson over for the visitors Oldham eased ahead in the second half with Southward scoring another great try holding off three defenders on his way to the line. Meanwhile the elusive Pitchford chipped in with a couple of tries.

Frank Pitchford leaves several Whitehaven defenders in his wake as he goes over for one of his two tries.
(18.04.1959)

April 20ᵗʰ 1959: BARROW 20   OLDHAM 21

W.B. Ganley, I. Southward, A. Davies, J. Noon, V. Nestor, A. Kellett, F. Pitchford.
K. Jackson, J. Keith, H. Lomas, C. Winslade, R. Dufty, R. Pugsley.
Goals: Ganley,6. Tries: Nestor. Noon. Pugsley.
Attendance: 6,247   Referee: Mr. R. Gelder – Wakefield.

Oldham set off well in this match with Davies capitalising on a handling error to put Nestor over and then Jackson carving an opening for Noon to score. These tries, along with four Ganley goals, put Oldham in the driving seat but Delves set up a try for Grundy just on half-time to give the home side some hope as they went in 5 – 14 behind. Wilson brought Barrow closer with a converted try before a break by Noon set up Pugsley to score under the posts. Barrow never gave up and two late tries from Rea and Wilson gave Oldham a nervous few minutes in the closing stages.

April 27th 1959: OLDHAM 15   ST. HELENS 14

W.B. Ganley, I. Southward, A. Davies, V. Nestor, R. Cracknell, A. Kellett, F. Pitchford.
K. Jackson, J. Keith, S. Little, C. Winslade, R. Dufty, R. Pugsley.
Goals: Ganley,3.   Tries: Keith. Nestor. Southward.

Attendance: 19,000   Referee: Mr. C. Appleton – Warrington.

St. Helens were the form team and victory in this match would have given them the Lancashire league title, whereas Oldham needed to win to qualify for the top four play-offs. Saints applied pressure from the start and after 14 minutes a neat reverse pass from Briggs put Murphy over.

Briggs converted but that was to be the only goal for St. Helens. Three unanswered tries, with Keith scoring the first and having a hand in the other two, put Oldham in control with three Ganley goals leaving the score 15 – 5 at the interval. The Saints forwards took command in the second half and tries for Van Vollenhoven (2) and Smith brought them right back into the match but the lack of a kicker cost them dear with the Lancashire league championship going to Wigan. Meanwhile, Oldham had qualified for the play-offs.

Perhaps they later wished that they hadn't!

Above:
Bob Pugsley and
Roger Dufty bring
down *Abe Terry*.

Left:
Alan Davies can only
watch as *Alex Murphy*
scores the opening try
of the match.

(27.04.1959)

1958-59

May 2nd 1959: ST HELENS 42 OLDHAM 4
Championship Top 4 play-off.
W.B. Ganley, R. Cracknell, A. Davies, A. Kellett, V. Nestor, F. Daley, F. Pitchford.
R. Rowbottom, J. Keith, H. Lomas, C. Winslade, R. Dufty, S. Little.
Goals: Ganley,2.

Attendance: 22,000   Referee: Mr. M. Coates – Pudsey.

It was a makeshift team that took on the champions elect with Frank Daley brought in and Sid Little acting as a stand-in loose forward. Saints showed no mercy and perhaps had an element of revenge in mind for the reverse earlier in the week. The writing was on the wall from the fifth minute when Terry put Large over and, although Ganley managed a couple of long range penalty goals, by half-time it was 16 – 4 and the match was as good as over. St. Helens finished the game with ten tries, including a 'hat-trick' for Large, as Oldham caved in. It was a shame that this proved to be the last senior game for Little, Cracknell and Daley. All three were deserving of a better finale.

*Left and Centre: **Ken Large** goes over for two of his three tries.*
*Right: A rare Oldham attack sees **Dick Cracknell** evade **Jan Prinsloo**.*
(02.05.1959)

May 5th 1959: Oldham v Halifax
Frank Daley benefit match
Oldham:
F. Stirrup, I. Southward, A. Kellett, A. Davies, T. O'Grady (Warr),
J. Edwards (Warr), J. Brennan (Salf).
S. Owen (Leigh), J. Keith, A. Mumberson, C. Winslade, R. Dufty, F. Daley.

Halifax:
Owen, Snowden, Burnett, Freeman, Sims (Oldham), Dean, Pratt.
Thorley, Shaw, Fairbank, Pierce, Turnbull, Fearnley.
Attendance: 3,559   Referee: Mr. R.L. Thomas - Oldham.

This was a much deserved benefit match for the popular Wiganer who served Oldham well in various positions for over ten years. Oldham, aided by several guest players, won the match which was played in a typical end-of-season manner with the man himself starting at loose forward. The talking points for the supporters were the debut of the newly signed Cumbrian prop-forward, Alf Mumberson and another wonder try from the mercurial Ike Southward.

*'Dancing Dan' - **Frank Daley***

1958-59

Most Appearances: Bernard Ganley, 41 out of a possible 44.
Most tries: Dick Cracknell 20.
Most goals: Bernard Ganley 190 - Most points: Bernard Ganley 383.

Bernard Ganley

Dick Cracknell

	1958-59	Played	Won	Draw	Lost	For	Against	Points
1	St. Helens	38	31	1	6	1,005	450	63
2	Wigan	38	29	0	9	894	491	58
3	Hunslet	38	27	3	8	819	493	57
4	**OLDHAM**	**38**	**28**	**1**	**9**	**791**	**477**	**57**
5	Wakefield T.	38	27	1	10	790	393	55
6	Swinton	38	27	1	10	691	442	55
7	Hull	38	25	1	12	796	413	51
8	Widnes	38	23	0	15	672	474	46
9	Warrington	38	22	0	16	780	585	44
10	Bradford N.	38	20	2	16	593	563	42
11	York	38	20	1	17	621	622	41
12	Halifax	38	19	2	17	695	594	40
13	Featherstone R.	38	18	3	17	597	613	39
14	Leeds	38	19	0	19	608	653	38
15	Keighley	38	18	1	19	560	629	37
16	Leigh	38	18	0	20	585	562	36
17	Barrow	38	18	0	20	573	602	36
18	Hull K.R.	38	18	0	20	542	619	36
19	Huddersfield	38	18	0	20	573	677	36
20	Workington T.	38	16	3	19	499	585	35
21	Whitehaven	38	17	0	21	659	627	34
22	Salford	38	16	1	21	603	680	33
23	Bramley	38	15	1	22	409	579	31
24	Blackpool B.	38	15	0	23	477	753	30
25	Castleford	38	13	0	25	527	732	26
26	Rochdale H.	38	11	1	26	398	649	23
27	Batley	38	10	1	27	433	679	21
28	Liverpool C.	38	8	0	30	476	954	16
29	Dewsbury	38	7	0	31	378	859	14
30	Doncaster	38	5	0	33	329	924	10

1958-59

SEASON	PLAYER	APPS	TRIES	GOALS	POINTS
1958-59	W.B. GANLEY	41	1	190	383
1958-59	A. KELLETT	40	18	1	56
1958-59	J. KEITH	39	13		39
1958-59	C. WINSLADE	38	6		18
1958-59	A. DAVIES	36	19		57
1958-59	F. PITCHFORD	36	13		39
1958-59	R. CRACKNELL	32	20		60
1958-59	S. LITTLE	30	6		18
1958-59	J. NOON	29	13	16	71
1958-59	D. McKEOWN	26	2		6
1958-59	D. TURNER	22	1	1	5
1958-59	K. JACKSON	22	1		3
1958-59	J. ETTY	21	6		18
1958-59	R. ROWBOTTOM	21	1		3
1958-59	R. DUFTY	20	1		3
1958-59	V. NESTOR	19	7		21
1958-59	G. SIMS	16	10		30
1958-59	H. LOMAS	14	2		6
1958-59	D. AYRES	11	3		9
1958-59	G. KELLY	11	1		3
1958-59	R. PUGSLEY	10	1		3
1958-59	I. SOUTHWARD	9	10		30
1958-59	F. STIRRUP	7	2		6
1958-59	D. VINES	5			
1958-59	S. QUINLAN	3	1		3
1958-59	P. GODDARD	3			
1958-59	J. EDWARDS	2			
1958-59	B. HATHERALL	2			
1958-59	F. DALEY	2			
1958-59	A. JONES	1			
1958-59	L. MEE	1			
1958-59	K. LLOYD	1			
1958-59	L. McINTYRE	1			
1958-59	R. SMITH	1			
1958-59	**TOTAL**	**572**	**158**	**208**	**890**

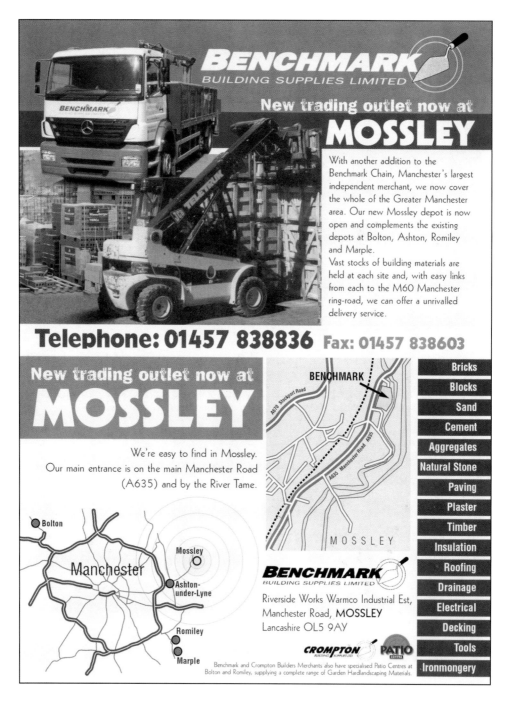

1959

The 1959-60 season started well enough, with the Law Cup being retained and impressive victories recorded against Leeds and Dewsbury in the opening two league games. At the turn of the year Oldham were in a good position, having only lost four matches in the league, but from this point on the form was erratic to say the least, as the season ended with the team having lost 15 league games, including five of the last six. Ironically, after the failures of their much-beloved predecessors, they did reach the semi-final of the Challenge Cup, for the first time since 1934, albeit on the strength of three home ties against Huddersfield, Walney Central (Barrow amateurs) and Bramley, only to lose a tense match (12 - 9) against Hull at Swinton. The three-year stranglehold on the Lancashire Cup was surrendered in the first round at Whitehaven, so often a difficult venue for the Roughyeds.

The 'great' team had now gone. Pitchford, Davies, Ganley and Winslade remained, but the core of that wonderful side was now retired or elsewhere. On the positive side, Nestor was as reliable as ever, Kellett was a great asset, Noon was proving to be a consistent performer in attack and defence, Ganley again proved that his goal-kicking prowess was as good as anyone in the game, as he finished the season with another fine total of 159, and the impressive Southward was scoring tries at an incredible rate. He managed 31 tries in just 25 appearances. However, his time with the club would be short-lived, and those exciting, entertaining and successful days of the previous four years were gone.

*Above: 'Two costly Cumbrians' - **Geoff Robinson and Ike Southward.***

August 8th 1959: Oldham 28   Rochdale H. 11
Law Cup
W .B. Ganley, I. Southward, D. Ayres, J. Noon, G. Sims, A. Kellett, B. Hatherall.
K. Jackson, L. McIntyre, P. Goddard, C. Winslade, R. Dufty, R. Pugsley.
Goals: Ganley,7. Kellett. Tries: Winslade. Sims. Dufty. Noon.
Attendance: 10,873   Referee: Mr. T. Watkinson - Manchester.

There was a home debut for Len McIntyre, who had been injured just after making his senior bow at Whitehaven on February 28th. Oldham dominated proceedings with two early penalty goals from Ganley and

a Kellett drop goal against a penalty by Jones for Hornets being the only scores for the first half-hour. Eventually the pressure began to tell as, first Winslade crashed over in the corner, followed a minute later by Sims finishing off a fine break by Kellett, to leave Oldham 16 -2 ahead at the interval. Smith got one back for Rochdale after snapping up a loose pass from Hatherall, but a try from Dufty and, then, the score of the match by Noon, set up by Pugsley and Hatherall, put Oldham clear, although Rochdale rallied with Short crossing twice for the visitors.

Roger Dufty touches down under the posts to score Oldham's third try.   (08.08.1959)

August 15th 1959: OLDHAM 27   LEEDS 12
W.B. Ganley, S. Quinlan, A. Davies, J. Noon, G. Sims, A. Kellett, B. Hatherall.
K. Jackson, L. McIntyre, P. Goddard, C. Winslade, R. Dufty, G. Robinson.
Goals: Ganley,6. Tries: Davies,2. McIntyre. Quinlan. Kellett.
Attendance: 14,212   Referee: Mr. R. Gelder - Wakefield.

This was a good show by an Oldham team featuring the newly-signed Geoff Robinson. The first try came on 15 minutes when Davies intercepted a Pycroft pass bound for Ward. Ganley converted and added two penalties, with just one goal from Hallas in reply. The Oldham forwards then combined well, with Robinson, Winslade and Goddard all handling before McIntyre touched down. With Oldham 14 -2 ahead at the break, Hallas got two points back for Leeds in the 42nd minute, and after a quiet spell Quinlan finished strongly in the right wing corner after an hour, to more or less seal the match. Don Robinson touched down for Leeds after a scramble near the Oldham line, but handling errors by the visitors set up tries for Kellett and Davies, both converted by Ganley. With the points in the bag Hallas cut through some indifferent defence for the final try, converted by Last.

August18th 1959: DEWSBURY 7   OLDHAM 35
W.B. Ganley, I. Southward, A. Davies, J. Noon, G. Sims, A. Kellett, F. Stirrup.
R. Smith, J. Keith, P. Goddard, R. Pugsley, R. Dufty, G. Robinson.
Goals: Ganley,7. Tries: Southward,3. Davies. Robinson. Stirrup. Kellett.
Attendance: 4,800   Referee: Mr. D. Davies. – Manchester.

A spate of injuries hit the Roughyeds before this match, but the reserves coped admirably, and none more so than coach Frank Stirrup, who displayed all his old skills with a masterly display at scrum-half. Ledgard gave Dewsbury an early lead with a penalty, but soon afterwards Davies put Southward away for the first try and a few minutes later looked to be doing the same again, before dummying the full-back on his way to score himself. Further tries before the break from Robinson, snapping up a loose ball, and Kellett, direct from a scrum, put Oldham firmly in command. Callighan got a converted try after 36 minutes, but that was as good as it got for the home side as the Roughyeds scored three more tries in the second half, with Southward, despite being injured in the first half, completing his 'hat-trick', complimented by one from Stirrup, who, along with Kellett, had tormented the Dewsbury defence throughout the match. Ganley? Seven from seven!

1959

August 22nd 1959: SALFORD 12   OLDHAM 12

W.B. Ganley, V. Nestor, A. Davies, J. Noon, G. Sims, A. Kellett, F. Stirrup.
K. Jackson, J. Keith, P. Goddard, C. Winslade, R. Dufty, G. Robinson.
Goals: Ganley,2. Stirrup.   Tries: Nestor. Noon.
Attendance: 8,000   Referee: Mr. C. Whiteley – Warrington.

Salford dominated possession by winning six of the first eight scrums, but had to wait until the 28th minute to take the lead with a Lowden penalty. However, the advantage did not last long before Winslade and Davies carved an opening for Nestor to score in the corner. Just before half-time Salford recaptured the lead when Jones rounded Sims to score an unconverted try, to leave the 'Red Devils' 5 – 3 in front. After the break Lowden and Ganley exchanged penalty goals, before Lowden attempted a drop goal, but to no avail. However,

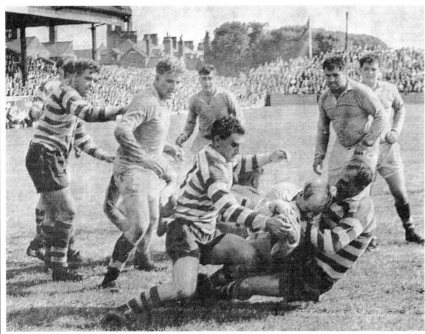

minutes later, Ganley showed how it was done to bring the scores level. Jones got his second try which, added to a later Lowden penalty, put Salford five points clear, only for Oldham to reply again, with Goddard making the break that led to Noon touching down at the posts. Ganley was left with an easy conversion, and the scores remained level with the Roughyeds somewhat fortunate to come away with a point.

Geoff Robinson and *Charlie Winslade* haul down *Billy Banks* near the try line with *Ken Jackson* and four Salford players in attendance.
(22.08.1959)

August 25th 1959: OLDHAM 6   WARRINGTON   10

W.B. Ganley, V. Nestor, A. Davies, J. Noon, G. Sims, A. Kellett, B. Hatherall.
K. Jackson, L. McIntyre, P. Goddard, C. Winslade, R. Dufty, R. Pugsley.
Goals: Ganley,3.
Attendance: 11,008   Referee: Mr. T. Watkinson – Manchester.

An out-of-sorts performance, with Oldham flattered by a score-line that does not show that Warrington's Gilfedder managed only two goals from ten attempts. A dull game saw the first quarter scoreless, with Ganley breaking the ice with a 21st minute penalty. Ten minutes later a series of prolonged Warrington attacks produced a 'walk-in' for Bevan, but two more penalties before the interval put Oldham 6 – 3 in front. The home forwards were quite disappointing whereas Major and Arkwright were having storming games for the 'Wire'. Gilfedder at last found some form to slot home two penalty goals, before Arkwright got the clincher three minutes from time after another bout of Warrington pressure.

John Noon wrestles with *Terry O'Grady* with *Alan Kellett* on hand if required.
(25.08.1959)

August 29th 1959: WHITEHAVEN 23   OLDHAM 5
Lancashire Cup 1st Round.
W.B. Ganley, V. Nestor, A. Davies, J. Noon, G. Sims, A. Kellett, F. Pitchford.
P. Goddard, L. McIntyre, R. Dufty, G. Robinson, R. Pugsley, J. Petley.
Goal: Ganley.   Try: Kellett.
Attendance: 5,500   Referee: Mr. M. Coates – Leeds.

After three successive victorious Lancashire Cup campaigns, the run was broken by another abject performance at Whitehaven in which ex-Warrington amateur John Petley made his only first-team appearance. Oldham had the perfect start, with Pitchford ghosting through to send in Kellett in the first minute. Ganley converted but that was it! Ably led by Tembey in the forwards and Davies in the backs, 'Haven' set about Oldham with left winger Stephenson the star of the show with four tries. Two came in the first half to leave the Cumbrians 8 – 2 in front at the break, with two more after the interval. There was one more from fellow wingman, Smith, and Bainbridge knocked over four goals to complete Oldham's misery.

September 5th 1959: HALIFAX 20   OLDHAM 27
W.B. Ganley, V. Nestor, A. Davies, J. Noon, G. Sims, A. Kellett, F. Pitchford.
R. Smith, J. Keith, P. Goddard, R. Pugsley, D. McKeown, G. Robinson.
Goals: Ganley,3. Tries: Pitchford,2. Noon,2. Nestor,2. Pugsley.
Attendance: 11,301   Referee: Mr. K. Rathbone - St. Helens.

After Owen had missed two penalty attempts, Oldham opened the scoring after eight minutes when Robinson and Noon combined to put Pugsley over. Halifax replied with a converted try from Burnett, but the lead was short-lived before a Nestor interception gave a try to the supporting Pitchford. However, the home side bounced straight back, with Jones dummying his way through just two minutes later. A Goddard break then set up a try from Noon. This was converted by Ganley, before Owen slotted home a penalty in the last minute of the half to see Oldham just 11 – 10 in front at the interval. The second period continued the to-and-fro scoring, but three tries in a 12 minute spell just after the hour mark swung the game firmly in Oldham's favour as Nestor, Noon and Pitchford each crossed for their second touchdown.

*Des McKeown tackles **Johnny Freeman** with try scorer, **Vince Nestor** and 'hero of the hour', nine goal, **Bernard Ganley** on standby if required.   (08.09.1959)*

1959

September 8th 1959: OLDHAM 21 HALIFAX 17

W.B. Ganley, V. Nestor, A. Davies, J. Noon, G. Sims, A. Kellett, F. Pitchford.
R. Smith, J. Keith, P. Goddard, D. McKeown, R. Dufty, G. Robinson.
Goals: Ganley,9. Try: Nestor.
Attendance: 12,003   Referee: Mr. A. Durkin – Dewsbury.

An amazing result which saw Oldham triumph in spite of being outscored by three tries to one! Five Ganley penalty goals set against a try from Sparks and three goals from Owen gave the Roughyeds a 10-9 half-time advantage. Williams punched the ball out of Pitchford's grasp and was controversially allowed to pick up and score, after which a Ganley penalty left the scores level at 12 – 12. After 53 minutes a high pass from Kellett was taken by Nestor, and he swept inside two defenders for a converted try, but Halifax responded when Burnett swooped on to a loose pass to score a converted try. With seven minutes to go the scores were still level, but a penalty by Ganley and another in the last minute gave Oldham an incredible win with one try and NINE goals!

September 12th 1959: OLDHAM 43 HUNSLET 9

A. Jones, S. Quinlan, A. Davies, J. Noon, G. Sims, A. Kellett, F. Pitchford.
R. Smith, J. Keith, R. Dufty, C. Winslade, D. McKeown, L. McIntyre.
Goals: Noon,8. Tries: Quinlan,2. Keith. Dufty. Davies. Noon. Jones. Sims. McKeown.
Attendance: 10,727   Referee: *Mr. J. Chadwick. – Dewsbury.
*Mr. W. E. Higginson (Touch Judge) - Warrington, took over part way through the match.

Another amazing result for a Roughyeds team that suffered a spate of last minute cry-offs but overcame the problems for a resounding win. Midway through the first half two Noon penalties against a try from Robins gave Oldham a single-point advantage. Then Quinlan knocked up a pass bound for Firn and re-gathered to sprint away and score. Hunslet responded with two tries from left winger Firn, and it seemed all the action was on that flank as Quinlan got over again to restore the Oldham lead. After the interval the makeshift team went from strength to strength, with the 'back three' of Winslade, McKeown and McIntyre leading the way. Seven more tries were added, including a spectacular score from Davies, who left half the Hunslet team in his wake on the way to the line.

Alan Davies scores one of the nine Oldham tries.   *(12.09.1959)*

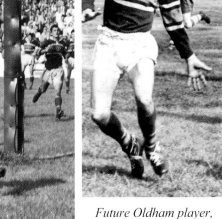

Future Oldham player,
Geoff Shelton *in action
for Hunslet at
Watersheddings in 1959.*

1959

September 19th 1959: OLDHAM 24 WIDNES 12

W.B. Ganley, I. Southward, A. Davies, J. Noon, V. Nestor, A. Kellett, F. Pitchford.
K. Jackson, J. Keith, R. Dufty, C. Winslade, D. McKeown, G. Robinson.
Goals: Ganley,6. Tries: Southward. Nestor. Winslade. Noon.
Attendance: 10,884   Referee: Mr. E. Clay – Rothwell.

Ganley opened the scoring with a penalty after seven minutes, and then the match came alive with a wonderful 70-yard move after 14 minutes ; Davies burst down the right and then turned the ball back inside to the supporting Pitchford, with Southward then getting inside him to take the pass and sprint away to the line. Five minutes later Keaveney scooped up a loose ball to give Myler a 'walk-in', but two more bouts of good handling produced tries for Nestor and Winslade to leave Oldham 13 – 7 up at half-time. An interception try from Chisnall gave the 'Chemics' some hope, but when Pitchford broke clear to put Noon over, the Roughyeds had enough of an advantage to see out the match comfortably.

1959

*Above: **Alan Davies** and **Charlie Winslade** contest a loose ball with the Widnes defence.*

*Opposite Top: **Charlie Winslade**, **Des McKeown** and **Geoff Robinson** put paid to a Widnes attack.*

*Opposite Bottom **Charlie Winslade** reaches out to score.*
(19.09.59)

September 26th 1959: BLACKPOOL B. 13   OLDHAM 29
W.B. Ganley, I. Southward, B. Pendlebury, J. Noon, G. Sims, A. Kellett, F. Pitchford.
K. Jackson, J. Keith, R. Dufty, C. Winslade,   G. Robinson, L. McIntyre.
Goals: Ganley,7. Tries: Kellett,2. Southward. Noon. Robinson.
Attendance: 3,000   Referee: Mr. H. Harrison – Horbury.

This match was the debut game for centre Brian Pendlebury. On the back of a massive possession advantage Oldham built up a substantial first-half lead, with Pitchford putting Southward over after 13 minutes, followed by Pendlebury setting up a try for Noon. Kellett added a couple more, to leave the Roughyeds 20 – 4 in front at the interval. The only Oldham try after the break came from Robinson, with Hutson getting a late consolation for 'Borough'. The downside for Oldham was a facial injury for Southward that would keep him out of the team for a month.

A full account of all the Oldham matches against the touring teams can be found in the book "Kangaroos, Kiwis and Roughyeds".

October 3rd 1959: OLDHAM 14   AUSTRALIA 25

W.B. Ganley, V. Nestor, A. Davies, J. Noon, B. Pendlebury, A. Kellett, F. Pitchford.
K. Jackson, J. Keith, R. Dufty, C. Winslade, G. Robinson, L. McIntyre.
Goals: Ganley,4. Tries: Davies,2.
Attendance: 17,621   Referee: Mr. C. Appleton – Warrington.

This match is well-documented for being a rough, explosive affair, and the reputation is well-merited, although there was some excellent rugby as well. After seven minutes Gasnier snapped up a fumbled Oldham possession to go in for try number one. Carlson added the conversion. There wasn't much to choose between the teams, and for the next quarter of an hour it was end-to-end stuff, with neither side able to break the deadlock. Then, on twenty five minutes, the ball was moved out swiftly by the Kangaroos from a scrum on their own twenty-five yard line until it reached Gasnier. The centre then turned on the pace to scorch through the Oldham defence for his second score. Carlson was again on target for the extra two points, and later added a penalty goal to put the visitors twelve points ahead. The Roughyeds were brought back on track by two of their most experienced players. Pitchford unlocked the tourists' defence with a sixty yard break that brought the crowd to its feet, and Davies got with him to finish off in style. Ganley added the conversion, and just before the interval he kicked a penalty goal, to leave the half-time score 7 - 12. The ill-tempered mood continued into the second period, and within a few minutes of the restart Carlson punished the Roughyeds for their continued indiscretions with another goal. However, the penalties were not all going one way, and six minutes later Ganley responded for Oldham. Australia increased their lead on the hour mark. Gasnier was again on hand to finish off, this time from close range after taking a pass near the try line. Oldham protested long and loud that there had been an obstruction but the whistle stayed silent and the score was allowed to stand. Still, Oldham would not bow down. When rugby football and not fisticuffs were on view the home side proved they also had some skill. A lively bout of passing culminated in Davies going over for his second try. The ever-reliable Ganley put over the conversion, to leave the Roughyeds just three points in arrears. Ironically, after Gasnier's sparkling performance, it was the right wing pair who settled the match for the Kangaroos. First, centre Boden went over, and then, five minutes from time, Carlson put the result beyond doubt with a try which he converted himself. Two minutes from time the game erupted! Muir had put in a late tackle on the Oldham hooker Jack Keith which went unpunished, and when a minute later he did the same again on Pitchford, the brawl started. Referee Charlie Appleton had already awarded Oldham a penalty, but the previously-lit fuse finally sparked the explosion with, once again, several players involved in fights. When order was finally restored Mr. Appleton pointed to the dressing rooms and rival scrum-halves, Pitchford and Muir, departed for the tunnel. A minute later the match was over.

The match officials go in to sort out one of the numerous brawls that marred this match while on the left another one erupts.   (03.10.59)

1959

*Above: **Reg Gasnier** scores one of this three tries in **Frank Pitchford's** tackle (other Oldham players) **Roger Dufty**, **Alan Davies and Len McIntyre**.*

Below: Another one of the fights!   (03.10.59)

1959

October 10th 1959: BARROW 22   OLDHAM 29

W.B. Ganley, D. Ayres, A. Davies, J. Noon, G. Sims, A. Kellett, F. Stirrup.
K. Jackson, J. Keith, R. Dufty, C. Winslade, D. McKeown, L. McIntyre.
Goals: Ganley,7. Tries: Davies,2. Kellett. Noon. McIntyre.
Attendance: 6,084   Referee: Mr. J. Senior – Bradford.

A try from Rea and a Dawes penalty got Barrow off to a good start, but bad handling cost the home side two tries, as first Kellett and then Davies capitalised on dropped possession to score. In between these two tries, Grundy had scored after a good break by Goodwin. The best try of the match came when Stirrup dummied his way past the initial Barrow defence and then sent a fine reverse pass to Davies, who finished off at the posts. 17 -12 up at the break, Oldham always had enough to keep the 'Furness-men' at bay, although it took a late try from McIntyre to make the match absolutely safe. The now customary fine display from Ganley with the boot was another decisive factor.

October 17th 1959: OLDHAM 28   WORKINGTON T. 2

W.B. Ganley, S. Quinlan, V. Nestor, J. Noon, G. Sims, A. Kellett, F. Stirrup.
K. Jackson, J. Keith, P. Goddard, C. Winslade, R. Dufty, L. McIntyre.
Goals: Ganley,7. Stirrup. Tries: Noon,2. Goddard. Sims.
Attendance: 7,597   Referee: Mr. A. Fairbottom – Hull.

After a scoreless first quarter, Lowden opened the scoring with a 20th minute penalty, but soon Stirrup carved open the Workington defence to put Goddard in at the posts. Kellett and Noon then combined to put Sims over. Ganley converted both tries and added a penalty, before Stirrup concluded the first half scoring with a drop-goal to leave Oldham 14 – 2 in front at the interval. The second period was a dull affair until Noon brightened up the proceedings with two tries in the last six minutes.

*Left: Cec Thompson is tackled by **Len McIntyre**.*

***Below: John Noon** dives over for one of his late tries.*

(17.10.1959)

292

1959

October 24th 1959: WARRINGTON 27   OLDHAM 8

W.B. Ganley, V. Nestor, A. Davies, J. Noon, G. Sims, A. Kellett, F. Pitchford.
K. Jackson, J. Keith, P. Goddard, C. Winslade, G. Robinson, L. McIntyre.

Goals: Ganley,4.

Attendance: 10,000   Referee: Mr. T. Watkinson – Manchester.

After seven consecutive league victories, Oldham came down to earth with a bump at Warrington, thanks mainly to the goal-kicking of Eric Fraser, who landed nine goals. The first try came on 27 minutes, when a collision between Davies and Challinor produced a loose ball that Edwards hacked on for the ever-reliable Bevan to pick up and score under the posts. Challinor added another to make the score 16 -2 at half time. Bad handling let Oldham down throughout the match, and although the defence was solid, the accuracy of Fraser punished any Oldham indiscretion. Ganley put over another three penalty goals, but a late try from Lannon emphasised Warrington's supremacy.

October 31st 1959: OLDHAM 20   BARROW 9

W.B. Ganley, I. Southward, A. Davies, J. Noon, V. Nestor, A. Kellett, F. Pitchford.
K. Jackson, J. Keith, P. Goddard, C. Winslade, G. Robinson, D. McKeown.

Goals: Ganley,7. Tries: Nestor,2.

Attendance: 10,131   Referee: Mr. L. Wingfield. – Normanton.

A close first half saw Barrow go in with a one-point advantage, with three Ganley penalties being offset by one from Dawes who also converted a try from Don Wilson, who charged over direct from a scrum to score under the posts. Five minutes into the second half, Ganley put Oldham in front, only for Ball to restore the lead for the visitors with another penalty ten minutes later. Davies and Sharpe had their names taken as some needle crept into the game. Second-row forward Ducie was stretchered off with a shoulder injury, after which Oldham took advantage of the extra man with Kellett and Pitchford setting up Nestor for a try in the 61st minute. He also added another late in the match to seal the win, with Ganley's seven goals, as at Craven Park three weeks earlier, ensuring that the points went to Oldham.

Geoff Robinson and
Des McKeown
bring down Barrow's
Mick Ducie.
(31.10.1959)

The Oldham team against
Barrow on October 31st
1959.
Back Row: C. Bradley,
Jack Keith, Ken Jackson,
Geoff Robinson,
Charlie Winslade,
Peter Goddard,
Des McKeown,
H. Goodwin.
Middle Row: Frank Stirrup,
Ike Southward, Alan Davies,
Bernard Ganley, John Noon,
Vince Nestor.
Front Row: Frank Pitchford,
Alan Kellett.

293

November 7th 1959: ROCHDALE H. 0   OLDHAM 45

W.B. Ganley, I. Southward, A. Davies, J. Noon, G. Sims, A. Kellett, F. Pitchford.
K. Jackson, L. McIntyre, R. Dufty, C. Winslade, D. McKeown, G. Robinson.
Goals: Ganley,9. Tries: Sims,3. Kellett,2. Dufty. Jackson. McIntyre. McKeown.
Attendance: 5,108   Referee: Mr. H. Harrison – Horbury.

Geoff Sims was drafted in as a last-minute replacement for Vince Nestor, who couldn't get away from his National Service commitments, and rewarded his selection by scoring a hat-trick in the first half hour of the match! After 36 minutes Noon forged an opening for Dufty to go over, and, with Ganley's conversions, Oldham were out of sight, leading 20 – 0 at the interval. The second half produced more of the same, although it should be said that Ledger had to retire after 20 minutes with a dislocated shoulder sustained in bringing off a desperate tackle on Southward.

November 14th 1959: OLDHAM 34   BLACKPOOL B. 5

W.B. Ganley, I. Southward, A. Davies, J. Noon, G. Sims, A. Kellett, F. Pitchford.
K. Jackson, L. McIntyre, P. Goddard, C. Winslade, R. Dufty, D. McKeown.
Goals: Ganley,8. Tries: Noon,2. Southward,2. Kellett. Dufty.
Attendance: 7,257   Referee: Mr. C. Whiteley – Warrington.

Another good day for Oldham, although 'Borough' took the lead after five minutes when prop-forward Brophy put Clayton over. The lead only lasted five minutes before Kellett weaved his way through to put Noon in for a converted try. Southward chipped in with a couple before the interval, with Oldhamer Ken Payne knocking over a penalty for Blackpool to leave the Roughyeds 15 – 5 in front at half-time. The second period was plain sailing for Oldham, with the pick of the tries being a 75-yard move started by Kellett, carried on by Davies, and finished in style by Noon.

Des McKeown, Geoff Sims and *Frank Pitchford* tackle a *Blackpool player into touch..*
(14.11.1959)

November 21st 1959: WHITEHAVEN 23   OLDHAM 9

W.B. Ganley, V. Nestor, A. Davies, J. Noon, G. Sims, A. Kellett, F. Pitchford.
K. Jackson, J. Keith, R. Dufty, D. McKeown, D. Cawthra, L. McIntyre.
Goals: Ganley,3. Try: Kellett.
Attendance: 3,700   Referee: Mr. G. Philpott – Leeds.

Another fruitless trip to Whitehaven, with a once-only appearance for Derek Cawthra, signed earlier in the week on a free transfer from Batley. McKeown (2) and Ganley had kicked penalty goals before, on 26 minutes, Gibson had a drop-goal disallowed as the ball had hit an Oldham player before clearing the crossbar. However, two minutes later, the same player dummied his way through for an unconverted try. Oldham responded with a magnificent 65 yard effort, with the ball passing through five pairs of hands before Kellett scored. Ganley's conversion made it level, but two more penalties from McKeown left the Cumbrians 11 – 7 up at the break. The Cumbrians had much the better of it in the second half, with further tries from Shepherd and Hughes and just a solitary penalty in reply from Ganley.

1959

November 28th 1959: OLDHAM 25 ROCHDALE H. 3

W.B. Ganley, I. Southward, A. Davies, J. Noon, V. Nestor, A. Kellett, F. Pitchford.
K. Jackson, J. Keith, P. Goddard, G. Robinson, R. Dufty, L. McIntyre.
Goals: Ganley,5. Tries: Noon,3. Southward. McIntyre.

Attendance: 8,747   Referee: Mr. D. Davies – Pendlebury.

This was a comfortable victory against neighbours Rochdale, with Pitchford and Kellett paving the way for Noon to score the first try after only two minutes. The Oldham centre went on to complete a first-half 'hat-trick', with further tries in the 18th and 39th minutes. In between these scores, Pitchford had put Southward under the posts, and it all added up to an 18 – 0 score-line at the interval. Ten minutes after the break McIntyre forced his way over direct from a play-the-ball, and the only consolation for Hornets was a late try from Thomas.

John Chisnall is too late to stop Ike Southward going behind the posts for Oldham's third try. (28.11.1959)

December 5th 1959: WIGAN 27 OLDHAM 7

W.B. Ganley, I. Southward, A. Davies, J. Noon, V. Nestor, A. Kellett, F. Pitchford.
K. Jackson, L. McIntyre, P. Goddard, C. Winslade, R. Dufty, G. Robinson.
Goals: Ganley,2. Try: Nestor.

Attendance: 19,678   Referee: Mr. T. Watkinson – Manchester.

Oldham were always second-best in this encounter, and it took good tackles from Ganley and Davies on Boston and Sullivan to keep their line intact early on, when their cause was also helped by five goal-attempt failures by Griffiths. Eventually all the pressure began to tell, and Cherrington put Ashton over for the first try. Again there was no goal, but when, after 29 minutes, Bolton and Sullivan combined to put Holden over in the corner; Griffiths duly obliged with the extras from the touch-line! He then followed it up with a try, which he again converted, to give Wigan a 13 – 0 lead at half-time. After the break Ganley and Griffiths exchanged a couple of penalty goals each, followed by a try from Nestor after good work from Noon. However, there was to be no come-back as late converted tries from Barton and Wright gave the score-line a more realistic look.

December 19th 1959: OLDHAM 46 DEWSBURY 7

W.B. Ganley, I. Southward, A. Davies, J. Noon, V. Nestor, A. Kellett, F. Pitchford.
K. Jackson, L. McIntyre, R. Dufty, C. Winslade, G. Robinson, G. Haynes.
Goals: Ganley,8. Tries: Southward,3. Nestor,2. Winslade. Dufty. Noon. Pitchford. McIntyre.

Attendance: 4,445   Referee: Mr. A. Fairbotham – Hull.

Gordon Haynes was brought in on trial from Swinton for this match, and impressed in what turned out to be another points-fest for the Roughyeds. The first two tries were set up by Noon for Nestor and Winslade, before there was a shock reply from Dewsbury in the 18th minute, Callighan breaking clear for Sutton to score. The try was converted, but a couple of touchdowns from Southward before the break left the score 21 – 5 in Oldham's favour. The Cumbrian international went on to complete his 'hat-trick' in a one-sided second half, with Haynes producing a solid all round display.

Gordon Haynes

December 25th 1959: OLDHAM 35   SWINTON 10

W.B. Ganley, I. Southward, A. Davies, J. Noon, G. Sims, A. Kellett, F. Pitchford.
K. Jackson, L. McIntyre, R. Dufty, C. Winslade, G. Robinson, G. Haynes.
Goals: Ganley,10. Tries: Southward,2. Kellett,2. Davies.
Attendance: 9,887   Referee: Mr. H. Harrison – Horbury.

Another amazing match for Ganley! Oldham led 10 – 8 at the interval on the back of five penalty goals from the 'Maestro', after the 'Lions' had roared in for two early tries, from Roberts and Stopford. Gowers had kicked one goal, and added another after the interval, but from this point the Roughyeds took control. First Pitchford and Noon put Davies over, who then in turn became provider, as Southward swept in for another two tries. Kellett also bagged a brace, with Ganley only managing to convert two of the five tries. However, his ten-goal tally still makes impressive reading, and prompted Swinton's veteran skipper Dai Moses to say, "There wasn't much between the teams… except they had Ganley."

December 28th 1959: OLDHAM 30   HULL 6

W.B. Ganley, I. Southward, A. Davies, J. Noon, V. Nestor, A. Kellett, F. Pitchford.
K. Jackson, L. McIntyre, R. Dufty, C. Winslade, G. Robinson, G. Haynes.
Goals: Ganley,6. Tries: Noon,2. Kellett. Southward. Winslade. Davies.
Attendance: 12,626   Referee: Mr. R. Gelder. – Wakefield.

This was another good show for Oldham to bring down the curtain on the 1950s, with an opening try after three minutes that had all the hallmarks of the team at their entertaining best. Pitchford found Noon with a long pinpoint pass, and he in turn put the ball out to Davies. Across went the Hull defence to snuff out the inevitable pass to Southward, but it was not to be. Instead Davies turned the ball back inside to Noon, who raced away to score under the posts. Haynes and Pitchford then put Kellett clear, and he duly obliged by leaving all chasers behind in a 45-yard run to the line. Bateson kept the 'Airle Birds' in touch with three penalties, to leave the score 10 – 6 at the interval. However, after the break, Hull were overwhelmed as Oldham turned on the style, with four further tries including the customary one from Southward, who would finish the season with 31 from 25 matches.

The race is on ! Action from the last match of the 1950s.
Alan Kellett *kicks the ball over the Hull defence as several players from each team give chase.*
(28.12.59)

1959

Most Appearances: John Noon 43 out of a possible 44.
Most tries: Ike Southward 31.
Most goals: Bernard Ganley 159 - Most points: Bernard Ganley: 321.

Bernard Ganley

Ike Southward

John Noon

	1959-60	Played	Won	Draw	Lost	For	Against	Points
1	St. Helens	38	34	1	3	947	343	69
2	Wakefield T.	38	32	0	6	831	348	64
3	Hull	38	28	1	9	758	474	57
4	Wigan	38	27	2	9	828	390	56
5	Featherstone R.	38	27	0	11	730	437	54
6	Whitehaven	38	22	3	13	594	533	47
7	Warrington	38	22	2	14	650	482	46
8	Swinton	38	22	2	14	654	503	46
9	**OLDHAM**	**38**	**22**	**1**	**15**	**744**	**461**	**45**
10	Hunslet	38	21	3	14	595	488	45
11	Leigh	38	20	4	14	600	502	44
12	Huddersfield	38	21	1	16	603	510	43
13	Hull K.R.	38	20	1	17	517	575	41
14	Leeds	38	20	0	18	641	573	40
15	Salford	38	19	2	17	629	583	40
16	Batley	38	18	3	17	476	506	39
17	Widnes	38	18	1	19	598	519	37
18	Castleford	38	18	0	20	561	630	36
19	Workington T.	38	18	0	20	448	530	36
20	Keighley	38	17	1	20	575	659	35
21	York	38	17	0	21	579	698	34
22	Halifax	38	15	2	21	627	561	32
23	Rochdale H.	38	15	0	23	435	519	30
24	Barrow	38	13	1	24	422	562	27
25	Bramley	38	10	2	26	393	673	22
26	Bradford N.	38	9	3	26	450	645	21
27	Liverpool C.	38	9	3	26	383	720	21
28	Blackpool B.	38	9	1	28	400	819	19
29	Dewsbury	38	4	1	33	337	982	9
30	Doncaster	38	2	1	35	284	1064	5

1959

SEASON	PLAYER	APPS	TRIES	GOALS	POINTS
1959-60	J. NOON	43	21	30	123
1959-60	A. KELLETT	42	19	1	59
1959-60	A. DAVIES	40	12		36
1959-60	R. DUFTY	40	5		15
1959-60	W.B. GANLEY	35	1	159	321
1959-60	G. ROBINSON	35	4		12
1959-60	L. McINTYRE	34	8		24
1959-60	C. WINSLADE	32	6		18
1959-60	F. PITCHFORD	29	4		12
1959-60	G. SIMS	27	7		21
1959-60	V. NESTOR	26	17		51
1959-60	K. JACKSON	26	1		3
1959-60	I. SOUTHWARD	25	31		93
1959-60	P. GODDARD	18	1		3
1959-60	D. McKEOWN	16	2		6
1959-60	J. KEITH	14	1		3
1959-60	G. HAYNES	11			
1959-60	B. HATHERALL	10			
1959-60	R. SMITH	9			
1959-60	A. JONES	8	2		6
1959-60	W. PAYNE	7			
1959-60	F. STIRRUP	5	2	2	10
1959-60	R. NEEDHAM	4	4		12
1959-60	R. PUGSLEY	4	1		3
1959-60	T. PARKER	4			
1959-60	S. QUINLAN	3	3		9
1959-60	B. LORD	3	1		3
1959-60	B. PENDLEBURY	3			
1959-60	A. MUMBERSON	3			
1959-60	T. GRAY	3			
1959-60	J. O'BRIEN	2	1		3
1959-60	W. PATTERSON	2		1	2
1959-60	J. CROOK	2			
1959-60	J. WARBURTON	2			
1959-60	J. PETLEY	1			
1959-60	D. AYRES	1			
1959-60	D. CAWTHRA	1			
1959-60	T. OGDEN	1			
1959-60	D. GODDARD	1			
1959-60	**TOTAL**	**572**	**154**	**193**	**848**

Regarding… some random comments (there were many more) of what the players and coach thought of their contemporaries.

BERNARD GANLEY:

"Even when we were doing badly or having an off day, Ganley's kicking would keep us in the game."
... Griff Jenkins.

"Bernard Ganley could have kicked a ball from our front step over the Herbert Street stand and landed it on the centre spot."   *... Dennis Ayres.*

"He was exceptional Bernard, but he designed it that way! He practised and made sure that he did everything that was necessary to convert a try or make a penalty count."   *... Alan Davies.*

"Bernard Ganley's goal kicking not only broke records, but won us more matches than any other player."
... Sid Little.

FRANK DALEY:

"It was Daley who called the moves. Daley was the gaffer, he had control."   *... Bryn Goldswain.*

"Daley was one of the best players I had to accomplish a mission. He was the man you needed to watch your opponents danger man."   *... Griff Jenkins.*

"Frank Daley was the most under-rated player of the time. A key player in the team."   *... Sid Little*

FRANK STIRRUP:

"Stirrup was a side-stepper and had a good football brain. My problem was to find a foil for him and that man was Frank (Dan) Daley."   *... Bryn Goldswain.*

"Stirrup was remarkable and I really class him as a genius. One of the finest players I ever encountered."
... Bernard Ganley.

"Stirrup and Willie Horne of Barrow were two of the cleverest players any coach could hope to have."
... Griff Jenkins.

"He had all the moves up his sleeve."   *... Derek Turner.*

"Frank was our football brain and had much influence in devising and refining set moves."   *... Sid Little.*

"Frank Stirrup was way above the normal. A thinking player! Thinking about how to bring about the downfall of the opposition and he was determined to motivate the players to do that."   *... Alan Davies.*

DEREK TURNER:

"Rocky Turner was the man we were looking for, he was on the go all the time, even when the other five were not. He never knew when he was beaten."   *... Frank Stirrup.*

"He was a great player when the team was in trouble. There are plenty who star when a team is doing well but Turner was at his best when the chips were down. To me that makes a great footballer."   *... Griff Jenkins.*

"He liked hard work. He absorbed and consumed hard work, and the impetus that gives to a team is enormous. He was a brilliant player."   *... Bernard Ganley.*

"Derek had that little bit extra. He had that determination to win at all costs. He put everything into it. Not only would he put everything into it, he made sure that everyone around him was involved totally to win the game."
... Alan Davies.

"Rocky Turner was surely one of the game's best loose-forwards."   *... Sid Little.*

DICK CRACKNELL:
"Cracknell was under-rated. He had marvellous judgement in reading a game. He was shrewd."
... Bernard Ganley.

FRANK PITCHFORD:
"Having been brought up as a player with Stirrup, Pitchford also developed into a fine thinker."
... Bernard Ganley.

"Young scrum-half, Frank Pitchford obviously had potential so I put him straight into the first team."
... Griff Jenkins.

"At his peak Frank's eye for an opening, and his ability to go through it in the blink of an eye, was devastating to the opposition."   *... Sid Little.*

JACK KEITH:
"With Keith playing it felt like we had 14 men. Not only could he win a fair share of the ball, but often you would find him backing up a wing on the far side of the pitch - after winning the scrum!"
... Griff Jenkins.

CHARLIE WINSLADE:
"The best second-rower in the world, in his pomp."
... Griff Jenkins.

ALAN DAVIES:
"An exceptional centre who had everything on and off the field. A charming, vociferous character. His performances on the field were outstanding over many years."
... Sid Little.

"He was a very fine player. Probably the best centre we ever had in Great Britain."
... Bernard Ganley.

JOHN ETTY:
"John knew where the line was and that the shortest distance to it was a straight line and if you got John half a chance he would make it to the line."   *... Alan Davies.*

GRIFF JENKINS:
"Goldswain baked the cake. Griff Jenkins iced it!"   *... Bernard Ganley.*

"Our coach insisted that we open the game out, give the backs a running chance and provide the football. The accent was on attack and it paid off."   *... John Etty.*

BILLY MITCHELL:
It would be remiss of me not to include praise for Billy Mitchell in this section. Without using direct quotes as above, I will only say that four of the most successful three-quarters of the era, Alan Davies, Terry O'Grady, Joe Warham and Dennis Ayres, have gone 'on record' as saying how much of a positive influence on their careers the Oldham-born Mitchell proved to be. All four extolled the inspiration they gained from such a positive and enthusiastic teacher of the three-quarter skills. Even coach Griff Jenkins, whose time with Oldham commenced just as Mitchell's playing career came to an end, was quick to acknowledge Billy's contribution. Gracing the line-up of the Roughyeds from 1937 until 1954, the Oldham club was indeed fortunate when they signed up William Sandiford Mitchell.

Epilogue

So, Oldham RLFC in the 1950s - magic or myth? Well I hope that in the previous pages there is enough information for people to make up their own minds.

Magic or myth? For those who say or said they were the best team of the era, definitely the latter.

It was by no means a 'wine and roses' scenario between the club and the players and during the decade transfer requests were frequent and there were numerous disputes between the players and officials with ultimatums issued by both sides. Indeed there were many mistakes along the way and to me the worst was the inability to retain the services of Derek Turner and the fact that while he was here, he was never made the club captain. Here was a tough uncompromising and inspirational player who led by example. These qualities were spotted by Wakefield where he was soon made the skipper of the team and led 'Trinity' to three Challenge Cup Final victories, two Championship Final appearances and two Yorkshire Cup Final successes in the period between 1960 and 1963.

During my research I asked a number of older supporters (approx 20) who they considered to be the most influential player of the era and to my surprise the first five answers were all different:

Ganley, Davies, Turner, Goldswain, Stirrup and from then on no fresh names were added with probably Stirrup and Turner emerging with the most votes.

Frank Stirrup

This is not to undermine the contribution of the other three players mentioned above. Where would the team have been without Ganley's goals or Davies's tries or Goldswain's initial guidance?

Perhaps I shouldn't let the subject go without mentioning; Cracknell, Ayres, Etty, Daley, Jackson, Keith, Vines, Little and Winslade. They were THE team. The Champions! And if they had the starring roles, then due mention should be given to their mentors and under-studies; Mitchell, Ogden, Warham, Leyland, Platt, Tomlinson, Anthony, O'Grady, Nestor, Noon, Kellett... and many more, especially coach, Jenkins.

Derek Turner

However, the players, officials and supporters of the time seemed unanimous with their appreciation of Stirrup's understanding of the game and his contribution to making the team become renowned for playing with flair and imagination. Stirrup, nicknamed 'Mr. Football', was indeed an entertainer!

Turner received similar, across the board, praise for his effort and determination.

Fact! When Turner arrived the club started to win trophies.

Fact! When he left the club stopped winning trophies. Turner was indeed a winner!

Magic or myth? For those who would argue that they were the best team to watch... well from the period from the start of the 1954-55 season through to the third consecutive Lancashire Cup final triumph in October 1958, all of the Rugby League community would agree it was magic!

Perhaps the legacy of the team is best summed up by the scribes of the time. Here are the words of Jack McNamara and Bill Dorran, the Rugby League correspondents for the Manchester Evening News and the Oldham Evening Chronicle in the 1950s.

"Oldham in the fifties did not so much rule the Rugby League, but more truthfully set a standard. They promised everything but never quite delivered all the goods. Yet it is not for their failures that this golden age of Oldham rugby will be remembered. They played wonderful, attacking football week after week with a consistency that now seems amazing. If they lost they usually lost gloriously!"
Jack McNamara.

"...But Oldham will be best remembered for its rugby - its charming, hair-raising, spine-tingling, heart-straining, honest-to-goodness fan-winning rugby."
Bill Dorran (WD).

THE OLDHAM RUGBY LEAGUE HERITAGE TRUST

The Trust was formed by a group of Oldham RLFC supporters who first met back in 1995 to discuss the formation of the club's Hall of Fame.

At that time it was realised that in and around the town there were a number of people who owned representative caps, medals and other awards won by Oldham players from bygone eras, some of whom wished to donate those items to the Hall of Fame.

To protect the ownership of this collection and at the same time ensure it was kept available for generations of Oldhamers to come, the Trust, under the guidance of the OMBC Museum, the Charity Commission and a local firm of solicitors, was formed.

Many of the items in the collection have been donated but from time to time the Trust bids for Oldham rugby- related items at auction, again in an attempt to either keep them in the Borough, or bring them back to the town.

As a result of the Trust's endeavours the people of Oldham now have access to one of the best rugby club collections of important memorabilia in the world.

In recent years, amongst other activities, the Trust has organised rugby related exhibitions, film shows and published books – Oldham R.L.F.C. in the 1950s is the sixth from the Trust's presses. It has also been involved in local youth and educational projects.

Should you visit the Trust's website www.orl-heritagetrust.org.uk, besides uncovering a mine of information surrounding the Oldham club's rich history and its players, you will find details of many books and publications that have connections with the club.

OTHER BOOKS PUBLISHED BY
THE OLDHAM RUGBY LEAGUE HERITAGE TRUST.

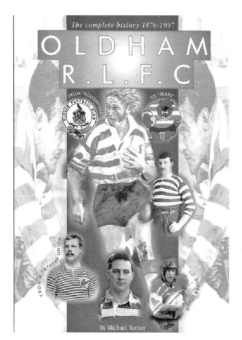

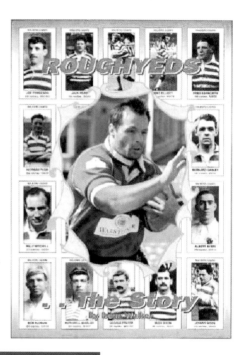

Top left:
Oldham R.L.F.C.
The Complete History
1876 - 1997
Michael Turner.

Top right:
Roughyeds … The Story
Brian Walker.

Centre:
Watersheddings Memories
Steve Brown - Mick Harrop
Michael Turner - Brian Walker.

Bottom left:
Oldham RLFC (Images of Sport)
Brian Walker.

Bottom right:
Kangaroos, Kiwis and
Roughyeds
Michael Turner.